LOVE+
TRUTH

THE ETHOS OF
BEING SPIRITUAL ART

LOVE+
TRUTH

ROBERT ALTHUIS

COPYRIGHT © 2023 SACRED GRACE TRUST

All rights reserved.

LOVE+TRUTH

The Ethos of Being Spiritual Art

FIRST EDITION

ISBN	978-1-5445-4221-8	Hardcover
	978-1-5445-4220-1	Paperback
	978-1-5445-4219-5	Ebook

I DEDICATE THIS BOOK TO YOU, the reader. By some miraculous amalgamation of innumerable variables and circumstances this book ended up in your hands. The probability of this actually occurring is, for all practical purposes, unfathomable, yet it happened.

And, for this very reason, we can know it's not random or a fluke. Somehow, the message contained in the words and language of this book was written to be read by you. I am merely a fairly insignificant piece of the puzzle as I am just the vessel through which these words, and whatever wisdom they might contain, found their way onto paper.

You, the reader, are the main act and the entire purpose this book found its way into existence.

So, let me leave you with this before you embark on your reading journey into this book.

"Worship the Teachings, never the Teacher. The true Teacher knows he's still a Student, the true Student knows she's already the Teacher."

You see, this book, me, anyone, or anything else cannot truly teach you anything. Only you can do that; you are your own guru, your own mystic, your own sage.

Truthfully, this is your book. I was just the typist.

CONTENTS

INTRODUCTION ... 1

PART I THE FOUNDATION

1. UNIVERSAL TRUTH ... 17
2. UNIVERSAL LOVE ... 24
3. THE OBSERVER ... 35
4. EVERYTHINNG IS ENERGY ... 45
5. COMPLEX LIVING SYSTEMS ... 55
6. FINITE GAMES AND THE INFINITE GAME ... 66

PART II THE ARCHITECTURE

7. DUALITY, POLARITY, & TIME ... 81
8. THE MASCULINE & CONSCIOUSNESS ... 93
9. AWARENESS ... 112
10. INTELLIGENCE ... 122
11. ENERGY ... 134
12. THE FEMININE & EXISTENCE ... 155
13. BEING ... 168
14. CREATIVITY ... 183
15. REVERENCE ... 192
16. MASCULINE & FEMININE ESSENCE ... 205

PART III THE GIFTS

17 POLARITY ILLUMINATES THE GIFTS 235

18 WISDOM 251

19 INTEGRITY 265

20 GRATITUDE 279

21 JOY 292

22 PEACE 308

23 BEAUTY 325

PART IV THE PRINCIPLES

24 COHERENCE ILLUMINATES THE PRINCIPLES 341

25 ONENESS 358

26 COMPASSION 378

27 GROWTH 392

28 HEALTH 407

29 ABUNDANCE 426

30 HARMONY 444

PART V LIVING A LIFE OF SPIRITUAL ART

31 AUTOPOIESIS & SELF-LOVE 471

32 FEAR—THE GREAT ILLUSION 487

33 THE ALL IS MIND 505

34 MIND MASTERY & STATES OF BEING 542

35 TO SURRENDER 563

36 SPIRITUAL SUCCESS 576

37 FLOWER OF LIFE—ALL CHANGE STARTS WITHIN 591

CONCLUSION ... 624

ACKNOWLEDGMENT ... 633

ABOUT THE AUTHOR ... 635

ADDENDUM   SACRED GEOMETRY & MATHEMATICAL POETRY ... 637

"A Tao that may be spoken is not the enduring Tao."

—TAO TE CHING, OPENING SENTENCE

INTRODUCTION

YOU DON'T REALLY NEED TO READ THIS BOOK. There's nothing in this book that you don't already know deep within you. The best this book can do is activate your remembrance.

So, to save you the trouble of reading, let me summarize this book for you.

Love is the secret sauce; Love is the only answer. This is the only truth, and honestly, we each know this, although we might not live it. Anything created, empowered, infused, bestowed, encircled, or embraced with love inevitably heals, thrives, grows, flowers, blossoms, unites, harmonizes, regenerates, and creates effervescent beauty in whatever form that might appear.

Love is the sacred elixir of Life itself, the magical energetic pixie dust of this universe—that which animates all of Creation. Love is infinitely intelligent, wise, and powerful, and when we awaken to this remembrance, the nucleus of Divinity deep within us is sparked and reignited.

You are Love—expressing and experiencing itself in a unique way. And, as Ram Dass reminded us, "We're all just walking each other home."

Home is Source Consciousness; home is Love.

In fact, all of Creation is Love, expressing itself in infinitely intelligent ways.

To see the Truth in this wisdom is to truly understand all of Life itself.

This wisdom has been forgotten by most, even though countless teachers and masters have come around for centuries to remind us. We only have to witness the state of affairs in the world to see what happens when we collectively forget to embody this wisdom in all we create. Examples that humanity has lost its connection with this wisdom are all around us: wars, violence, hate, racism, injustices, inequalities, widespread famine, epic pollution, environmental degradation, and the list continues.

Yet, deep down, we each know there's a deeper meaning and purpose to life than just accumulating worldly success and shiny objects. No matter how faint this inkling is stirring our soul, it's always there for each of us. Except, we cannot solve this puzzle with our mind as this stirring extends far beyond the reaches of logic and rational thought. We have to access (more accurately perhaps, "return to") a grander form of intelligence, which can only be found in our heart.

INTRODUCTION

It's been said the journey from the head to the heart is the longest journey we'll ever make. All I have to add is that it's only long when we make it so.

One reason to read this book is to go on a quest of remembrance to shorten this journey from the head to the heart. This book is a roadmap for bringing the formless into form. Or, in other words, how to bring spirituality into our existence. Or, in yet other words, how to make our life an expression of spiritual art.

What do I get for making my life spiritual art? This question is powerful, and it is the right question to ask. We'll dive much deeper into this throughout the book, but for now, the thing to know is that there's the "game *man* plays" and the "game *spirit* plays."

The game man plays is, essentially, worldly success; this is what we call a Finite Game with a beginning and an end, which on a personal level, we call birth and death. This game has its own set of rules, and the outcome of play determines the winners and losers. For the most part, this game is all about fame, fortune, and applause. This game is played in our Outer World, and even though we can experience a certain level of happiness, peace, and fulfillment in this game, it's always fleeting. As we'll discover, the Outer World is unstable, chaotic, ever-changing, and highly dynamic, so happiness, peace, and fulfillment that's tethered to the events and circumstances in our Outer World mean we are a hostage on the roller coaster called life.

The game spirit plays is a very different one; this is the Infinite Game with no beginning and no end—it goes on into eternity.

This game has its own rules, and it's completely unconcerned with what we would call winners or losers. Its only objective is infinite growth and expansion through infinite experiences. We call this process self-realization, and in the broadest terms, we could call it realizing our full potential. This game plays out in our Inner World—where we can find and access a state of enduring happiness, peace, and fulfillment regardless of what plays out in our Outer World.

This is the big game playing out at all times; the game man plays is the small game, played within the confines of this big game. By definition, the Finite Game mankind engages in plays out within the Infinite Game spirit plays.

So, the question then is, do you want to play small ball, or do you want to get into the big game? It's actually a very rich proposition, because to get into the big game, we don't have to give up playing small ball. In fact, almost universally, as we advance in the big game, we become exponentially better in playing our individual game of small ball, although it will also inevitably change how we play the game man plays.

Once we see, we cannot unsee.

> "No man is free who is not master of himself."
> —EPICTETUS

This book is a primer to explain the big game, the rules, and how we can become masterful players in the only real game this universe is playing for eternity.

INTRODUCTION

When I refer to becoming a masterful player at Life itself, I am specifically talking about you becoming a spiritual Poet, expressing yourself into all of Creation. A spiritual Poet is a person devoted to self-poetry, where that poetry is not the composition of a literary masterpiece but, rather, the creation of a masterpiece of being spiritual art. And, to avoid any doubt, this masterpiece I am referring to is you. You are the spiritual art being expressed as self-poetry; I wrote this entire book to help you create a true masterpiece.

We'll go much deeper into all of this, especially in Part V, but I want to nip any idea in the bud that connects "mastery" with worldly success. This universe is entirely unconcerned with the number of zeroes in your bank account, your house's size or zip code, or the fanciness of your cars, boats, toys, or any other shiny objects. It doesn't care about exclusive memberships to private clubs or any sort of title, prestige, status, celebrity, privilege, or ranking within any business, organization, society, culture, or even country. These are all nice decorations that can make for a comfortable or even fun experience here on the Earthly plane, but we're going to progressively dismantle these old and worn-out ideas of success to make room for a new paradigm of success in alignment with the only real game the universe is concerned with.

To help us do all of this, this book is broken down into five parts that work together to form the Love+Truth Framework. These five parts are sequential and organized, so each successive part is solidly anchored in the philosophical foundation created by the previous part(s). Except for air castles and mythical fairies sprinkling fantasy pixie dust, most things are best served by being well-grounded, directly relatable, and understandable; spirituality is no exception, so this has been the North Star in the birth and creation of the Love+Truth Framework. Of course, let's not lose sight of the fact that this book, the Love+Truth Framework, or this North Star is *not* our destination. Becoming a spiritual Poet and "being spiritual art" is our destination, so all of these are merely navigational aids to help us get there.

In Part I, we'll lay the foundation; this part creates the bedrock of a common language and foundational understanding of some key building blocks of this universe we call our reality, allowing us to explore the depths of what spirituality actually is.

In Part II, we'll discuss the grand architecture to gain a fundamental appreciation and in-depth understanding of the Masculine and the Feminine, the principal energetic polarity that governs our universe.

This sets us up to explore the Gifts of this principal polarity in Part III and how these Gifts are instrumental to the process of self-realization, ascension, and enlightenment. Incidentally, in colloquial terms, we call all these things becoming a more whole and beautiful person. In my silky use of words, I call this becoming a spiritual Poet and "being spiritual art."

Don't get hung up on words or language; it's the Gifts that are important in Part III, as they dovetail into Part IV, where we explore the principles of this universe. These principles are by no means arbitrary or trivial as they are the immutable laws that govern all of Creation. By the time we get to Part IV, it will likely already be abundantly clear these immutable laws and principles didn't just drop out of thin air. There's some absolute supreme source, and whether we call this God, Creator, Source, Great Spirit, Monad, or Infinite Intelligence is irrelevant. By the time we've completed Part IV, we're ready in every way for the capstone part of the Love+Truth Framework.

In Part V, we're going to amalgamate all four previous parts and go step-by-step through how we make all of this not just an intellectual understanding but an embodied expression of Life itself. One of my masters used to tell me almost daily, "Robert, your spirituality means nothing unless it changes how you do the dishes." What we're talking about here is the rubber meeting the road. This Love+Truth Framework is beautiful, but unless you embody it and make this your spiritual art and expression into Life itself, it's little more than a perfectly good tree wasted on creating a book. Part V is where you will be left with one final question—an invitation, if you will—are you ready to now become the spiritual Poet that deep down you already know you are and always have been? The only question then becomes if I did a good enough job throughout these five parts to bring you into remembrance.

In taking you on this journey, this book has a singular yet bold purpose: to illuminate what has been hiding in plain sight for eternity.

> "A pure heart—open to light— will be filled with the elixir of Truth."
> —RUMI

I am by no means the first to do this, nor the most enlightened, nor is any of this my original discovery.

All ancient wisdom traditions point at the same thing and a great many truly enlightened teachers—Jesus, Buddha, and Lao Tzu, just to name a few—spoke about everything you'll read in this book in the language of their time.

To better understand why this purpose is bold, we may look for some clues in the opening quote I used for this book:

> The Tao that may be spoken is not the enduring Tao.

Traditionally credited to the sage Lao Tzu, the Tao Te Ching is a Chinese classic text containing eighty-one verses written about 400 BC, which forms the foundation of Taoism. "Tao" translates as "The Path," and "Tao Te Ching" roughly translates as "The Path of Integrity," but for a deeper understanding, we can interpret this to mean "The Path of Truth."

All ancient wisdom traditions and their respective foundational scriptures—whether it's the Bible, the Upanishads, the Koran, the Torah, the Zohar, and many others, including the Tao Te Ching—express in words, which is content, that which is beyond words, beyond content, beyond any language.

This is what this quote means. Using words, we can only point at, describe, refer to, and infer the absolute or universal Truth that underpins all of Creation.

So, this book is not *the* Truth. It merely points at it, and my intention and commitment are to point at it in the most truthful way available to me.

INTRODUCTION

> "Writing cannot express all words,
> words cannot encompass all ideas."
> —CONFUCIUS

Spirituality is simply not an exact science; no amount of intellect or math will ever transmute the formless into form. So, reading any spiritual text that way will yield little more than a theoretical understanding of the arrangement of words.

If our genuine aim is spiritual growth or even mastery, we must seek to go beyond intellectual understanding to enter the domain of Higher Knowing. Higher Knowing is still not the same as the Truth, but within Higher Knowing, we can get very close. There is a level beyond Higher Knowing where we merge with the Truth, but that's well beyond the purpose of this book, any language, and my spiritual paygrade, for that matter.

Where intellectual understanding comes to us through learning or accumulating knowledge, Higher Knowing comes to us through remembrance. You recognize Higher Knowing more so than that you logically understand it.

The Golden Rule—do unto others as you wish to be done unto you—is a beautiful example. We might not all live by this rule or not all the time, but we all intuitively know this rule to be truthful. We even all intuitively know that if we all lived by this rule, the world would be a profoundly different place. There's no need for any of us to try to intellectually understand this rule; our Higher Knowing immediately recognizes the Truth within this rule. Even very young kids immediately recognize the Truth within The

Golden Rule. That's remembrance; something within us recognizes the innate and inherent Truth of something. It's no coincidence, by the way, that a variation of The Golden Rule is part of virtually every single ancient wisdom tradition.

The way to read this book is to be open to encounter remembrance. My sole intention is to speak to your Higher Knowing. But, to do so, I need to get past the "defense," which is your logical mind. Your logical mind likes form, diagrams, theories, math equations, and tangible specifics. Spirituality is intangible by nature—beyond language and words—and your logical mind absolutely abhors the formless. It's a nonstarter in the perception of the logical mind as it considers the formless simply not real. In fact, it's worse; it considers the formless dangerous as the mind's greatest fear is the unknown.

So, to appease and neutralize the defenses of your logical mind, I purposely designed this book to be a logical sequence of spiritual truisms. That means that although this is not your usual book, you can certainly read it that way. Usually, we read a book front-to-back and then add it to our bookshelf collection. Many books we don't even ever finish as books struggle to hold our attention. All of that is perfectly fine, so that's one possible approach.

When I first started reading Jiddhu Krishnamurti's books some years ago, this is exactly what happened. I could recognize the depth of his work, but I couldn't quite assimilate and internalize it into deep knowing. I've come to discover this is how Truth operates. Truth has this remarkable quality to touch us even when we can't yet fully wrap our whole mind around it. Truth also has layers. I've gone back time and again to Krishnamurti's and many other books and wisdom teachings, and the truly profound texts always unfolded layers of Truth I simply couldn't see before.

I am, by no means, suggesting this is a profound book—that's for you to decide. But I can tell you this book has many layers of Higher Knowing. I know because this Higher Knowing didn't come from me; it came through me.

I understand that might sound like an oddity to some of you; less than a decade ago, it would have to me, also. In hindsight, I now realize my intuitive capacities of claircognizance and clairsentience were switched "on" from a very early age only to become suppressed and repressed as they didn't fit our modern world of science, math, and that which can be measured and observed. They were always there, though, and never fully muted. In mostly unconscious ways, I even used and, at times, abused these innate capacities in business and my personal life, but a major shift happened in 2015 when I experienced a major spiritual awakening event in my life. Until then, I had been pursuing (with a vengeance) the same American dream of worldly success as almost everyone else. By way of an Ivy League MBA, a fast-track career in the corporate world of big business, and then becoming a successful entrepreneur, I made it to the proverbial mountain peak by 2015, when I sold most of my business portfolio. I was a big success by all the standards of our world, yet somehow—deep inside—I felt empty and as if I had bankrupted my soul.

At the time, I had no real idea what this was or why it was happening to me, but one of the knock-on effects of this spiritual Crucible was that my claircognizance and, a little later, my clairsentience became—for all intents and purposes—fully reactivated and permanently switched on. So, when I say it "comes through me," I am humbly admitting that this Higher Knowing is coming from a Higher Source, and I am merely a vessel for this information. The authorship is not Robert's brilliance or enlightenment; it's a Higher Source of intelligence using me as a messenger to receive, synthesize, and share information of a Higher Order. Humans have been "channeling" higher dimensions since antiquity; this isn't something new or even all that special as we all have the hard wiring in place to do this, which is to say, literally, every single person alive has this innate capacity. You can even get certified in Mediumship, which I did as I wanted to perfect my art by gaining a deeper understanding of the science.

This same Higher Knowing that came through me to form these words also informed me to reread this book several times as it was coming through me. And, each time I did, more layers revealed themselves. One key thing it revealed to me is that this entire teaching framework is designed to serve as a reference guide, much like the sixty-four hexagrams of the seminal *I Ching* is designed to be read and incorporated into our practice of Life itself.

It's totally up to you how you consume this book, but this is how I would do it. First, read it front-to-back without worrying one bit about what information you're able to receive or not receive. This book is a scenic journey; it will guide you on a walk unto the pathless land. The point is not to memorize the walk but to simply experience it.

Next, I would flip back and reread the parts that call me to do so. If there are none, the bookshelf will do.

Finally, I would put this book on my stack of other books I frequently reference. I have about eight to ten next to my bed. Whenever it calls me to do so, I pick up the book that's calling my name, and I use my intuition to guide me to what I need to read. Sometimes it's a paragraph; sometimes, it's three chapters. I don't argue with the guidance; I just follow it.

In this way, this book will become an endless treasure trove of remembrance of Truth. Whatever Higher Knowing you need in that exact moment, it will provide to you. Trust it will, and your trust will be richly rewarded.

My wish is that this book will help you remember as there's nothing in this book that, at the deepest level, you don't already know.

Oddly enough, it's truly just that simple.

PART I

THE FOUNDATION

"All truth passes through three stages.
First, it's ridiculed. Second, it's vehemently
opposed. Third, it's accepted as self-evident."

—ARTHUR SCHOPENHAUER

CHAPTER 1
UNIVERSAL TRUTH

THE TRUTH IS, WHATEVER YOU OR I consider to be the truth, is merely relative truth. Barring those who might be at the highest levels of enlightenment—the true sages and mystics of which there might be a handful living among us at any given time—all we will ever possess is relative Truth as we are inherently biased by our perception.

In that sense, our relative Truth is truthful. It's how we perceive the world and reality, and so, for each of us, this is unique. In Hindu philosophy, the Sanskrit word "Maya" points to this. Maya means magic or illusion, and the process of awakening is referred to as awakening to the veils of illusion that prevent us from seeing reality as it really is.

Our level of awakening (i.e., level of consciousness), personal circumstances, and cumulative life experiences from the day we are born color the lens through which we perceive life. And, for most of humanity, this lens is foggy as many are not awakened yet.

They're completely unaware of even the existence of these veils of illusion, so they have not even begun the process of awakening and burning through them. This book will reveal many of these veils, even though it's not specifically written to point them out.

> "Everything we hear is an opinion, not a fact. Everything we see is a perspective, not the truth."
> —MARCUS AURELIUS

So, how does our lens get so foggy? We'll explore this in Part I as we discuss and lay the foundation of the Love+Truth Framework. We'll not only look at but parse out seemingly obvious concepts like Love and Truth, so we envelop them with definitional rigor and make them not mere notions but actual workable concepts within Life itself. From there, we'll explore the fundamental insight that we are "The Observer," which is the pivotal passageway into understanding who we truly are and, perhaps equally important, who we are not.

Next will be two chapters—"Everything is Energy" and "Complex Living Systems"—on the essential nature of this universe, which we must fathom at a basic level, or we have no context to understand what we are an integral part of. Finally, we'll close out this Part I by examining the deeper purpose of this universe and Life itself. Hence, in this last chapter, called "Finite Games and the Infinite Game," we anchor in the fundamental and age-old query of what Life itself, including yours and mine, is truly all about. So, now that we know where we will be going in Part I, let's start at the very beginning: Universal Truth.

We are each born into a fishbowl called culture, religion, and societal beliefs. Our upbringing, schooling, life experiences, and media exposure, just to name a few, all add dense layers—veils—to our understanding of the world and reality. We swim in this fishbowl from the day we are born to the day we die. We might jump to another fishbowl from time to time and then, swimming in those waters, we take on those colors also. The more fishbowls we dare to swim in, the more our understanding of the world gets nuanced. As Mark Twain said, "Travel is fatal to prejudice, bigotry, and narrow-mindedness."

We're also born into a body that has a gender, skin color, creed, sexual orientation, and all sorts of other identity markers that impact our perception of the world as well as how we interact with the world. All of these experiences are processed by our mind, and through pattern recognition, our mind forms a basis of understanding that it uses to navigate us through life.

It's unavoidable then that we each have a unique vantage point, as not a single person will ever walk a mile in our shoes. We might find others with similar life experiences based on our race, socioeconomic status, the culture or country we were born in, etc. And these people might view the world very similarly, but never exactly the same. This is why each of us walking this Earth possesses only our own relative Truth, which is singular.

However, there's more than just fishbowls to swim in; we can also jump into the wide-open ocean and swim there. When we venture on the spiritual path, this is, in essence, what we're doing. The ocean is not colored by what's ultimately man-made. Culture, societal beliefs, religion, ideologies, etc., are all man-made. And the more we swim in the ocean, and the deeper we dare to dive to explore the depth of this vast ocean, the more we tend to lose all the conditioned thinking that stuck to us by swimming in the fishbowls. This is the spiritual purification process of remembering who and what we truly are. In a way, we're simply clearing the fog off our lens so our relative Truth may become even more truthful to absolute, fundamental, or universal Truth.

I prefer to use the term universal Truth, but absolute or fundamental say the same thing; words are just labels. Universal Truth is the truth beyond any fishbowl coloration. It stands on its own, always holds true in all circumstances, and is completely independent of any religion or ideology. It might correspond with Truths held in religion or ideology, but, in fact, it supersedes it.

Universal Truth is not subject to time, place, culture, race, creed, or gender, and it holds true as much on Earth as on the far ends of the universe. Universal Truth is self-evident, indivisible, integral, complete, and not subject to human opinion, interpretation, or manipulation.

Universal Truth is beyond words and language as well. We can merely point at it and describe it with words, but language cannot capture its full vastness nor the depths of its purity. This is because language is a tool of the mind, and our mind is finite in its capacity to grasp the infinite. We'll get much deeper into this as we explore further on this journey of revealing the essence of the Love+Truth Framework.

So, how do we gain access to universal Truth?

The answer is the intelligence of our heart, which is the portal that gives us access to Higher Knowing. Higher Knowing is that which is beyond logic, linearity, theories, concepts, frameworks, or any thought-forms that are merely psychological constructs.

As we'll uncover in this book, universal Truth lives at a frequency and vibration of absolute purity, which makes it beyond the reach of our mind, which is inherently colored by perception. Through the intelligence of the heart, we can gain access to these higher frequencies and vibrations, but to do so, we have to learn—perhaps remember is a better word—the language of the heart.

The language of the heart is feeling, sensing, direct knowing, and intuiting. Where the mind is loud and noisy, producing an incessant stream of thoughts in the form of language and images, the heart speaks to us in very subtle and understated ways. So, one of the first things we need to learn to gain fluency in this language of the heart is to quieten the mind.

True mind mastery from a spiritual perspective is the ability to create the stillness of our mind. From a neurotic bully to a serene servant, and within this process of mastering the mind, we not only become the director of the orchestra, but we gain the power to masterfully orchestrate the harmonics of the music. It's the harmonics of the music within us that corresponds with the infinite harmonics within our universe, and through the harmonic phenomenon called sympathetic resonance, this creates what we call our reality. We'll delve deeply into all of this throughout this book, so don't worry if none of this makes any sense right now. Just allow me to take you on this walk, and I'll lay bare all of it for you in the best way I know how.

Stillness of the mind allows the intelligence of the heart to reveal itself to us. There's actually very little to learn here; the language of the heart comes to us through remembrance. We each have an innate capacity to feel, sense, directly know, and intuit. For most of us, these are dormant capacities, though—long dismissed by Western society as inconsequential or illogical as humanity went on the search for Truth in its rational faculties of the mind.

Universal Truth is far beyond the reach of logic and the mind. And we see evidence of that abound in the world today. Our world today is created by the dominance of the mind's neocortex, so it's no surprise we see so little universal Truth reflected in its Creation.

The universal Truth I point at in this book, using words and language, is something you can only really access with the intelligence of your heart. Universal Truth is a frequency and vibration that goes beyond words, but it's directly accessible through feeling, sensing, direct knowing, and intuiting. I specifically use the word accessible, as you cannot possess universal Truth much like you cannot possess sunlight. You can only access it, as you cannot own or possess that which governs you.

The way to read this book, then, is to allow it to touch you. Allow the sunrays of universal Truth to penetrate your deepest being. Resist the temptation to want to understand it logically; that approach will not get you beyond the words. The gold is not in the words themselves, it's in the frequency and vibration these words hold.

Sympathetic resonance spontaneously occurs when we tune in and connect with the frequency and vibration of the words. We just know as that's how direct knowing works.

The universal Truth then reveals itself to you through sympathetic resonance. It will literally resonate with you; it's that simple. In fact, everything in this universe unfolds and reveals itself to you through sympathetic resonance, and we'll go on a journey of unpacking this universal Truth throughout this book as well.

Just like Truth resonates or vibrates at a higher octave or frequency than Falsehood, so does being spiritual art. Living in Truth, ascending into higher and more refined octaves of consciousness, and being spiritual art are all deeply interwoven.

> "Even if you are a minority of one, the truth is the truth."
> —MAHATMA GANDHI

Universal Truth is not just a fundamental concept; it's a fundamental essence of universal Love, as we'll discover in the next chapter.

CHAPTER 2
UNIVERSAL LOVE

UNIVERSAL LOVE IS THE ONE UNIVERSAL TRUTH, which is why this chapter follows universal Truth—without knowing what a universal Truth is, we have no framework to place universal Love.

The one universal Truth is that the only Truth there is, is that Love is all there is. Universal Love gives birth to universal Truth is another way to view it. I recognize this could use some more words to land what I am pointing at, so we'll do just that in this chapter. For now, just know that much like a master tailor of bespoke suits needs to know the nuances and intricacies of fine fabrics, a spiritual Poet devoted to mastering being spiritual art needs to move and come into deep and intimate accord with Love as the sacred fabric of Life itself.

> "In the silence of Love you will find the spark of life."
> —RUMI

To kick this exploration off in the proper direction, let me first clarify that I am talking about "love the energy" and not "love the emotion." Throughout this book, we'll refer to these as "Love (the energy)" or "Love (the emotion)" to clearly delineate as these are two very different qualities of Love itself. Love (the emotion)—that warm and glowing feeling we have toward someone or something—is what most people perceive to be Love. We can love a person, our family, our pet, our house, our job or career, and all of this would be Love (the emotion). It's personal in nature, not universal. It's neither wrong nor unreal, but it has a few specific hallmarks that are absent in Love (the energy).

Exclusion.

Within Love (the emotion), we love some people or things but not others. We can see this in love for our race, creed, religion, ideology, culture, and country, to name just a few. Love (the emotion) is defined by exclusion. And, because it's defined by exclusion, it's limited; other words for that would be finite or conditional. Hence, that brings us to yet another specific hallmark of Love (the emotion).

Perishable.

Another undeniable hallmark of Love (the emotion) is that it tends to be fleeting and unstable, which could be considered conditional, but I prefer to use the word "perishable" as most people hopelessly confuse their "conditional love" for "unconditional love," which itself has been diminished to a spiritual buzzword—more on that later. Love (the emotion) is perishable because we love a person one day, and for whatever reason, not the next day. We might love our car, house, career, hobbies, favorite musicians, or politicians one day and not the next. We can even fall out of love with our own race, religion, and country. In fact, this happens all the time, even if it hasn't happened to you. When something is perishable, it means it can go bad, and we all know and have examples in our own life where Love (the emotion) went sour.

Just by observing these two hallmarks, we can see that Love (the emotion) has polarity or an opposing side.

The flip side of the Love (the emotion) coin is indifference. Why indifference and not hate? When we withdraw Love (the emotion) from someone or something, we don't necessarily hate them or it now, but we become indifferent. Hate holds a lot of negative energy; that's why it can be so destructive and is often expressed in violence. So, hate is a surplus of negative energy toward someone or something. The opposite of that is idolizing or even aggrandizing, which is the surplus of positive energy toward someone or something.

We see this play out in the world everywhere. We idolize and aggrandize our own people, religion, ideology, or country, for instance, and hate others. This, and wanting someone else's resources, is the catalyst and rationale for most wars and violent conflicts throughout history. On the other hand, we Love (the emotion) our family and friends and will come to the rescue time and again when they fall on hard times. Yet, we're indifferent to the suffering of billions of people we don't personally know.

The point to take away from all of this is that Love (the emotion) holds within it exclusion, it's perishable, and there's the presence of polarity. Love (the emotion) isn't necessarily bad; we all know it's amazing to feel Love (the emotion) when it's unbridled and activates and flushes our system with the potent cocktail of love hormones. Falling in love and being in love is a beautiful thing—one of the most beautiful experiences available to us—but just those words alone tell us something profound.

If we can "fall *in* love," it means we can "fall *out* of love." If we can be "*in* love," it means we can be "*out* of love." And all of that is Love (the emotion).

So, now let's take a look at Love (the energy).

The defining qualities of Love (the energy)—universal Love—is that it's unlimited and infinite as well as enduring, which means it's not perishable. Moreover, universal Love has no polarity. Please note that the terms universal Love and Love (the energy) are interchangeable; I merely used the term Love (the energy) to contrast it with Love (the emotion). For the remainder of this chapter and book, I will use the word universal Love, or whenever I use the word Love with a capital "L" it means universal Love.

Now, let's start unpacking all these defining qualities and more.

All major ancient wisdom traditions and all the great teachers—Jesus, Buddha, Lao Tzu, and Rumi, to name a few—pointed at universal Love. But, just like universal Truth, universal Love is beyond words, beyond content, beyond any language. So, all we can do is point at it, describe it, refer and infer and recognize that words can never completely encircle its vastness.

Universal Love is self-evident, complete, integral, stands on its own, holds true in all circumstances and across all geographies and timelines, and is completely independent of any religion or ideology. It's, therefore, unlimited and infinite. There's no beginning and no end; it simply just is.

Universal Love knows no exclusion because of what it is; it doesn't just encompass everything in this universe; it is this universe, as we'll discover later. In most religions, universal Love is described as God's love. However, I usually steer clear of religious interpretations as most religions have evolved around the core premise that their version of God's love is the only real and true one. That's exclusion showing up again, so we know it's not universal Love, even though it's attempting to point at the same thing.

The fact is, universal Love supersedes any religion. God is ultimately just a word—a label—which we can substitute with Creator, Source, Spirit, Infinite Intelligence, Universal Mind, or whichever word we prefer. Universal Love doesn't deny anyone's religious beliefs or preferential words, but the thing to take away is that universal Love cannot be possessed or claimed by any particular religion.

Any religion that operates with and within universal Love, and to the extent its teachings align with universal Love, can be of great beauty and serve humanity in profound ways. When exclusion is introduced into any religious doctrine, it's trying to divide that which is indivisible.

This is the essential quality of infinity. Universal Love is unlimited and infinite; it cannot be divided, partitioned, or even excluded.

Even the offenders of the worst atrocities in history were still held by universal Love. There are many other intelligent ways that the universe bestows the responsibility of our karmic lessons squarely on our Soul's shoulders, but excluding us from universal Love is not one of them. We are never without universal Love—even when we have drifted so far into darkness that we can no longer perceive its light.

Universal Love is also enduring as it's eternal. It's simply not perishable; there's no off button. It does not wane, diminish, decay, rot, or perish—ever. There's nothing you have to do, accomplish, maintain, or achieve to be held in universal Love. That said, there are karmic consequences for not aligning with universal Love, as universal Love governs this entire universe.

The word to particularly erase from your conscience is sin. Sin leads to guilt and shame, and these are two very disempowering levels of consciousness. There's no such thing as sin in universal Love. All is held equally in universal Love; it's enduring in that you cannot be abandoned by it no matter how hard you try. What you can do is retreat so deep into darkness that you can no longer perceive its light. Just because you can no longer perceive it doesn't mean it's not there. It is, always, as it's enduring and eternal.

Unfortunately, throughout history, we have seen many examples of people venturing into the deepest abyss of darkness and inflicting unthinkable acts of cruelty and suffering on others. And we continue to see many examples of this in our world today. And it's not limited to others; look at what we do to animals and Mother Earth.

As we witness this darkness, it can be very challenging to know that this universal Love is omnipresent within each of us and within all of Creation. The spiritual truth that might help you is to know that all actions by all people are recorded in their karmic records. Universal Love also means that we are responsible for purifying our karmic records over all our lifetimes. This isn't a matter of sin; it's solely a matter of karmic responsibility. In that way, the universe can be said to be indifferent to what you do in this lifetime, as it knows you cannot escape your karmic records.

> "Don't take revenge. Let karma do all the work."
> —BUDDHA

We, as humans, are not asked to opine on, judge, or condemn others. We are not equipped to do so, as we cannot look across lifetimes and timelines. We are merely invited to observe others, and then learn, grow, and expand from all we observe and experience by focusing solely on living our own life as truthfully as we can to universal Love.

The power and effervescent beauty in that is that all it takes is the free will decision to shift your life onto the pathless land of the spiritual realm—don't worry, I am going to show you exactly where to find that realm later. For now, we need to create some foundational understanding first, so we have solid footings to build upon. Because, as you venture onto this pathless land, each step, word, action, and thought becomes who you are so understanding the fundamentals is paramount. Universal Love is not just a decision we make about how we live our life but about Life or all of Creation itself. This isn't so much about becoming anything or anyone as it is about who we decide to be. As the name alludes, there can be no actual roadmaps for the journey *into* this pathless land, as the whole point is for you to walk your unique path and leave your own trail. However, the Love+Truth Framework in this book will provide you with all the navigational aids you require to walk the pathless land with purpose, courage, and direction. Be and live this framework—this Ethos—and your life expression cannot help but become spiritual art.

Let's now touch on "unconditional love," which has become the spiritual buzzword du jour. There's nothing wrong with unconditional love per se; it's mesmerizingly beautiful and divine. However, "unconditionality" is just one of many aspects of universal Love, which is vastly grander than unconditional love, which I will showcase throughout this book. The best I will ever be able to do is give you a glimpse of universal Love; words could simply never contain it fully. Yet, words are powerful and can taint things, especially when culture takes a run with it. This has happened with unconditional love; it's being used rather casually these days and often gets confused and comingled with—what's in truth—conditional love or Love (the emotion). How do I know? Well, these days, we have all sorts of so-called gurus, sages, mystics, healers, and teachers preaching about unconditional love, and then they turn around and say or do all sorts of things that are a far cry from what they preach. This has spilled over into spiritual circles and now the mainstream, which has overall sullied the reverence for unconditional love in our use of language; it's become just another buzzword we use casually, with most not having the faintest idea of its significance.

When I contemplate the deeper meaning of universal Love—which I do daily—I remind myself each time that I am entering a space of absolute purity, reverence, and power. This space is an omnipresent field of pure Divinity—and it's within each of us. There's nothing casual about it, as we're touching on the very core of Life itself—the one true essence of all of it, and this book aspires to show you not just this Divinity but that it's within you. For I know, if I can succeed in just that, universal Love will become as real and palpable to you as burning your hand on a piping hot stove. And, like that hot stove, we can only truly revere what's real to us. I want to make it real to you, so real it becomes your knowing. To be clear, you may call it anything you wish after that, including unconditional love; in the end, words are just labels.

> "The center of the universe is everywhere."
> —BLACK ELK

As previously mentioned, universal Love has no polarity. You may consider it the only thing in this universe with no polarity, and the origin of that is that universal Love is Source Consciousness itself. Again, Source Consciousness is just a word—a label—much like God, Creator, Source, Great Spirit, Yahweh, Adonai, Elohim, Allah, Abba, Monad, The All, Universal Mind, and Infinite Intelligence are all just labels to point at a Supreme Being or what some refer to as the Absolute. You can substitute any of these with the word or label of your preference, as that doesn't change its essence.

Let's recall that universal Love is Love (the energy). Through our advances in quantum physics, we know this entire universe is a field of energy, and we also know that at the quantum level, we are each energy expressing itself in human form. We'll go deeper into this in later chapters, but for now, it suffices to know everything is energy.

We also know there was a Big Bang event of some sort that, to the best of our understanding, brought this whole universe into being. What we don't know—i.e., can't scientifically prove—is what was there before the Big Bang.

That's been an enduring mystery for scientists, although mystics and even Jesus have pointed to this truth since ancient times. A singular Source Consciousness of infinite awareness, intelligence, and energy is expressing itself—in infinite ways—for eternity, through all of Creation, which includes the 100 billion galaxies known to us today, the 100 billion or so galaxies believed to be beyond what we know, and anything that might be beyond that.

Now, the essential nature of this Source Consciousness is universal Love. And since you and I—as well as all of Creation—are each an individual yet unpartitioned expression of Source Consciousness, our essential nature is universal Love. We are Love, and we are each the center of the whole universe.

> "What you seek is seeking you."
> —RUMI

Of course, I made some pretty big frog leaps there, so the rest of this book will unveil and reveal this grand mystery at the very core of human existence and its quest for the Truth. Much like we need to learn to crawl before we can walk and walk before we can run, you'll find each next part builds upon the prior part, and similarly, each chapter will build upon the prior one. All of this is by design, as our aim is not just to learn how to run but how to run and chew gum at the same time. That is, just knowing the information—i.e., learning how to run—is great but, at the same time, mostly meaningless unless you can also bring it into embodiment—i.e., chew gum at the same time—in your daily life. All "embodiment" really means is that it becomes your expression into Life itself or all of Creation, and this is what being spiritual art is all about.

However, don't believe my word for it yet; just read on and allow resonance to activate remembrance on this journey of discovering your and my true nature. Of course, this begs the question: *what is this true nature to start with*? Let's dig into that as we explore the next chapter, aptly titled "The Observer."

CHAPTER 3
THE OBSERVER

PERHAPS THE SINGLE MOST profound revelation—remembrance, if you will—is when you realize that you are the Observer. It's a critical threshold to cross from which the journey of awakening starts in earnest.

This doesn't mean we can't access universal Truth or universal Love before we cross this threshold, but the true depths don't reveal themselves until we self-realize and can observe ourselves as the Observer.

In our unawakened state, we identify with both our mind, believing we are our thoughts, and our body, thinking we are our body. The unawakened state is akin to being hypnotized as within this state you're simply not aware that you are unawakened. You are for all intents and purposes in deep hypnosis operating under the illusion you are your Ego or personality that's part and parcel with your body. Nothing could be further from the truth. You have a personality; it's yours, but it is not you. Similarly, you have a body; this is also yours, but you are not your body. There's a lot to unpack here and all of this has far-reaching consequences in your entire perception of reality as we're going straight for the jugular in terms of the veils of illusion.

Let's start with the mind.

Our mind is a marvel of ingenuity, a human supercomputer. Besides all the bodily functions it commands autonomically (meaning spontaneously and outside your conscious control), our mind produces thought. However, when we look inside the human skull, we don't find the mind; we find the human brain, which is an organ.

The human brain is comprised of about 100 billion nerve cells called neurons, which are interconnected with trillions of connections called synapses. Thoughts are electrochemical signals that pass from one neuron to another, and synapses allow this connection—or neurotransmission of thought-form—to occur. This operation of the brain is what we call the mind.

So, right there we can see that the mind is not real in terms of something we can physically touch. The brain is, but not our mind.

Where our brain is biological in nature, our mind is psychological. And all thoughts or thought-form are, therefore, psychological constructs. Thoughts might appear real and palpable to us, but they're all psychological constructs.

Carl Gustav Jung, a Swiss psychiatrist and psychoanalyst who lived in the first half of the twentieth century, gave us great insights into the structure and nature of our mind or psyche. This is now referred to as Jungian psychology. He posited that three components comprise the human psyche: our conscious mind, our subconscious mind, and our collective unconscious.

> "Your vision will become clear only when you can look into your heart. Who looks outside, dreams; who looks inside, awakes."
> —CARL JUNG

Even though Jung was a classically trained psychiatrist, he is—by many—considered the most influential thought-leader of his era in such diverging fields as psychiatry, anthropology, archeology, mythology, philosophy, and psychology, as well as religious studies. He was truly a polymath, but underneath all this academic excellence lived a true spiritual genius. Jung was really a mystic and sage disguised as a world-renowned psychiatrist; the depths and profoundness of his whole body of work are truly mesmerizing.

In Jungian psychology (also known as analytical psychology), the collective unconscious incorporates patterns of memories, instincts, and experiences common to all mankind. These patterns are inherited, evolutionary in nature, and can be arranged in the archetypes we find in Joseph Campbell's illuminating body of work encompassing mythology. This is the story of humanity we each carry within us. The fact they're inborn and ancestral doesn't mean we lack the spiritual potential to rise above them. We can; we are in no way sentenced to be chained to our ancestral "baggage" indefinitely. But illumination of these patterns comes organically when we first focus on the other two personal parts of our psyche, so that's a far more productive place to start.

Our conscious mind is like the top of the iceberg floating above the water line, whereas the subconscious mind is the invisible body of the iceberg submerged below. Like the iceberg, our conscious mind is relatively small—about 5 percent—and our subconscious mind is the other 95 percent, give or take.

Compared to our subconscious mind, which has virtually unlimited processing capacity and memory, our conscious mind operates at a much lower bandwidth and has limited storage capacity. All our bodily functions are commanded autonomously by our subconscious mind drawing on some vast reservoir of intelligence which is unconscious to us; we don't even have to think about it with our conscious mind.

Other than when we sleep, our five senses are inundated with data every waking moment, and most of that slips right past our conscious mind, yet it's all recorded by our subconscious mind. The filter that determines what the conscious mind registers and what passes through is called the reticular activating system or RAS. Interestingly, the conscious mind instructs the subconscious mind what it wants to register, and the subconscious mind autonomously commands the RAS. This interaction between our conscious and subconscious minds is at the very core of mindset work. Because, absent clear instructions from the conscious mind, our subconscious mind will just run its default programming, accumulated throughout your lifetime from pattern recognition.

The default programming comes from our upbringing, schooling, culture, societal beliefs, religions, etc.; cumulatively, this becomes our conditioned thinking. Conditioned thinking is how we think the world works, who we are, and what's possible and not possible for us or within reality in general. If there are limiting beliefs within this conditioned thinking, these will function as glass ceilings of what you (mistakenly) believe is possible for you. Limiting beliefs can be the cause of great suffering as within any belief we hold—whether we hold that belief consciously or subconsciously—is the premise that it's true.

All default programming in our subconscious mind can be reprogrammed; this is essentially what happens in therapeutic hypnosis. But we hold no power to reprogram anything as long as we believe we are our thoughts, which brings us to the Ego, which, within the context of the Observer, is interchangeable with "personality." However, throughout the remainder of this book, I will be using the term Ego.

The Ego is a psychological construct of self, created and held within our conscious mind. As covered earlier, psychological constructs are thoughts or thought-form, which are not real. So, this psychological construct of self is basically a thought, an idea, or perception, if you will. Yet, since about 80–85 percent of humanity lives in an unawakened state, most people identify with this self. They believe they are the thoughts and voices chattering on incessantly in their head. Now, the Ego has an important role to play, so it's not a faulty design by nature, but it's not who we truly are. So, let's explore that further and reveal that Truth as being able to see and clearly delineate between the Ego (or "small Self") and the Observer (or "true Self") is fundamental to raising our game of being spiritual art to a higher octave.

Jiddhu Krishnamurti (1895-1986) was a preeminent philosopher and spiritual teacher who spoke about this topic in great depth for almost six decades. The essence is this: if there's no thinker, there can be no thought. If there's thought, there must be a thinker. These two are essentially one and the same; one cannot exist without the other. While it's difficult if not impossible to observe the thinker, we can observe thoughts. In fact, that's what we do all the time. We do nothing but observe thoughts and voices all day long. So, since that's a fact and we know the thinker and thought are one and the same, we cannot be the thinker producing thought.

To put this in other words, our psyche is the thinker which produces thought. We cannot observe our psyche per se, but we can observe the thought it produces, and from above, we know they are one and the same.

> "It's the mark of an educated mind to entertain a thought without accepting it."
> —ARISTOTLE

This leaves only one option for that which we truly are. *That* which observes our thoughts. Hence, we are the Observer; it cannot be any other way.

So, what is this Observer, then?

Consciousness—or what we colloquially refer to as our Soul. Later, we'll delve much deeper into what Consciousness is, but for now, the essential takeaway is that we are not our thoughts. We are the Observer of our thoughts. So, we are not our Ego or psychological construct of self. This persona or personality only exists in thought-form within our psyche; in that sense, it's not real. It's an idea.

Now, don't worry if this requires some time to digest. Just run with it for now and allow resonance and remembrance to do their work as we continue this journey.

The revelation that we are the Observer opens up a host of profound insights, but let's first address our body. If we are not our Ego (or thoughts), we can rule out that we are our body because our body isn't what governs our human experience. Just take away our psyche or the Observer, and we can see that our body is something we have, but it's not who we truly are.

> "You are a little soul carrying about a corpse, as Epictetus used to say."
> —MARCUS AURELIUS

The Observer—Consciousness or Soul—has a psyche and a body. We can see this even more clearly when we think about death. Our body dies, our psyche, including our Ego, dies with it as our brain dies with the body, and what's left is the Observer or our Consciousness. This part of us never dies as it's eternal.

Our life on Earth is our Soul taking on finite form—our body—for this lifetime, only to return into the infinite and formless until it reincarnates into finite form again, and this process repeats itself into eternity as we ascend to ever higher levels or octaves of consciousness throughout our countless lifetimes.

As we explore all of this much deeper, this insight alone will reveal many revelations about ourselves and how so many things we witness in the world are just complete madness from a spiritual vantage point.

Things like race, creed, culture, nationality, gender, and even such highly sensitive topics as sexual orientation and gender identification all reveal themselves as psychological constructs or identification with our body's biological or physical characteristics. Take me, for instance: from the vantage point of the Observer, I am *not* a 6' 5" Caucasian male. I have a body which measures 6' 5" in height, is genetically predominantly of Caucasian or Europoid ancestry, and is considered biologically male based on my XY chromosomes and male genitalia.

> "Respond intelligently even to unintelligent treatment."
> —LAO TZU

If humanity can awaken to the vantage point of the Observer, there wouldn't be any racism, as we would consider it downright foolish. Most wars make no sense anymore if we no longer identify with a certain culture, religion, or nationality. From the vantage point of the Observer, sexual orientation is just a physical attraction or sexual preference, but it has no bearing on who we truly are. Even gender identification becomes an entirely different discussion than we witness in the world today. First, when we awaken to the spiritual Truth that we are the Observer, any identification with our body greatly diminishes or even dissolves entirely. But, more importantly, our gender identification loses significance as we're no longer defined by it. We're no longer defined by any of our identification markers; we might still hold them internally, but they become soft and fluid enough so no outside opinion can offend us anymore. We no longer need any validation or recognition from others as we're no longer tightly identified with any of these parts of our humanity living in finite form on Earth.

This is not to say or suggest any form of racism, bigotry, hate, violence, or any other form of oppression of others' freedom to fully express themselves is in any way acceptable. But, awakened to being the Observer, none of this would ever cross your mind as that would be akin to abandoning your spiritual North Star, which is living a life in alignment with universal Truth and universal Love.

The only way out is the collective awakening of humanity, as at the level of consciousness most are today, they simply have no concept of this spiritual North Star, so they cannot see the universal Truth that we are all equal yet unique expressions of Source Consciousness.

The Observer, on the other hand, can only see the sanctity of all life and knows no other way but to respect all others and their unique expression in this lifetime.

Admittedly, this is a high spiritual bar, and we're all imperfect humans. Still, we can all start by aiming for it. As the saying goes, practice makes perfect.

> "To be wronged is nothing
> unless you continue to remember it."
> —CONFUCIUS

Now that we have defined—or perhaps redefined for some of you—who we truly are in terms of our inner world, let's take a closer look at our outer world in the next chapter, so we clearly define that also.

CHAPTER 4

EVERYTHING IS ENERGY

THIS CHAPTER IS A FUNDAMENTAL puzzle piece as without understanding the essential nature of this entire universe, we're stuck living our life in 1 percent of reality.

That's right, our physical world and our existence within it—as we perceive and experience it through our five senses—is a mere 1 percent of all there is. What we perceive as being physically real and solid turns out not to be solid at all.

> "Ninety-nine percent of who you are is invisible and untouchable."
> —R. BUCKMINSTER FULLER

To lay all this bare, we must go on a journey from Newtonian physics to quantum physics, as the field of physics has already discovered all of this. Before we do, it's important to note that scientific discovery does not make something come into existence, let alone a universal Truth.

For starters, the notion of humans "inventing" anything is a misnomer, which is why I specifically use the word "discovery." Everything, including what we refer to as a human "invention," already exists as a potentiality in the Infinite Field of Possibilities. Any human invention, therefore—in the truest sense—is merely a discovery we made. A potentiality became an actuality through human discovery.

So, when we make advances in something like the field of physics, what we're doing is discovering something that was already there. Gravity existed from the moment this universe was born. Newton's discoveries didn't invent gravity; he merely realized, for humanity, a scientific understanding complete with mathematical proof of a universal Truth of this universe. And to be even more truthful, Newton's discoveries weren't all his own.

There were countless scientists whose work he built upon that enabled him to crack the code, so to speak. We see this everywhere; we love to worship heroes, but the humble fact is every hero we worship—in whichever field—is an amalgamation of all that went before him or her. This is the universal principle that we are each born into co-inherited wealth, which among other things, constitutes all knowledge, discoveries, and wisdom of all of humanity that went before us. This principle also applies to our personal success—whether spiritual or material—as we'll discover when we examine the role of symbiosis and facilitating factors in Complex Living Systems. Awareness of this principle is why all true greats are graced by humility, something to remember for each of us when the lotto of life treats us favorably.

All the above goes for quantum physics; in the last one hundred years or so, humanity made huge advances in scientifically understanding the essential nature of this universe. At the same time, every self-respecting quantum physicist will admit with humility there are still countless mysteries we have yet to discover. Nevertheless, our scientific understanding has reached far enough to encompass everything covered in this chapter, which is all we really need to know as foundational knowledge to delve deep into the subject of Love+Truth.

From the perspective of Newtonian physics, we and the world we perceive with our five senses are just a bundle of building blocks called atoms. Atoms that come together form molecules, and molecules that come together form cells. Cells that come together form tissue, which can be muscle, intestines, or any other part of our body. All of this appears solid. Anything we can see or touch in our physical world has this same architecture, whether it's a single-cell organism, a giraffe, a rock, or a grain of sand. None of this is untrue; it's just not a complete picture.

> "Reality is merely an illusion, albeit a very persistent one."
> —ALBERT EINSTEIN

When we look inside an atom, we find three subatomic particles: protons, neutrons, and electrons. Protons are positively charged, electrons are negatively charged, and neutrons have no electrical charge. Protons and neutrons live together in the atom's nucleus; the electrons orbit the nucleus. We refer to these subatomic particles as sub-particles or quanta, which is the plural of quantum. The field of quantum physics is concerned with quanta.

However, 99.999 percent of an atom is what we call "empty" space, as the quanta are infinitesimally small compared to the atom itself. To put this in perspective, the Hydrogen atom is roughly one hundred thousand times larger than its nucleus. So, if the nucleus was the size of a ping pong ball, c. 0.4 inches (c. 1cm), its electrons would be in orbits about 0.62 miles (c. 1km) away. That's a lot of empty space; however, note that empty space here doesn't mean nothingness.

We have established now that our physical world, including our bodies, which we perceive as solid, is, in fact, mostly empty space. So, where we started—1 percent of reality—is actually generous; in terms of quantum physics, it's even much less than that.

So, let's now take a closer look at quanta.

Quanta, or sub-particles, are actually energy that we discovered have two distinct states: a wave state and a particle state. So, at the quantum (subatomic) level, everything in this universe is energy.

Researchers at the CERN Institute in Switzerland discovered the Higgs boson—colloquially known as the "God particle"—using the Large Hadron Collider, a seventeen-mile loop that's the most powerful particle accelerator on the planet. This discovery was monumental because, before its discovery, scientists could only hypothesize its assumed existence as it validated the existence of the wave state.

The particle state was already known, as the particle state represents the wave state (a potentiality) locked into time and space (an actuality). An actuality is something we can physically or scientifically observe because this is when something appears in our physical reality as matter or an occurrence. Every "thing" in our universe is quanta locked into time and space, making it an actuality. In other words, quanta—which is energy—express themselves as matter or an occurrence through a change from the wave state to the particle state.

Another key scientific discovery concerning quanta is the Heidelberg uncertainty principle, named after German physicist and Nobel Prize winner Werner Heidelberg, who discovered (in layman's terms) that to observe a "thing" is already to change its outcome as the interaction of observation collapses the wave function (potentiality) into a particle state (actuality).

Observation is the introduction of Consciousness, specifically Awareness, which is a cornerstone of Consciousness, as we'll unpack further in Part II. For now, the key concept is that when Awareness meets—i.e., observes—Awareness, something happens: a potentiality becomes an actuality.

> "In this flow, mind and matter are not separate substances. Rather, they are different aspects of one whole and unbroken movement."
> —DAVID BOHM

If all these concepts are novel to you like they once were to me, it's perfectly normal for all of this to make your head spin a bit. We are used to knowing the outer world or what we call reality through our experience living in it. Our experience is, at its core, a perception of our mind, so our experience of the outer world actually lives and resides in our mind, not in the outer world. Even though, in our perception—which creates our experience—our entire Life plays out outside of us in the outer world.

The key takeaway is that there is a distinct paradox between how we "experience" our reality through our five senses versus how this "experience" of reality actually comes into existence through our own Awareness. No worries if all of this is not fully digestible right away; we're going to continue to pick this apart and look at it from various angles throughout this book, so just follow along, and the building blocks will all fall into place.

So, to build further on this notion of Awareness meeting Awareness, we also know that even a single-cell organism has awareness as it is aware of its surroundings and, in fact, has a symbiotic relationship with its surroundings. The same goes for trees, plants, animals, and all of nature. All of this is well documented in science. We can therefore infer that everything in the physical world demonstrates some level or form of Consciousness, however minute it might be.

Physicists have also concluded that what we refer to as "empty" space is not nothingness. In fact, this empty space is full of an infinite amount of energy. So, all that exists physically—including us humans—is energy expressed in physical form in a vast ocean of energy in wave form.

Everything is energy.

In other words, the 1 percent of form we call reality somehow originates from this 99 percent of formless energy. As mentioned before, this 1 percent is not a scientific number—in actuality, it's far less, but for practical purposes, we can work with it as the essence is in the concept and not the exact scientific number.

The best way to visualize this is to picture a 100 percent ocean of formless energy, of which 1 percent then expresses itself in what we call form, which leaves the remaining 99 percent formless. Without fully solving the scientific puzzle of how all of this is possible, some of the greatest physicists of the last century, such as Albert Einstein, David Bohm, Nikola Tesla, and numerous others, discovered many of the properties of the universe we'll explore next. We tend to view these men as genius physicists and brilliant scientists; however, the better way to view these men is as spiritual prodigies with a physicist genius.

> "If you want to find the secrets of the universe, think in terms of energy, frequency and vibration."
> —NIKOLA TESLA

Since this is pretty much where the scientific breadcrumbs end at this point, for the rest, we can look to the philosophical legacy of the brilliant physicists already mentioned (there are too many to list) and other great philosophers, inventors, and spiritual teachers ranging from R. Buckminster Fuller to Leonardo da Vinci to Yogananda. All the great ancient wisdom traditions, including those from Indigenous cultures, speak to the same basic premise in the language of their time and culture. The specific words they each use might be different, but if you can learn to see the correlations in the symbolism used, the breadcrumbs all appear one after another.

Everything in this universe—the form and formless—is Consciousness, of which Energy is a second cornerstone (we already discovered Awareness), which we happen to be able to have some scientific understanding of as it has properties we can observe and, to some extent, quantify mathematically.

In this vast 100 percent ocean of Consciousness, some parts "appear" in form when the wave function collapses and gets locked into time and space. This is a potentiality becoming an actuality, the formless taking form. As Tesla alluded to, we also know frequency and vibration play an essential role in orchestrating how the formless becomes form through what's called sympathetic resonance.

The vast formless aspect of this ocean of Consciousness functions as an Infinite Field of Possibilities. In other words, everything already exists in potentiality and something, some mechanism, converts this enfolded state called a potentiality into an unfolded state called an actuality in terms of matter or occurrence in what we call reality.

For the astute observer, it's quite clear there's some form of Infinite Intelligence that's orchestrating all of this, animating and expressing enfolded potentialities into unfolded actualities.

Hence, we found the third and final cornerstone of Consciousness. Intelligence.

Incidentally, enfolded and unfolded states are terms David Bohm used to describe his most advanced thinking of the workings of the universe. He referred to this as the holographic nature of the universe; we'll explore what he meant later. The key point to take away, for now, is that all of this is deeply interwoven with work done by the most brilliant physicists, both past and alive; nevertheless, my aim here is not to give you a PhD in quantum physics or advanced mathematics as we don't need that to get a PhD in Love+Truth (so to speak).

The goal is to give you a practical understanding—a basis from which to work so we can place many other puzzle pieces in place and start filling in this magical puzzle. Whenever in doubt or if any of this eluded you for the moment, don't worry—just remember, as far as we know, Jesus and Buddha had no concept of quantum physics, but there's zero doubt they had a very deep understanding of Love, Truth, and all of Creation, which is what this book is about. Conversely, countless scientists can do all sorts of mathematical magic but don't have the faintest clue about Love, Truth, or the intelligence of Life itself.

There's a lot more ground to cover and dots to connect to bring all of this together in a cohesive understanding, but the essence to take from all of this is that everything is energy. Energy is the fundamental fabric of this entire universe and everything within it, including each one of us.

We're still just building the foundation, and in the next chapter, we'll get very specific and tangible about how Complex Living Systems are foundational to the fundamental structural design of our universe.

CHAPTER 5
COMPLEX LIVING SYSTEMS

WE LIVE IN A WORLD UTTERLY LOST in logic and rationalism. We can more or less pinpoint the start of the Renaissance as that's when a nearly 1,700-year religious lockdown on science and exploration came unhinged.

Nicolaus Copernicus, a Renaissance polymath, mathematician, and astronomer who placed the Sun (rather than Earth) at the center of the universe, died in 1543, the same year he published his major work, saving him the outrage of and possible execution for heresy by religious leaders. But, unbeknownst to him, he started what's now called the Copernican revolution, advancing science as the basis of understanding our universe instead of religion.

The religion of science was born.

Until this point in history, humanity's capacity to exploit, destruct, and obliterate nature was somewhat limited and benign. Science and technology—coupled with exponential population growth—would come to change that in dramatic ways.

With the advance of science came global exploration. Within the sixteenth and seventeenth centuries, several seafaring nations like Holland, England, and Spain would quickly become global empires. These empires produced vast riches, creating sizzling economies and copious wealth the world had never seen before. All this trade and financial wealth needed financial systems, currencies to trade in, ways to manage risks, and ways to invest surplus capital. Banks, money, and stock exchanges emerged, industries were born, and feudalism began its inevitable decline as capitalism came to age as the preeminent ideological bedrock of Western societies.

The religion of money was born.

Agricultural societies transformed into industrial societies, urbanization started in earnest, and with the introduction of railroads, cars, electricity, and mass production, every person became a source of labor and every source of labor an end-consumer. Fast forward and post-World War II, we can see how consumerism has come to dominate our lives; it's center stage in an economic theory premised on infinite compound economic growth, which views human and natural capital as mere inputs to an economic system that reigns supreme.

The religion of consumerism was born.

This is the trifecta that has us at the edge of extinction as we unabatedly continue to destroy our home planet, foolishly guided by the conflux of these three religions, which as of today, still go mostly unchallenged.

While flawed, it's arguably not these religions themselves that are faulty, but the embedded reductionist thinking that resides at the core of each of them.

Reductionist thinking or reductionism is the idea that complicated behaviors or phenomena can be better logically explained, understood, examined, or managed by reducing them into small, simple pieces. In this chapter, we'll explore and relate reductionism to the current state of affairs of our world and humanity at large—which is all connected and interwoven with humanity rising to become more refined spiritual art.

> "There is nothing wrong with the reductionist method, so long we don't confuse the method for how the world really works."
> —WES JACKSON

Reductionist thinking purposely ignores or sidesteps relationships and context—complexity—to solve something that's now reduced to being complicated. Reductionism views everything as a mechanical toolkit where individual parts can be optimized, maximized, or minimized, as the case might be, without any relationship or effect to any of the other parts.

This is both logical and rational, yet the problem is not that our world or this universe is complicated but that it's infinitely complex.

Truthfully, this whole universe is a self-organizing complex living system made up of countless embedded, smaller, complex living systems. Earth is a complex living system within this universe;

the world's oceans and the Amazon rainforest are complex living systems within Earth. The Atlantic Ocean is a complex living system within the world's oceans, and the North Sea is a complex living system that connects to the Atlantic Ocean.

But it's not just limited to nature. Any country is a complex living system among all other countries, and within countries, there are regions, states, provinces, cities, neighborhoods, etc., which are all complex living systems nested within each other.

The national economy is a complex living system within a country or society, as well as the regional or global economy. Culture is a complex living system within a society, and subcultures are nested within cultures. A business is a complex living system within an industry which itself is a complex living system.

You get the picture; just about anything is a complex living system nested within larger ones with smaller ones nested within.

Finally, our body is a complex living system nested within a larger environment, which is a complex living system, with countless complex living systems nested within our body, like our biome, which has billions of organisms operating within a complex living system in our guts.

All life and Creation on Earth—including humanity—are underpinned on the premise of complex living systems—self-organizing life forms maintained by flows of information, energy, and matter that operate in highly dynamic interdependent relationships that collectively make up the environment.

> "When we try to pick out anything by itself,
> we find it hitched to everything else in the universe."
> —JOHN MUIR

What all of this means is that everything connects to everything else. Changing one thing changes everything.

Complex living systems cannot be explained, understood, or examined—let alone be managed by the reductionist method. Reductionism is a tool to solve something complicated that can be isolated. Reductionism cannot handle complexity.

We need another approach to solve complexity; we call it "holism."

Holism doesn't strip away relationships and context. It looks at things in the most comprehensive and holistic way possible to address the inherent complexity in complex living systems while acknowledging that there's a limit to how much complexity can be managed in the first place.

Holism leans heavily on the embedded wisdom of nature. It looks to the laws and principles that govern nature (and this whole universe, the ultimate complex living system) to see what makes nature self-sustaining, regenerative, abundant, adaptive, and always gravitating back to balance and harmony. Holism is focused on the overall vitality of the system, not optimizing any arbitrary parts to the detriment of the whole system. The field of biomimicry specifically looks to see how the processes of nature can be replicated in such diverse fields as real estate development, healthcare, manufacturing, product design, waste management, and countless others.

Any complex living system is very capable of enduring small and large temporary shocks. However, even relatively small chronic unbalances in one area can cause catastrophic degradation over time to the health and vitality of the whole system.

This is where the world is today.

By and large, we have lost our connection with nature. Moreover, the religion of science has us not only believing we're not part of nature but that we are above nature. Nothing could be further from the Truth; the outcomes have been catastrophic.

We live stressed-out lives, spending most of our time behind desks, in artificial light and air-conditioning, and exposed to copious amounts of EMF and toxic chemicals. We eat processed, fast, and GMO foods—devoid of any nutritional value. We drink tap water laced with fluoride and vast quantities of sugary soft drinks. Our clothes, furniture, and household products are all made with toxic dyes and chemicals. We lack movement, exercise, sunlight, and fresh air, and our human connections have hollowed out as we all have 1 million friends on social media, but we know nobody.

We have an endemic obesity problem, exponential growth in chronic illnesses, an opioid crisis, rising rates of alcoholism and suicides, addictions to everything from shopping to gambling to porn, rising emotional and domestic abuse, and the list goes on.

When we zoom out from the micro to the macro, we see unconscionable wealth concentration, deep ideological schisms in society, rising polarization in politics, enduring unaddressed inequalities and injustices, and the destruction of Mother Earth. Wars, violence, hate, epic pollution, and about 1 billion living in abject poverty, with almost half those in starvation.

These are the inevitable outcomes of the trifecta of religions that rules our modern times. This is what happens when the world is stuck in reductionism.

> "That which is not good for the beehive
> cannot be good for the bees."
> —MARCUS AURELIUS

Our current Neoclassical economic theory is based on reductionism. The embedded premise and core objective of infinite compound economic growth in a world of finite resources is fatally flawed. The math simply doesn't work. Moreover, an economic system primarily concerned with profits and growth is ignorant of its many relationships to the whole. Economic theory and models don't factor in what's healthy or in the best interest of people, society, well-being, equality, justice, or Mother Earth; it's no surprise, therefore, that it tramples those over and over as a stampede of wild broncos unless reeled in by regulations.

There are green sprouts, though; a new paradigm called regenerative economics or capitalism is emerging, which is based on holism and how complex living systems are designed and work.

Our practice of industrial mono-cropping agriculture and feedlot livestock rearing is also a multi-faceted disaster and, again, a product of reductionist thinking. Mono-cropping and heavy tilling have depleted our soils, which now are dependent on ever more use of glyphosate, pesticides, and herbicides—all chemicals which are ruinous to our biome. This, combined with GMO seeds, has directly contributed to an exponential growth in chronic illness over the last five decades; we're literally poisoning ourselves. Bare soils also release CO_2 stored in the soils, aggravating our climate challenge. Barren soils cannot absorb and store water, depleting natural aquifers, and we find ourselves with droughts and wildfires left and right. To make it all worse, our government heavily subsidizes this whole system that's disrupting our own complex living system, the Earth's, and the complex living system called our biosphere.

The solution is staring us straight in the face; it's called regenerative agriculture, although it goes by various other names as well. It addresses all the issues with our current food production system and could have a dramatic positive impact on our health, water supply, and our ability to draw down CO_2 from the atmosphere. In addition, it's more profitable, so all subsidies can be phased out after the farms transition, which takes only two to three growing seasons. What's in the way is incumbents, big businesses that draw their rich profits from the status quo.

Healthcare is another example. Western medicine is based on reductionism; the idea is that our body is a biological, mechanical toolkit where we can tinker with parts with impunity. It's a system based on pharmaceutical intervention which mostly treats symptoms but not causes; hence, the exponential growth in chronic illnesses. Staying chronically ill is very good for business, you getting healthy is not. A notable exception is trauma-related injuries; Western medicine is brilliant at replacing your hip or getting you a new knee—that's a good example of where and how reductionism can be suitable in specific applications.

Again, there's hope on the horizon; there's a new field in Western medicine called functional or holistic medicine, incorporating much of the intelligence and wisdom found in Eastern medicine into Western medicine. Eastern medicine, like Ayurveda and Chinese natural medicine, including acupuncture, recognize our body is an intelligent complex energy system. The underlying premise of this new field is that the body is a complex and intelligent living system, that food is medicine (Hippocrates), and that most chronic illnesses are not so much genetically determined as they are diet and lifestyle related.

The point is this: we have to shift the lens through which we view all of Creation, including ourselves. There's art and poetry to discover in the infinitely intelligent ways Creation is designed and works. There's radiant and exquisite beauty, abundance, vitality, and life in each and every complex living system, from the very small to the very large—from the nature-made to the man-made.

But, to shift our lens, we must shift our way of thinking to holism. You dance with complex living systems as they each have a cadence and rhythm; you become part of complex living systems instead of trying to dominate or manipulate them. All of Creation is not an inanimate mechanical toolkit. Instead, it's a highly dynamic, always evolving, and infinitely intelligent system of life which is deeply interconnected and teeming with vitality and creative potential.

When we start having eyes for the awe-inspiring beauty, intelligence, and divine magic within all complex living systems—within all of Creation—we start to merge into all of Creation as sculptors, creators, and artists. All of Creation is a canvas we help paint through the spiritual art of our life. What we do and how we do things matters greatly; we are each critically important as all of Creation is co-created. Your life is the creative genius you imprint on the canvas of all of Creation. It's your true enduring legacy, no matter if any other human gives you applause or accolades for it. Creation craves and beckons your genius, your most beautiful art, and it will hold it sacred for eternity.

Most of all, ignoring the nature of complex living systems doesn't make them go away. This is the fundamental design of the universe at all levels of Creation; you simply cannot reduce away through logic those forces that govern you.

And the universe, with its Infinite Intelligence and creative potential, governs us, not the other way around.

Understanding complex living systems, then, is the keystone to understanding the essential nature of all of Creation in our physical reality. I promise you that much like Mozart knew how to capture symphonies in musical notation, Michelangelo knew how to work with marble, and van Gogh knew the intricacies of working with paint colors, the spiritual Poet knows and appreciates the importance of understanding the essential nature of all of Creation. Not in the sense that mere knowing produces spiritual art but in that knowing enables the being of spiritual art.

> "Don't fight forces, use them."
> —R. BUCKMINSTER FULLER

CHAPTER 6

FINITE GAMES AND THE INFINITE GAME

TO NOT UNDERSTAND THE GAME all of Creation is playing is to not understand Life itself. Our world today is a reflection of humanity being utterly lost in playing a game that's not the real game.

We could easily call this ignorance, but what it truly is, from the perspective of universal Love, is an unknowing form of childish innocence—no matter the sheer gravity of suffering and ugliness the ignorance within this innocence produces.

Either way, it's still steeped in incognizance, unawareness, obliviousness, and nescience. However, it's innocent until you know. Once you know, it becomes ignorance. Absent knowing, it's simply not a choice you can decide on—this is the innocent nature of simply not knowing. Within knowing, we have a choice on what we decide, and innocence then becomes ignorance.

To truly be an expression of spiritual art, we need to lose our innocence and rise above ignorance. For the first, we need to expand our knowing; for the latter, we need to make a decision. So, just for fairness in advertising, my sole intent in this chapter is to rob you of your innocence and inspire you to rise above ignorance.

> "A finite game is played for the purpose of winning, an infinite game is played for the purpose of continuing the play."
> —JAMES P. CARSE

To set the stage for this chapter, I will create a lay of the land of games by freely paraphrasing from James P. Carse's seminal work *Finite and Infinite Games*, which is impossible to read for the intellectually curious without making an indelible impression.

Finite Games have various defining features, which are how we know it's a Finite Game and not an Infinite Game. For starters, a Finite Game is not just played for the purpose of winning, but it has a precise beginning and definitive end, or we cannot establish a clear winner. So, Finite Games have temporal boundaries.

A Finite Game has numerous other defined boundaries, such as spatial. There must be a defined area in which the Finite Game takes place. In a tennis match, this would be the tennis court. In business, this could be the stock market or an industry. For nation-states, this is the global geopolitical arena. Spatial boundaries are ultimately determined by the players. Spatial boundaries might be codified by written rules, but players freely participating in a Finite Game is what really ratifies the spatial boundaries.

One cannot truly win a game with one player. So, another key characteristic of Finite Games is they cannot be played alone. This is a numerical boundary; there must be more than one player. A player can be an individual or a team. A team can be a set number of players, like a soccer team, a business, or even an entire nation. Either way, a team is ultimately a player in a Finite Game.

In addition, a Finite Game might have the entrance and exit of new players, but it cannot be that any player can just walk on and off the field as they please, as that would make it impossible for an eventual and clear winner to emerge from among the players in the game. It needs to be clear who's playing so one player can win.

There's a beautiful self-orchestrating mechanism within Finite Games that takes care of this conundrum. Players choose to play freely, but they derive their license to play from other players in the game. This also means that any player can be removed from a Finite Game when the other players revoke this license.

Let's, for instance, take a Wimbledon final or the Super Bowl. Players or teams choose to play in this pinnacle championship Finite Game; however, they can only do so if the opposing player or team shows up to play. The license to play is derived from the opposing player or team and revoked when they choose not to play. You might still get the trophy, but nobody would truly view you as the winner of that game.

Hence, trophies are just memorabilia of a Finite Game we played. But the actual "winning" comes from the other players acknowledging the player that won as the winner. Referees and spectators have a role to play, but they merely confirm the winner determined by the players that lost through concluding (referees) and applauding (spectators) that the Finite Game was won by the winning player.

Trophies come in many forms. They might be actual trophies or medals, but also fame, fortune, and applause. Titles, diplomas, certifications, status, prestige, and recognition are also all trophies we gain when we win Finite Games.

Not all is lost when we don't win the Finite Game we're playing; as in many Finite Games, we can get ranked. Being the richest person in the world is a Finite Game in all the dimensions described before, and if we're not *the* richest, we get ranked up to a certain point of relevance to the players in the Finite Game. The Forbes 500 cuts the relevance off at 500, so if you're the 501st richest person, you have no relevance in that particular Finite Game and don't get ranked.

Some Finite Games have the appearance of continuous play, but closer examination will tell us otherwise. Political parties play in the Finite Game called elections even though it appears on the surface they're playing continuously. Businesses compete in the Finite Game of quarterly earnings, yearly results, or market share, which are all Finite Games continuously played but with clear temporal boundaries. People play in the Finite Game called worldly success, but winners are defined by our current standing in the rankings, so there's a temporal boundary. Worldly success itself is a spatial boundary as we measure success in our material gains. So, what can appear as continuous play in Finite Games is really just Finite Games played back-to-back.

Finally, there can be Finite Games played within Finite Games. There can also be Finite Games played within Infinite Games. But, what's not possible is for an Infinite Game to be played within a Finite Game. Infinite Games can be perceived as being played within larger Infinite Games, but a more truthful description would be to say Infinite Games play alongside and in collaboration with each other.

There's really only one dimension in which Finite Games and Infinite Games are identical, and it's a crucial one. It's an immutable principle of all play that whoever plays, plays freely. Whoever *must* play, cannot *play*. All credit goes to James P. Carse for this insight; its depth is profound as we'll get to uncover.

So, let's take a look at Infinite Games.

As mentioned, Infinite Games are played for the purpose of continuing play indefinitely. This means there are no temporal, spatial, or numerical boundaries, and although there are players, there are no "winners" as Infinite Games have no defined end. Another way to look at that is everyone is a winner just for freely choosing to be a player.

Even though the principal purpose of an Infinite Game is to continue play for eternity, there can be deeper layers of purpose, which are always subservient to this principal purpose. That is, a subservient purpose may not cause play to stop as that would violate the principal purpose. Some examples of possible subservient purposes are growth, expansion, evolution, experiences, health, vitality, happiness, joy, fun, art, beauty, and the Creation of living poetry through the process of Creation itself.

All of Creation is not just an Infinite Game—it's *the* one Infinite Game. Incidentally, all the above subservient purposes are part of it.

There's something noteworthy about it, though. We—humanity—are part of it also, but we're not necessarily players. As we covered already, to be players in this Infinite Game (or any game, for that matter), we must freely choose to play.

To be just part of it—which we cannot freely choose not to—is to *have* to play. When we *must* play, we cannot *play*. Can you see that?

Being unknowingly part of the Infinite Game all of Creation or Spirit plays is to be an actor who doesn't know which movie he or she is in. They're lost in subplots called Finite Games, mistaking the subplots for the whole movie. This is the unawakened state most of humanity is in. That's neither good nor bad; there's zero judgment in any of this, it's just a neutral fact. Awakening is the realization we've been playing in Finite Games—lost in subplots—that occur and play out within *the* one Infinite Game.

To choose to play in *the* Infinite Game, we must first know there's a choice to play. The moment you understand the previous few paragraphs—truly understand them at a very deep level through resonance and remembrance—you have both lost your spiritual innocence *and* gained the option to freely choose to become a player in *the* Infinite Game. Mind you, this realization comes with a hefty spiritual responsibility as well, as not freely choosing to play in *the* one infinite game after losing your spiritual innocence is in fact choosing to be ignorant by default.

Once you see, you cannot unsee.

But as history has shown us time and again, "seeing" doesn't necessarily stop us from turning a blind eye. We must make a choice, which is a decision of what we will embody in this lifetime. How we choose to live our life—i.e., express our spiritual art into Creation—is where the rubber meets the road and ignorance is alchemized into ever-higher octaves of spiritual awareness and realization.

Freely choosing to play in *the* one Infinite Game is going on our Hero's Journey from the Ordinary World into the Spiritual World.

The Hero's Journey, a term coined by famed writer and mythology scholar Joseph Campbell, is the spiritual arc of ascension, which is deeply rooted in the evolutionary history of humanity. You will find this spiritual arc in all ancient civilizations, all ancient wisdom traditions, and all Indigenous traditions; it is deeply rooted in storytelling and mythology, which is how humanity continues to evolve even though storytelling has now also taken on the form of movies, TV, audiobooks, etc.

Once we're aware we have this choice, the timing or when we freely choose to play and go on our Hero's Journey onto the pathless land of the Infinite Game is up to us.

However, the journey itself is not optional.

> "Opportunities to find deeper powers within ourselves come when life seems most challenging."
> —JOSEPH CAMPBELL

Not to worry though, the universe will remind us often. This will show up as feeling empty, restless, unfulfilled, or even depressed. It might appear as crisis, catastrophe, or calamity that disrupts our life. All of these are just divine gifts wrapped in sandpaper; freely choosing to play means you accept the invitation to unwrap them.

Often, we might not feel ready or fully understand what we're beckoned to do. We fear the unknown; our attachment to what's known and therefore comfortable—even though it might actually be very uncomfortable suffering—holds us back from freely choosing to play. So, we numb ourselves with all sorts of distractions and addictions like chasing more trophies in the form of accumulating ever more trinkets and shiny objects, fame, fortune, and applause. Or we submit to alcohol, nicotine, drugs, gambling, sex, porn, change out partners or indulge in extramarital affairs thinking that might solve it.

It won't, you're treading water but only you can freely choose to play in *the* Infinite Game. Only you can freely choose to go on your Hero's Journey. The Infinite Game is in no particular rush for you to freely choose to play. It's playing an Infinite Game, so it's the patience of the Infinite Game played into eternity against your patience for your inner suffering.

Everything is always in perfect order. Everything always happens for our greatest growth, greatest prosperity, and greatest evolution. These are some of the rules of *the* Infinite Game you'll get to discover through remembrance once you freely choose to play.

There's one more layer to uncover in the principle "whoever *must* play, cannot *play*" as it pertains specifically to Finite Games. Remember the fishbowls we swim in and the coloration of the waters we take on as conditioned thinking? To the extent conditioned thinking is why we choose to play in a Finite Game, we're not choosing freely because the conditioned thinking is compelling us to play.

> "Everyone is born a genius,
> but the process of living de-geniuses them."
> —R. BUCKMINSTER FULLER

A son or daughter who's raised in a family of doctors and is ingrained with the conditioned thinking his/her family is a family of doctors so he/she must continue that legacy, is virtually incapable of freely choosing to play in the Finite Game of becoming a doctor. How many people do we know who chose to be a businessman, lawyer, accountant, rabbi, Army colonel, college graduate, politician, athlete, or take over the family business or what have you because they felt that was expected of them by their upbringing, social class, society, or even religion?

What's important to note is that when we *must* play a game, we cannot *play*, and it's only when we *play* that we can access our unique genius. We are each born with innate talents, gifts, and superpowers—no exceptions—but those can only be accessed and activated when we *play* a game; they go dull and muted when we *must* play. We might still become successful in the worldly sense, but we're leaving our genius—and therefore full potential—unrealized.

Finally, the embedded objective of Finite Games is not just to become the winner—or ranked if winning is not attainable—but to become somebody. Within becoming somebody, there's a distance created where we are right now at this moment and this somebody we're striving to become. When our aim is becoming a partner at a prestigious bulge bracket law firm, we inadvertently hitch our happiness and joy to becoming this somebody. We're not *playing* anymore; we now *must* play this defined Finite Game to become this somebody.

We can see this play out everywhere in our world that's obsessed with and measures success almost solely in the gaining of trophies and rankings. Those not ranked or without trophies are deemed worthless. Ranking or gaining trophies—becoming somebody—is a never-ending carousel, as the moment we gain a trophy we bask in its temporary glory and then move the goalposts for the next trophy we want to gain (read: somebody to become). This is the rat race of being compelled to play in Finite Games through our mistaken conditioned beliefs of what the game of life is all about.

It should be becoming clear now it's not the compulsory playing of Finite Games.

There's only one way off this Finite Game carousel: we freely choose to play *the* Infinite Game. The essence of the Infinite Game is to become nobody at all and within becoming totally okay being nobody we are liberated and totally free to be anybody.

Being totally free to be anybody, we can now freely choose to *play* any Finite Game. We can pick and choose whichever Finite Game we want to play in, unleash our genius as an experience we wish to experience, and be totally free whether it wins us any trophies or whether we get ranked.

We don't care, it's nice to win them, but we're really just playing the Infinite Game which is about continuing play indefinitely. We're already a winner, trophies then lose both their significance and claim on us. We're free; we're just playing.

To directly know this deeply—from a place of resonance and remembrance—is to understand the only real game there is to play. The rest of this book—if you will—is to show you the rules of the game Spirit plays; *the* one Infinite Game. Turns out these rules have a magnificently intelligent grand architecture to them, so that's what we'll explore and reveal next in Part II.

And guess what, as we choose to devote ourselves to the mastery of *the* one Infinite Game, by some miraculous occurrence of Divine Providence, we tend to become exceptionally good at whatever Finite Games we freely choose to play as our true genius—through *play*—now goes unleashed.

There's only one real game. Now you know, choose wisely.

PART II

THE ARCHITECTURE

"The only person you are destined to be
is the person you decide to be."

—RALPH WALDO EMERSON

CHAPTER 7

DUALITY, POLARITY, & TIME

TO RENDER THE FUNDAMENTAL ARCHITECTURE of all of Creation something we can bring into our own Creation, we must first develop a clear understanding of some essential principles of this Grand Architecture. I will be using the terms "Grand Architecture" and "Architecture" with a capital "A" interchangeably; just know they refer to the same thing. When I use either of these terms, I am referring to the totality of the Formless and the Finite World of Form. The term "Fundamental Architecture" of all of Creation refers specifically to the Finite World of Form.

From there, we can start to uncover what animates or brings these principles to life within us, which is what's covered in the rest of Part II. At the very heart of this Grand Architecture is the principal polarity in our universe—the Masculine and the Feminine—and this Part II is dedicated to delving deep into both of these principal polarities and then exploring and revealing how they are complementary and interdependent. In turn, this Grand Architecture sits at the very core of the Love+Truth Framework, and later, as we explore and layer in Part III and Part IV, this will all become strikingly clear. Even if you cannot yet "see" the whole house we're building, please know there's a blueprint we're following. Just trust the process; the foundation is now in place, but we still have more building to do.

Duality is the elemental quality of the "Finite World of Form" or that which we perceive and experience as our physical reality. This is the world or reality we perceive with our five senses, which we refer to as a dimension. If you recall from the chapter "Everything Is Energy," the Finite World of Form is only "1 percent" of reality; this is why it's referred to as a dimension as it's only a dimension of reality. In spiritual lingo, this dimension is often referred to as the third dimension or 3D. Labels aren't necessarily important; those are just words, so when we speak of the Finite World of Form, physical reality, or 3D, we're all pointing at the same thing. However, I specifically use the term "Finite World of Form" throughout this book as what's not widely understood by most— even in spiritual circles—is that what "3D" is really referring to is a level of Consciousness, and what we call our physical reality is just an effect, reflection, product, or derivative—whatever you wish to call it—of the density or octave of the cause which in all circumstances and across all dimensions is Consciousness. We'll explore all of this at great depths so don't worry if these words are not landing yet; all you need to know is that Consciousness is the cause of all effects across all dimensions. Consciousness is what creates realities—which is to say turns the formless into form—and the level or octave of Consciousness determines at which density of dimension Consciousness is able to manifest realities. In all of this, labels themselves are not so important, but the way in which we use specific words is.

Not to get too nerdy, but it is important to understand that the "Finite World of Form" is specific and not interchangeable with the "World of Finite Form." In the strictest sense, there's no such thing as "finite form," as nothing in the Finite World of Form is either static or finite. Even a mountain, which appears static, behaves like a wave if we project its evolution over hundreds of millions or billions of years. It just appears static because of our own time warp, meaning there's a distortion in how we experience time because human life—from an evolutionary perspective—is insignificantly short. Similarly, nothing in the Finite World of Form can actually be measured because everything is infinite. It only becomes finite because we round the measurement off at some arbitrary level of measurement. We measure the distance between two places, typically in miles or kilometers, maybe rounding it to the first decimal because, for practical purposes, that has sufficient utility for us. But you can always expand decimals when measuring anything, which means all measurements become infinite. The same goes for measuring time, size, volume, etc.

All of this is consistent with our scientific understanding of fractals—the infinitely complex patterns that are the building blocks of all form-based Creation—which can scale down (smaller) and up (larger) into infinity. If you wish to understand fractals on a deeper level, I encourage you to read up on the work of renowned mathematician and polymath Benoit Mandelbrot (1924–2010), who discovered what's referred to as the Mandelbrot Set. His work was a revolutionary breakthrough in the field of fractal geometry, which in turn, revealed great new insights into sacred geometry. Finite form, then, is a theoretical concept; it doesn't truly exist in the "real" Finite World of Form.

The above elaboration is key to fully appreciating the intrinsic nature of duality, which is that duality is one of the veils of illusion. What we perceive with our five senses as static, or largely unchanging finite form, is, in fact, a finite world—dimension—of infinite, dynamic, and ever-changing form.

Duality comes into existence through the creation of our Ego. As you might recall from the chapter "The Observer," the Ego is a psychological construct of self, created and held within our conscious mind. We also uncovered psychological constructs are thought-forms; that is, they're not "real." The Creation of this sense of self by default creates the sense of "others." Without the Ego, we would have no concept of what delineates "ourselves" and everything else. Our Ego is what allows us to perceive and experience our form, called our body, within the larger Finite World of Form. This is duality or the dualistic principle of the Fundamental Architecture of what we call reality, which is the Finite World of Form.

It's quite the eye-opener. Basically, that which is not real—our Ego—is perceiving, experiencing, and interacting with that which is not real—other Egos—in a dimension that appears real but is actually just energy masquerading as matter.

> "You're not a drop in the ocean, you're the ocean in a drop."
> —RUMI

Duality is an integral part of the Fundamental Architecture of the Finite World of Form because, without duality, Source Consciousness would have no way to experience itself in relation to itself. If you recall, all of Creation—you and me included—is individuated yet undivided parts of Source Consciousness expressing themselves into form. Duality, then, is form recognizing form.

Polarity, often confused with duality, is another fundamental quality of the Finite World of Form. Polarity is a continuum with opposite poles and a still point in between, which is the Fulcrum of the continuum. Remember this Fulcrum—we'll get back to that and its significance in later chapters. We see Polarity throughout the Finite World of Form, but the principal Polarity of all of Creation is Masculine vs. Feminine.

Before we delve deeper, let's clarify some essential nomenclature, so we don't get confused. When I refer to Masculine and Feminine, I am principally referring to energy, some of which I will describe as qualities, properties, or essences. When I refer to biological gender, I will use the words male/female or man/woman.

> "You do you, and I will do me."

I will bypass the whole topic of gender identification altogether, and nothing contained in this book should be interpreted or viewed in the context of that topic. Gender identification, in its entirety, is strictly anthropological in nature and has no bearing on spirituality. At its root, gender identification is a psychological construct (thought-form) about form in the Finite World of Form. Universal Truth and universal Love—spirituality—transcend the Finite World of Form as they each have their origins in the formless realm or dimension, so gender identification has no application in this dimension, and everything I speak about in this book applies to everyone equally regardless of biological gender, gender identification, sexual orientation, or any other possible identification of form like race, creed, ancestry, nationality, etc. Spirituality is color-blind, gender indifferent, and knows no cultural, societal, or national boundaries. Instead, it's infinite, eternal, and formless.

Now that we have that cleared up, back to Polarity. We'll unpack the Masculine and Feminine polarity in-depth in this chapter, as it's the driving force that animates all of Creation, but before we do, it's helpful to illustrate how it's Polarity that gives us dimension to our experiences.

We cannot experience joy unless we know sorrow. There's no day without night. Beautiful is born from ugly or vice versa. Yes needs no as much as light needs dark as without this polarity the other cannot exist. The essence of polarity is beautifully captured in the ubiquitous Yin/Yang symbol called "Taijitu."

The Taijitu is deeply embedded in ancient Chinese philosophy, and it is an integral part of Taoism. The symbol is represented by Yin (Feminine, black half with white dot) and Yang (Masculine, white half with black dot) and describes how seemingly opposite or contrary forces are actually complementary, interconnected, and interdependent. In this symbol, Yin also represents Chaos, and Yang represents Order, which we'll explore deeply when we reveal the essence of both Yin and Yang in this chapter.

The essence to grasp from polarity is that, in spiritual terms, there's no such thing as good or bad, right or wrong in an absolute way. It's all an abstraction—a perception that is a relative Truth—as everything lives on a continuum. Good is part of bad and vice versa. This is what the small dot represents in the Taijitu. If there were no bad, we would have no way of discerning what's good.

I recognize your mind might be protesting right now; how can there be no such thing as "right" or "wrong"? Let me first explain the principle at work here. For instance, we all can probably agree that beauty is in the eyes of the beholder. What's beautiful to some is ugly to others. It's an abstraction—a perception, in other words—on a continuum with opposite poles called beautiful and ugly.

Now, let's dissect "right" or "wrong." Let's assume for a moment that principally we all believe killing someone is wrong. Yet, when one nation goes to war with another, we send "our" soldiers into combat where they will kill others and now most of us believe this is "right" or justified. You see, even right or wrong are an abstraction—a perception of reality—on a continuum.

The context in which to view Polarity is outcomes or consequences. When we shower someone with kindness, we'll likely get favorable outcomes like a deep connection, an exchange of love, or a beautiful interaction or even friendship. When we shower someone with hostilities, we're very unlikely to be reciprocated with loving kindness. So, our choices have outcomes and consequences, and in that sense, we can use the words "good" and "bad" or "right" or "wrong." But, in an absolute sense, these words are just an abstraction on a continuum that we refer to as Polarity.

Polarity is an essential key to cultivate the level of spiritual discernment necessary to start navigating through the Finite World of Form with more grace and wisdom. This is mostly because this spiritual discernment allows us to get psychologically and emotionally untangled from our relative Truth—in other words, we start to get the fog off the lens through which we perceive life.

> "The separation between past, present, and future is only an illusion, although a convincing one."
> —ALBERT EINSTEIN

The final essential quality of the Fundamental Architecture of the Finite World of Form to explore is time. At closer examination, the linear time in which we perceive and experience physical reality appears very real, yet in reality, it's entirely fungible.

First, it's important to understand that our Earth time measurements (i.e., year, months, days, hours, minutes, etc.) are fairly logical and very practical yet completely arbitrary. Basically, we made it up. What we call a year is Earth's full revolution around the Sun, which takes 365 Earth days, six hours, and about nine minutes. We make up for these six hours and nine minutes by having a leap year every fourth year and adding a day to the month of February. I mention Earth days because the seven other planets in our solar system orbit around the Sun at different orbital speeds in different orbits in terms of relative distance from the Sun. So, for instance, one Mars day equals 1.0275 Earth days, and one Mars year is roughly 687 Earth days. Clearly, what we call time is relative and arbitrary, but it's practical, so we work with it.

Another attribute of what we call time is that it's linear. We typically consider the Big Bang the beginning of our known universe. In scientific circles, it's generally accepted the Big Bang happened about 13.8 billion years ago, give or take a few hundred million years. Our Gregorian calendar, introduced in 1582, starts at the birth year of Jesus Christ, and we preface anything before that year with BC ("Before Christ"), and technically anything after is AD ("anno domini"). All of this is linear and moves in one direction—forward-moving—which creates what we call past, present, and future.

This linearity is native to the Finite World of Form, but the forward-moving attribute is relative and arbitrary as it relates to language. Let me explain. If we had created a calendar that counted down—let's say Jesus Christ was born in the year 10,000—then as of the writing of this book (2022), we would now be in the year 7,978, and so linear time would, in effect, be backward-moving.

My point is this: it's always "Now."

> "Ultimately, all moments are really one, therefore Now is an eternity."
> —DAVID BOHM

Superimposing the framework of linear time—which we already concluded was practical yet entirely arbitrary—to our physical reality does not change the fact that it's always "Now." We can refer to the past, but it's an abstraction as we can't go there. We can refer to the future, but that's an abstraction also, as it hasn't happened yet. We're stuck in the present—the moment called "Now"—for eternity.

Time then, as we just defined above, is a perception of our experience in our physical reality or this dimension we call 3D. It's an essential quality of the Fundamental Architecture of the Finite World of Form, which we can observe and experience, yet, much like duality, it's not truly real.

The opposite of "time" is "no time." Now we're in the formless spiritual realm or dimension which knows no time or space.

It's important to note that the forward-moving attribute of linear time is a product of how we interpret time to move; it's not intrinsic. If it were intrinsic, the opposite would be backward-moving time which leads to the premise of retro-causality as the explanation of syntropy—a topic we'll uncover later. Retro-causality might work well with our current mathematical formulas of how the universe works, but a working math equation doesn't make a phenomenon a universal Truth.

However, our current scientific understanding and explanation of syntropy are directionally pointing in the right direction. I recognize this might yield me some poisonous arrows aimed in my direction, but, for me, spiritual Truth trumps what some will deem scientific heresy. But, with Albert Einstein and David Bohm on my side, I feel confident my understanding is supported by what these and various other physicist geniuses were pointing at, not to speak of what we can discern from ancient wisdom traditions and various master teachers who have graced this Earth.

The key takeaway from all of this is that time is something we perceive and experience in our physical reality as it's an essential quality of the Fundamental Architecture of the Finite World of Form. It's unique and exclusive to the dimension of physical reality and ties into the second law of thermodynamics, which we refer to as entropy. As we explore, we will uncover how entropy and syntropy are closely related, although not mirror opposites in all aspects.

In the formless dimension of the metaphysical world—spirituality and Consciousness—there is "no time."

Finally, since the Finite World of Form is nested within the formless infinite metaphysical realm, we can say, in reality, there's "no time" at all as it's always "Now."

I know, this stuff is deep. Don't worry if this hasn't fully arrived yet; we'll keep exploring, and we'll look and explore this from various angles and perspectives, sometimes even using different words to describe the same thing because different words land differently for different people. Invariably, as we turn over more and more puzzle pieces, the puzzle will start to come together.

Now that we have anchored in a shared understanding of these three fundamental aspects (i.e., Duality, Polarity, and Time) of the Grand Architecture, we're well prepared to dive into the principal polarities. We'll start with the Masculine first, followed by the Feminine, and then we'll close out this Part II by going deep into how these two principal polarities are each a sacred aspect of one inseparable harmonious unity commonly referred to as Source or Source Consciousness. Although, as mentioned before, don't get hung up on labels. We're only really concerned with the essence, not labels.

With that said, let's explore the Masculine.

CHAPTER 8
THE MASCULINE & CONSCIOUSNESS

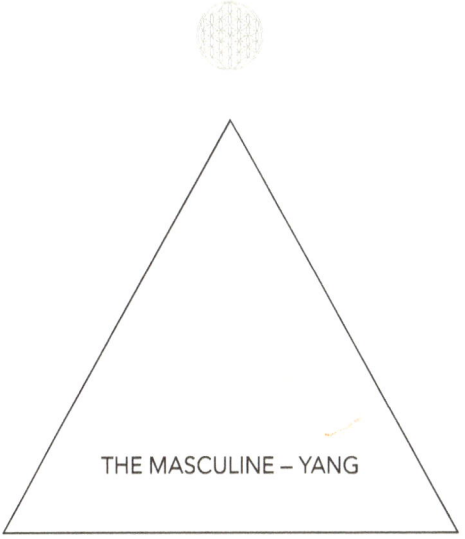

LET'S START AT THE END, so we know where we're going: Consciousness = Love.

Before we go on a journey to explore why that's so, let's revisit that all of Creation has a Grand Architecture, and much of this we can retrace in such things as sacred geometry, principles like self-organizing complex living systems, fractal patterns, elemental qualities, frequencies, and constituent attributes.

It's an immaculate design, originating from within Source Consciousness—the Infinite Intelligence that designed, orchestrates, and governs all of Creation in infinitely intelligent ways. This is the fundamental basis of the universal Truth that everything is always in perfect order.

The Love+Truth Framework we'll now start to unfold one layer at a time was born from sacred geometry, which is evident in the graphic representation. As much as I might have written this book, the Truth is the content was revealed to me through sacred geometry so let's define what that is first.

The rest of Part II, Part III, and Part IV will be a progression of how, from the initial compilation of the elementary forms of two basic equilateral triangles, the encoded wisdom within the sacred geometry of these forms was revealed.

Sacred geometry is a field of study as old as antiquity. It ascribes symbolic and sacred meanings to certain geometric shapes, patterns, and their respective geometric proportions and ratios. Sacred geometry is where mathematical principles intersect with the premise there's a geometric design that is the foundational underpinning of the Creation of the cosmos. We can observe and witness sacred geometry in all of Creation—both in all life forms as well as in all inanimate objects. We can retrace sacred geometry back to all great civilizations like ancient Egypt, the Roman Empire, and the Chinese dynasties; across all major world religions such as Taoism, Hinduism, Islam, Judaism, and Christianity; and all esoteric wisdom traditions like Buddhism, Stoicism, Gnosticism,

Hermeticism, etc. Literally, sacred geometry is anywhere and everywhere, even in the fields of science, music, and art.

So what? You might wonder.

Excellent question, and the simple answer is just one single word: Divinity. If I do my writing job well, you will come to see the sheer brilliance, magnificence, and absolute magical beauty within sacred geometry, and sacred geometry then becomes an access point to see the Divinity within and throughout all of Creation. And I know if I can move you to see the Divinity within all of Creation, I am a mere hairline away from you being able to recognize the Divinity within yourself and to feel how you're an interwoven part of this magical web of life. Now, once that happens, we're on the home stretch as now you cannot help but come to see and recognize that same spark of Divinity in all others. This trifecta of Divinity remembrances—which might occur in any order—is the ultimate game changer, literally and figuratively. As once you fully internalize that you are a unique spark of Divinity expressed as spiritual art, being "that" becomes self-evident and any doubts about which game you're here to play on the Earthly plane dissipates like morning dew does before the rising sun.

Let's start unpacking; we still have much more ground to cover.

As mentioned in Part I, Source Consciousness itself is whole, the perfect integral unity of all things in perfect harmony. It needed Duality to experience itself, the principle of form recognizing form. It then brought all of Creation—form—into existence through

Polarity when the perfect integral unity bifurcated itself into two principal polarities: the Masculine and the Feminine. The subatomic representation of this bifurcation is the proton (Masculine, positive charge) and the electron (Feminine, negative charge), and all of Creation can be reduced back to these two principal polarities. The Fulcrum or still point is also represented at the subatomic level in the form of the neutron, which is our first glimpse of the holy trinity, which we'll discover is interwoven into all of Creation in all sorts of poetic ways.

The sum of Source Consciousness can be retraced in the Masculine and Feminine parts—two essences that combined restore the unity of Source Consciousness.

A full restoration of Source Consciousness, sometimes referred to as Unity Consciousness or Singularity, is the ultimate form of enlightenment. But rather than seeing or setting enlightenment as a goal to achieve, it's more helpful to see it as a spiritual path—an adventure—we choose to go on. This is the spiritual path of stepping onto the pathless land toward Unity Consciousness—this is *the* one Infinite Game. Before we can venture onto this spiritual path in earnest, we first need to awaken, which is to realize this path even exists. And, as we explored earlier, it's only when we know the path exists that we can freely choose to play in the Infinite Game.

With all that said, let's begin.

First, please note the terms "the Masculine" and "Masculine-energy" and "Yang" are interchangeable. Conversely, the terms "the

Feminine" and "Feminine-energy" and "Yin" are interchangeable as well. I might use any of these terms interchangeably, depending on the context or syntax.

We each have both Masculine and Feminine energy within us—no exclusions. One energy might be highly dominant while the other is said to be dormant or not integrated, but there's no such thing as a human being with only Yang or only Yin. Men, by and large, are Masculine-energy dominant, and women vice versa. This is not a hard rule, though, and biological gender or gender identification plays no role in this. We're each wired differently, so men can be naturally Feminine-energy dominant, and women can be Masculine-energy dominant. In reality, this is quite rare; what's more often the case when we encounter them is that these men or women are non-dominant, meaning their Yin and Yang are naturally close to being balanced. We perceive these men as being more Feminine and women as being more Masculine because of the contrast with their respective archetypes.

When a man is Masculine-energy dominant, he will embody Masculine-energy archetypal attributes, not to be confused with cultural male archetypal attributes, which can vary significantly from culture to culture. A "manly man" in American culture differs from a "manly man" in Latin or, for instance, Japanese culture. Even with the same general culture, there can be subcultures of each that have their own archetype of what constitutes a "manly man."

A typical man that's Masculine-energy dominant but who has not integrated his Feminine-energy is energetically disharmonious. This will illuminate the shadow side of his Masculine-energy which we'll cover in-depth in the final chapter of this Part II, together with the Yang archetypal attributes. The same goes for women the other way around.

Finally, it's important to note that none of this has anything to do with sexual orientation or preferences. For instance, gay men can be Masculine-energy dominant, have balanced or neutral energies, which would make them appear more Feminine, or in rare cases, be Feminine-energy dominant. The same goes for lesbian women in reverse and any and all sexual orientations in between.

As mentioned earlier, Masculine-energy is one of two essences of Source Consciousness. Each of these two essences was endowed with three constituent attributes from Source Consciousness, which is to say each essence is incomplete—i.e., not whole or integral—without the other essence. However, restoring unity between these two essences is not about realizing perfect balance—it's about realizing perfect harmony. Recall that Source Consciousness is formless and biological gender is exclusive to form. So, Source Consciousness is always in perfect harmony; the balance within Source Consciousness is fluid and dynamic as it's everything or the entire continuum between the Masculine and the Feminine.

Masculine-energy has three constituent attributes, which we'll, at times, refer to as cornerstones going forward. These are Awareness, Intelligence, and Energy, which are the constituent attributes of Consciousness itself. Hence, the Masculine represents the essence of Consciousness within Source Consciousness. When we refer to the essence of Consciousness, it would not be an understatement to suggest we could easily replace essence with genius. All of Source Consciousness is pure genius, so Consciousness is one essence or reflection of its genius.

There's a chapter dedicated to each of the cornerstones of Awareness, Intelligence, and Energy, but let's explore Consciousness itself further first. As we do, please remember words—which are content—can only point at something that's beyond words, beyond content, and beyond language.

Consciousness is the infinite stillness that contains everything. It's infinite, eternal, and omnipresent, omnipotent, and omniscient. Consciousness is the Absolute, there's nothing beyond it, and everything is contained within it. Literally, everything in this universe is Consciousness expressing itself both through form and the formless, which is the "nothingness" we refer to as space.

If you wish to view it this way, Source Consciousness is what existed before what we call "reality" was created and will remain whenever "reality" ceases to exist. Reality contains not just humanity or planet Earth, but all the billions upon billions of galaxies known to us, as well as the entire known universe and whatever may extend beyond it. This entire reality—as far as science can tell us today—had an origin and is seemingly headed for an eventual collapse and terminus event (don't worry, this event is billions of Earth years from now). Source Consciousness or the Absolute, of which all other forms of Consciousness (including you and me) are an aspect, was here before reality was created and will still be here after it ceases to exist. It can be no other way as this reality exists within this Consciousness and, at the same time, is made of this Consciousness. Don't worry if this is not fully landing yet;

this is deep and fundamental existential knowledge about the nature of "our" reality, so we're going to pick this apart from all angles throughout this book. I have no doubt the puzzle pieces will all come together as you read on.

To visualize Consciousness, you could liken it to an omnipresent invisible electromagnetic field that encapsulates everything. From now on, I'll use the term "Infinite Field of Consciousness" when I refer to this infinite, eternal, omnipotent, omniscient, and omnipresent field that encompasses both the formless and the Finite World of Form. Don't worry if it's challenging to conceptualize Consciousness at this moment. When we start exploring its three constituent attributes, we'll start adding dimensions to Consciousness that will help greatly in internalizing what Consciousness truly is.

Since Consciousness is formless and infinite, it is also not time or space. We can say then the Masculine is the infinite—that of no time and no space—living in the Finite World of Form, which is time and space. The formless living in form.

The Finite World of Form is subject to entropy. Entropy is the second law of thermodynamics that states that all form (living or inanimate) is subject to dissipating energy, which is to say it eventually will rot, decay, and dissipate or die. Entropy is the process from Order into Chaos. So, the finite or form = Chaos.

> "There is nothing more real than what cannot be seen and there is nothing more certain than what cannot be heard."
> —CONFUCIUS

The formless—Consciousness—then is Order. In fact, it's infinite or perfect Order. Systems Science, an interdisciplinary field concerned with understanding systems, has confirmed so much as the consensus is that Consciousness appears to be a spontaneous, self-organizing intelligent system with omnipresence. We're back to self-organizing complex living systems. Can you see the connection?

In neo-Confucian Chinese philosophy, "Li" is the principle or law or organizational rights considered to be the underlying reason of the perfect order of nature. "Li" is said to be the intelligence that orchestrates "Chi," which is energy or life force. "Li" is not something we can observe directly with our five senses, but we can study it by observing how it works and directs nature, and in neo-Confucian philosophy, it was held that the master can see the underlying Order through the apparent Chaos of all of Creation.

David R. Hawkins, MD, PhD, in his seminal book *Power vs. Force* introduced to the world the first scientifically evidenced levels of human consciousness, which he called the Map of Consciousness. The map depicts the vibration of the various levels of human consciousness; we'll discover the true significance of this in the chapter about the constituent attribute Energy. It's trademarked, so I can't share a graphic in this book, but I highly encourage you to look it up and study it closely.

> "Everything in Nature contains all the powers of Nature. Everything is made of one hidden stuff."
> —RALPH WALDO EMERSON

Perhaps you noticed I stated "levels of human consciousness." This is intentional as systems scientists have also arrived at the conclusion that literally everything in this universe appears to have some form of Consciousness. Of course it does; to be an integral part of self-organizing complex living systems, something has to design, animate, orchestrate, and govern all of this. All animals from the highest intelligence ones all the way down to single-cell organisms, all inanimate objects like rocks and a grain of sand, and every star, planet, or meteorite not only have Consciousness, but they are also an aspect of Source Consciousness expressing itself into form. And the most precious self-organizing complex living system to us humans—Mother Earth—most definitely has Consciousness. Measurable even, it's called the Schumann resonance and holds a frequency of 7.83 Hz.

Each human being then is Consciousness expressing itself into form. To be even more specific, each human being is an individuated aspect or expression of Source Consciousness. Again, don't worry if this is not quite landing yet; we're going to pick this apart with surgical precision as well throughout this book and even take it a few levels deeper.

So, how is all this possible? Well, all Consciousness has the same three cornerstones except, for instance, the DNA sequence of a rat or a monkey is different than that for a human and the level of Awareness, Intelligence, and Energy within Consciousness can vary greatly, so what it can potentially express into form is infinite. Incidentally, humans share about 50 percent of DNA with bananas and close to 98 percent with dolphins. So, biologically, humans are just a few chromosomal rearrangements away from all of the rest of nature, which reconfirms humans are an integral part of nature.

The level of Consciousness determines what amplitude of Awareness, Intelligence, and Energy is accessible and this is the core premise of Hawkins' Map of Consciousness. We can quite readily equate "levels" of Consciousness with "octaves" where there are lower octaves and higher octaves. At higher octaves, the amplitude—meaning mass, volume, or magnitude—of Awareness, Intelligence, and Energy is going to be higher than at lower octaves of Consciousness. In other words, at higher octaves Consciousness becomes ever more refined, powerful, insightful, and enlightened and we are literally able to see, understand, and discern reality at greater depths. Hawkins' scale of levels of human consciousness runs from 20 all the way to 1,000, which is basically Unity Consciousness or enlightenment. It's important to note the scale is logarithmic, meaning 400 is not twice as much as 200. With a base 10 logarithmic scale, 400 means 10 to the power of 400 (10^{400}), which is exponentially higher than 10 to the power of 200 (10^{200}).

The implications of this are enormous. At current, Hawkins estimates 80–85 percent of humanity resonates at consciousness levels of 200 or below. 200 is a critical threshold as Consciousness below this level is ruled by levels which are governing through negative states of being such as shame, guilt, apathy, fear, and anger. Above the critical Consciousness level of 200, positive states of being like courage, reason, love, and joy become governing.

Moreover, Hawkins' extensive research showed that humans vibrating below levels of 200 are Ego-identified (i.e., mind and body). Ego-identification is strongly correlated to being Mind-dominant where we're not only governed by logic and rational thought but primarily driven by our primal survival instincts. From this Mind orientation we view others (and the Outer World) as separate from ourselves and objects or means to personal survival and we're primarily guided by the seeking of pleasure, predation, and personal gain. Neurosensory inputs from our five senses pass directly through the Amygdala, so instinctual and habituated emotional responses are triggered before intelligence and cognition. We'll further define Intelligence from the perspective of the universe later in the chapter. Intelligence as our prevailing collective human understanding is severely skewed by this Mind-dominance and the suppression and dismissal of the intelligence of our Heart.

The Amygdala is our fear trigger, it's hypersensitive and interprets every neurosensory input from the perspective of being a potential threat to personal survival. Further, when we're Ego-identified and Mind-dominant we're in a trance of our inevitable enculturation (conditioned thinking); we literally can't see past or through the fog on our lens, which skews our views of life into Falsehoods, which we're convinced are Truths.

As mentioned, Mind-dominance means we're governed by logic and rational thought. We see evidence of this all around, as through logic we justify away all the unintelligent outcomes humanity creates like war, violence, hate, racism, inequalities, injustices, rampant pollution, and the destruction of Mother Earth just to name a few. At this level of Consciousness, we really only have access to Love (the emotion), so we commit cruel and barbaric atrocities left and right and our moral compass is very loose as evidenced by the prevalence of the abuse of power and the pervasiveness of self-dealing, greed, malfeasance, corruption, crime, and the general indifference to human suffering of others. This world is misguided by the use of Force and dog-eat-dog competition and identifies strongly with an ill-fated misperception of Darwinism. And we justify all of it away based on identification with race, creed, political ideology, nationality, religion, and even economic ideologies. This is a world governed by a predominantly Ego-identified humanity which is Mind-dominant. We'll circle back to this Mind-dominance later and explore it in-depth.

Truthfully, the idea most have that humanity is a very advanced species is a complete illusion. What we by and large are is a species with advanced technologies running on primal survival instincts.

This picture changes dramatically when our level of Consciousness rises above the level of 200. At that inflection point of Consciousness, we start to gain access to the intelligence of our Heart and we transition from being governed by primal survival instincts to spiritual energy or our Divinity. Neurosensory inputs are now fast-tracked to the prefrontal cortex, but more importantly the suprarational intelligence of our Heart takes over from the Amygdala as the predominant filter of our neurosensory inputs. This marks a sea change shift from perceiving the world from the perspective of separation and survival instincts to the lens of unity and Higher Knowing. Rather than viewing ourselves as separate and distinct entities from the Outer World, we start viewing all others and the Outer World as one, which is the premise of Oneness, which we'll cover in-depth in Part IV, The Principles.

When the intelligence of our Heart comes online, it's literally as if we're getting infused with a higher intelligence; our world views and perception of others change radically as we're starting to gain access to Love (the energy) or universal Love. It's not even gaining access, Love (the energy) starts to permeate our entire state of being—this is basically the process of our innate Divinity coming online. All of this is very challenging to describe to a person below level 200—it's like describing the color orange in a sea of red to the color-blind.

At levels above 200, the use of Force transmutes into the proper use of Power—the power of Love, that is, which for the avoidance of doubt is what we referred to earlier as Love (the energy). Our orientation toward fierce winner-takes-all competition turns into an openness to seek win-win-win collaboration, which is aligned with the principles of nature (symbiosis) and countless Indigenous wisdom traditions which were all but eradicated by colonialism and later imperialism.

In fact, one of the great prevailing distortions in humanity today is the interpretation of Darwinism. People worship the notion of "survival of the fittest" or "survival of the strongest" and use it as a favored battle cry and justification (again) for the abuse, harm, damage, and suffering they inflict on others and their environment. All of this is not just steeped in deep ignorance of Darwin's work but in the ignorance of lower octaves of Consciousness, which have no access to seeing the interconnectedness of all of Creation. Darwin's research concluded that it appears in the evolutionary process of species, *not* the strongest but the one most fit to adapt in an ever-changing environment appears to become the dominant or surviving species.

This nuance changes everything, as, from this vantage point of Darwinism, the single most important question before all of humanity now becomes: *Of what value is humanity to the self-organizing complex living system called Mother Earth?* We have miserably failed at being good stewards of Mother Earth; our cruelty and harm caused to others, animals, and the biosphere is nothing short of barbaric, and we cheer at the idea the way out is colonizing Mars. In our current manner, Mother Earth is far better off without humanity as, left to its own devices, nature is just fine. The first step out of this disastrous conundrum is not even raising our level of consciousness; it's cultivating a sense of humility so we can start to take an honest look at the mess we made. Trust me; this wasn't what God had in mind in Genesis 1:26–28.

> "We are in a race to raise human consciousness."

The process of enculturation leads to dominant states of being, which is how we perceive reality and what determines our views on life, which in turn, determines our thoughts and actions. As described, at these lower negative states of being, there's a limited range of Awareness, Intelligence, and Energy we have access to, so we resort to Force. All the enduring unintelligent outcomes in the world, like wars, violence, hate, racism, inequalities, injustices, rampant pollution, etc., are all due to most of humanity being at a low level of consciousness, which we could call the collective unconsciousness of the many.

If Fear (100) is our governing state of being, we don't have access to the same level of Awareness, Intelligence, and Energy we have at the governing state of being of Love (500), for instance. In fact, below the critical threshold of 200, we're survival driven as we perceive the world to be a dangerous and unsafe place. We justify and rationalize greed, malfeasance, and corruption and are capable of harming or even killing others as we lack empathy and reverence for the sanctity of all life.

Above 200, we start to progressively gain access to exponentially greater levels of Awareness, Intelligence, and Energy, which opens up whole new ways of solving problems and challenges, seeing opportunities and self-evident higher order solutions where none were visible before, and gaining the power to create positive outcomes. Frankly, this is the only way out from where the world stands today. The way out is to raise the collective level of human consciousness, which we can each only contribute to by raising our own. As we continue, this book will reveal step-by-step how all these puzzle pieces fit together and how we can ascend to higher levels (which can also be seen or referred to as "octaves") of Consciousness by bringing this wisdom into our own embodiment.

The logarithmic scale has another significance. One person at a level of consciousness above 200 counterbalances multiples of people below 200. For instance, one person at 300 counterbalances 90,000 people below 200. At 500, this becomes 750,000 people below 200, and at 600, it becomes 10 million. Without this counterbalancing effect, humanity would have likely already self-destructed, as the negativity would have no offset. This also demonstrates how relatively few people raising their level of Consciousness can cause a tipping point to occur, which would trigger a phase transition in accordance with the Adaptive Cycle model of change for humanity (as we'll further uncover in Part IV in the chapter "Growth"). There are clear signs this might actually be happening right now; more on this later.

> "As mentioned before, awakening = remembrance."

Awakening of the Masculine involves no longer getting lost in the finite, which is form. Unawakened, Yang is lost in playing Finite Games, chasing worldly success, and is driven by a lust for trophies and worldly power. At a deeper level, this is due to the unconscious belief of the unawakened Masculine that it can control and dominate the Finite World of Form. It's seeking itself—Order—in the Finite World of Form, which is False Order since the Outer World is entropic or Chaotic.

The deep Yang lesson is to surrender, which is letting go of control of the Finite World of Form. We'll circle back later to what the Masculine must surrender to, but the key takeaway for now is that awakened Yang emerges through the illumination that true inner freedom for the Masculine is in *being* Order (Yang) within holding an ocean of Chaos (Yin) without.

In other words, the Masculine is the stillness of the eye of the hurricane. In a fully awakened and illuminated state, the Masculine surrenders to allow the storm (Life itself or Outer World) to be what it might be and finds its freedom in being the eye of the hurricane regardless of what plays out in the Outer World. Only from this place can the Masculine truly freely choose to play any Finite Games as it knows the real game it's playing—*the Infinite Game*.

This eye of the hurricane—this place of total stillness and perfect Order—is the source spring of universal Love. In Hinduism and Buddhism, the Sanskrit word "Samadhi" is used to refer to this state of total bliss where our Consciousness merges with Source Consciousness, which has been universally described as being engulfed in an ocean of Love.

To experience this as a continuous, uninterrupted state of being is to be enlightened at exceptionally high levels of Consciousness. On Hawkins' Map of Consciousness, this would be c. 700 and above, and there might be a handful of beings on Earth right now at that level of Consciousness. Jesus, Buddha, and Lord Krishna are the only ones known to have calibrated at 1,000, so that's the rarest of rare throughout human history.

However, at levels of 200 and above, we can start having experiences where we come close or touch Samadhi, even if ever so briefly. Its mere palpable presence to us will break the seal of universal Love within, and it will start seeping ever so slowly into our whole being and life's expression.

This process of ascension—which is our Consciousness expanding or rising into higher octaves—is how Love (the energy) becomes something we not only directly know but steadily becomes the force field that permeates and illuminates our entire being. We literally become luminescent to others and our mere presence becomes undeniable for the awakened and unawakened alike. And so we end where we started: Consciousness = Love.

Now, I fully appreciate that just this one chapter probably hasn't connected all the dots for you to feel and embrace that Consciousness = Love. We need to trek much further and deeper into Consciousness as there are many more dots to connect before we can ultimately connect all of this back to being spiritual art.

So, let's now explore the constituent attributes of Consciousness—Awareness, Intelligence, and Energy—at deeper levels so we can start internalizing what Consciousness truly is.

CHAPTER 9

AWARENESS

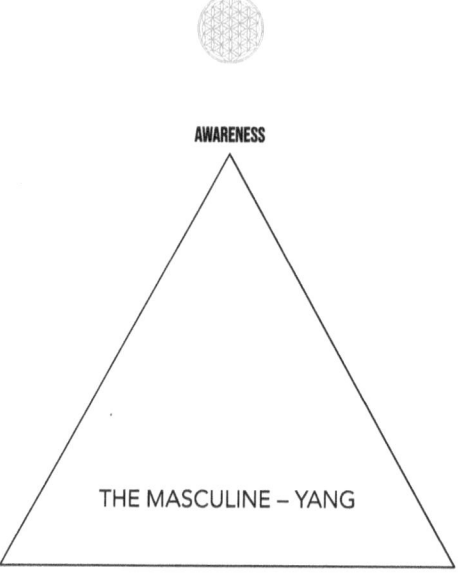

LIKE CONSCIOUSNESS ITSELF, ITS FIRST CORNERSTONE— Awareness—is somewhat nebulous and amorphous. We all have an intuitive sense of what it is, but when asked to define Awareness, it gets tricky fast.

Fortunately, there's quite a bit to say about Awareness, so a clearer picture reveals itself, and the ambiguous becomes far more distinct.

For starters, let's build on the premise that all of Creation in the Finite World of Form is Consciousness expressing itself into form. All of Creation then has some level of Awareness as Awareness itself is a cornerstone or constituent attribute of Consciousness. In other words, there's no such thing as Consciousness that doesn't have any Awareness.

Advances in biological science have confirmed so much; we now know that even single-cell organisms have Awareness as evidenced by their interaction with their surroundings. We could state that these simplest of life forms have an innate awareness of the boundary between self and their surroundings. Single-cell organisms are not only aware of their surroundings, they interact and communicate with, and are in an interdependent relationship with their surroundings. We once again see this pattern of self-organized complex living systems—in this case, a single-cell organism—being nested in larger self-organized complex living systems and there being an undeniable symbiotic relationship between nested systems.

We can also see Awareness has an element of sensing in it. When Awareness meets another life form, it's really sensing the Awareness in the other life form. Form recognizing form is truly Awareness meeting Awareness. The interesting thing is we know this phenomenon is not exclusive to the Awareness of any life form meeting the Awareness of another life form, whether that's a human, animal, tree, or plant, all of which have been scientifically proven to have some level of Awareness. In fact, trees and plants have been proven to have nervous systems and intelligence, and they can communicate through their root systems. None of this would be remotely possible without some level of Awareness. The kicker is that this same phenomenon is also apparent when Awareness meets the Awareness of inanimate forms.

Starting with this chapter, we're now going to traverse into and reveal yet a deeper layer of reality within, for example, something as seemingly inconspicuous as "awareness." Almost all of us have an understanding of what "awareness" constitutes, yet for the most part, our understanding tends to be incomplete or even wholly off base as we've never actually explored for ourselves what something means. Instead, we've just adopted what our upbringing, school system, culture, society, religion, etc., informed us "things" mean, so what we believe to be our innate understanding of "things" is, in fact, extrinsic, acquired, and therefore truthfully not even really our own. We'll go much deeper into all of this in later parts, but for now, the key takeaway is to open up to explore deeper layers of meaning and spiritual truth within regular words we all think we already understand. This goes for Awareness but equally as we mine the depths and richness of spiritual truth within Intelligence, Energy, Being, Creativity, and Reverence. Like a painter needs to master the composition of color for his/her paintings to come alive with the art within him/her, so does the spiritual Poet need to plumb the depths of the constituent attributes to allow their spiritual art within to come alive in their whole being.

> "Ultimately, the entire universe has to be understood as a single undivided whole."
> —DAVID BOHM

To understand this, we have to get back to subatomic particles and that everything is energy. As explained before, these subatomic particles can take on a wave-state (potentiality) or a particle-state (actuality). In modern physics, there's an experiment called the "Double-Slit Experiment," which conclusively proved that the mere observation of a subatomic particle changes its behavior. The mere observation of a subatomic particle in a wave-state locks this wave-state subatomic particle into time and space, which is to say it takes on the particle-state. So, we can deduce from this that when Awareness (through observation) meets the Awareness of a subatomic particle in the wave-state, the subatomic particle takes on the particle-state. This is also referred to as "the observer effect."

This observer effect has a deeper layer because what it's revealing to us—in scientific terms—is what mystics have been pointing at since time come. And that is that all of Creation—the Finite World of Form—comes into existence through our Awareness. Your Awareness—observation—is what locks subatomic particles into time and space, which is to say, it becomes an actuality. I recognize this is hard to grasp as, through our five senses, we perceive the Finite World of Form as static and unchanging. This is an optical illusion that is possible because the phase transition from wave-state to particle-state is such an infinitesimal amount of time that we could say it's instantaneous, which is why we experience form as continuous.

The conundrum is that this is not provable as the mere introduction of observation changes the state of a subatomic particle instantaneously. Even inanimate objects like a camera have

Awareness since we already concluded everything is Consciousness expressing itself into form, and there's no such thing as Consciousness without Awareness. Don't misinterpret this to imagine the camera itself has Consciousness like you would think a human has, but a camera can be seen as a collective of atoms, and each atom is Consciousness expressed into form. Even though most of science still has little idea of what Consciousness truly is, its presence is now widely accepted, which is science confirming what the mystics have been pointing at for millennia. If this whole topic escapes you, don't worry because being unable to internalize any of this doesn't in any way prevent you from living and embodying the spiritual wisdom contained in this book. Understanding physics is simply not a prerequisite for making your life an expression of spiritual art, but for some of you, knowing this will create a bridge from the observable world to the formless or spiritual realm, which is a bridge from the domain of the mind into the realm of the heart.

So, let's climb out of this rabbit hole of quantum physics and explore Awareness from a more familiar and palpable perspective.

We are all familiar with the concept of conscious Awareness, which occurs when we become consciously aware of someone or something, which could be form but also an occurrence, situation, or event. Conscious Awareness happens when something registers—appears in thought-form—in our conscious Mind. We have no conscious Awareness of what's in our subconscious Mind until it rises up, so to speak, to the level of our conscious Mind. Remember though, it's what we call the Observer that's aware of what appears as thought-form in our conscious Mind, not the conscious Mind itself. We just connected a major dot, if you noticed: Awareness—which is a cornerstone of Consciousness—resides at the level of the Observer.

We can liken our conscious Mind to the tip of the iceberg that's above sea level and the subconscious Mind, the invisible—unconscious—body of the iceberg that's below sea level. This tip of the iceberg is consciously aware the bottom part is there, but we just have no conscious Awareness of what's within this bottom part.

Conscious Awareness does not just pertain to our subconscious Mind, though that's only part of it. It pertains to our entire perception of all of reality. As we covered before, our perception is the relative Truth as all of our perception is colored by the lens through which we perceive life. And our perception dictates how we experience our reality. We all know that two people can perceive the exact same reality—occurrence—and experience it very differently.

Let's take the example of two business partners: their company goes bankrupt, and they're both in financial ruin. One might experience this as disastrous, become destitute, and end up as a homeless person or, worse, commit suicide. They were broken by the experience. The other licks their wounds and starts rebuilding their life; they see an opportunity in this gift wrapped in sandpaper and perhaps chart in a direction with their life they've always wanted to go in but weren't able to because of their commitment to the business. The point is, how we experience reality is completely entangled with our perception of reality, and this perception comes from the coloration of the lens through which we perceive life.

We can only "see" what we're consciously aware of, and this could be an opportunity—understanding a situation or why an occurrence in our reality could not be any other way. We don't even have to know or understand why any occurrence is the way it is; the mere Awareness of our perception of it—which dictates our experience of it, whether positive or negative—gives us the power to change our perception and, therefore, our experience of it. The "thing" doesn't change; our perception of it changes, which changes our experience. Any "thing" in our Outer World is truly out of our control; however, our Inner World perception of it is fully under our control to the extent of our Awareness of our perceptions.

> "The root cause of all pain and suffering is ignorance."
> —BUDDHA

We can say then that when we're not consciously aware, we're ignorant of that thing we're not consciously aware of. What logically follows is that when we expand our (conscious) Awareness, we become less ignorant.

In Buddhism, ignorance as the root cause of all pain and suffering refers to a fundamental misperception of the true nature of the self and all phenomena. That is, we confuse the small Self (i.e., Ego) for the true Self and we allow Outer World phenomena to dictate our Inner World state or experience. This same premise is a fundamental cornerstone of Stoicism. Here are some quotes from some of the greatest Stoic philosophers that all point at the exact same thing in different words.

> "Men are disturbed not by things, but by the view which they take of them."
> —EPICTETUS

> "If you're distressed by anything external, the pain is not due to the thing itself but your estimate of it; and this you have the power to revoke at any moment."
> —MARCUS AURELIUS

> "We are more frightened than hurt; and we suffer more in imagination than in reality."
> —SENECA

In the chapter "Mind Mastery & States of Being" in Part V, I will provide practical instructions on how we can change our perception—and, therefore, experience—through mastering our Awareness. But before we get there, though, we have a lot more ground to cover first, so we establish a solid foundation of spiritual Truth to work from.

When we expand our Awareness, we are not only reducing our ignorance, but we inevitably raise our level of Consciousness. When we raise our level of Consciousness, the other two cornerstones—Intelligence and Energy—expand as the rising tide of one constituent attribute causes the tide to rise for all. This means that an expansion of our Awareness will inevitably give us access to greater levels of Intelligence and more refined mastery of Energy as we'll come to define those cornerstones when we explore them at deeper levels. This ties back directly to Hawkins'

Map of Consciousness, which plots and reveals the levels of human Consciousness.

All of this does beg the obvious question: *How do we expand our Awareness?*

We expand our conscious Awareness first and foremost by coming to know the true nature of reality, which is universal Truth. The Ethos captured in this book is a roadmap and framework to lay bare this universal Truth of the true nature of reality. I am by no means suggesting this book contains everything there is to know about universal Truth or the only place you could find it, but it contains sufficient breadth and depth to enable you to start living a life of spiritual art. Part II provides the Architecture, Part III the Gifts that follow from this Architecture, and Part IV the Principles of this universe. When all of this becomes conscious Awareness to you, you will have everything you need to freely choose to play *the* Infinite Game, and within that choice, you will start the process of *autopoiesis* or self-poetry. Living and embodying the universal Truth contained in this book cannot do anything but raise your level of Consciousness and transform your life into an expression of spiritual art.

We can conclude then that the mere Awareness your life *could* be self-poetry and spiritual art is where it all starts. Or, better yet, "resumed" as you have always been art as in the words of Leonardo da Vinci:

> Art is never finished, only abandoned.

By getting this far into this book, you're already well on your way to making the art that is you no longer abandoned. Let's continue by delving into the next constituent attribute: Intelligence.

CHAPTER 10

INTELLIGENCE

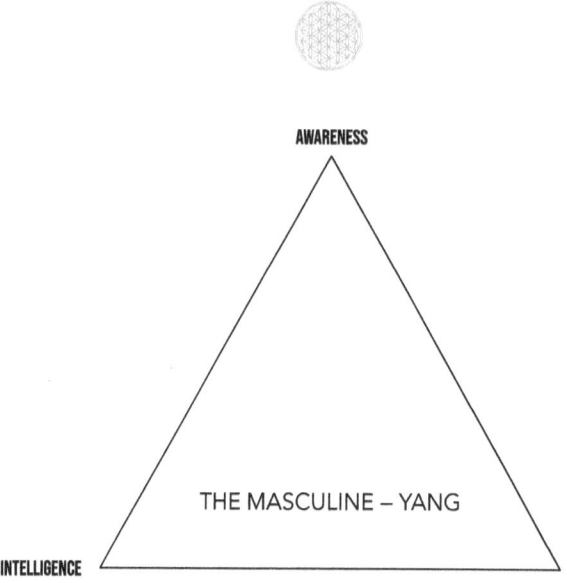

I SINCERELY HOPE BY NOW you're starting to get at least a glimpse of the awe-inspiring flawless design of the intelligence of Life itself—that which governs all of Creation. As referenced earlier, in neo-Confucian Chinese philosophy, the cornerstone of Intelligence was captured in the concept of "Li."

This chapter will reveal another layer of depth to this flawless design, and within this layer of Intelligence, there are yet still deeper layers. So, even within the Grand Architecture of the intelligence of Life itself, we can retrace a fractal quality, which is an element we'll see come back many times throughout this book on what—at first glance—might seem disparate topics. Nothing is truthfully disparate as everything is connected to everything else, but more specifically our beingness of spiritual art is fractal in nature also, and we most clearly see this in the ripple effect of all we do. The downstream effects of our "being" are vast and powerful, so much so it's unknowable to us exactly how massive of an impact each one of us has on all of Creation. We might not view ourselves as powerful or even creators, but that's exactly what we are, and we powerfully create 24/7/365 whether we know it or not. All of our outside world—physical reality—is a mirror reflection of our creation and co-creation with all others. If you wish to see a different reality, all you need to and actually can do is uplevel the spiritual art you express into this world. It's that simple, just not so easy.

Let's start with the quite apparent and obvious, there's a self-organizing Intelligence that orchestrates all of Creation. Take your body; from the day of your conception until the day you die some self-organizing Intelligence contemporaneously orchestrates a multitude of complexity that's almost unfathomable, and your conscious Mind has virtually nothing to do with any of it. It just works.

From a single cell for about the first twelve hours after conception, this self-organizing Intelligence comes online and will develop, create, and instruct the construction and ongoing maintenance and regulation of a complex living system called your body, which will grow to have roughly 7 octillion (7×10^{27}) atoms, 100 trillion cells, and a brain with on average 80 to 100 billion neurons just to mention some staggering quantities of what's being managed somehow. This Intelligence will autonomically regulate your heartbeat, blood pressure, digestion, immune system, hormone balance, and too many other critical bodily functions to mention. And, somehow, it manages this infinite amount of complexity in real time through a mind-boggling system of positive and negative feedback loops down to the subatomic particle level and all of this is communicating and functioning in harmonious interdependent relationship with each other. Seriously, think about it, this is pure magic. What it certainly is, is pure Intelligence.

And we know this Intelligence is already present in the first single cell where it all starts as otherwise it could not know to divide itself into two cells. Please don't interpret this statement in the pro-life or pro-choice context, this book is solely concerned with *the* Infinite Game, not the Finite Game of politics. This Intelligence I am pointing at is present in all of Creation. This Intelligence is what knows how to make a giraffe when a giraffe needs to be created, an Alaskan king crab when an Alaskan king crab needs to be created and so on and so forth. It also knows how to make mountains, rivers, oceans, rainforests, planets, galaxies, and entire universes.

How do we know? Because all of these exist. All of Creation is some form of self-organizing complex living system that's dynamic, ever-changing, evolutionary, adaptive, and embedded with an innate Intelligence that orchestrates all of it. Yes, even inanimate, or man-made objects because at the subatomic level we can still find this same Fundamental Architecture. Again, not surprisingly, because the whole design of all of Creation has a fractal quality. Hence, since all of Creation is Consciousness expressing itself into form, we now know Intelligence is the constituent attribute of Consciousness that orchestrates this eternal symphony of Creation from the grandest complex living system—the entire universe—to the smallest subatomic particle.

But there are more layers.

However, to explore "Intelligence" at a deeper level we have to first define Intelligence from the perspective of the universe or the intelligence of Life itself.

In human terms, we tend to define Intelligence very narrowly like IQ. In the last twenty years or so, there have been many psychological studies conducted and countless books released that further define Intelligence in various distinct categories such as spatial intelligence, bodily-kinetic intelligence, musical intelligence, linguistic intelligence, logical-mathematical intelligence, interpersonal intelligence, intrapersonal intelligence, and naturalistic intelligence. Depending on the book or researcher, there might be more or less. At its core, all of this is reductionism at work, breaking down the complex into digestible parts that we can logically analyze and understand.

None of this is necessarily bad and it can even be very helpful, but this is not how the universe defines Intelligence.

> "Knowledge is not intelligence."
> —HERACLITUS

The truth is, the universe is entirely indifferent to how complex a math equation you can solve. It's unconcerned with whatever genius you might have in any of these reductionist parts of human intelligence.

To the universe, Intelligence is defined as one single premise:

> "Intelligence creates intelligent outcomes; Unintelligence creates unintelligent outcomes."

So, what's an intelligent outcome is the obvious next question? Anything that's conducive to Life itself, which can be defined as the greatest growth, greatest prosperity, and greatest evolution of Life itself.

Well captured within this definition of intelligent outcomes is Love, Truth, joy, happiness, fulfillment, health, peace, harmony, vitality, abundance, expansion, and the list goes on. However, Life itself is all of Creation, not just merely our own individual growth, prosperity, and evolution. And this is entirely logical because we are each a self-organizing complex living system nested within larger self-organizing complex living systems and within us are smaller nested self-organizing complex living systems and so on and so forth. As Marcus Aurelius said: "that which is not good for the beehive cannot be good for the bees."

Now, let's take a closer look at unintelligent outcomes.

If we look at our world today, we see wars, violence, hate, crime, racism, greed, corruption, malfeasance, self-dealing, inequalities, injustices, rampant pollution, and a complete annihilation of Mother Earth, which is the very planet that allows us to live.

I can go on, but I think you get the picture. These are all unintelligent outcomes as they are not conducive to Life itself as we previously defined it. From the perspective of the universe, it's really just that simple.

So, what we can see revealed then is that the human interpretation of Intelligence with all its reductionist variations doesn't necessarily produce intelligent outcomes. In fact, it creates a dizzying list of unintelligent outcomes. This is because our human understanding of what constitutes Intelligence is not just slightly flawed; it's categorically in conflict with the intelligence of Life itself that governs all of Creation.

Now, to be very specific, this isn't necessarily a human computing power—IQ—problem but a level of Consciousness problem. With 80-85 percent of humanity below 200 on Hawkins' Map of Consciousness we—humanity—simply don't have sufficient access to Intelligence as the universe defines it. We're mired in survival mode, Fear, and short-sightedness, which leads to self-dealing, greed, malfeasance, corruption, manipulation, and, most of all, indifference to the health and vitality of the system.

Unfortunately, if that picture is not dim enough, it gets worse as now we have artificial intelligence or AI as well. AI computing power has been growing exponentially for the last forty to fifty years. It is often referred to as Moore's law. It's not really a law, just an observation by Gordon Moore dating back to 1965 that computing power (measured in dense integrated circuits) doubles roughly every eighteen to twenty-four months. AI computing power is now approaching the computing power of a single human, and it's anticipated that cumulative AI computing power will surpass the collective human computing power in the next ten to fifteen years, likely sooner. This pivotal inflection point is often referred to as the technological singularity—or simply singularity—and marks the point in time where technological growth, in theory, becomes uncontrollable and irreversible.

Here's the real rub with all of that. AI is often touted as being "self-learning," but this is actually a critically ignorant misnomer. AI was not only designed by humans but was largely designed after the pattern-recognition learning of the human brain. So, by and large, AI "self-learns" patterning after humans. This is logical, as human intelligence cannot create an AI that's more intelligent than its own. What it can do through AI is amplify the computing power, or in other words, AI computing power can be made faster and more precise in terms of the sheer volumes of variables it can process.

So, what we have with AI is amplified computer power self-learning from our collective human Intelligence, which is creating a multitude of catastrophic unintelligent outcomes. Perhaps you're familiar with the saying that money is an amplifier. If you're a wholesome person, money will make you more wholesome. If you're an asshole, money will only make you a bigger asshole.

AI is an amplifier. The question is, *What are we going to have amplified?* As I mentioned before, we're in a race to raise human Consciousness so we—humanity—can start to access higher levels of Intelligence, defined as creating intelligent outcomes. At these higher levels of Intelligence, AI can amplify and become a huge aid in solving the world's greatest challenges.

This higher level of Consciousness—and therefore true Intelligence—is regretfully sparse today among the technocrats and scientists leading the charge with AI. So, there's legitimate cause for concern, but there are also green sprouts to report. It's my personal conviction that in the inevitable phase transition we're arguably already in, we'll start seeing a shift that can't come too soon. Either way, the race is on.

> "You can't solve a problem with the same level of mind that created it in the first place."
> —ALBERT EINSTEIN

What Einstein was pointing at with "level of mind" is "level of intelligence," which has a deeper meaning than just creating intelligent outcomes vs. unintelligent outcomes.

Let me explain.

Since the early days of the birth of the religion of science—about five hundred years ago—humanity has come to define Intelligence as the exclusive product of the Mind, the neocortex, to be specific. We idolize logic and rational thought and have become entirely dismissive of there being any other source of Intelligence. We are lost in the cobwebs of our Minds.

Nothing could be further from the Truth. As the HeartMath Institute has scientifically researched for decades and conclusively proven, our Heart is another vital source of Intelligence. In fact, there's more data going from the Heart to the Mind than vice versa, and our Heart has neurons similar to our Mind. The intelligence of our Heart is quite different, though, and we can only access it through the language of the Heart, which is sensing, feeling, direct knowing, and intuiting.

Whereas the Mind is loud and chaotic with a never-ending stream of thought, our Heart speaks to us in subtle ways. We have to quiet our Mind, as only in that stillness can we effectively tune into it. But, when we do, we gain access to a vast ocean of Intelligence, which in countless ways, is far superior to our Mind's intelligence.

> "Society speaks and all men listen.
> Mountains speak and wise men listen."
> —JOHN MUIR

Our Mind's intelligence is limited—finite—to its experiences, which it can gain through life, learning, reading, studying, analyzing, etc. Over our lifetime, the Mind accumulates and stores knowledge, and then it draws from this finite database of information to produce thoughts, solutions, ideas, and strategies. The Mind is exceptionally skilled at linear, logical thought, solving math problems, learning a language, or synthesizing novel ideas from its database of information. It's also inherently limited as its perceptions are colored by the unavoidable enculturation process, which is how it forms its prevailing worldviews and beliefs about life.

The intelligence of the Heart taps into an entirely different and much higher level of Intelligence available to us: universal Intelligence.

As we covered before, this entire universe—the Formless and the Finite World of Form—is made up of Consciousness, and recall we could visualize Consciousness as this omnipresent Infinite Field of Consciousness. Well, this field holds an infinite amount of information, everything that has ever happened (actualities in the form of events, actions, thoughts, and feelings) in this universe since the beginning of time, and all possible future possibilities, which are each a potentiality. This infinite amount of information—sometimes referred to as "Akashic records"—is stored in the energy that is the third constituent attribute of Consciousness which we'll explore in the next chapter. For now, it suffices to know it's stored in this energy.

Our Heart is the portal to this vast ocean of universal Intelligence. Every precognition, foreknowledge, foresight, or extrasensory perception is information from this universal Intelligence coming to us through the intelligence of the Heart. But it's not limited to that; when we become fluent in the language of the Heart, we can tap into the suprarational intelligence of the Heart, which is directly connected to this omnipresent field of universal Intelligence, and gain access to insights, genius, and wisdom that's far beyond the linear computing power of our Mind. We colloquially call this our Higher Knowing. In Part V, in the chapter "The All Is Mind," we'll explore this deeper.

This is where true Intelligence comes from, that is, Intelligence defined as creating intelligent outcomes.

Below levels of 200 on Hawkins' scale of human Consciousness, we have very limited access to this level of Intelligence. The Heart's intelligence becomes progressively more accessible as our level of Consciousness rises. When we gain access to the intelligence of our Heart and learn its language—sensing, feeling, direct knowing, and intuiting—our life starts to shift in dramatic ways. Much of the pain and suffering so prevalent below levels of 200 starts to melt away as we start creating ever more harmonious intelligent outcomes in every area of our life. The framework of this book, when brought into genuine embodiment, will crack the portal of your Heart wide open, and this higher level of Intelligence will become something that guides you through life.

John Muir's quote refers to the premise that this universal Intelligence is omnipresent; the universe "speaks" to us every moment of every day in subtle and sometimes not-so-subtle ways. However, our Mind doesn't speak its language, so when we're entangled in the cobwebs of our Mind, we're tone-deaf and color-blind to this higher level of Intelligence of our Higher Knowing which otherwise would be available to us.

Nature is perhaps our greatest teacher, but so are the myriad of occurrences, events, and situations we encounter daily, which

—when we fail to see the deeper meaning—are lost on us. We can draw no wisdom from them. There's no such thing as an accident, fluke, coincidence, or random event in this flawlessly designed, infinitely intelligent universe. Literally, everything contains a clue, an answer, or a yet unseen solution or guidance but the only way to gain access is through the intelligence of the Heart.

Let's explore the next cornerstone—Energy—and reveal more of this Grand Architecture of the universe so we can connect even more dots. And, in many ways, very much like the "Connect-the-Dots" game we all played in our childhood, all we're really doing as we progress through the parts and chapters of this book is revealing a picture—a deeper understanding—that was already and has always been there except it's not visible until we connect enough dots. Imagine the poetic simplicity and sheer wisdom in that, knowing all we really need to do in Life itself is connect enough dots, and the picture—a deeper understanding—by magic and operation of cosmic law reveals itself.

> "If you can't explain it simply, you don't understand it well enough."
> —ALBERT EINSTEIN

CHAPTER 11
ENERGY

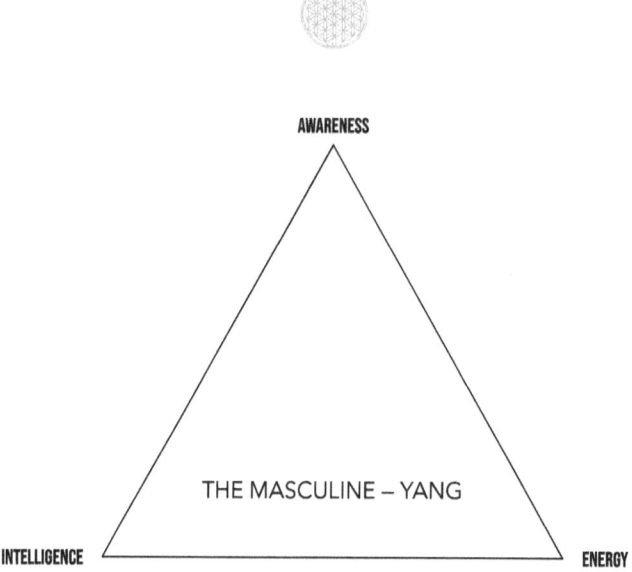

WE ALREADY CONCLUDED THAT EVERY SINGLE THING is Energy. However, there's a lot to learn that will reveal Energy is not just the elemental building block of all of Creation but also the force field that gives rise to all occurrences.

Let's begin with Energy in terms of Life Force, the cosmic atomic energy that gives rise to all life forms. Life Force is also known as

Life Force Energy, vital energy, vital principle, spirit energy (or just Spirit in Christianity), and other variations. It's been known to mankind since time come; in Chinese ancient wisdom traditions and natural medicine, it's referred to as "Chi," and in Ayurvedic medicine and yogic traditions, it's called "Prana," which loosely translates as "breath of life." We'll work with just Life Force.

We could easily view Life Force as the fuel that gives birth to, animates, and powers life forms. As Consciousness decides to enter into form with the creation of a first single cell, all of Consciousness—Awareness, Intelligence, and Energy—is what creates this first cell from commanding subatomic particles from the wave-form (potentiality) into particle-form (actuality) no matter that from a biological perspective we consider this occurs because male sperm fertilizes a female egg. Consciousness gives rise to form, not the other way around. Life Force is the fuel source within Consciousness that enables this to happen.

In the way Life Force is the fuel source of Life itself, food is the fuel source of our biological body. This reconfirms that Consciousness gives rise to form, as without Life Force—i.e., when we die—food does nothing to give rise to form. Being brain-dead means our organ called the brain has gone offline or has become inoperative, so we lose our cognitive abilities as the brain gives rise to our Mind. This reconfirms that our brain does not give rise to Consciousness either. In other words, the Observer is separate and distinct from our brain and therefore Mind. There's been extensive academic research done on near-death experiences (NDE) that has conclusively confirmed all of this.

So, for all life forms, Consciousness—and therefore Life Force—continues to animate and power the life form until Consciousness leaves this life form, which we call death. All finite forms, including life forms, are subject to entropy (dissipating energy or, let's say, "wear and tear") over their lifetime. However, at death, the entropic process of rotting and decaying accelerates, and the life form disintegrates and is released back into the formless Infinite Field of Possibilities (i.e., "nothingness" or the field of formless Consciousness) as subatomic particles in wave-form.

> "Space is not empty. It is full, a plenum as opposed to a vacuum, and is the ground for the existence of everything, including ourselves. The universe is not separate from this cosmic sea of energy."
> —DAVID BOHM

As the first law of thermodynamics tells us: "energy can neither be created nor destroyed, only converted from one form of energy to another." In that sense, our entire universe is a closed-loop system. Thankfully, this closed-loop system contains, for all intents and purposes, an infinite amount of Energy that is the fundamental basis of the premise that we live in an abundant universe.

So far, so good; this is really all we need to know about the Life Force aspect of the constituent attribute Energy, so let's move on.

The field of physics has taught us light—photons—is a form of electromagnetic or radiant energy native to Energy. And it's been known for some centuries that light contains information. Since the Infinite Field of Possibilities contains an infinite amount of Energy, it also contains an infinite amount of light and, therefore, an infinite amount of information.

In the prior chapter, we briefly touched on the term "Akashic records," which refers to everything that has ever happened (actualities in the form of events, actions, thoughts, and feelings) in this universe since the beginning of time and all available future possibilities which represent all potentialities. All of this infinite amount of information is held and stored within the constituent attribute Energy that's native to the omnipresent Infinite Field of Possibilities, which is also sometimes referred to as the Akashic field. This is where the name Akashic records derives from.

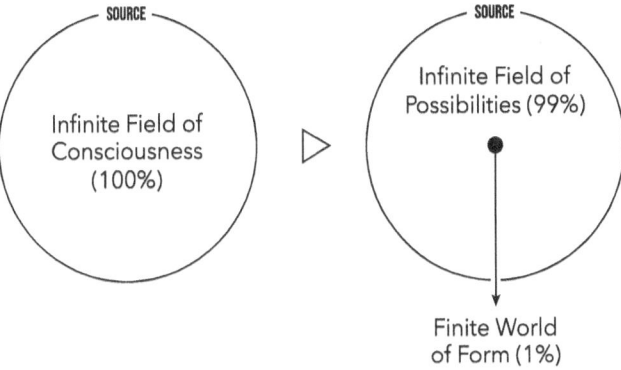

Just to clarify the nomenclature, for the rest of this chapter, when I refer to the "Infinite Field of Possibilities" I am referring to what we've previously also referenced as the formless, formless Consciousness, field of formless Consciousness, space or nothingness, or now Akashic field. In science and physics especially, they often refer to this as the Quantum Field or just Infinite Field, and we also previously referred to this as the formless "99 percent" of reality we can't witness or experience with our five senses. It's all pointing at the same thing.

I will use the term "Finite World of Form" when I refer to what we typically consider the material world or our physical reality. In different contexts, I might also refer to this as the Outer World, all of Creation, Life itself, and later on, when we explore the Feminine, we'll introduce the term "Existence." We also referred to this as the "1 percent" of reality we *can* witness and experience with our five senses. It's all pointing at the same thing, yet in different contexts, different labels work better.

Finally, when I point to the Infinite Field of Possibilities *and* the Finite World of Form combined, I will use the term "Infinite Field of Consciousness," which refers to the totality of everything there is and ever will be—the "100 percent" of everything known and unknown, past, present, and future. In all instances, when I use adjectives like infinite, eternal, formless, or omnipresent, it's only to accentuate what I am pointing at. Theoretically, in the absence of any form, nothing has been created, and everything is just a potentiality; the Infinite Field of Consciousness and the Infinite Field of Possibilities are one and the same. Can you see that? Now, can you also see that everything is Consciousness, and Consciousness can appear in either one of two states, namely formless or form?

I fully realize this all might sound a bit confusing to have so many names for the same thing, and from the perspective of our linear, logical Mind, it might be. But I am not speaking to just the cognitive part of your Intelligence or preparing you to take a test on this. This will likely all come together for you in Part V in the chapter "The All Is Mind." Until we get there, I request you just trust me; it's intentional and serves a distinct purpose related to resonance and remembrance, which does not occur at the level of our logical Mind.

> "I am trying to awake the energy contained in the ether. These are the main sources of energy. What is considered empty space is just a manifestation of matter that is not awakened."
> —NIKOLA TESLA

Please recall, at the end of the day, everything is Consciousness in either the formless state or form state. The formless state we also call a potentiality, and the form state is an actuality.

Now that we have that clarified, let's take a look at some of the work of David Bohm, widely considered one of the greatest physicists of the last century. Bohm's work and scientific legacy hold some important clues to the inner workings of the universe. Bohm was fascinated with what he described as appearing to be a living and creative universe with a distinct holographic quality. His observation was that subatomic particles in wave-form appear to have infinite potential to become anything in the particle-state.

He called the wave-form the "enfolded state," which is a potentiality with infinite creative potential, meaning it can be expressed in an infinite number of different forms. This makes total sense as we know the entire Finite World of Form is made up of subatomic particles in particle-form, but despite the differences in the form, these subatomic particles themselves are indivisible and identical. In other words, a tree is made of the same subatomic particles as a human, an elephant, a mountain, or even a planet. The difference is the expression of these subatomic particles.

The particle-form he called the "unfolded state," which is an actuality locked into time and space—it's now been expressed into form and thereby entered the Finite World of Form, which he likened to a holographic reality that has the appearance of following linear time. He considered this holographic reality a dimension—one aspect—of a totality of reality that we happen to experience as our physical reality through our five senses.

Bohm's use of the word "holographic" is not exactly as the process used to create a three-dimensional holographic image, so referencing that process mentally will steer you down the wrong alley to fully appreciate his work. What he pointed at is there appears to be an infinite and formless ocean of seemingly "nothingness," which is actually not nothingness as it contains everything in an enfolded state. In other words, everything already exists as a potentiality in this nothingness. He was pointing at the Infinite Field of Consciousness.

Within this infinite and formless ocean of nothingness, any formless potentiality can change state from enfolded to unfolded, which occurs when it changes from wave-state to a particle-state. When this occurs, the formless becomes form and thereby becomes visible or experiential to our five senses. It's holographic in that this all occurs within nothingness or the Infinite Field of Consciousness. It's all the same thing, just in a different state.

The significance of his work and legacy is that he started to bridge the world of physics and science with what ancient wisdom traditions and spiritual teachings have been pointing at since the earliest days of human civilization.

Let's build further on this foundation.

If I have done a half-decent job at connecting the dots so far, it should be becoming apparent that it's Consciousness—through its three cornerstones of Awareness, Intelligence, and Energy—that somehow creates, orchestrates, and animates all of Creation. The logical question then becomes: *through what process or mechanism does this occur?*

The answer is sympathetic resonance.

> "If you want to find the secrets of the universe, think in terms of energy, frequency and vibration."
> —NIKOLA TESLA

This quote is so significant it warrants repeating. Tesla knew. We will never know if he solved all the mathematics to prove his statement, as so much of his invaluable research and scientific discovery work was seemingly "lost," but there's very little doubt he figured out the mechanism by which this universe—Consciousness—manifests the Finite World of Form, which incidentally includes all occurrences or events within this Finite World of Form.

Let's start with the fact that every single subatomic particle in this closed-loop system called our universe vibrates. There's no such thing as a subatomic particle that's static or without vibration. Hence, our entire universe and everything within it is vibration in perpetual motion. Even something that appears solid and stable, like a hard tabletop surface, is just very densely packed molecules vibrating at a relatively low (literally "dense") frequency, which gives the appearance to us of the surface being solid. Molecules are, of course, made up of atoms which are made up of subatomic particles. The vibration actually originates at this subatomic level and reverberates from there.

So, let's uncover what vibration is and how it relates to frequency. Vibration, in its essence, is a disturbance of the equilibrium and has what's called a Sinusoidal Waveform or sine wave.

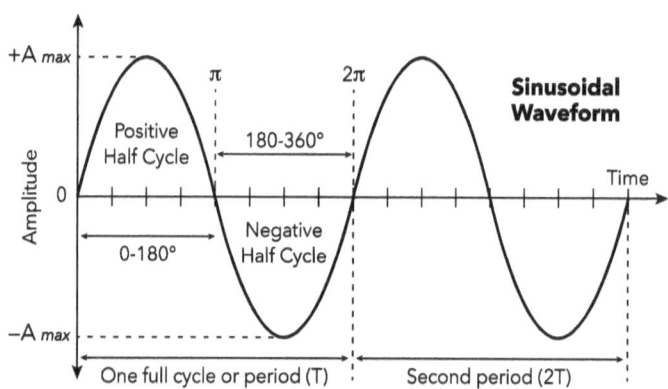

A vibration has an amplitude, which is the height and lows of the peaks and troughs; in an audible wave or sound, this would be the volume. A vibration also has an oscillation rate, which is the cycle of the amplitude as measured in time. One cycle is one peak and one trough. The oscillation rate is called the frequency of the vibration. Since a frequency can be any number above zero, theoretically, with decimals running to infinity, there's an infinite amount of unique frequencies in our universe. For practical purposes, frequencies are conventionally rounded at the fourth or fifth decimal for scientific purposes, as any measurement beyond that is deemed non-material and outside the range of detection of most scientific measurement equipment.

I also want to point out the still point or Fulcrum in the sine wave. One full cycle has one peak and one trough; from the peak to the trough, it passes through a neutral point, and this is the still point or Fulcrum within the sine wave. Please note when we're talking about sine waves and low or high frequencies, we're still talking, for the most part, about incredible speeds that are not detectable by the human eye. This is why form appears solid to us; we can't detect this sine wave or the Fulcrum, at which point, theoretically, form is "off" and not solid at all.

We measure frequencies in Hertz (Hz), where 1 Hz equals one cycle per second. So, 100 Hz is 100 cycles per second. As indicated before, a very low frequency is considered dense, and a very high frequency is considered light. Intuitively, we all know this firsthand as when we are "vibing high," we feel happy, open, and light, and when we have "low vibes," we feel down, closed, and dense. A harmonic frequency is an integer multiple of a fundamental frequency, so 200 Hz, 300 Hz, 400 Hz, etc., are harmonics of the fundamental frequency of 100 Hz. We call vibrations combining together "contributing vibrations," and the pattern that is created is the "resultant frequency." This is the Fourier synthesis named after Joseph Fourier (1768-1830), who first developed the mathematical proof of this phenomenon.

Walter Russell (1871-1963), in his magnum opus *The Message of The Divine Iliad (Vol. I & II)*, revealed a significant clue to both the origin and continued workings of the entire universe. In his explanation, the birth of the universe occurred when Source Consciousness—the unified and integral whole of all there is—emitted a vibration (the Big Bang) in the form of the original sine wave from which all of Creation followed. This original sine wave had a Masculine pole (the positive charge) and a Feminine pole (the negative charge), which is reflected in protons and electrons and consistent with our scientific understanding of vibration. If you recall, we referenced the Masculine and Feminine as the principal polarity of this universe; now you know its origins, and of course, we can see this reflected throughout nature where—in biological gender terms—male and female come together to create new life.

As you can tell on the graph above, the sine wave travels through a neutral point, which Russell also referred to as the Fulcrum or still point. This is reflected by the neutron in the nucleus of an atom which, through nuclear force, bonds with the proton around which the electron orbits through electromagnetism. Russell explained that the entirety of Source Consciousness is contained within this Fulcrum, and the Masculine and Feminine essence are each reflections of this still point, which is to say the sum of the Masculine and Feminine is the totality of Source Consciousness.

Russell was actually, first and foremost, an impressionist painter, sculptor, and author who, after experiencing what he referred to as a "cosmic illumination," could perceive all motion (of energy) and became newly aware of all things. Of course, many people scoffed at this, especially classically trained scientists, and so during his lifetime, much of his work was met with great skepticism and even mockery. This actually put him in great company as most truly revolutionary thinkers, artists, and science mavericks like Pythagoras, Plato, Seneca, Copernicus, Galileo, Bruno, Steiner, Tesla, Buckminster Fuller, and countless others paid for their contribution to humanity's advancement with ridicule, scorn, and many times, their lives. There's no doubt Russell was an eccentric maverick, a medium deeply connected with a source of intelligence that was octaves above the scientific "thinking" of his era, but I will leave it to you to explore his work and come to your own conclusions if he was a madman or a genius ahead of his time.

So, although in the strictest sense, he was not considered a scientist, most of his findings are aligned with our current scientific understanding that our entire universe is an ocean of vibrating subatomic particles, that vibrations have a positive (Masculine) and negative (Feminine) pole and that the sine wave passes through a neutral point. We also know that much like a single cell can split into two cells and so forth, a single origin vibration has the potential to create something into form (through sympathetic resonance). Creating just one single element of form within the formless Infinite Field of Consciousness would then trigger a change—however minute—in this same field, which would now constitute the Infinite Field of Possibilities and a Finite World of Form made up of this single origin element of form. This singular change would set off a cascading of new vibrations at different frequencies—evolution—which, over 13.8 billion years, evolved into what we now consider our universe and everything within it.

I know, it sort of sounds fantastical that this previously completely formless omnipresent Infinite Field of Consciousness could evolve into the universe we know today through a single origin vibration. You should know this, though: every single vibration in the form of a frequency, once transmitted, travels through this universe for eternity and is registered in the Akashic records within the Akashic Field. To put this into context, all the episodes of "I Love Lucy," which aired from 1951–1957, still exist in the Akashic records and, provided you have the technology or clairsentient abilities to tune into the Akashic records, you could theoretically watch the reruns into eternity.

If you think this sounds far-fetched, you should know there are computer scientists in very advanced stages of being able to download information from the Akashic field, and in the coming years, with the advent of AI, this will, without a doubt, become viable if it isn't already. Theoretically, the history of all of mankind and all karmic debts will be accessible when this technology comes online, much like it already is for those with clairsentient abilities. The Truth always comes to light, as they say, or in Mark Twain's words, "If you tell the truth you don't have to remember anything."

The point here is, don't underestimate the reverberant potential of a single frequency as they exist for eternity. All of this provides a plausible and logical explanation of how one single origin vibration could evolve into an infinitely complex mosaic of vibrations over 13.8 billion years, which we scientifically know is where we are today. So, even if we dismiss Russell's work entirely, we still are where we are today.

We have already concluded that the range of possible frequencies is infinite, and we can visualize each unique frequency like a radio channel. To hear, which is to "experience," the 99.7 FM radio station, we have to tune our radio receiver exactly to this channel; if we tune it to 99.6 or 99.8 FM, we will not pick up its signal—in other words, we won't be able to connect to the resonant frequency sent out by that radio station. Said another way, 99.7 FM is a potentiality on our radio receiver until we tune exactly to that frequency, and then it becomes an actuality we experience. In yet other words, until our radio receiver's resonant frequency is tuned to exactly match the resonant frequency of the radio station, we cannot experience that frequency.

Now, what humans can actually "hear" is limited by our audible frequency range. For example, Mother Earth has a resonant frequency of 7.83 Hz, which is colloquially referred to as Mother Earth's natural heartbeat, but the official name is the Schumann Resonance, named after a German physicist named Winfried Schumann (1888-1974) who first confirmed this frequency.

The Schumann resonance is not audible to humans because our audible frequency range is c. 20 Hz to 20,000 Hz. If our range extended to, let's say, 5 Hz, the Schumann resonance of Mother Earth would appear to us as a constant buzzing noise with slight pitches as Schumann resonance is not static at 7.83 Hz; it has minor variations in amplitude. Resonant frequency then refers to what's called "natural frequency," which is the rate of vibration range determined by the physical parameters of the vibrating object.

Finally, while our audible frequency range is somewhat limited, our tactile frequency range is very expansive, so we can feel, sense, interact with, and be influenced by a very broad range of frequencies well beyond our audible frequency range. For example, scientific studies have been conducted where people were placed underground in a concrete bunker, which disconnected the study objects from the Schumann resonance, and the outcomes were startling. It disrupted the circadian rhythm and cycles, caused hormone imbalances, and led to such things as "foggy brain," feelings of emptiness, and even depression. When the Schumann resonance was reintroduced in the bunker, all these symptoms disappeared. We will delve deeper into this in Part IV in the chapter "Health."

> "Physical reality, at its core, is nothing but the harmonics of vibrations."

This holds another essential clue, each finite form—whether live or inanimate—has a natural frequency. To put this in other words, subatomic particles in particle-form apparently have a natural frequency. Yet, in other words, the frequency determines what the subatomic particles in particle-form become or are in form. So, we could say the constituent attribute Intelligence within Consciousness commands "what" and the constituent attribute Energy is both the fuel source (subatomic particle) and mechanism through its rate of vibration, which is frequency. In this orchestra of the creation of form, the constituent attribute Awareness is the composer, Intelligence is the director, and Energy is the musical notes that culminate in what we experience as frozen music (i.e., physical reality). Music, as we all know, is, at its core, nothing but the harmonics of vibrations. I already stated above what physical reality really is.

What's commonly referred to as manifestation is, in David Bohm's terms, an enfolded state of potentiality becoming the unfolded state of actuality. The formless becoming form-based, or wave-state becoming particle-state. I am pointing at the same thing in as many ways possible, as different words work for different people.

All potentialities already exist in the Infinite Field of Possibilities; what manifestation really is, then, is converting a formless potentiality into an actuality in our Finite World of Form, which we experience as our physical reality. Recall—an actuality is not exclusive to form; it can be an occurrence or event in the Finite World of Form as well.

So, how does that work?

> "Everything is energy, and that's all there is to it. Match the frequency of the reality you want and you cannot help but get that reality. It can be no other way. This is not philosophy, this is physics."
> —ALBERT EINSTEIN

To get there, we have to first understand that when an atom vibrates due to the vibration of its subatomic particles, it creates electromagnetic waves unique to its natural frequency. These electromagnetic waves create a field that has a unique frequency signature, and one of the properties of Energy is that like-energy attracts like-energy. Now, sympathetic resonance is a harmonic phenomenon wherein a vibratory body responds to external vibrations to which it has a harmonic likeness. In the examples of two equally tuned tuning forks—that is, the same natural frequency—when you "excite" one of the tuning forks (the "external vibration"), the other one (the "vibratory body") will start to vibrate as well provided, of course, they are in close enough proximity. The greater the volume or magnitude of the external vibration, the further away the vibrating body can be to get excited. If the tuning forks do not share the same natural frequency, exciting the first one will not excite the second one.

So, what Einstein pointed at is that every potentiality in the formless Infinite Field of Possibilities is a vibratory body with a unique frequency signature. When this vibratory body gets "excited" by an external vibration with the exact same natural frequency, it will start to vibrate at that frequency; we already covered how this triggers the whole orchestra of the creation of all form.

We—humans—have a natural frequency that is heavily correlated to our level of Consciousness. Generally, the higher our level of Consciousness, the higher our vibration. Love vibrates a lot higher than Fear. But we're complex beings with lots of thoughts and emotions as we travel on the roller coaster of life. So, the way to view this is that we have a natural frequency range. Within this range, we have a potential peak frequency, which is the highest level of Consciousness accessible to us in this lifetime, and we can also fall below our natural frequency.

This can be momentary, like in the instance we lose a loved one and are in deep grief. This will lower our vibration significantly while we mourn our loss, but then we tend to process our grief and revert back to our natural frequency range. We can also fall below our natural frequency for prolonged periods; this happens, for instance, when we submit to addictions like alcoholism or drug use, or we find ourselves in a toxic relationship or even the wrong career. Prolonged periods below our natural frequency will cause dissonance in our energy system, which can show up as illness, moodiness, feeling empty, restlessness, depression, or even suicide. It can also show up as occurrences and events which cause great suffering, like divorce, financial ruin, or other crises and catastrophes.

Finally, we transmit a multitude of frequencies at the same time through our various bodies, like our physical body, emotional body, mental body, and spiritual body. We even know certain organs within our physical body resonate at different natural frequencies. So, we are each a very complex mosaic of frequencies and transmit a multitude of vibrations at different frequencies and amplitudes (i.e., power or volume). Multiply this times 7.8 billion people and add in the rest of physical reality, and you have a mind-blowingly complex web of life, and yet, it still somehow is all orchestrated by the Infinite Intelligence that underpins all of Creation.

But, as Einstein alluded, what we call our Life or reality is something we principally attract through sympathetic resonance, even though below levels of 200, we perceive and experience these as the fruits of our labor, good fortune, bad luck, or maybe ascribe them to fate. That's all fine; it's just not really how this universe actually works, so from that limited state of Mind, we cannot evolve to become a powerful conscious co-creator of our own reality.

> "Consciousness is the Creator; the Finite World of Form is the Creator's Creation."

Every spoken word, thought-form, and action affects our vibration. Thought-form or thoughts and beliefs are the dark horse here—literally and figuratively—as these can be conscious but also unconscious. And it's these unconscious thought-forms that have an outsized impact on the creation and manifestation of our reality, as only about 5–10 percent of our total thought-form is conscious. Hence, the vital importance of mastering our conscious Awareness as what spins around unguarded in your subconscious Mind can act as a major silent saboteur in manifesting and creating the life you truly desire.

All of this is because your whole life is a direct reflection of sympathetic resonance. Like-energy attracts like-energy. Now, being a "good" or "bad" person or "sin" has very little to do with this. The universe is indifferent in the sense that sympathetic resonance holds true whether you are a good or a bad person. Financial riches gotten through ill means is a potentiality with a unique frequency signature; if you vibrate at that unique frequency signature, that will manifest in your reality as an occurrence no matter what the "how" might look like in the physical world.

True love, abundance, health, happiness, joy, fulfillment, integrity, compassion, and gratitude are all examples of things that have unique frequency signatures, and as humans, we can emit a multitude of frequencies at the same time. When they're within our natural frequency range, we're not only able to manifest these occurrences or events, but we will be and remain in energetic coherence, which in biological terms, we call homeostasis or great health as all our bodily systems are functioning optimally. When we introduce dissonance to our energy system, we become the source of our own suffering, however that might show up in our life.

In that sense, we are each what David Hawkins calls a morphogenetic field or Attractor Field with a gravitational force. You are the co-creator of your own reality. Your vibration then determines what attracts to you, i.e., shows up in your physical world as your reality. I say co-creator as we are each a complex living system nested in the larger complex living system called humanity, which is nested within the even larger complex living system called Mother Earth, which is nested in the yet larger complex living systems of our galaxy, our universe, and whatever might be beyond.

Finally, occasionally I get the question, *If all this is so, why should I care about being a good or bad person? If I can get rich, powerful, and just enjoy myself, why bother being a "good" person?* The answer is quite simple: you cannot escape your Karmic records, which include your Karmic debts. What you do here in this lifetime is your Karmic responsibility; you cannot escape it as all of this is *the* one Infinite Game played out over eternity whether or not you're hopelessly lost playing insidious Finite Games in this lifetime. This is why the hallmark of a truly awakened human being at more advanced levels of Consciousness is compassion toward those who are living ignorant lives. They understand the Infinite Game at a deep level, so they cannot help but love you regardless and have immense compassion for you.

In my experience, both from having been there and now working with people that seemingly have it all, there's definitely not a 1:1 ratio between worldly success and true happiness. People at low levels of Consciousness suffer through life; they might have worldly success—lots of fame, fortune, and even applause, but their Soul is aching—if not bankrupt. At levels below 200, there's a persistent and palpable murmur of suffering woven into the fabric of our existence. We might not even be aware of it as we might have come to believe that's just how life is. We might have grown numb to it, or we might be numbing it out, but it's there. It's always there.

The only way out is discovering you have a choice and then freely choosing to play *the* Infinite Game.

That takes us to Earth school or our Existence here on the physical plane, which leads us to the Feminine; let's explore that principal Polarity next.

CHAPTER 12

THE FEMININE & EXISTENCE

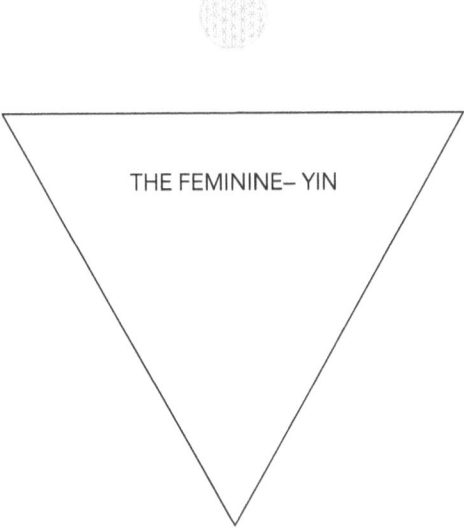

LET'S REPEAT WHAT WE DID BEFORE and start with the end: Existence = Truth.

Existence is the Finite World of Form, which is symbolically represented for us humans by Mother Earth. In Chinese ancient wisdom traditions—including both Taoism and Confucianism—Earth represents the Mother or the Feminine (or Yin), and the Heavens represent the Father or the Masculine (or Yang). The Heavens refers to Consciousness which in Native American indigenous traditions is referred to as the Great Spirit. It's all pointing at the same thing. Again, words are just labels, so when studying spiritual teachings, it's key to look for the symbolic meaning rather than making literal interpretations.

Existence is also just a word and therefore a label. For instance, we could substitute "Existence" with "Creation," and it wouldn't change the essence of what's contained in this book one iota. So, if for any reason the word Existence doesn't resonate with you, feel free to substitute it in your Mind with Creation, Life itself, Outer World, or even physical reality.

The parts or essences of the Feminine and the Masculine are the sum of Source Consciousness; we can see this reflected back because when we combine Earth and the Heavens, we're back to the totality of everything (Source Consciousness).

Whereas the Masculine—formless Consciousness—can be challenging to visualize, the Feminine or the Finite World of Form is intimately familiar to each of us. This is our physical reality, the world we perceive and experience with our five senses.

Our physical reality, of course, is characterized not just by form but by time and space. If you recall, the Infinite Field of Possibilities *and* the Finite World of Form combined live within the eternal and omnipresent Infinite Field of Consciousness. So, the Feminine then is the finite—that of time and space—living in the infinite, which is no time and no space much the same as all Finite Games play out with *the* one Infinite Game.

So, why is it that Existence = Truth?

Universal Truth, as we covered in the very first chapter, is that which is indivisible, integral, and beyond any culture, ideology, or religion. It holds true across all timelines, all geographies, and cannot be manipulated, changed, or corrupted by mankind. For all intents and purposes, universal Truth is the inviolable and immutable Constitution of this entire universe, including our physical reality.

Again, if you recall, all things are illuminated through Polarity. We cannot know (or see or experience) beauty unless there's ugly; we cannot know bad unless there's good, and so on. In the same way, we cannot discover Truth unless there's Falsehood.

The Finite World of Form—our physical reality—is where each of us, as an individual expression of Source Consciousness, can experience life in physical form, and through the veils of Duality and Polarity we can then illuminate Truth from Falsehood. I often call this Earth School, as that's essentially what it is. We're each here to rediscover—through resonance and remembrance—Truth from Falsehood. It should be becoming quite clear now what Maya or veils of illusion are truly pointing at as well. It's all connected and for the true spiritual student connecting the dots between all the various ancient wisdom traditions, sacred Indigenous wisdom teachings, and teachings of countless great masters and teachers throughout history becomes a deeply inspiring journey of remembrance.

Once again, spiritual teachings and texts point at something. Reading Rumi's work literally will only get you to skim the surface. This is the fundamental disconnect with most religious scholars who, over the millennia, have taken mostly a very literal interpretation of the words written in such profound texts as the Bible, Koran, Torah, and Tao Te Ching.

> "A woman is a mystery to guide a wise and open man."
> —RUMI

This relates back to levels of Consciousness, which determine the level of Intelligence in terms of spiritual wisdom we have access to. Spiritual texts written by teachers and masters calibrating in the 600s or 700s cannot be understood at their full depth of wisdom by someone calibrating below 200, for instance. People calibrating below the level of 200 are fundamentally guided by primal survival instincts and view themselves and others as separate and distinct. They still seek worldly power, which, once acquired, is likely to be abused by the use of Force. They rationally justify corruption, malfeasance, crimes, and atrocities like torture and killing under the guise of righteousness. They invent such Falsehoods as "sin" and "heresy" to gain power and control over others through seeding shame and guilt, some of the lowest vibrations on the Map of Consciousness.

The Truth is that if we take an honest look at the world's great religions, we can see exactly this. This is not to say any of these religious teachings are not profound and contain much Truth. They do; I revere many of these Teachings and reference and quote them often. But the institutions of religion have been the direct cause and catalyst for unthinkable human suffering throughout history, and this continues to this day.

Throughout history, wars have been principally fought over resources, ideology, or religion. Historically speaking, most of these wars have been contested over religion. Still today, there's an enduring conflict between Israel and the Palestinians; the underlying conflict is a difference of religion, even though it's being fought over land rights (resources). Steeped in righteousness, both sides justify unthinkable acts of violence and inflict incredible human suffering. It is noteworthy to say that Israel is justifying its own brutalities and use of Force based on a deep ancestral wound left from centuries of persecution, with the apex being the holocaust of WWII. However, their religious righteousness is blinding Israel to see they are repeating history in that the land rights constituting the State of Israel forcefully displaced a Palestinian population that had lived in that same territory for generations. Except this time, they are the ones using more Force as they have the economic and military might weighing heavily in their favor.

The enduring Israel-Palestine conflict is a human tragedy on both sides, yet it cannot be resolved at the level of Consciousness these two sides calibrate. From a higher level of Consciousness—universal Truth—both sides would look at this enduring war and violence and see the complete and utter madness in it. At its core, this conflict is people killing other people over beliefs held, which God rules supreme. Beliefs, as we discussed earlier, are thought-form or psychological constructs; they're not absolute Truth. We are not our beliefs, which are a product of the Mind; neither are we our body. We're each an individual expression of the same Source Consciousness. It makes no difference what you call this Source Consciousness, how you pray to it, or what rituals you adopt to worship. All people are one; there's no separation. Only at levels of Consciousness above 200 do we start to gain access to Love (the energy) from which place it's obvious to see Truth from Falsehood that we are all one.

The institutions of religion have produced such things as the Inquisition, a blood-stained chapter in the history of the Catholic Church, which killed, tortured, persecuted, and maimed non-Catholics for several hundred years. During the colonization of Latin America especially, under the auspices of the Catholic Church, barbaric crimes were inflicted on the native people and entire Indigenous cultures were ruthlessly eradicated as if they had no right of life or Existence. More recently, the Catholic Church has been paying out hundreds of millions in legal settlements for sexual abuses by its priests, and much of this sexual abuse was known or condoned in the highest offices of the Vatican, and priests were simply reassigned.

I just pointed out two examples to highlight the Truth about the institutions of religion, but I could fill pages with all the other human suffering inflicted by the myriad of other religious wars and tyranny throughout history, which is still ongoing today. The Taliban, ISIS, the enduring conflict between Pakistan (Islam) and India (Hindu/Sikh), and persecution in China (Communism, an ideology) of the Tibetans (Buddhism) and Uyghurs (Islam) are all evidence of the prevalence of levels of Consciousness below 200 among the majority of humanity. What characterizes all of these conflicts is the use of barbaric Force in the name of righteousness.

All of these religions and teachings have profound wisdom in them, and all of them contain a great deal of shared spiritual wisdom. For instance, the Golden Rule, in some form or fashion, can be retraced in every single one of them. But, as institutions of religion, none of them truly live the Golden Rule. That's because these religions all originated from great masters and teachers who calibrated very high on the Map of Consciousness; however, the institutions were created and ruled over the millennia by religious leaders below the level of 200.

> "You do you."

There's a great golden opportunity, though, within all of this. Should the current religious leaders rise in their level of Consciousness, these religious institutions have within them the Power (of Love) to transmute and effect great change since, collectively, they have billions of followers. Pope Francis is showing signs of great humility and has been making concerted efforts to build bridges to the other great religions of the world. This is the only way toward unification of all people, to move away from war, violence, and the insidious use of Force, and to work toward the spiritual *and* universal Truth that all is one. We are one humanity, all life is sacred, and all people matter and are valuable beyond any measure. And, within that premise, there's room to honor everyone's beliefs and dedication to their own God and their own religion.

Finally, what goes for religions, as described above, we see mirrored in ideologies. What typically starts with noble intentions gets distorted over time and turns into mental dogma in the form of theories that are just thought-form, not universal Truth. Communism, fascism, socialism, nationalism, racism, capitalism, environmentalism, atheism, nihilism, minimalism, hedonism, wokism, and even spiritualism are just some examples of theories and schools of thought that, at their core, are just a set of irreducible beliefs—which are thought-form—about the nature of righteousness. Ideologies then become no different from how religions are used by the institutions of religion as weaponized versions of beliefs.

Back to Rumi's quote.

What Rumi is pointing at with the word "woman" is the Feminine, and the word "man" points to the Masculine. So, let's restate that quote:

> The Feminine is a mystery to guide the wise and open Masculine.

Substituting a few keywords, this becomes: "The Finite World of Form is a mystery to guide the wise and open Formless" or "Existence is a mystery to guide a wise and open Consciousness." This is Earth School, and Existence is where we get to discover Truth from Falsehood, which is the remembrance of our true nature.

So, let's uncover some more Falsehoods.

We have already peeled back many layers on the illusion that constitutes physical reality. Everything is Energy, and the Finite World of Form is truthfully Consciousness expressing itself into form.

Humanity as a whole is caught up in playing Finite Games, but the only real game there is *the* one Infinite Game. Being lost in these Finite Games is why our world looks the way it does. All wars, violence, hate, racism, inequalities, injustices, chronic illness, addictions, abject poverty, starvation, rampant pollution, and the complete destruction of Mother Earth can be deduced back to humanity being utterly lost in playing Finite Games. Why is humanity lost in playing these Finite Games? Levels of Consciousness below 200.

Humanity has come to believe that it's not part of nature; we even started to tinker with the sacred codes of nature with disastrous effects on our health and well-being as well as the health of Mother Earth. GMO foods, chemtrails, global weather manipulation, genetic manipulation through medicine, synthetic fertilizers, pesticides, herbicides—the list goes on—are all examples of seeds we planted on an ill-fated path we went on, which we are now starting to harvest in the form of catastrophic consequences.

The religion of consumerism has enculturated humanity with the belief that fame, fortune, applause, and the never-ending accumulation of trinkets and shiny objects—*Never Enoughitis*—are the pathway to happiness, joy, peace, and fulfillment. In the meantime, we're living stressed-out lives, obesity and chronic illness are endemic, addictions like alcoholism and opioids are rampant, the divorce rate is above 50 percent and steadily rising, and our biosphere is in critical condition and dangerously close to going into hospice care.

The whole religion of consumerism is underpinned on the deeply flawed Neoclassical theory of modern capitalism, which is steeped in reductionist thinking. Perhaps the most critical flaw is that infinite compound economic growth is possible on a planet of finite resources in terms of its capacity to regenerate those natural resources. In our modern-day school of economics, human capital (humanity) and natural capital (Earth's resources) are mere inputs—"cogs-in-the-wheel"—in service to financial capital.

Our entire way of life violates the principles of self-organizing complex living systems, which is the Grand Architecture of this entire universe.

> "Love is the answer,
> Truth is the only way."

Existence shows us Falsehoods so we can discover Truth. We discover Truth through resonance and remembrance. We rediscover who we truly are, our true nature, and as we do, we rise in our levels of Consciousness, which reveals to us that we have collectively made Earth School hell on Earth, whereas it should and could be heaven on Earth.

Existence, the Feminine, Yin, or our Mother teaches us Truth from Falsehood. The only real Truth is we're each an individual expression of Source Consciousness, and as we uncovered earlier: Consciousness = Love.

> "Awakening = Remembrance."

Awakening of the Feminine involves no longer getting lost in the infinite, which is the formless. Unawakened Yin is lost in seeking herself—Life itself or Earth or Existence or all of Creation—in the formless. At a deeper level, this is due to the unconscious belief of the unawakened Feminine that the Order is in Creation and the Chaos is in the infinite.

Both Yin (Chaos) and Yang (Order) are seeking themselves so they can experience their essence. Unawakened Yin or Yang are both seeking it in the wrong place due to misplaced unconscious beliefs.

Let me explain.

The Feminine represents Life itself. She is Existence, the Finite World of Form, or all of Creation itself. Her true nature is Chaos, as all of Existence is Chaos existing within Order. The Finite World of Form, which is Chaos within the Formless, which is Order. The Feminine (Chaos) is the river of life, which runs through the structure of the Masculine (Order).

Awakened Yin then is the Feminine knowing she is Life itself—Chaos—and she learns to accept that the Order is in the formless or infinite. Seeking Order in the Finite World of Form = False Order or a Falsehood.

The deep Yin lesson is to become grounded in the Chaos of the Finite World of Form.

The Feminine as an energy is wild, untamed, and free. She's the whirlwind of Life itself, the poetic beauty within the non-linear messiness of all of Creation. For the Feminine to become truly free and liberated, she needs to come out of her head and into her body where she can feel and experience Life itself instead of thinking about it. She's sensory, flowy, creative, and unstructured but only up to a certain point as her river runs through the structure of Order. Spiritual awakening of the Feminine is knowing she's held by Order so she can relax into *being* Creation. She can now be her true nature, which is Chaos. In the next chapter on the first constituent attribute of the Feminine—Being—we will delve much deeper into the essence of *being* Creation as it holds such a pivotal relationship to our beingness of spiritual art.

> "Her freedom is being Chaos (Yin) in an ocean of Order (Yang)."

Again, we're speaking here of the Feminine essence, which is one part of the whole of Source Consciousness. All men and women have the Feminine essence within—regardless of gender identification or sexual orientation—even though women are typically Feminine-energy dominant and represent the embodiment of the Feminine essence for that reason.

Also, Chaos shouldn't be interpreted here as something negative or inferior to Order. It's mesmerizingly beautiful and poetic and it's an integral part of Life itself, Polarity, and the Grand Architecture of all of Creation.

Chaos counterbalances Order, and all of Creation is just a poetic dance between Chaos and Order. Life itself, all of Creation, is a never-ending oscillating and dynamic flow of occurrences, whether in form or experiences. Just like the Taijitu symbol illustrates, the seed of Order is held within Chaos, and the seed of Chaos is held within Order. Chaos, then is every bit as beautiful, meaningful, and important as Order despite the Western civilization Masculine-dominated and Order-oriented cultural beliefs.

In the final chapter of this Part II, we'll delve deeply into the dynamic and interplay of the Feminine and Masculine essences. We'll discover how our prevailing cultural views have shaped history, our world, and our whole reality through the endemic oppression of the Feminine and how it's only through restoring the Feminine in its Divine sovereignty that we can restore harmony not just within ourselves—male or female—but our entire world.

But before we can do that at any meaningful depth, we must first explore the cornerstones—constituent attributes—of the Feminine, which are Being, Creativity, and Reverence. Because remember the respective constituent attributes of both the Masculine and Feminine, and later the Gifts and Principles we'll add in Parts III and IV, respectively, are our colors with which we paint our spiritual art unto the canvas of Life itself or all of Creation.

Let's continue with exploring Being first.

CHAPTER 13

BEING

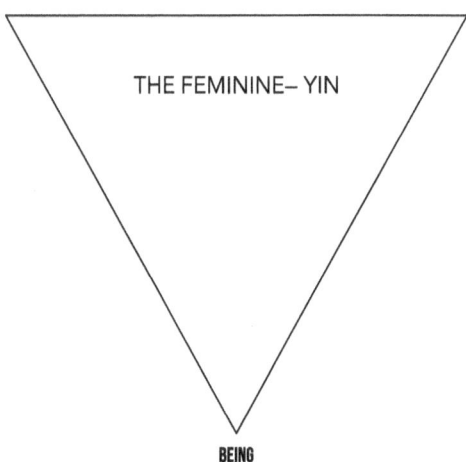

WE ARE HUMAN *BEINGS*, although if you were an alien visiting Earth for the first time, you would be easily fooled into believing we are human *doings*. Being and Doing are opposite poles, whereas Being is the first constituent attribute of the Feminine, and Doing has a distinct Masculine quality to it.

Most of us have no concept of what it means to just be. Yet just Being is our very essence. From the moment we're born, take our very first breath, and the umbilical cord is severed, we don't just come to exist as a sovereign human being—we are already enough and complete.

Not complete in the sense we don't still have to develop many of our faculties, our physical body, and learn to become self-sufficient. But complete in the sense we're already a complete human being from a holistic or spiritual perspective. So, we're already enough; nothing we'll come to do, achieve, or gain in material wealth, fame, fortune, or applause in life will make us "more" or "less" of a human being. No experience from the moment we're born until the day we die will make us more of a human being.

We're born whole.

The notion we have to do something to become someone is one of the most stubborn misperceptions—veils of illusion—held by almost all of humanity regardless of race, creed, nationality, culture, or religion. This pernicious Falsehood must be completely dismantled if we are to escape the endless carousel of Finite Games the matrix informs us we must play. The "matrix" doesn't—and will never-volunteer to inform us of the axiom that "when we *must* play, we cannot *play*," as its entire psychological hold on us is based on milking and exploiting our ingrained understanding that we must become someone, hence we *must* play which is *being* in Doing, not Being. Read on, and we'll unravel all of this one strain of spiritual spaghetti at a time.

Almost universally, the moment we're born, our parents, family, and culture place enormous expectations on each one of us of what we might become. Any signs we might have some natural ability or talent are immediately translated and projected on us, becoming something that's deemed worthwhile or noteworthy.

So, whether it's our ability to throw or catch a ball, speak or read a word, carry a tune, or solve a puzzle is absorbed by our loved ones' dreams and aspirations for us and projected back on us incessantly. Enormous significance is put on our *"doing"* in school, starting as early as preschool, sports, music, arts, etc. and none of this really stops until the day we die. And, so, from the earliest days of our lives, we're enculturated that our worth, purpose, and aim in life is Doing on the way of becoming. Our whole life becomes just about achieving milestones, resetting the goalposts, and becoming the next "someone" we need to become to be whole and complete.

So, as soon as we graduate Kindergarten, our goals are set on Elementary School followed by Middle and High School. Then College, perhaps a Graduate degree, or maybe we start our professional career. Maybe it's becoming an Olympic athlete or world-class musician, or maybe just getting a job so we can pay our bills and then start accumulating toys and shiny objects. Maybe it's becoming a wife, a mother, a husband, or a business tycoon. Maybe it's becoming thin, fit, or muscular, or maybe it's becoming powerful, influential, and famous. Perhaps it's having a certain net worth, a certain rank in the Army or Fire brigade, or it might show up in a wall full of diplomas or a retirement account fully funded at age sixty. It doesn't really matter; our world is monomaniacally focused on Doing. In the eyes of society at large, our worth—including self-worth—hinges on what we do and, therefore, become.

If you're courageous enough to really look at it, you will find this to be so. I know this ruled my life; I spent a whole lifetime focused on *doing* on my way to becoming.

The universe is entirely unconcerned with your tireless worldly *doing* and what you become because of it in the worldly sense. It doesn't care about your achievements, trophies, diplomas, or fame. The universe is only concerned with one thing: your Being and, more specifically, the truthful *being* of your authentic Self.

Your authentic Self is not the same as your image of self or the Ego, which is just a psychological construct. Your authentic Self is the true you, the Observer and timeless spiritual essence we could call your Soul.

Your Ego, deeply enculturated over a lifetime of swimming in society's fishbowl, is caught up in playing Finite Games. Lost might be a better word. The Ego is desperate to be seen, recognized, and validated, so it willingly adopts society's vision of what it means to be someone and, without a second thought, loses itself in tireless Doing. And in this context, even the "rebels" that abhor society's rules and are hellbent on breaking them are still fueled by the same underlying motivation. So, even they are still lost in Doing, even when that Doing is *doing* seemingly nothing, *doing* what society deems bad or wrong, or just *doing* what's contrarian.

"Being" a "rebel without a cause" or "anarchist" is still *doing* as it's manufactured by your *doing* down to the way you speak, act, and dress. As long as you're busy becoming someone, you're Doing and not Being.

To understand this at a deeper level, it's helpful to revert back to the nature of playing Finite Games and *the* Infinite Game. First, if we're lost in playing Finite Games, we cannot freely choose to play, so we *must* play. When we *must* play, we're, by definition, lost in Doing. As we learned, when we freely choose to play *the* Infinite Game, we can now freely choose to play any Finite Game as all Finite Games play out within *the* one Infinite Game. Within freely choosing to play a Finite Game, we have the opportunity of Being while *doing*—as in playing—whatever Finite Game we decide to play.

The nuance is in that when we "must play" we're in "Doing" and when we "freely choose to play" we're in "Being." In Doing, the trophies and what we become matter; they're the whole and the sole reason we're *doing*. In Being, we're seeking an experience through the playing of any Finite Game—we're not caught up in the trophies that come with it or becoming anyone in particular. In Being, we're detached from the outcome of the Finite Game we freely choose to play. In Doing, the outcome of the Finite Game is what we're playing the whole game for.

I recognize this nuance is challenging to see when you've been caught up playing Finite Games your whole life believing you were freely choosing to play them. Believing that you were *doing* it for the experience of playing and not the gaining of trophies, and believing at your very core that your sense of self is in no way hinged on any of these Finite Games you've been (unknowingly) playing your whole life.

So, let's strip this down further to see what wants to be revealed. If trophies—which can be money, titles, social status, prestige, recognition, validation, acceptance, etc.—were of no concern to you, would you be *doing* what you do? Would your life look the same? Would you be married to the same person, live in the same place, have the same career, or even dress the same way, just to name a few?

For most people, if they had the courage to be honest with themselves, the answer would be "no" to some or maybe even all of these questions.

But then, almost instantaneously, our logical mind kicks in at the behest of our Ego, which cannot afford its whole psychological construct of self to come tumbling down. So, the Ego immediately protests and says, "But I have responsibilities and bills to pay," "This is just how the world works," "There's nothing wrong with all my *doing*," "I accomplished a lot in life," "I love what I do," and so on and so forth.

Nobody is a "bad" person for *being* lost in Doing. There's no judgment when we *must* play Finite Games because our enculturation has shaped our beliefs—colored our lens—in such a way that we simply have no alternative, as that's what we perceive life is all about. Still, where we really want to go is not just merely living but *being* truly alive, which we have no access to unless we ground ourselves in Being over Doing.

Just like there can be no Infinite Game within a Finite Game, there can be no true Being within Doing, which, after all, is mere *doing* without truly Being. However, there can be all sorts of *doing* within Being, much like all Finite Games are played out within *the* one Infinite Game.

This might appear to be a 2mm distinction, but the difference is oceans apart. The fundamental difference is our Awareness of what game we're choosing to freely play.

If we're not even aware there is *the* one Infinite Game, we're by default caught up in playing Finite Games, and nothing is freely chosen, and we play because we must play. We're merely *doing* life according to our enculturated beliefs about life from this level of Awareness. If we're aware of the Infinite Game, but do not freely choose to play in it, we're still just caught up in Doing. Only when we freely choose to play *the* Infinite Game can we access *doing* within Being and become truly alive.

> "Becoming 'awake' involves seeing our confusion more clearly."
> —RUMI

Ironically, the critical threshold we have to cross is becoming a sovereign critical thinker. We cannot access truly Being without first crossing this threshold, and the reason is we have to rise above all the enculturated beliefs we hold. We have to start piercing through the veils of illusion that hold us in the illusion we're freely choosing to play the Finite Games we're, in fact, hopelessly lost in.

This is no easy task, as these enculturated beliefs are everything we've ever known to be true about life, how the world works, and our role in it. But, unless we get the fog off our lens, we will remain stuck in seeing the world through our own distortions of reality. We even believe we're already sovereign critical thinkers; that's how deep this programming truly runs.

Unless you've already started awakening, chances are you're not a true sovereign critical thinker. If you're still closely identified with societal norms and values, ideologies, religion, nationality, race, creed, social status, or the importance of any sort of trophies, you're not yet a true sovereign critical thinker.

If you are still caught up in the theater of politics, the countless shenanigans of big business, the disingenuous manipulation of advertising and marketing, the endless barrage of false narratives spun by mainstream media, or the hero worship of all things that yield fame, fortune, and applause, you're still blind to what's truly in front of you. If you're still playing along with fashion trends, concerning yourself with things like social status, prestige, and how others might perceive you, then you're not free yet. You might be able to read a dense publication about a multi-faceted topic and arrive at a salient intellectual understanding together with a balanced analysis of the pros and cons—but this is a variety of academic intelligence which is not to be confused with true sovereign thought. What I am referring to is being able to see through the veil of illusion. In spiritual terms, we would call that knowing Truth from Falsehood; in colloquial terms, we call this seeing past and through all the bullshit.

As the awakening process unfolds, we're organically nudged toward becoming a sovereign critical thinker. The veil of illusion gets thinner; we start to see more, question more, inquire more, and think deeper about all of it. We slowly but surely gain not only the ability to see through the veil of illusion, but moreover, we gain the courage and spiritual fortitude to stand in our own Truth.

When you move forward on the path of becoming a true sovereign critical thinker, your enculturated beliefs will start to dissolve for you, and you will start seeing how our entire world is literally inverted from Truth. Like the pulling of the proverbial one loose string, the whole sweater will start to come apart. This is both an eye-opening and somewhat disturbing experience; it's deeply challenging and can be borderline traumatic at times as we're starting to see Falsehood after Falsehood in its naked Truth. In the awakening process, we experience this as part of what's commonly referred to as the "deep night of the soul," where our whole known reality seemingly disintegrates all around us.

Deep "night" is really deep "nights," we'll have countless of these *deep nights* as we start piercing the veils of illusion and see Truth from Falsehood. However, we must pass through this stage to get to "Being," as an integral part of Being is *being* a true sovereign critical thinker.

> "A seeker of truth looks beyond the apparent and contemplates the hidden."
> —RUMI

Being a true sovereign critical thinker is quite rare; it requires being totally at peace with having a Truth that puts you in the minority, even when that minority is just you standing alone in your Truth. In Gandhi's famous words, "Even when you're a minority of one, the Truth is the Truth." *Being* in our Truth means we live it completely; we can't be in Being while *doing* what's not our Truth. This is why it's so rare—knowing Truth is one thing, but truthfully *being* your Truth is a whole different level of self-mastery.

Next, we have to be willing and open to search for, look into, and consider all viewpoints. Not only do we need to proactively seek to get out of our echo chamber whenever and wherever possible, we cannot be too fragile to engage with new information or opposing viewpoints and have everything throw us into an emotional tailspin or dislodge our mental equanimity. In Epictetus' wise words: "It's impossible for a man to learn what he thinks he already knows." In Buddhism, they call this "Shoshin," which translates into "beginner's mind." Marcel Proust said all of what we're pointing at in these prophetic words: "The only true voyage of discovery would be not to visit strange lands but to see known lands with new eyes."

So, now we know we cannot truly access Being unless we have freely chosen to play *the* Infinite Game, *and* we have become a true sovereign critical thinker. But what does this constituent attribute Being look like and actually do for us?

Presence.

A person grounded in Being—even while *doing*—has Presence. Not *presence* in being impressive, but true *presence* in being fully Present. Most people are lost in Doing, meaning they're busy in their mere *doing*, scurrying about, rushing to go somewhere or to become someone, and in turn, they're never really Present. They don't really listen, don't really observe, and don't really think critically. It's all mechanical, mostly commanded by their subconscious mind autopilot, and typically quite unoriginal and inauthentic. Their true Being is masked by all their busy *doing*.

However, most of us would never know what their Being really looks or feels like because all we know is being really busy *doing* while Doing. We think it's normal, which is why true Presence in others often also goes unnoticed, as only in *being* Present can we discern true Presence in others. However, even those lost in Doing occasionally cease all their *doing* for a moment, and when they encounter a person with true Presence during one of these mini-breaks it makes a lasting impression. Because someone with true Presence is authentic, which is a palpable Truth when we're Present for it.

True Presence comes from truly *being* totally in this moment—the "Now"—which is the only moment there is and ever will be. Truly *being* in this moment requires our mind to be calm and still. We cannot be right here, right now, while our mind is bouncing frantically around like a Mexican jumping bean from past to future and back again with a few momentary pauses in the present. So, what does that tell us? Presence exists in the still point or Fulcrum, which is the present moment or eternal Now, whereas past and future signify the continuum or Polarity of linear time.

As we quiet our minds, we start to be Present for what is. The Feminine is deeply grounded in fully Being in the Now. Her home is the Fulcrum, as that's the only place where Life itself can flow through her as the still point of all of Creation. In this Fulcrum, we start to fully embody our body and be totally *present* with it, which will inevitably give us more Presence to others already. We start to truly listen and not hear the words but the deeper meaning within them. We start to truly observe and start having eyes for all sorts of details, clues, signs, solutions, serendipities, and even opportunities. And we start to think critically from a place of sovereignty, meaning we don't allow any of our mind's enculturation to stand in our way of recognizing Truth from Falsehood.

The reason that women are deemed more intuitive than men is because when she is deeply grounded in her Yin, she's grounded in this Fulcrum. In that still point, she's naturally receptive to Life itself—she sees, hears, feels, and intuits all sorts of things that men lost in ceaseless *doing* upon *doing* have simply no receptivity for. She's tuned into Life itself while he's too busy *doing* in Doing.

Fully Being in the Now—the only moment there ever is—has a frequency that is noticeably distinct from the frequency of *being* in never-ending Doing. The frequency of Being is light, soft, coherent, and calming, whereas the frequency of Doing is dense, edgy, frantic, and restless. These frequencies are closely linked to our autonomous nervous system, which has two states. In Being, we're in the parasympathetic nervous system—rest and relax—where our energy-system is in coherence, which has a calming effect and gives us access to alpha and even theta brainwaves. In Doing, we're in the sympathetic nervous system—fight or flight—where our energy-system is in survival mode and we are predominantly in beta brainwaves.

We'll delve much deeper into these two states and their corresponding brainwaves in Part V in the chapter "Mind Mastery & States of Being." What you should take away, though, is that within *being* in Being you will have an unmistakable Presence about you which has a distinct and palpable frequency all others who are Present for it will take notice of.

Our Presence is not just something the Outer World will take notice of; it will radically change the eyes with which you view the Outer World. Presence is what allows us to see and experience what was always there to start with; we were just not Present for it, including what's next.

Being Alive.

> "It's not death a man should fear, but
> he should fear never beginning to fully live."
> —MARCUS AURELIUS

This is how you know if you're *being* alive or just *doing* life. People busy *doing* life cannot sit still, do absolutely nothing, and be totally content. Almost immediately, they get bored, restless, uncomfortable, or even mildly irritable. They feel they should be *doing* something, even if that *doing* is *being* entertained, making a new to-do list, or mentally lamenting what they could be *doing* instead of just *being*. Even *being* lazy is rooted in *doing* as in true Being. There's no such thing as *being* lazy; you're just *doing* nothing in Being. If you recognize yourself in any of the above, you're busy *doing* life and too busy in Doing for there to be any sense of truly *being* alive. This is because life runs through us, but when we're in Doing we're too busy running through life by incessantly *doing* to be truly Present for what's truthfully running through us.

The incredible richness, magic, and poetry of Life itself are mostly invisible to us unless we're fully Present in Being, even when that Being is *doing* something in the moment. If Doing is a black-and-white movie without sound, Being is a movie in 4D LED high resolution with stereo Dolby sound. When we become Present in Being, the movie of life comes fully alive for us, and with it, we start truly *being* alive. Life becomes a fully immersive experience of *being* alive, grounded in just Being. From this place, our *doing* is no longer just a means to an end; our *doing* is the end as we're *doing* it from a place of authentic Being.

We can readily witness the cornerstone Being in all of nature and Mother Earth, and if anything, she is truly the quintessential representation of the Feminine. All animals, trees, plants, and even phenomena like the weather are busy *doing* just Being. You'll only find a tree busy *doing* Being a tree, a squirrel busily *doing* Being a squirrel, and an ocean is only concerned with *doing* Being an ocean. No part of nature is ever confused about what it should be *doing* in Being or what it is because nature doesn't confuse what it does with what it is.

You are not what you do. Human beings are not defined by what they do; they are defined by their *being* in Being. In Being, you are already enough, already complete, and truly free to do all sorts of *doing* without any of it defining you.

This is the constituent attribute of Being, truly *being* alive vs. busy *doing* life.

Of course, some would argue what you do—i.e., "accomplish" in the outer world—does define who you truly are. True, but only in the sense that your *doing* of Being or Doing will define who you are in terms of the level of spiritual art (or lack thereof) that's in your human beingness. Because, if you recall, the only real game the universe is playing is *the* one Infinite Game and this game is concerned with one single thing: the continuous raising of the refinement of your spiritual art through your beingness. The universe is entirely unconcerned with the trophies (or ranking) that are at the very core of Finite Games. We'll get much deeper into all of this in Parts III and IV as we start to form a complete picture of the full-color palette with which we—as spiritual Poets—get to "paint" our spiritual art.

Before we get there, let's explore the second cornerstone of the Feminine: Creativity.

CHAPTER 14

CREATIVITY

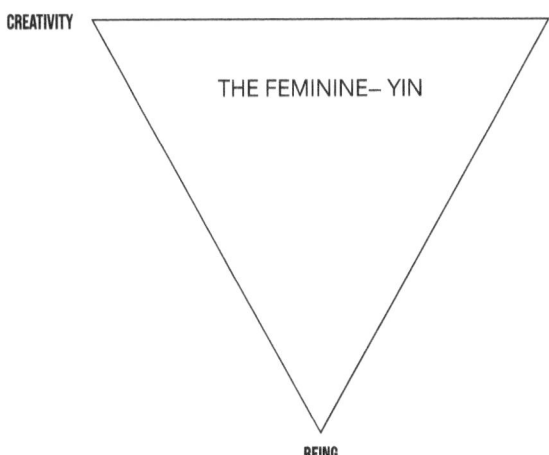

CREATIVITY IS NOT JUST THE juice of life; it's Life itself. This entire universe, all of Creation, is a never-ending dynamic flow of ever-changing Creation. And the Feminine is the true creatrix at the very center of all Creation.

The word Creativity is derived from the Latin word *creare*, which means to create, to make, or to produce. The antonym then is to destroy, to destruct, or to dismantle in terms of rendering something unproduced. Therefore, the opposite pole of Creativity is Destruction. The creation of Life vs. the destruction of Life, which is death. The Feminine *is* Existence, she is Life itself, and within *being* Life, she is the creatrix through which we discover Truth from Falsehood.

Delving a little deeper into the word Creativity reveals a lot more about this cornerstone of the Feminine. Some words closely associated with Creativity are imagination, artistry, genius, brilliance, virtuosity, flair, playfulness, luminosity, inspiration, ingenuity, inventiveness, resourcefulness, adaptability, and originality.

All of these words point to the essential qualities of Life itself and the hallmarks of those who have become true masters of not just Life itself but creating a life of *being* fully alive by *being* fully immersed in the playful Creation of Life.

But, again, if we *must* play, we cannot *play*, and playful Creation then becomes something we don't have access to. Seeking pleasure and gain is not the same as playful Creation, as there's a goal or outcome attached to our *doing*. Playful Creation is creating for the sake of creating and is deeply rooted in Being.

When the outcome of what we create is some form of destruction—degeneration or death—then it wasn't truly Creativity that got us there. We can see this very clearly in our world today. Humanity has "created" many things, but regretfully many of these things were highly destructive in their outcome. In the chapter "Intelligence," we referred to these as unintelligent outcomes; it's all connected and pointing at the same thing. War, violence, hate, racism, inequalities, injustices, rampant pollution, and the annihilation of Mother Earth are all things humanity created and continues to create.

We've created weapons of mass destruction and continue to make more and more advanced weaponry so we can kill with ever more precision and velocity. Humanity has created GMO and heavily processed foods that are devoid of any nutritional value; industrial agriculture practices which have rendered most of our soils depleted and barren; plastics and other synthetic materials which aren't readily biodegradable have caused havoc to Mother Earth; and a host of synthetic pharmaceuticals and medicines treat symptoms but don't restore our health. I could fill dozens of pages with more examples, but you get the picture.

Humanity has created economies that view people as a mere input in the system, caused huge disparities in income and wealth, and in turn, produced an ever-widening political divide that is destabilizing society. Humanity has created a model of life that has resulted in an ever-increasing decrease in community, family life, and connection between people. The divorce rate is above 50 percent and rising, domestic violence and abuse are endemic, alcoholism and opioid abuse are widespread, chronic illness has grown exponentially over the last four to five decades, and depression and suicide rates have been steadily rising as well.

All of the above is symbolic of the decaying and diminishing of Life itself, which is the entropic process of death, however slowly. It's highly destructive and degenerative, so by definition, none of this can be rooted in Creativity even though humanity created it.

> **"Creativity is intelligence having fun."**
> —ALBERT EINSTEIN

So, from this, we can clearly see that for there to be true Creativity within Creation, the Creation itself must be conducive to Life itself.

Anything conducive to Life itself is in right relationship with everything else it touches or affects; this is a fundamental design principle of self-organizing complex living systems. Within Creation, there must be a contribution or value to the whole system that's far greater than the resources it takes from or the harm it causes to the system. Again, Intelligence is defined as *that* which creates intelligent outcomes.

This is exactly where so many of humanity's Creations fail as we are hungry for instant gratification, short-term oriented, and so many negative effects are simply not factored in or given any weight through the reductionism lens we perceive the economy, society, or our own lives. But there's a deeper layer to this, as all of this originates from a level of Consciousness that simply cannot even see how its own enculturation, including what we value and worship most, is driving all of this.

We're back to being in a race to raise human consciousness as, at the current prevailing levels below 200, there are no real solutions since our own collective ignorance and survival mode mental state don't allow us access to the higher Intelligence solutions we need. So, for example, we fumble around with setting sustainability goals that don't nearly move the needle enough, and most everything else, we "greenwash" away with empty slogans and lofty aspirations that are too soft to make a dent in anything. We're stuck in the core of the psycho-cybernetic loop of our own limited perceptions of reality, which block true Creativity from emerging as the truly novel, inventive, imaginative, and creative always happens on the edges of any system.

> "The world is but a canvas to the imagination."
> —HENRY DAVID THOREAU

What we witness on the macro level (society, economy, etc.), we can also see on the micro or personal level. The deep enculturation of most of humanity acts like a trance of conditioned thinking; it's so pervasive and omnipresent that people are like the proverbial fish that cannot see the water it's swimming in. As if hypnotized, most don't really pause to question the norms and values of society, the life of Finite Games prescribed by their culture, or what the world deems as successful. So, most chart into this world to "create" a life that's confirmative, unimaginative, and uninspiring to their Soul. It's the mechanical repetition of the playbook prescribed by their society, so it's no surprise, then, that we seek escapes in the form of addictions, entertainment, vacations, and even retirement. We need this because our lives lack a vital ingredient: true Creativity.

Grounded in Being, with our sovereign critical thought fully online, we start to see the narratives of society and culture that govern our life. Once we see, we cannot unsee, and so this process of seeing starts to create the space for our true Creativity to come alive and be expressed in our life. This is where our world becomes the canvas of our imagination, and our authentic creative expression can start to flower and blossom.

This doesn't mean we become anarchists or fight society's norms and values, as that's still being stuck in Doing. Instead, we start to create our own narrative of Truth, and we let go of Falsehoods, not by fighting them, but by setting them aside, which is to say consciously ignoring them. Within ignoring them, we feed these Falsehoods no more energy, which allows us to simply be in Being. This process does require courage, as we need to be willing to stand in our own Truth unabashedly.

Generally speaking, most people don't want you to change, and they especially don't want you to break the ancestral mold. This mold is not just their perception of reality but their mental crutch and emotional safety blanket. It's deeply challenging for others to be confronted with someone that liberates themselves from the tribe's enculturation; it's a mirror they are likely not ready to look into. So, in this process of liberating ourselves from our own enculturation, we are typically faced with difficult choices we have to make for our own health and well-being. Not everyone is ready to accompany us on our journey of freely choosing to play *the* Infinite Game, which really is our liberation from enculturation. Hence, we're often forced to lovingly distance ourselves from those loved ones, family members, or friends that unconsciously hold us back from going on this journey.

> "If you love what you do, you'll never work a day in your life."
> —MARK TWAIN

Expressing our own unique and true Creativity into our lives is infusing our life with the deepest sense of purpose, fulfillment, and joy. This is the juice of Life itself. We are each born with unique talents, gifts, and superpowers—no exceptions—and when we allow the truest expression of our own Creativity to come through us, these talents, gifts, and superpowers are inevitably activated. This might prompt an accomplished lawyer to realize her true purpose is being a painter or vice versa.

It truly doesn't matter *what* we do in life; what truly matters is *why* we do it, as the *why* determines the *how*. The *how* here only refers to one thing: is our *how* coming from Doing or Being? There's art, beauty, and poetry that can be expressed in any *what* we might do. It makes no difference if you're a doctor, master plumber, schoolteacher, devoted mother, business tycoon, or world-famous opera singer. In fact, it makes no difference if *what* you do is just living life and has no label at all. What matters is your *why*, or in other words are you expressing your truest Creativity into this world through your life's expression, or are you *doing* what your enculturation instructed you to do and become?

All of humanity is a brilliantly complex mosaic of unique puzzle pieces called human beings. You are a unique puzzle piece that contains within it some unique art with effervescent beauty, and an invaluable contribution to the whole, and only you can express that puzzle piece to perfection. Your art is needed, and only you can do you like you can. This is at the heart of your Creativity that you have within; it wants not only to be expressed, but this universe wants to receive it. This universe is craving your true Creativity to be expressed, and it will even come to your aid when you do.

Physical reality shows us the corresponding nature of this universe through corresponding with our creative expression. This is why when we do nothing, are stifled by self-doubt, fear of rejection or failure, or are hostage to our own procrastination, it cannot come to our aid as we give the universe nothing to correspond to. Life itself—the Feminine—is all about movement. For there to be Life itself and thus Creativity, things cannot be stagnant, dormant, or restricted.

This is not to say we cannot rest. Rest and sleep are a natural temporary pause of movement; it's restorative in nature and therefore conducive to Life and an integral part of the cycles we see in nature, such as the four seasons and even our own circadian rhythm of sleep and waking states. However, when things go stagnant or dormant—they're indefinitely paused—we see Life itself, and thus Creativity, go stale, then in decline, until it starts to disintegrate, degenerate, decay, and ultimately dies.

When we move, act, create, and express our Creativity into Life itself, we're giving the universe something to correspond to. Our only real job is to turn the small wheels—that which we control—and the universe will turn the big wheels in the form of serendipities, fortunate coincidences, "lucky" breaks (there's no such thing as "luck"), and all sorts of other occurrences that aid the expression of our Creativity into physical reality.

We can see then that the Feminine doesn't just create Life itself; she also receives it. In other words, the Creativity we express into Life itself is incomplete unless we can learn to be receptive to the universe. Existence is a dance with Life itself; the expression of our Creativity—our art and poetry, no matter what form that comes—comes fully alive when we engage with the universe in a dynamic flow of giving and receiving. Coming to see and know the universe as our co-creator is a sign of emerging spiritual maturity, as the level of our receptivity to the universe determines how much of our true Creativity we're able to express into Life itself.

When we have no eyes—no receptivity—for how the universe is aiding and guiding us, our Creativity will be muted, stifled, or worse, misguided by our enculturation. On the other hand, when we start having a deep receptivity for the universe's aid and guidance, it will provoke our creative genius to come fully alive. None of this is to be confused with the recognition, validation, or applause of others. That's always welcome and encouraging, but just remember that throughout history, there have been countless artists, philosophers, scientists, and other great masters whose genius and brilliance were not recognized during their lifetime. So, if this is you, just know you're in good company.

The sovereign Feminine Is fearless in the expression of her Creativity from a place of Being; she creates for the sake of Creation. However, her art is always conducive to Life itself as the constituent attribute Creativity is always expressed in service to Life itself.

Which is the perfect segue into the third cornerstone of the Feminine: Reverence.

CHAPTER 15

REVERENCE

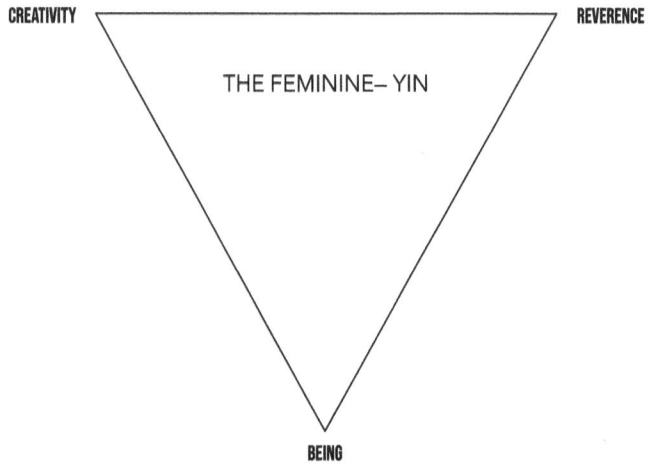

THE THIRD CONSTITUENT ATTRIBUTE of the Feminine is Reverence, which is often misunderstood to mean the same as *respect*. Respect is beautiful, but Reverence has a far deeper meaning and, therefore, far greater gravity to it.

We can already clearly see this in the Merriam-Webster Dictionary, which defines Reverence as:

Profound adoring awed respect.

Reverence, then, is the gold standard of all things we consider "respect." We can be or act respectful yet still hold no true respect; in other words, we can play or fabricate it. We cannot be truly reverential without it coming from true Reverence. So, there's a depth and purity to Reverence that goes well beyond "ordinary" respect, and this level of deference will prove instrumental as, without Reverence, we have no way to access our own Divinity within, and without this access our spiritual art will remain superficial in depth, muted in radiance, and lacking in integrity.

> "If we could see the miracle of a single flower clearly our whole life would change."
> —BUDDHA

If you recall, the Feminine represents Existence or Life itself, and this third cornerstone of the Feminine points us directly at the "Sanctity of all Life." All of Creation is sacred and holds infinite value, not the least of which, every single human life. Reverence then points at Reverence for all of Life itself, for all of Creation.

The oppression, devaluing, and diminishment of the Feminine essence over the millennia is probably no more obvious and visible in the utter irreverence of humanity for Life itself, the unthinkable brutalities and suffering inflicted on others, and the desecration of all other life forms, including Mother Earth herself.

For all our pride and hubris about humanity's historical accomplishments, technological and scientific advancements, and so-called intelligence, we're completely blind and ignorant to see that—truthfully—humanity is the greatest threat to Mother Earth and all its diverse life forms. In plain terms, we are the greatest savages on this planet, operating at very low levels of intelligence as the universe defines it.

And, at the very root of this is that we collectively lack the spiritual maturity of Reverence. We have no eyes to see the miracle of a single flower, let alone all of Creation. If we did, the world would look radically different.

We cannot even see the sanctity of every human life as evidenced by the countless wars, acts of violence, hate, racism, inequalities, and injustices that are pervasive in our world, still today. We have diminished the sanctity of a human life by measuring it in its utility to the economic system and the financial net worth of the individual. Human life has been reduced to a number; it's disposable and dispensable. How else can you send soldiers into wars to butcher the "enemy" or accept abject poverty, famine, and starvation by almost a billion people?

We're able to do all these things because we're collectively lost in the cobwebs of our minds and utterly disconnected from our Hearts. Our enculturation blinds us to see these heinous things for what they really are: atrocities by mankind. We glorify our respective military prowess and celebrate our war heroes and victories and so justify and rationalize the unthinkable brutalities of war. We dismiss abject poverty, starvation, and intolerable human suffering as an abstraction, an unfortunate byproduct of the advancement of mankind to be solved in due time.

To the Heart—which resides in Reverence—these aren't mere abstractions; they represent the gross Unintelligence that's governing mankind's selfishness in the values and priorities we hold most dear. All of these atrocities and abominations perpetrated by mankind on its own kind are infinitely solvable. There's no lack of food, money, or resources to solve all of these almost overnight. Except, without Reverence, we have no access to the true Intelligence and spiritual maturity it requires to address our own human inadequacies.

> "Just as white light consists of colored rays, so Reverence for Life contains all the components of ethics: love, kindliness, sympathy, empathy, peacefulness, and the power to forgive."
> —ALBERT SCHWEITZER

Albert Schweitzer (1875-1965) was a renowned German philosopher, writer, humanitarian, physician, and theologian who used the word "ethics" to describe what he concluded were not only the principles but the ultimate purpose of Life itself. Reverence was a central theme as he saw this as what differentiated what he called a truly alive person from someone who merely existed no matter how successful this person was in a worldly or material sense. So, here we can see—again—the connection between Doing and Being, whereas Reverence can only come into play for us when we're in Being, or in other words *being* alive.

Reverence goes even beyond morality, ethics, or being a "good" person. Reverence is *the* ethos of *and* for all of Life itself. It's a lens through which we perceive all of Creation, and in that way, it becomes our inner North Star. A North Star overrides our primal need and desire to be right, righteous, or solely seek personal pleasure and gain. We—all of humanity—must heed the call to rise above race, creed, nationality, patriotism, religious or political affiliations, and most of all, acting solely out of self-interest.

When Reverence comes into our perception of reality, a whole new reality emerges. We start to see the madness, fallacies, and even idiocies of what drives mankind to such barbaric actions and unintelligent outcomes. Looking at the world from our Heart opens up a whole new dimension and infuses us with Love and compassion for all others. None of us is responsible for changing the whole world, but we are each responsible for our own slice of the whole. The below quotation is a poignant reminder we each have a duty to all our fellow humans to come to the aid of those who need our help and we each have an important role to play in creating a more beautiful and just world:

> "To be wealthy and honored in an unjust society is a disgrace."
> —CONFUCIUS

Having said all the above, please note there's nothing inherently wrong with creating a beautiful and abundant life for ourselves. In fact, it's near impossible to be deeply spiritual when we struggle for survival, so ensuring we're in a good place ourselves is a prerequisite for even being able to serve as a life raft for someone else. However, when our pursuit of abundance harms others, we run afoul of the laws of this universe.

Harm comes in many ways, some of which we might turn—consciously or unconsciously—a blind eye to. When we lend our careers to companies or governments that extract, exploit, and degenerate natural or human capital, we're participating in causing harm. A multinational in the chocolate or candy business going about business as usual in the cacao supply chain is a participant in the exploitation of impoverished farmers. A Wall Street firm financing the fossil fuel industry is participating in the destruction of Mother Earth. It's convenient to say, "But I am not the CEO running the multinational or the oil company," but the fact is we're participating by lending our time and energy to these sorts of industries. The same goes for what we purchase (i.e., consume), the gas-guzzling SUV we decide to drive or idle incessantly while we pick up our kids from school, the single-use plastic we casually discard, the warmongering politician we vote for, and the list goes on.

Of course, in this day and age, it's nearly impossible to live a 100 percent harm-free life, as just about anything has a negative consequence. However, you'd be surprised how many adjustments, large and small, we can make by just becoming aware and committed to Reverence as a principle guiding our life choices.

No longer tacitly accepting by approving of any form of war, violence, hate, racism, inequality, or injustice is a life choice we make. From the perspective of our Heart, it's simply indefensible, no matter the rhetoric by politicians and the media. Reverence is not just a noble quality we grow into; it's a conscious decision we make about how we live, view, and approach all of Life itself.

Of course, there's no more obvious place to see humanity's Irreverence than how we treat other life forms, animals, nature, and all of Mother Earth. In fact, we've started polluting the universe as we shoot Tesla cars into space and casually abandon used-up space equipment, much like we do here on Earth. Reverence doesn't stop with how we treat other humans; moreover, the case could be easily made that Reverence might begin with how we treat everything non-human. Because if we can foster Reverence for all of Creation, surely we will extend this Reverence finally to our fellow man, woman, and child. There's no pick-and-choose in Reverence; we either have Reverence for all of Creation, or we have Reverence for none of it—everything is connected to everything else.

> "Learn how to see. Realize that everything connects to everything else."
> —LEONARDO DA VINCI

Let's take a look at animals. Besides the ongoing extinctions of all sorts of wildlife, the way we treat industrial-farmed livestock is nothing short of ruthless and barbaric. Confined for a dramatically abbreviated life while fattened on a non-natural diet of GMO corn, soy, and wheat, we then take conscious animals like cows, pigs, and chickens through the harrowing experience of imminent death as they're rounded up in queue to be slaughtered. We know these animals all experience terrifying fears as they release copious amounts of fear hormones in this process. We then mechanically slaughter these fully aware mammalian animals, and estimates are that up to 10 percent of them are still alive when they're hoisted upside down and cut open. The entire process of industrial livestock farming lacks any sort of Reverence and, arguably, humanity.

In commercial fishing, we see similar irreverence for fish and aquatic life. For example, "bycatch" is the term commercial fishermen use for anything caught in their nets that they do not want, cannot sell, or are not allowed to keep. Each year, millions of endangered shark, dolphin, and whale species find their unjust death this way, destroying entire aquatic ecosystems, which is why we now have Chinese fishing trawlers encroaching on Chilean territorial waters just to highlight one such example.

Dolphins and whales are highly intelligent mammals, by the way, with rich social lives, apparent communities, and their own form of language and communication. It's widely accepted among marine wildlife biologists that they likely vividly experience their horrific deaths in the very same way we humans would. Yet, in the Faroe Islands, they still hold their annual dolphin round-up, where they bludgeon 1,000 to 1,500 dolphins to death with machetes.

This isn't an advocacy to become vegan, and certainly, don't take it as a promotion of the lab-derived fake meats that are flooding the market, as most of these are devastating for your health. However, let's start by stating the fact that our choice of meat consumption is primarily a cultural choice. A Hindu would choose to fast rather than eat cow meat, an orthodox Jew wouldn't even contemplate eating pig meat, and a Chinese person views dog meat as a typical staple. Meat consumption is first and foremost a choice and not a life necessity as you can live to a ripe old age being a vegan or vegetarian for life—in various cultures around the world, they have done this for millennia. Even more so, in today's world any vitamin or mineral deficiencies can be supplemented.

Here in the West, we do overconsume meat in general, so just for health purposes alone, we would show Reverence for our own health by reducing our meat intake drastically. But there's also a cycle of life in nature, and we are part of nature. In addition, the science is undeniable that there are vitamins and minerals in animal meat (inclusive of fish) that are beneficial to our health, which is not to say these couldn't be found possibly in other foods or supplemented. Hence, eating meat or animal products per se doesn't make us less of a spiritual person—having no Reverence for the meat or animal products we eat does.

> "To me, every hour of the light and dark is a miracle. Every cubic inch of space is a miracle."
> —WALT WHITMAN

To move toward Reverence for all Life as it relates to meat or animal products, it's inherent that we first and foremost concern ourselves with the quality of life these animals enjoyed while alive. *Did they graze or roam freely? Did they eat their natural diet? Were they kept free of hormones and antibiotics?* These are all key questions to ask. Basically, *were they raised with Love, compassion, and Reverence?* Second, *Were they humanely slaughtered?* Now, the process of taking life—slaughtering—is inherently violent and somewhat barbaric. Yet, this can still be done with Reverence. Most Indigenous cultures have long-standing hunting or fishing traditions, but their Reverence for the life they took is pervasive in the whole ritual of hunting the animal and honoring the animal once it's killed.

Indigenous cultures recognize the miracle of what they call the Great Spirit. All of Life itself and all its representations within all of Creation, including animals, are miracles of the Great Spirit, and since they're representations of this Great Spirit, they hold all of it sacred. There's great natural wisdom in Indigenous cultures that we would do well to learn from and weave into Western civilization.

It's my personal belief that everyone that consciously decides to consume meat or animal products cannot truly do so truly consciously unless they have at least witnessed the slaughtering of an animal or, better yet, done so themselves. You cannot consciously consume meat unless you have deeply connected with the cycle of life process. There are many butchers who will not slaughter, and there's a reason for that—it's a gruesome act, and it is difficult not to have it affect you deeply. So, if you wish to consciously choose to eat meat, there's no judgment in that, but I encourage you to seek the experience of slaughtering an animal so you can viscerally connect with your choice. If you're incapable of looking the animal in the eye and consciously connecting with the experience of taking its life, you are incapable of consciously eating its meat.

Finally, there's simply no place for recreational killing of any animal to coexist within Reverence for Life itself. As thrilling as it might be to hook a big fish or kill a full-grown buck, the act of killing any life for entertainment purposes is representative of levels of consciousness below 200. As Leonardo da Vinci pointed at, everything is connected. There's simply no way we could even consider this fun, interesting, or justifiable at higher levels of Consciousness. Again, I am not passing any judgment because I am not responsible for the Karmic debts of others, but just know if you view this as entertainment or a fun way to spend your free time, it's a clear indicator that you are not fully connected with your spiritual Heart yet.

> "If a man loses his Reverence for any part of life,
> he will lose his Reverence for all of life."
>
> —ALBERT SCHWEITZER

It's perhaps easier to see how our treatment of live animals is reflective of Irreverence or Reverence, but all of Creation includes all life forms and the whole of Mother Earth. Forests and oceans are life forms, and so are lakes, prairies, and the ice caps at our poles. All are teeming with life, and we're even constantly discovering new proof of Consciousness and Intelligence in these life forms previously unknown. Trees communicate through their root systems, fungi collaborate and form intricate webs of life, and ants and bees have crucial roles in supporting and enabling all sorts of life forms. Ground cover affects local temperatures and micro-weather patterns, which collectively influence macro-weather patterns.

Basically, when humans treat the Biosphere and Mother Earth with complete Irreverence, we're destabilizing the entire web of life that enables our very existence on this planet. And, despite the naysayers and people that like to argue climate change is a hoax, there's no denying global temperatures are rising, ice caps are melting at an accelerating pace, the oceans are littered with plastic, and we're losing ancient forests like the Amazon at the rate of roughly 150 acres per minute.

Humans have been treating Mother Earth with complete Irreverence for at least five hundred to six hundred years. Since WWII, the problem that is humans has only been exacerbated by dramatic population growth and the advancement of technologies that enhanced our capacity to cause harm to the environment on an industrial scale, where in earlier times, we were far smaller in numbers and had only primitive tools. When your most advanced technology is hunting with a bow and arrow, your capacity to affect Mother Earth on a global scale is negligible.

Many scientists believe we're well on our way to extinction as we push Mother Earth to the tipping point of no return. There's a zone of vitality within which our planet can self-organize and regenerate itself; beyond these limits, our children will inevitably come to live their life in a *Mad Max* movie.

At the very core of the changes we—humanity—need to make is Reverence for Life itself. We have to make a choice if our current way of life, including its economic theories and priorities, is conducive to Life itself. These might be hard choices because change is never easy, certainly not on a global scale, but these choices are quite obvious.

We simply must adhere to the principles of this universe, or the universe will ultimately break us. Reverence for Life itself is one of those core principles, which is why it's a cornerstone of the Feminine as she represents Existence itself.

> "Reverence awakens in the soul a sympathetic power through which we attract qualities in the beings around us which would otherwise remain concealed."
> —RUDOLF STEINER

A more beautiful world—a better world—organically originates from Reverence. The corresponding nature of Life itself responds powerfully when we dwell in Reverence. When we can live from a place of Being Love, kindliness, sympathy, empathy, peacefulness, and cultivate the power within to forgive, then Life itself has no way but to correspond to us in that way. Like-energy attracts like-energy.

So within, so without.

Like everything else, Reverence is an inside job. No matter how unloving, unkind, or unfavorable the Outer World might seem or treat us, we still have the capacity to have unwavering Reverence for all of Creation. We can pour this Reverence into our relationships, our work, our way of life, and all of Life itself that we touch or encounter.

When we successfully saturate our entire Being with Reverence, we inevitably come to experience Reverence in all areas of our life. Within this constituent attribute of the Feminine, we will find a powerful catalyst to transform our life and readily ascend in Consciousness above 200 as the mere recognition of the Sanctity of all Life is a profound and life-altering insight.

In Parts III and IV, we will uncover how Reverence connects us to the divine Feminine Gifts and universal Principles, but before we do so, we'll close out this Part II of the Architecture by revealing the unity and interconnectedness of the Masculine and Feminine Essence.

CHAPTER 16
MASCULINE & FEMININE ESSENCE

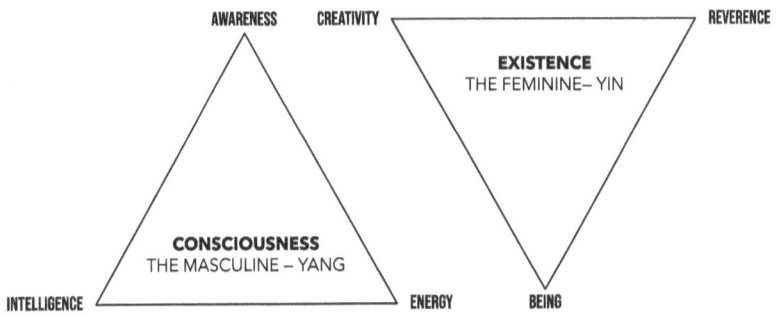

FOR A QUICK REFRESHER on the first chapter of this Part II, the Masculine and Feminine are two essences of the whole of Source Consciousness. One essence is not more valuable or significant than the other; they're different yet fully equal in all respects.

Regardless of biological gender, we each have Yin and Yang energy within. Men generally are Masculine-energy dominant and women vice versa, and none of this has anything to do with sexual orientation or preferences. We are also each different and unique; each of our respective essences will be harmonized a little bit differently.

Depending on the environment, situation, or our interaction with others, we might situationally change our dominance as there's fluidity within our capacity to access our Masculine or Feminine essence within. We do each have a natural harmonious state between our Masculine and Feminine Essence, which is not balanced per se but our own unique true nature in terms of harmony between these two essences.

We can be out of harmony with our own unique true nature by being dominant in our non-dominant essence. For a Feminine-dominant woman, this would be leading her life from being predominantly in her Masculine, and for a Masculine-dominant man, it would be the opposite.

We can also be out of harmony when we're integrated, yet one or more of the constituent attributes of either or both of our Masculine and Feminine are still in dissonance. More on that later.

Finally, when our non-dominant essence is suppressed, we refer to that as not being integrated, which is to say we're out of harmony with our own unique true nature. When we're not integrated, we lack access to the qualities or constituent attributes of the suppressed essence. Paradoxically, it's the suppressed non-dominant essence we have to heal and integrate to restore our non-suppressed dominant essence into true Sovereignty. Of course, true Sovereignty is interlinked with the harmonious integration of the Masculine and Feminine within and a prerequisite to ascending into the higher octaves of consciousness, which is to say, an ever-higher level of refinement of our spiritual art. In many ancient wisdom teachings, the reference to "the Alpha and the Omega" is truly a reference to the Masculine and the Feminine. Christianity adopted this to refer directly to Christ, but what's lesser known is that the underpinning of this reference was that Christ embodied what's called "Christ Consciousness," which is the fully integrated Alpha and Omega. We'll touch more on all of this later in Part V, but for now, we still have many essentials to uncover to do that discussion justice.

"Healing" our non-dominant essence typically involves bringing this essence into coherence, after which we can work toward integrating this essence harmoniously. You cannot harmoniously integrate an essence that's in dissonance. In other words, true Sovereign Masculinity or true Sovereign Femininity represents the harmonious integration of a fully coherent Masculine and Feminine essence in accordance with the unique harmonious true nature of that person.

Harmony and harmonious are the key operative words; this is because the Polarity continuum is governed by the universal Principle of Harmony, which we'll cover in-depth in Part IV. The crux is that without Harmony between these two (coherent) essences within, our dominant essence cannot be sovereign—as in "be in its power"—because the still point or Fulcrum goes out of its harmonious pivot point.

It's important to understand this harmonious pivot point is not the midway or center point as that's associated with balance, and as mentioned, the Yin/Yang Polarity continuum is governed by

Harmony. It must be because Life itself is dynamic and ever-changing, so this continuum within us operating harmoniously with Life itself is dynamic and ever-changing, which also then means the Fulcrum is dynamic and ever-changing.

This is a fundamental understanding in love relationships as well as opposites attract. So, in a typical love relationship, one lover would be Feminine-dominant (typically the woman) and the other Masculine-dominant. In the new age Polarity relationship coaching space, the belief is widely held and taught that the Masculine-dominant lover is leading because of his Masculine-energy, which allows her to surrender into trust and relax into her true Feminine nature of receiving, flowing, and sensuality. Chaos being held by Order. Albeit maybe monogamous instead of polygamous, this actually creates a quasi-concubine/master role play, as it's based on false Order.

True Order is, by definition, in the harmonious pivot point—the still point—and so the dynamic the Polarity relationship coaches are after requires the Masculine to take command of the Fulcrum. Taking command here doesn't mean he plays boss, but he masterfully controls and shifts this Fulcrum along the continuum whereby he leads, and she can truly flow along. The Masculine's constituent attribute Awareness is so finely tuned into her, the relationship, and the circumstances that he anticipates what's needed in the moment and shifts the Fulcrum accordingly. Sometimes he needs to be firmer and stronger in his Masculine; sometimes, he needs to be more soft and gentle in his Feminine. This doesn't mean the Masculine serves or accommodates the Feminine's every whim; it just means for the Masculine to truly lead and *be* Order, he must command the Fulcrum.

Incidentally, this dynamic goes for all Yang-based leadership, whether it's a love relationship, business, or politics. For instance, Sun Tzu's ancient Chinese military treatise *The Art of War* is basically all about commanding the Fulcrum in the context of military strategy, and this book has later been extrapolated in the context of business strategy by dozens of business authors and thought leaders.

> "In warfare, there are no constant conditions. He who can modify his tactics in relation to his opponent will succeed and win."
> —SUN TZU

The way to look at all of this is a dance between these essences within. Sometimes one will lead, at other times, the other, but the whole dance is about being fully integrated while being in harmony with our own unique true nature. When we realize this, we become truly sovereign, as in being in our spiritual power. So, when we refer to the Sovereign Masculine, we're really pointing at a fully integrated Masculine and Feminine Essence in harmony with its own unique true nature, which in the case of the Sovereign Masculine would be Masculine-dominant. The same goes for the Sovereign Feminine the other way around.

Before we go deeper into all of this, let's build a foundation of understanding of our various bodies, so we all speak the same language. We'll use the below representation of Leonardo da Vinci's "Vitruvian Man" to illustrate these bodies.

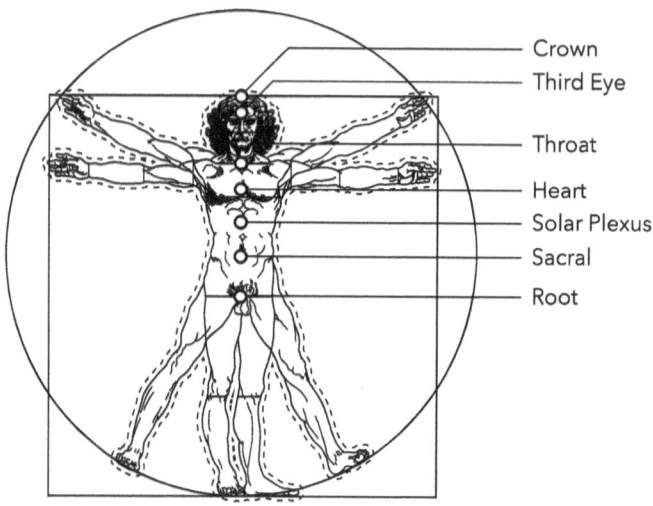

First, we have our physical or biological body. This body is the densest in terms of vibration (i.e., low frequency), which is why it appears solid to our five senses. Second, the halo indicated by the dotted line around the physical body represents our emotional body; this is the second densest yet already ephemeral in nature, so we cannot observe it with our five senses. Next is the square, which represents our mental body, which is yet a little less dense than our emotional body. Please note the square is symbolic and not an actual rendition of what our mental body looks like. Symbolically, the square in ancient Chinese wisdom traditions refers to Earth, which is consistent because our Mind is a product of the brain, which is on the Earthly plane. Finally, the circle represents our spiritual body. This body is the least dense of these four. The circle also represents the "Heavens" or spiritual realm in these same ancient Chinese wisdom traditions, so, again, symbolically, this fits perfectly.

There are more granular representations of the bodies we have, just like we have many more Chakras than the main seven commonly referenced and also shown here in this depiction of the Vitruvian Man. For purposes of this book, this is all we need to get to all the depth we're seeking to go to. Our Chakra system plays a key role in our energy system and energy regulation and is a topic more than worthwhile to master, but that subject alone requires a full book in and of itself to do it any justice. I finally opted not to cover it for that reason, as Chakra system mastery is not a prerequisite in making your life an expression of spiritual art, and any book can only have so many layers.

Just like we discovered with self-organizing complex living systems, these bodies are nested and directly relationally connected and interdependent. Trauma, which is an emotional wound stored in our emotional body, will affect our physical body as well as our mental and spiritual body, albeit in different ways. Similarly, an ancestral wound stored in our spiritual body will affect all the bodies nested within, and so on and so forth. Western medicine—in the form of integrative medicine—is even coming around to the core premise on which Chinese natural medicine and India's Ayurvedic medicines are based, which is that every physical illness or injury has its root cause in higher bodies meaning the emotional, mental, and/or spiritual bodies.

This is because everything—including our physical bodies—is ultimately energy. Energy in each of these bodies is either in coherence or dissonance. The dictionary describes dissonance as the "lack of harmony," and coherence then refers to harmony or the harmonious state of energy. In biological terms, we refer to coherence as homeostasis and dissonance as illness or injury.

When we look at the Masculine and Feminine, we can see their respective constituent attributes also have a coherent and dissonant state. Or, in colloquial terms, a healthy and unhealthy state as follows:

Essence	Coherence	Dissonance
Masculine (Yang)	Awareness Intelligence Energy	Ignorance Unintelligence Impotence
Feminine (Yin)	Being Creativity Reverence	Doing Destruction Disregard

It's important to note that there can be no such thing as coherent Masculine or coherent Feminine if one of their respective constituent attributes is still in dissonance. There are infinite layers of depth we can cultivate in each of these cornerstones as our level of Consciousness rises, but all must be at a base level of coherence before we can speak of any sort of coherence. This goes even before fully integrating our non-dominant (also fully coherent) essence and creating harmony between our two essences within. Clearly, there can be no real harmony within our true nature with any essence or cornerstone remaining in dissonance, as that's like having one section or one instrument in the orchestra out of tune.

Let's explore how all of this relates to the Masculine first.

Since we already explored the coherent states of the Masculine cornerstones in-depth, we'll focus on the dissonant states. The opposite pole of Awareness is Ignorance; we're simply not aware or unconscious. Although Awareness is a quality we ripen and deepen with conscious practice and application, unconsciousness is ultimately still a choice we make. At varying levels, we each have the innate ability to raise our Awareness, so ignorance is—at the end of the day—a choice no matter how unconscious we might be to the fact we're making it.

The opposite pole of Intelligence is Unintelligence. Remember, we're defining Intelligence in terms of how the universe defines it, i.e., Intelligence is *that* which creates intelligent outcomes. Unintelligence, then, is *that* which creates unintelligent outcomes.

Energy at its core is Life Force, and so the opposite pole is Impotence. Not merely in physical form, but the word Impotence generally refers to inadequacy, incapacity, and the lack of sufficient ability, energy, and power. When the Masculine lacks access to Energy, it feels and suffers its own Impotence within Life itself, which we then see reflected in resorting to Force. For instance, any abuse of power, money, or influence is resorting to Force and has its origins in Impotence, possibly only amplified by Ignorance and Unintelligence. Despondency, despair, dejection, depression, etc., are all reflections of Impotence which then will produce such things as poverty, lack, paucity, and scarcity, which can show up in any or all areas of life. In that way, people that believe they lack the power to change their circumstances indeed create that very reality. This is why poverty is so sticky and tends to become generational; at the same time, we know poverty can be escaped as there are those that escape. Unequivocally, those who escaped didn't suffer Impotence; they had the Energy to literally empower themselves out of their circumstances.

Often, we can refer to the dissonant state as the shadow state, which produces telltale shadow sides, which we'll get into later. But, in our Masculine-dominant world today, we can readily see evidence of all these shadow states—Ignorance, Unintelligence, and Impotence—all around. In fact, most of our world today was created by men with unintegrated Masculine Essence (i.e., suppressed Feminine) in deep dissonance, which is to say levels of consciousness below 200.

Historically, women were treated and considered by men as inconsequential until about sixty to seventy years ago, so from an evolutionary perspective, there's little to blame them for in terms of the endemic problems in our world. Despite the many advances in women's rights in most parts of the world, we're still living in a world whose fundamental architecture in terms of politics, business, and society was designed, built, and controlled by men over the last 200,000 years. Since these men were overwhelmingly unintegrated, there was not even any Feminine essence bleeding through their Masculine, so the world we see today is what gets created by a dissonant and non-integrated Masculine where the entire Feminine is suppressed.

Let's take a look at the Feminine now.

The opposite pole of Being is Doing, as we explored at great length earlier. Similarly, Destruction is the opposite pole of Creativity as we defined it, and Disregard is the shadow state of Reverence.

The Feminine-dominant (woman typically) that's in dissonance with her own constituent attributes will be lost in her shadow states of Doing, Destruction, and Disregard. This might not be obvious at first, but when we add the insight that the Feminine Essence is oriented toward introversion and the Masculine Essence is oriented toward extroversion, we can readily see how this pattern shows up as the Feminine will hurt itself first and foremost in her self-destruction, and the Masculine will inflict pain and suffering on others first and foremost before self-destructing.

In dissonance, the Feminine becomes self-destructive, which we witness when she hollows out her health and well-being in too much Doing and not enough just Being. Or when a lack of Creativity flowing through her life causes stagnation of joy and freedom of expression, which is a form of Destruction. Or a lack of Reverence for herself and her body as she allows society to guilt and manipulate her into believing she needs breast implants, Botox, tummy tucks, toxic makeup and beauty products, and all sorts of other artificial contortions to be worthy or good enough.

Now we can also clearly see what happens when the extroverted-oriented Masculine-dominant is not integrated with the Feminine as, by default, this puts his Feminine in a suppressed or dissonant state. The Masculine-dominant men who have ruled the world for millennia have been utterly lost in Doing, Destruction, and Disregard for all of Creation, and so many have inflicted unthinkable pain and suffering on others, most notably women, minorities, and those deemed weak or inferior.

Conversely, the Feminine-dominant with a non-integrated Masculine Essence will be lost in her own Chaos as there's no structure—Order—of the coherent Masculine for the river to flow through. This can show up as an inability to create her own financial abundance and independence, lack of a clear purpose and direction in life, erratic emotional mood swings, or endless procrastination and indecision, just to mention a few.

> **"A man's heart away from nature becomes hard."**
> —STANDING BEAR

It's been said the longest journey we'll ever make is from the head to the Heart. Nothing could be more true for the Masculine-dominant man who's both in dissonance in his Masculine and non-integrated with his Feminine. Even though this is commonly referred to as the "wounded" or "toxic" Masculine, I prefer to use the term dissonant Masculine when referring to the Masculine Essence. I will use "wounded man" when referring to a dissonant Masculine-dominant man who's non-integrated and "shadow states" when referring to constituent attributes that are in dissonance.

The Mind is the fortress of the Masculine, whereas the Heart is the citadel of the Feminine. A non-integrated Masculine-dominant man then has no access to his heart or its Intelligence. He's literally heartless and lost in the cobwebs of his logical Mind. This, combined with a dissonant Masculine, is the toxic cocktail that creates the Masculine shadow sides.

Disconnected from his Heart and dwelling in his shadow states, the wounded man is easily recognized by how he shows up in life. The wounded man might wear a self-confident mask but internally is fragile and susceptible to dogma, groupthink, and enculturation as he has no access to sovereign critical thought, let alone the courage and strength to stand alone in his Truth. He lacks empathy, and as his Heart hardens over time, Love and compassion become inaccessible to him. His self-worth is entirely dependent on validation and recognition from others, so he pursues Finite Games and trophies to prove his self-worth, hereby confusing fame, fortune (net worth), and applause for his self-worth as a man.

Emotionally, he's very easily triggered, always needs to be right, and will quickly resort to Force, which is a direct reflection of his Impotence. The wounded man is self-centered, and he cleverly disguises his inner insecurity with arrogance and bravado. However coy, at the end of the day, he's flashy with his trinkets, shiny objects, trophies, status, and deep-down views women as arm candy as that completes his image as a "successful" man.

He's highly prone to succumb to infidelity, greed, hubris, corruption, malfeasance, and abuse of his power and influence, as he lacks the Heart to be steadfast in his integrity. Comfort in the form of pleasure and gain easily sway him away from what's right and just, as that takes real bravery and requires true courage. The wounded man thinks of and portrays himself as a lion, but in truth, he's a feeble opportunistic sheep masquerading in lion's clothes. No matter his worldly success, which is just a thin layer of glossy veneer, there's actually very little real substance and no spiritual backbone to speak of. In every sense, the wounded man is still a boy in a man's body.

When the wounded man's Masculine dissonance spirals out of control, we start seeing the truly toxic nature emerge from his own darkness. He becomes cold, calculated, malevolent, violent, cruel, and capable of participating in, directly committing, or tacitly approving unthinkable atrocities and barbaric acts. The narcissist, sociopath, and psychopath is nothing but a wounded man spiraled out of control, which is to say, lost in his Masculine shadow states and completely disconnected from his Heart—which is his Divinity, which is his Feminine.

Regretfully, at this moment, most men in places of power and influence—business or politics—are wounded men at levels of consciousness below 200. Looking at the chaos, destruction, suffering, and general disarray in the world today, we can even conclude many of them are spiraled out of control. Their ignorance of the pain and suffering their Unintelligence causes is, at times, almost unbearable to witness for those that have their eyes wide open. Their Impotence is reflected in their deeply unconscious use of Force, which is guiding the world toward an Orwellian surveillance state reality. Barring a remarkable ascension in Consciousness, these self-anointed "elites" are not the ones who are going to create a better, more beautiful, and more just world. Instead, their agenda is dark and aimed at consolidating worldly wealth and power to the detriment of all others.

Despite these puppet masters' seemingly unlimited wealth, power, and influence, it's important to note that their claim to power is, at its core, merely a carefully fabricated and brilliantly advertised narrative sold to humanity as the absolute Truth. However, the Machiavellian Finite Game they're playing is just a story; it's not real. And all it takes is to see the story for what it is, and the story loses all its power. They know this also, which is why they will use more and more Force to coerce others into subservient obedience to their narrative, which is the sole tent pole holding up their Finite Game.

The only true freedom is inner freedom. The path to freedom then is to awaken to this story and see it for what it is, which opens up the pathway to freely choose *the* one Infinite Game. And, within freely choosing to play *the* Infinite Game, we can freely play in any Finite Game we choose, even theirs. The moment you freely choose to play *the* one Infinite Game, you have existentially exited their Finite Game—the "Matrix" if you will—and they no longer have any real power over you. Trust me, the "elites" are keenly aware of this and will do anything to stop you from making this choice as they know if enough of us "non-elites" do this, their Finite Game—which is just a story—collapses.

Game over.

For the wounded man, the only way out is to go within. He must go on his Hero's Journey from the Ordinary World into the Spiritual World. This awakening process involves an inevitable deep process of letting go of all worldly attachments. He must find the courage to let go of everything he's known to date and venture onto the pathless land of his Heart. In this spiritual purification process, the universe will strip him naked of all his Falsehoods until he surrenders to his Heart by allowing the Feminine within to illuminate his Divinity.

The Divinity within, which we can only access through the intelligence of our Heart—once recognized and embraced—is what will finally guide him to restoring full coherence in his Masculine. He will emerge from this arduous spiritual metal-forging process a true lion—courageous, wise, humble, and virtuous—as he will have activated his true Masculine superpower: Love & Compassion.

His signature hallmark is now unwavering integrity. A man in his Sovereign Masculine has an unmistakable presence about him, his charisma is luminescent, and his powers transcend anything worldly. Now, in devoted service to the whole, he's become a fully embodied guardian of Truth. And Truth, if you recall, is the Feminine, Existence, Life itself, or all of Creation. She's safe now in his mere presence, as nothing will ever happen to her on his watch.

True Order is restored, at last.

> "Truths and roses have thorns about them."
> —HENRY DAVID THOREAU

The Feminine has its own shadow sides stemming from dissonance or her shadow states, and we could easily say she's a beautiful rose with thorns that can cut deeply. We should first note that her shadow states (or the Masculine's shadow states, for that matter) are not her true nature. Her true nature is coherence or the cornerstones of Being, Creativity, and Reverence. Only when she's out of harmony with her own true nature are the shadow states activated and produce the shadow sides.

Here, I'll refer to the Feminine-dominant woman who has not integrated her Masculine as a "wounded woman." Similar to the wounded man but in reverse, her path to coherence is first healing her Feminine dissonance, and she will then become anchored in her Sovereign Feminine when she fully integrates her Masculine within.

The wounded woman lives in hurt, a deep visceral pain stemming from feeling unseen, unheard, and unloved. Typically, this originates from real-life experiences with others—especially wounded men—and the Outer World in general. As real and traumatic as these experiences might have been—some even stem from abuses as a young girl—her hurt is perpetuated by the continued seeking of love, validation, and recognition in the Outer World.

If her trauma was inflicted by men, she will unconsciously seek out love, validation, or recognition from men, but this perpetuates the cycle even more as wounded women inherently attract wounded men. The reason is twofold. First, wounded men are weak themselves and prey on the weakness in others, so with both wounded men and women being vulnerable, they are the targets of choice. Second, a woman in her Sovereign Feminine won't give the wounded man the time of day, so he's relegated to seeking out wounded women, which he, in his heartless unconsciousness, is almost destined to hurt and harm even more.

In reality, her way out of her inner hurt—dissonance—is radical self-love. When the wounded woman awakens to radical self-love, she heals. No other—especially not any man, wounded or otherwise—can do this for her; it's an inside job. From this place of radical self-love, coherence is restored, and integrating her Masculine typically happens organically, at which time she blossoms into her Sovereign Feminine. A woman in her Sovereign Feminine is a force of nature—an absolute powerhouse—fully embodied in her magical Feminine superpowers: Divinity & Creativity.

Needing no more validation or recognition from others, she revels in her freedom, wildness, and untamed artful life expression. With her Masculine fully integrated, she's a natural leader and effortlessly navigates worldly affairs—e.g., creating financial abundance and independence as desired—but will always do so with a distinct Feminine flair and playfulness. She lights up any room when she enters and is cherished like a true rose. You will only experience her effervescent beauty and lucent Intelligence, but the thorns are still there to remind anyone that she's to be handled with respect and care. She's nobody's prize anymore but her own, as she's truly sovereign in her entire Being.

The wounded woman is also easily recognized. Her inner pain and suffering are expressed in becoming stubborn, unyielding, bitter, manipulative, resentful, vindictive, jealous, hardened, cold, unreasonable, and perhaps even mean-spirited. None of this is her true nature; she's just in deep pain and has abandoned herself through—consciously or unconsciously—withdrawing radical self-love from herself. Where the wounded man expresses his inner suffering by inflicting pain and suffering onto the world, the wounded woman mostly inflicts the pain and suffering on herself and resides in anger and bitterness toward the world.

In today's still Masculine-dominant world, the Feminine remains suppressed. In fact, the Feminine has been suppressed for millennia, and historically, it wasn't that long ago women deemed witches were burned at the stake or drowned in rivers. In the US, it was only in 1920 that women were granted the right to vote, and to this day, there are pay discrepancies, lopsided representation in corporate C-suites and boards, and the US is still to have its first female resident. In other parts of the world, girls still can't go to school, and women can't vote, hold political office, or even decide to walk down the street without face cover. Clearly, the Truth is the Feminine, as represented within women, is still suppressed in many ways, although things have significantly improved in Western developed countries. Unwillingness to see this stark Truth is choosing to live in ignorant Falsehood.

At the same time, it would be ignorant to overlook that all women's rights, freedoms, and privileges gained in the last century have principally been possible because men chose to make this possible and acquiesced to the ever-louder protests and demands of women (rightfully) fighting for their rights. There are only two ways to break an existing power structure of any kind. You overthrow it with some form of Force or it's in some way relinquished by those holding the power.

Perhaps this is going to be a somewhat bitter fact to swallow down and digest for some, but women cannot overthrow with Force any power structure held with Force by men. Where abuse of the law is, the law itself is not Force, as laws need to first come into the body of legislation for anyone to avail themselves of their rights under such laws. Force, however regretful, has to do with the capacity to inflict damage and harm. We can debate this all day long, but we only have to look at Iran, Afghanistan, and countless other countries where women and girls are oppressed to see the inherent Truth in the statement that women cannot overthrow with Force a power structure held with Force by men. Governments, regimes, and power structures are overthrown when men willing to fight and die for the cause concern themselves with the revolution; women and children in this regard are paper tigers. You might argue, "But what about board rooms or CEOs?" Guess what, an all-male board of directors would have to vote in favor to bring in the first female board member, something that has only been happening at a snail's pace. Same goes for the appointment of senior executives including CEOs and, incidentally, the US is yet to have its first female President. This will inevitably happen at some point, but only when enough men support this with their vote.

The second way to change an existing power structure is through acquiescence of those holding the power. Therefore, it's of paramount importance for men, and especially men in places of power and influence, to rise to higher levels or octaves of consciousness as the necessity and importance of moving toward a completely level playing field for men and women becomes entirely self-evident at higher levels of consciousness. In this sense, the ascension of men holds more weight than the ascension of women in terms of accelerating the creation of a more beautiful, just, and livable world that honors and recognizes the inherent value and worth of men and women equally. As it's only when men volunteer to relinquish their chokehold on the power structure of societies, boardrooms, and companies that the Feminine—women and girls—will truly have the level playing field to blossom and flourish.

For any of you offended by these observations, please note this is simply reflecting how the real world functions and operates today. This isn't a political statement, or a suggestion women or girls are of any lesser value or significance than men. It's a factual explanation of how existing power structures can be broken down and how this relates directly to the fact we're in a race to raise human consciousness.

So, continuing where we left off before, whereas wounded men are disconnected from their Feminine and lost in the shadow states of their Masculine, we see many wounded women that felt compelled—consciously or unconsciously—to abandon their Feminine in order to play in the Masculine-engineered playground called business and careers. This playground, which is premised on structure, hierarchy, linearity, and logic, is heavily skewed toward rewarding Masculine qualities and traits and dismissing Feminine qualities and traits.

To succeed in this playground, you only have two options: (1) play by the rules; or (2) change the rules. In a male-dominated playground, women have not had the power and influence to change the rules, although the feminist movement has made some inroads and marginal changes. But fundamentally, the playground is still male-engineered and dominated, and so it's not surprising then that women, almost by invisible force, leaned ever more heavily on their Masculine—to the detriment of their Feminine—to succeed in this playground.

Hence, we're now in an era where many women have become Masculine-dominant, which in the case of a naturally Feminine-dominant woman, means her Masculine is predominantly leading. We can clearly see this in how they dress, walk, talk, act and generally show up. It has a distinct Masculine rigidness to it, nothing like the natural flair and playfulness of the Feminine. However, her constitution is not designed to be predominantly led by her Masculine, which shows up in various ways.

Illnesses like thyroid disorders (hormones), adrenal fatigue, irregular cycles, low libido, and infertility are all indications of the stress put on her body by being predominantly in her Masculine. It also reveals itself in love relationships. The Masculine-dominant man is hard-wired to lead and will find the opposite pole—a Feminine-dominant woman—naturally attractive. Just to be clear, we're talking energetics here, not biology, chemistry, or even aesthetics. Incidentally, in a sacred union, the Feminine is in no way inferior due to her submission to his leadership, as she chooses to follow his lead based on a deep trust he must earn first and then maintain throughout the relationship, so in fact, all the power rests with her.

We see this same dynamic in healthy courtship. He pursues, but she decides so, truthfully, she's in control. This tension of Polarity between the Masculine and Feminine is also what creates passion or sexual chemistry. Two equally Masculine/Feminine balanced individuals might develop a beautiful relationship, but they'll likely be more roommates than passionate lovers.

By the way, all of these dynamics apply equally to gay couples; sexual chemistry requires Polarity regardless of sexual orientation or preferences. So, a woman who leads with her Masculine will not attract a Masculine-dominant man like two positive poles of magnets won't stick together. Since her true nature is Feminine-dominant, she will not be naturally attracted to men who lead with their Feminine, and so this is why love can seem elusive or disappointing for many women leading with their Masculine or why many emasculated men find courtship, dating, and relationships challenging.

Wounded men leading with their Feminine have their own set of health issues, most notably low testosterone, which can show up for men as general lethargy, low sex drive, erectile dysfunction, weight gain, man breasts, and thinning or loss of facial and body hair, just to name a few. Wounded men in dissonance with their Masculine also have telltale illnesses, which we now believe are just normal. Heart attacks, strokes, clogged arteries, cirrhosis of the liver, high blood pressure, diabetes, cancer, and even alcoholism and suicide are all significantly more prevalent in men than women. These are all stress-induced symptoms or outcomes of the root cause called dissonance. Operations and pharmaceuticals will treat these symptoms; however, only restoring coherence will truly cure them where that's possible.

> "Archetypes are the unconscious images of the instincts themselves, they are patterns of instinctual behavior."
> —CARL JUNG

As the great work of the renowned mythologist Joseph Campbell revealed, all of humanity's deepest nature reveals itself in archetypes that seem like blueprints for all of mankind. They are remarkably similar across history, geographies, cultures, and civilizations. The Masculine and the Feminine can be seen as the master Archetypes from which all others are derived. The Father, Warrior, Wizard, Villain, King, and countless others are all derived from the Masculine archetypical architecture. Similarly, the Mother, Virgin, Mystic, Seductress, Queen, etc., are all derived from the Feminine archetypical architecture.

Archetypes are ingrained in our culture, and so through the process of enculturation starting when we are mere toddlers, these archetypical blueprints are downloaded into our subconscious Mind as instinctual patterns of our innate humanity. This enculturation process has an implicit and explicit aspect. Explicit would be what we are directly taught, see on TV or in movies, and experience in life. Implicit is that which is subtly woven into the fabric of our upbringing, schooling, culture, customs, societal values, religion, and the prevailing worldviews of our race, creed, or country. These patterns are dynamic yet highly resilient and never exactly the same in any two people as we each perceive our reality through our own unique lens.

The cultural patterns also follow a distinct fractal pattern meaning they scale infinitely. A clever meme can go viral in minutes or hours but often doesn't live more than a day or two. Fads are short-lived cultural phenomena, whereas trends typically last for years. Values and behaviors evolve over decades, and ideology and worldviews can last many decades or even centuries. Learning and the adaptation of any cultural patterns (i.e., enculturation) happen through tribal regulation—tribal conformity is encouraged through rewards (e.g., inclusion, love, recognition), and tribal rebellion is discouraged through punishment (e.g., exclusion, hate, ridicule).

All of these cultural patterns also follow the adaptive cycle model of change, which is native to nature's self-organizing intelligence: the rapid growth phase, then the conservation phase, then the release phase, followed by the reorganization phase, and then the cycle reiterates.

The reason all of this is relevant is because it's nearly impossible to awaken our Awareness to something that's so deeply engrained it appears irrefutable. Most of our enculturation is hardly irrefutable; they're just cultural customs adopted by collective tacit societal agreement. Archetypes, however, run deeper; these we cannot refute, but we can become aware of them. And, in our Awareness of them, we bring them into our conscious realm where we can recognize and even work with them to our advantage, as these archetypes are what instinctually drive the behaviors of all of mankind. There's a treasure trove of deep wisdom and great beauty within archetypes, and studying this field is deeply inspiring as it magnetizes us to reach for our full human potential.

> "Woman is the light of God."
> —RUMI

Finally, the Masculine and Feminine archetypical architecture is also distinct and recognizable in how its (coherent) energy feels and is experienced by others. The Sovereign Masculine's energy is firm, powerful, penetrating, and emanates depth and presence. It's anchored in Love & Compassion, which is the Sovereign Masculine's true superpower. The Sovereign Feminine's energy is soft, nurturing, enchanting, and radiates grace and sensuality.

Sensuality is not to be confused with sexuality here, as sensuality points to her sensory nature, not sex or sexiness. The Sovereign Feminine's energy is anchored in her magical superpowers: Divinity & Creativity.

The Masculine is the formless—Consciousness—which is Love. The Feminine is the World of Finite Form—Existence—through which we discover Truth. Yang is the Order within the infinite, Yin is the Chaos within the finite, and the seed of each resides within the other. She's also Life itself, all of Creation, the Sanctity of all Life, and therefore represents Divinity and Creativity. In service to her Divinity, he will discover his own Divinity within. In his Love and Compassion, she will see her own Divinity reflected back to her. This is the eternal cosmic dance toward unity in Source Consciousness between the Masculine and Feminine played out in our physical reality. To see the art, poetry, and beauty in all of this is to see all of Life itself as a Gift.

This concludes Part II—The Architecture—which sits at the very center of the Love+Truth Framework, and all of this will become visual in Part IV—The Principles—where we start to transpose and reflect all of this unto the sacred geometry shapes that underpin the entire Love+Truth Framework. But, to get there and have it make sense, we first are going to reveal the next layer of the Love+Truth Framework, which emerges when we combine the sacred geometry triangles (two-dimensional "tetrahedrons") of the Masculine and the Feminine.

And, what truthfully emerges are the sacred Gifts from the Masculine to the Feminine and vice versa. But that's not all that emerges as starting in Part III, we'll start to see the miraculous mathematical poetry and deeper spiritual meaning of sacred geometry embedded within the Love+Truth Framework become inescapably visible.

So, let's journey on with Part III—The Gifts.

PART III

THE GIFTS

"When I let go of what I am, I become what I might be."
—LAO TZU

CHAPTER 17
POLARITY ILLUMINATES THE GIFTS

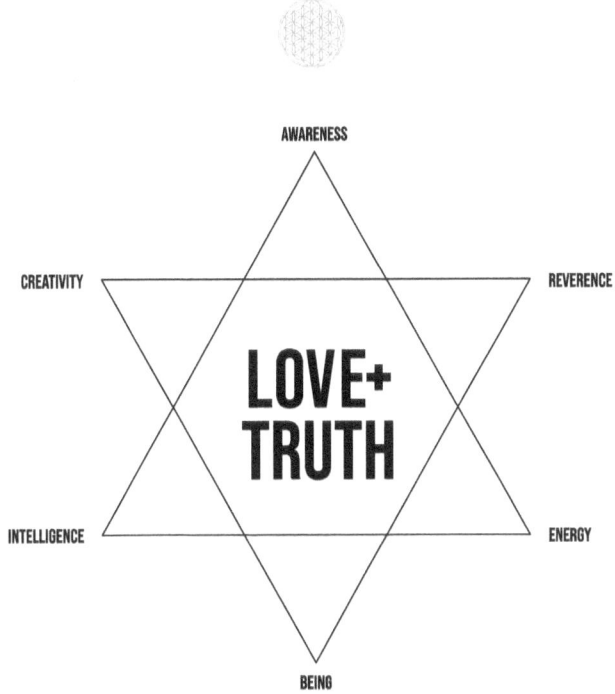

IF YOU WILL, WE COULD LIKEN the Grand Architecture to the primary colors of the painter's color palette. The Gifts then become the secondary colors which are created by fusing two of the primary colors, i.e., combining red and blue creates purple and so on and so forth. In this way, the Love+Truth Framework very much mirrors "chromatics," which is the science of color.

Not coincidentally, what we call "color" is actually electromagnetic radiation vibrating at a particular frequency multiplied by the speed of light, and when the corresponding wavelength (in nanometers or "nm") is between 380 to 740, it's within what we call the visible light spectrum for humans. There are many more colors, such as ultraviolet rays and infrared rays, that we can't see. Here's the point: the human light spectrum is completely workable for our purposes as humans here on the Earthly plane. In the same way, the Love+Truth Framework synthesizes and distills that which has infinitely more dimensions (as in "colors" or "aspects") into a spectrum that's beautifully workable for us here on the Earthly plane. There are more colors, but the ones captured in the Love+Truth Framework—in all their apparent simplicity—already provide such a vast depth of spiritual "chromatics" we don't need more colors to paint an incredible depth and richness into our spiritual art. What we each—myself included—really need is more mastery, not more colors.

However, don't take my word for it yet; let me prove it to you.

When we converge the Masculine and Feminine two-dimensional tetrahedrons, a perfect six-pointed star emerges, which in sacred geometry is sometimes affectionately referred to as the "Mandala of the Hexagram." In Western civilization, many will recognize this as the Star of David, which is a sacred Judaic symbol; however, the use of this symbol predates Judaism by at least 5,000 years, as archeological records of ancient Egypt and Indian civilization have revealed. For all intents and purposes, this highly revered sacred symbol of sacred geometry has been around since the dawn of human civilization and has been discovered in all corners of the world.

Even though derived from Hebrew, the religion-neutral name often used is "Merkaba Star" or simply "Merkaba" (alternative spelling: "Merkabah") and is widely considered to be the Taijitu (Yin/Yang symbol) of Western civilization as it represents the unity of the Masculine and the Feminine. However, as we're about to discover, the Merkaba is far more than that.

> "Already at sixteen, my mind was a battlefield: my love of pagan beauty, the male nude, at war with my religious faith. A polarity of themes and forms: one spiritual, the other earthly."
> —MICHELANGELO

Merkaba means "chariot," and in ancient Biblical texts (Ezekiel 1:4–26), is even referred to as the "Throne-Chariot of God." In today's language, we would simply refer to it as "vessel." When broken down phonetically, the word Merkaba reveals to be constituted of three distinct words: Mer—Light; Ka—Spirit; and Ba—Body. In metaphysical terms, the unity of Spirit (Masculine or Consciousness) and Body (Feminine or Existence) creates Light. Light is energy, so this unity creates an energy field which is our Light Body, or in other words, our energetic vessel. The Spiritual, Mental, Emotional, and Physical Bodies are all nested—each at progressively lower or more dense frequencies—within this Light Body, which is created and activated by a vortex.

This energy field is sometimes referred to as the Merkaba effect and not only symbolizes the formless pathless land—the land we humans must traverse to become spiritually enlightened—but it's the actual field, when activated, that allows our Consciousness, which is our Soul, to travel interdimensionally. For most, their

Merkaba is dormant as they have not developed the ability to activate it. When our Merkaba is dormant—that is, we're unconscious of it—we only experience the 3D dimension of physical reality, which renders us a multi-dimensional being living in a singular dimension.

There's nothing wrong with that; except for a very few of us, we all go through a process of amnesia at birth where our remembrance of being a multidimensional being is temporarily erased and hidden beyond the veil of illusion of physical reality. Chances are, you are a master of activating your Merkaba and have done so countless times for eternity in between and perhaps even during other incarnations. I realize this might sound far-fetched and perhaps even delusional to some of you, but every person that has experimented with Indigenous plant medicines like Ayahuasca, Bufo Alvarius, Peyote, or Psilocybin ("mushrooms") has experimented with altered states of Consciousness, which was like experiencing a distinctly different dimension of reality than the one we refer to as 3D or physical reality.

There's been extensive academic research done at the University of Virginia and many other institutions on what's called near-death experiences ("NDEs"). NDEs are by now well-documented and provide conclusive evidence that our Consciousness travels interdimensionally during an NDE, after which it returns to reinhabit our physical body.

My point here is not to prove the validity of our interdimensional nature and take you through the preponderance of all the scientific evidence available; I am merely providing this backdrop to lower any skepticism you might have, which would then mentally block you from assimilating any of the material I am about to cover. I am not asking you to believe any of it at face value—just remain open to it, and remembrance will do the rest. In fact, at an even deeper level of understanding—"innerstanding" really—we come to see remembrance as *that* which refines and enriches the tapestry of our spiritual art. You will learn and take from this book what you're supposed to at this very moment; that's an inviolable law of this universe. If you read this book again in five years, you'll find it's an entirely different book even though, clearly, the words or content will not have changed.

> "Male and female are the first things we learn because they represent the polarity of existence."
> —FREDERICK LENZ

This sacred Merkaba energy field created by the unification of the Masculine and the Feminine doesn't just point at our own Divinity; it directly points at the Sanctity of all Life as down to the quantum level, we can see all of Creation is created by the unification of the Masculine and the Feminine. Another way to see this is that everything has its origins within Source Consciousness—the Divine or Divinity—as that's all the reunification of the Masculine and the Feminine ultimately is. Furthermore, the upwards pointing Masculine tetrahedron symbolically refers to the Heavens, and the downward pointing Feminine tetrahedron symbolically refers to Earth. The Formless or Consciousness ("Heavens") and the Finite World of Form or Existence ("Earth").

> "When will you begin that long journey into yourself."
> —RUMI

Now, here I am going to impart one spiritual Truth that's a pivotal keystone, arguably even the most valuable paragraph of this entire book. When we refer to Heavens vs. Earth, Consciousness vs. Existence, Formless vs. Form, and the many other ways we point to the Duality principle of the Grand Architecture of Life itself, we're inclined to fall into the mental trap of interpreting this as *that* which we are seeking is outside of us. It's there somewhere in the distant Heavens, much like the mental image religions paint of the Heavens of this faraway place we might get to go to when we die.

Paradoxically, all of the Heavens are within you. Your deepest Inner World *is* the Heavens, *is* Consciousness, and *is* the Formless. As the earlier poetic Rumi quote stated: "you're not a drop in the ocean; you're the entire ocean in a drop." Heavens, Consciousness, the Formless, the universe, the "above" in the Hermetic "so above, so below" and so forth are all accessed by going within into the deepest part of our Inner World. The Merkaba, albeit a Light Body seemingly outside of us, is also accessed and activated by going within. Nothing of any spiritual nature is ever outside of you other than in the symbolic use of words and language; it's all within you. I cannot overemphasize the essentiality of this knowing as you'll never find what I am pointing at in this book searching outside of you.

Let's continue.

Much deeper layers are revealed when we bring the sacred geometry of the Merkaba into 3D, which reveals the true tetrahedron form of four equilateral triangle faces, six edges, and four vertices or corners. This is also called the Star Tetrahedron or, again, simply Merkaba. In sacred geometry, the Merkaba is contained within Metatron's Cube, which is considered the essential building block of this entire universe that gives "form" to all of Creation. We'll explore the mystical mathematical poetry of Metatron's Cube later in Part IV.

In 3D, we can also see how the Light Body or energy field is created by the Merkaba. The top Masculine tetrahedron rotates counter-clockwise, and the bottom Feminine tetrahedron rotates clockwise in an asynchronous 34:21 Fibonacci ratio. These opposing centrifugal forces create the vortex of energy—energy field—that is, our Light Body. Much like the eye of a hurricane and completing the holy trinity, the still point or Fulcrum in the Merkaba is our Heart chakra. This is not coincidental (nothing is), as our Merkaba is activated by deep, reverent Love and Compassion. This is also why at lower levels of Consciousness below 200, our Merkaba is dormant since we cannot yet access the universal Love within Christ Consciousness.

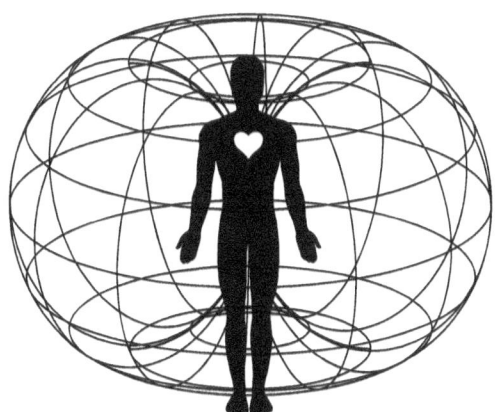

Our Light Body itself is pure white light, but like a veil, to an array of colors our aura can shine through. The colors of our aura are a derivative of the vibration of our various bodies, like the physical, emotional, mental, and spiritual bodies. Vibration creates sound; sound holds a frequency which in turn creates notes, and notes times C2 (speed of light) produces a specific color. Since all our various "bodies" or layers within our Light Body vibrate at a different frequency, our aura becomes a luminescent palette of all the colors of the rainbow, with each color representing different frequencies. The width of our fully activated Merkaba Light body can extend upwards of fifty to sixty feet; when our Merkaba is dormant, only the metaphysical structure of our Merkaba is there. The size or width of our aura varies greatly from a few feet to upwards of twenty to twenty-five feet in all directions. This is a reflection of our expansiveness, whereas high levels of vibration (i.e., Consciousness), such as Love, are very expansive, and low levels of vibration, like Fear, are contractive.

> "Dogs, also, bark at what they do not know."
> —HERACLITUS

Everyone has the "machinery" to activate their Light Body; however, as mentioned at Consciousness levels below 200, this Light Body is inaccessible and, more likely than not, the Egoic Mind is highly resistant to the mere notion of the existence of our Merkaba or Light Body. The Egoic Mind abhors that which it cannot conclusively verify through the five senses as that represents its archnemesis, the "unknown." So, at lower levels of Consciousness and in the dormant state, our Merkaba is basically set at the pilot light setting waiting to be flared up—expanded—by us reaching higher levels of Consciousness.

Although some of this might be new information, especially about the Merkaba, we all already know the aura firsthand. We have all "felt" someone else's energy; this happens anytime when someone else's energy field comes in contact or connection with ours. I say connection because we can sense this over the telephone or even text as much as in person, provided we're open and receptive to it. We all have the innate capacity to "read" energy in this way; however, at lower levels of Consciousness, our Mind's incessant noise drowns out our ability to listen to our Heart. It's our Heart's intelligence that gives us access to this innate capacity through feeling, sensing, direct knowing, and intuiting, which constitutes the language of the Heart.

It's important to note that we're each incredibly sensitive to others' energy and especially group energy which is just the amplification of multiple energy fields. Surely, you've walked into a party at some point and immediately felt a great vibe in the room; this is group energy, and walking into such a room will inevitably lift your spirits and own vibration. Or it might actually turn you off if you're in a very low vibration—you're literally not vibing with the positive vibe. This is why joyful people can be highly irritating to people in low vibration; it can even make them angry and resentful.

Conversely, we've all walked into a meeting at some point, and the vibe was grim, perhaps even ominous. We immediately sense this and will inevitably tense up unless we can consciously maintain our own high vibration, which is the sort of mastery that comes with high levels of Consciousness. When we witness rioting soccer hooligans in Europe, violent rioters, and looters at demonstrations, or even armies like Nazi Germany's infamous SS unit, we can see the grave danger within this phenomenon. Because otherwise common everyday people—albeit at Consciousness below 200—can collectively get swept up in a very low group energy of anger or false pride and proceed to carry out unthinkable acts of violence and destruction that are generally totally out of character.

Having a deeper understanding, as well as learning to intuitively sense and read our own aura and energy field, is foundational to becoming more masterful at managing our own vibration, recognizing and navigating group energies, and even utilizing our own higher vibration to help lift and heal others.

Finally, when we superimpose the Merkaba on a male and female body, we can also see the origins of why the archetypical architecture of men is to be Masculine-dominant and vice versa for women. In the below picture, we can see the leading edge for men is the Masculine, and for women, it's the Feminine.

STAR TETRAHEDRON

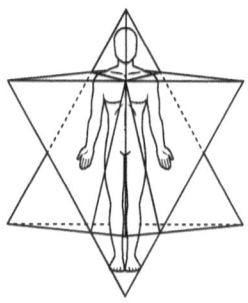
Orientation in Men

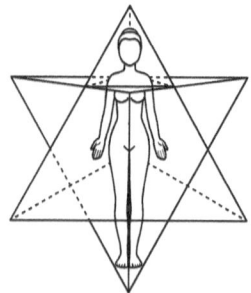
Orientation in Women

Just to over-emphasize this point once more, all humans are equally sacred, equally divine, and only in the unification or integration of the Masculine and Feminine within can any human—regardless of gender, sexual orientation, or gender identification—walk down the path of true spiritual self-realization. Literally, "God," so to speak, doesn't care about your gender, what you do in the bedroom, or which pronouns you prefer. And, frankly, this is why for any person genuinely walking down the path of spiritual self-realization, this entire contentious and highly divisive societal debate about these topics is not much more than a cultural soap opera played out in the theater of political agendas and opinions, only to be exacerbated by an insidious schism-hungry social and mass media landscape. It's irrelevant in spiritual terms, provided only you cause no undue harm to others; you do you, and I will do me.

> "The superior man thinks always of virtue,
> the common man thinks of comfort."
> —CONFUCIUS

This brings us to the sacred Gifts that are illuminated when we converge the Masculine and Feminine two-dimensional tetrahedrons, and the Merkaba is created.

The symmetrical intersection of the Masculine and Feminine tetrahedrons creates six smaller equilateral triangles, which we colloquially call the star points. For the astute sacred geometry observer, we can immediately spot that if these six star points were to be folded inwards, it creates a perfect hexagon—the honeycomb shape. The honeycomb shape is another revered sacred geometry shape with equally remarkable geometric and mathematical properties we see come back in everything from nature to human architecture. Perhaps you can even see in the graphic below that, from a 3D perspective, the honeycomb shape reveals a perfect cube.

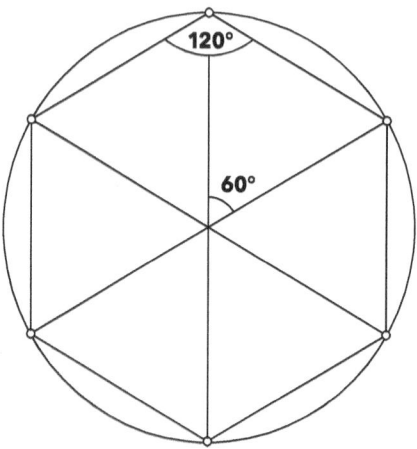

For the enthusiasts, the Addendum explores sacred geometry and its mathematical poetry in greater depth. My aim with sharing all of this is not to give you a PhD in geometry, but to expose the mathematical poetry within sacred geometry, which is the very foundation of all of Creation. What we don't know, we cannot see. What we cannot see, we cannot value. And what we don't value, we will never treasure. So, just see the miraculous poetry in all of it as that will serve as a powerful pathway to see the poetry within your own expression of being spiritual art; the rest is details for the curious student.

Returning back to the six star points, which represent the sacred or virtuous Gifts, we can see that three of them are created by the lines connecting the vertices or corners of the Masculine triangle and vice versa. Each of the three star points of the Masculine point at a Feminine constituent attribute and, again, vice versa. What emerges symbolically then is that the Gifts derived from the star points created by intersecting Masculine lines are the Masculine Gifts to the Feminine and, again, vice versa.

Since a picture tells a thousand words, let's walk through an illustrated example of this. In the graphic below, the line that connects the Masculine cornerstones of Awareness and Intelligence creates a star point that points at Creativity, hence the Gift to the Feminine.

The actual convergence or amalgamation of the constituent attributes Awareness and Intelligence creates the first Gift to the Feminine: Wisdom.

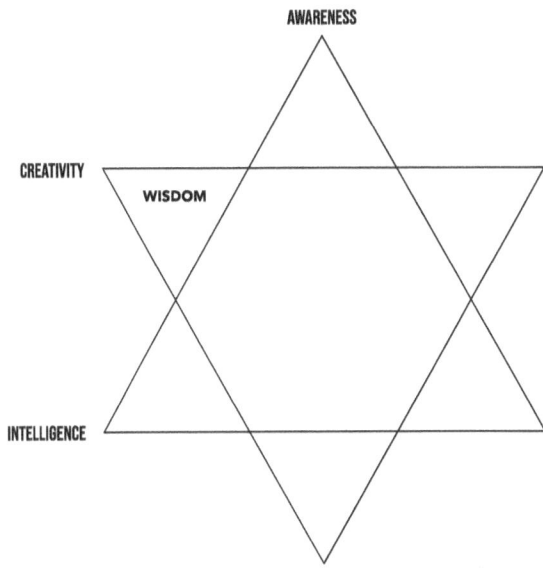

We'll cover Wisdom and the other five Gifts in great depth in the rest of this Part III. And, since Polarity is an integral part of the Grand Architecture of this universe, each virtuous Gift also has an opposite pole as well. This non-virtuous state is the dark side or shadow state of the virtuous Gift and comes into play when one or both of the respective constituent attributes are in dissonance. The level of depth or virtuousness of the Gifts, then, is a derivative of the level of coherence within the constituent attributes, with the lowest denominator between the two being the weak link that holds the virtuousness of the Gift down from where it could be.

Conversely, the level of dissonance in one or both of the cornerstones determines the amplitude of the level of absence of virtue, or in other words, the lack of that Gift being accessible. For instance, the shadow of Wisdom is Imprudence. So, dissonance in our Awareness or Intelligence (or both) will lead to Imprudence, which we can also easily call inability, ineptness, thoughtlessness, or stupidity, just to name a few.

Another way to see this is for us to deepen our Wisdom, we must raise our Awareness and Intelligence, as Wisdom is a derivative product of these two cornerstones. You'll find this to be both practical and insightful, as now we have a roadmap for where to seek growth on our never-ending inner journey.

Whereas in the Architecture of the Masculine and Feminine and their respective constituent attributes, we discovered the foundational building blocks of who and what we truly are, within the Gifts, we find the sacred virtues that come from spiritual embodiment of this Grand Architecture. The Gifts are what we animate and bring to Life itself. Another way to look at this, the Gifts are what we come to exude into and, therefore, experience in Life itself as we get the mud off the spiritual diamond buried deep within each of us. The Gifts are the fingerprints we'll leave on all of Creation, all we interact with, and all of our relationships with others. These Gifts have their own energy signature, which we'll be known for as they become an unmistakable part of our sheer Presence and, ultimately, it's our Presence we are all remembered by.

> "I saw the angel in the marble and carved until I set him free."
> —MICHELANGELO

For as much as we cannot become a skilled spiritual sculptor without having a foundational understanding of the art of spiritual sculpting, my deepest wish for writing this book is to show you there's a magnanimous Divine Being—a true spiritual Poet—in the marble that only you can set free as you are both the sculpture and the sculptor.

For me, from where I am viewing all of Life today, I cannot help but see the miraculous poetry, art, beauty, and intelligence in all of Creation. And I cannot help but see the Divine Beings or true Poets in the marble all around me. Too busy chasing trophies in Finite Games, I didn't have any eyes for any of this most of my life. If this can occur for me, there's absolutely nothing preventing you from having this same occurrence.

So, as we move forward with this book, I will do my very best to convey the mystical beauty, Divine poetry, and sheer magnificence of Life itself. I hope you can start to see the poetry in all of it and, most importantly, yourself. You are pure unadulterated living poetry craving to be expressed in its most beautiful form. Just as you are today, you're already perfect; however, in repeating Leonardo da Vinci's words: "art is never finished, only abandoned."

We might call going on the spiritual path doing "the work," but truthfully, what we're doing is making art. You are art—an individual expression of the Divine with unlimited potential waiting to be carved out of marble.

Let's start with the first virtuous Masculine Gift: Wisdom.

CHAPTER 18
WISDOM

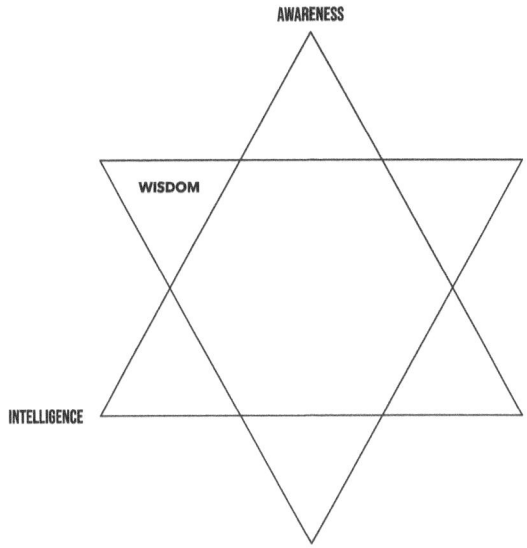

THE FIRST VIRTUOUS MASCULINE Gift of Wisdom is highly paradoxical in nature: those that never question if they possess it typically don't; those that often wonder if they possess it typically do.

Let's go on a journey into Wisdom to find out why.

As the graphic shows, Wisdom is derived from the amalgamation of Awareness and Intelligence. This becomes abundantly obvious when we look at the dissonant states of these two constituent attributes of the Masculine. As a refresher, for Awareness, this dissonant state is Ignorance, and for Intelligence, it's Unintelligence.

> "Abundance of knowledge does not teach men to be wise."
> —HERACLITUS

Unintelligence, again, is defined by the universe as *that* which creates unintelligent outcomes, which is anything that's not conducive to Life itself. War, violence, hate, crime, racism, illness, misery, pain, suffering, inequality, injustice, greed, malfeasance, oppression, pollution, etc., are all unintelligent outcomes not conducive to Life itself. Clearly, when our level of Consciousness resides at the level of Ignorance and Unintelligence, this will not yield any sort of Wisdom. In fact, it will produce Imprudence, the shadow state of Wisdom.

From the above example, we can already glean quite a bit of insight. First, Awareness is almost a precursor to Intelligence, as, from a place of Ignorance, it's near impossible to consciously access the sort of Intelligence that creates intelligent outcomes. We might still create some intelligent outcomes, but it will be mostly—for lack of a better word—accidental.

Conversely, as we raise our Intelligence—as defined by the universe—it's also nearly impossible not to reduce our Ignorance, which is to say, raise our Awareness. So, these two cornerstones grow and evolve in lockstep because they're interdependent and enjoy a symbiotic relationship. Wisdom, the derivative of these two constituent attributes, becomes the proverbial ship that will inevitably also rise when the tide of Awareness and Intelligence rises. We'll see this pattern repeat itself as we explore all the Gifts.

> "Mankind will never see an end of trouble until lovers of wisdom come to hold political power, or the holders of power become lovers of wisdom."
> —PLATO

In our society, Wisdom suffers from a similar misperception as Intelligence does. We equate raw intellectual horsepower—measured as our IQ—or our ability to solve a complicated math problem with Intelligence in the same way we mistake the accumulation of copious amounts of knowledge with Wisdom. Becoming a walking encyclopedia of staid knowledge has nothing to do with true Wisdom because even with all the knowledge in the world, you can still be in Ignorance and Unintelligence.

Nothing could be more prominently on display in our world today. Ironically, with this collective misperception, we worship and idolize many people who—quite frankly—are often a mild insult even to Imprudence. It's one thing to buy their music, watch them on TV or in movies, or religiously follow their mindless superficiality on social media, but regretfully, we even vote them into office and appoint them as CEOs of major corporations. People who know a lot but have little Wisdom to show for it.

Alongside his illustrious Greek peers Pythagoras, Aristotle, and Socrates, Plato was a luminary philosopher among a cadre of the most preeminent philosophers the world has known. In fact, all of history's true greats were polymath philosophers first and foremost. Polymath means they studied multiple disciplines, and all major discoveries by mankind came from the cross-pollination of what's called the Quadrivium. The Quadrivium is considered the foundation of all of Creation and is made up of numbers, geometry, music, and cosmology. All roads of the Quadrivium lead back to Thoth in ancient Egypt, Hermes Trismegistus in ancient Greece, and Mercury in ancient Rome, and if you keep following this thread throughout history, you'll unavoidably come across the Knights Templar and perhaps even discover what this mystical order of Knight-Priests was really all about.

If you then follow this thread into the Renaissance, you'll find this lineage of preeminent philosophers continues with Leonardo da Vinci, Michelangelo, Galileo Galilei, Nicolaus Copernicus, Rene Descartes, Baruch Spinoza, Isaac Newton, and, skipping a few centuries; we get to Albert Einstein, Nikola Tesla, and David Bohm. This isn't the complete list by any means, and I don't mention these things to prepare you for Trivia questions; I am pointing at something and leaving breadcrumbs the size of boulders in case you wish to become a philosopher yourself.

So, what really is a philosopher? The word philosophy comes from the Old Greek *"philosophia,"* which comes from *"philo,"* which is *"loving,"* and *"sophia,"* which means *"wisdom."* So, to be a "philosopher" is to be a "lover of wisdom." Now read the quote above again. We'll revisit philosophy and the Quadrivium again in Part V in the chapter "The All is Mind"; let's pick up now where we left off.

Wisdom is not just mastery of the intelligence of Life itself but deeply knowing Life itself, which means we must live and experience it deeply and consciously. When you are young, you can certainly be wise "for your age," but *true* Wisdom comes with age and experience.

Most ancient and all Indigenous cultures revere the Elders of their tribe. As Indigenous men aged into maturity, they no longer were as suitable for hunting or tribal warfare, but their accumulated Wisdom would make them ideal tribal leaders, councilmen, or shamans. They would be deeply involved in the tribe's politics and community and would lead the process of passing on ancestral tribal knowledge to youngsters, especially boys and young men. Similarly, Indigenous women past their childbearing years would become the wise female Elders that had a prominent role in grooming young girls into womanhood, conveying their knowledge and wisdom of herbal medicine and crafts to the younger generation, and would be central to the tribal community.

> "Wisdom is the daughter of experience."
> —LEONARDO DA VINCI

In modern Western civilization, which is obsessed with youth, we practically disregard the Wisdom of our Elders, especially women who are culturally relegated to second-rank citizens once they enter middle age. Forget about anyone beyond retirement age; we steer them to fifty-five-plus communities before we park grandpa and grandma in a retirement home. We would do well for our society—both young and old—to learn a thing or two from Indigenous cultures, as there's a vast amount of untapped Wisdom within our Elders that's getting lost to Sudoku games and afternoon bingo.

Being merely an Elder isn't enough, though; for Wisdom to emerge, we must have cultivated a high level of sovereign critical thought, as only through this ability will we have the required level of discernment to see through our own enculturation. Our enculturation is the lens through which we perceive reality, and discernment acts as a fog-clearing agent of that lens. Without sovereign critical thought, we become parrots of dogmatic thinking.

We especially see this distortion phenomenon these days in politics but also in business, science, medicine, and religion. Dogmatic thinking and its cousin group think leads to self-righteousness, which has within it the capacity for violence. We become so enamored and intoxicated with our own beliefs that we no longer have the capacity to objectively examine our beliefs or the intellectual courage to test their validity. Any narrative contrary to our beliefs is then interpreted as a personal attack, which leads to using Force to defend our position. This is what righteousness inevitably leads to, and this righteousness can exist only because we lack the discernment to see the colors we've taken on from swimming in a cultural fishbowl. Arguably, our blindness to our own ideology is more dangerous than any ideology itself.

As we covered earlier, the only way out of any fishbowl coloration is cultivating a deep sense of sovereign critical thought—the courage to see where our ideology has steered us into righteousness.

WISDOM

> "Every man takes the limits of his own
> vision for the limits of the world."
> —ARTHUR SCHOPENHAUER

We are each born with a peculiar factory-standard defective bias in our perception of reality. This defective bias is two-fold. We only see a very limited sliver of reality and assume that's all there is, and we assume everyone sees the same reality we do.

The first part points at our relative Truth, which is uniquely tainted by the lens through which we view life. This lens, as already discussed, is colored and fogged over by our inevitable enculturation. The process of defogging and decoloring this lens is done by expanding our Awareness. This takes time, devotion, and commitment as we have to rewire and retrain our Mind, but with the Awareness directed at expanding our Awareness, we have the remarkable capacity to get this lens ever clearer and expanded.

The second part, the embedded assumption everyone else sees the same reality we do, is hardwired in. It's more subtle and sneaky as we never really question this assumption; it's just there lingering in the background. This bias can be more readily dispelled and what it takes is a decision that overrides this hardwired assumption. That decision is to make the base assumption that nobody sees reality the way I do. When we make this the operative command for our subconscious Mind, we hardwire in the notion that others, more likely than not, see reality differently. This opens up the curiosity valve and closes down the self-righteousness valve to a trickle. Curiosity is what prompts us to start asking questions, engaging in dialogue and conversation, and listening to others so we may get a better picture of what they're seeing and experiencing. This is the number one antidote to the societal phenomenon of "gaslighting" we've seen flare up in recent years. Gaslighting is rebutting people with some form of statement or argument that what they are seeing, feeling, or experiencing is not true. Underlying gaslighting is this ethereal and very shifty subconscious bias that all others see and experience reality the same way we do. We don't, and we never will.

Addressing this twofold bias in our factory-standard Awareness is a prerequisite then to move toward embodying true Wisdom. If we can't perceive beyond our relative Truth, we have no hope of dismantling it. And, stuck at our relative Truth, the false limits of this relative Truth will dictate the false limits of a world we simply cannot see truthfully.

> "The only way to make man trustworthy is to trust him."
> —HENRY L. STIMSON

There's an outgrow of the above bias, which is closely related and equally important to touch upon: cognitive bias. Cognitive bias is the tendency of our Mind to dismiss facts and information that are in conflict with its understanding of what the facts and information should be. This bias is well-known in scientific circles as well, and in robust scientific research, all sorts of robust precautions are taken to guard against this very pervasive and stubborn bias. The art and science, so to speak, in combating cognitive bias is to lean into "feeling" and "sensing" what the facts or information are telling us versus solely relying on our Mind's interpretation.

Feeling and sensing connects us with the intelligence of our Heart, which is our center of suprarational intelligence, which is more holistic and expansive yet inclusive of the rational intelligence of our Mind. In Part V, we explore all of this on a deeper level, but the point I want to drive home here is that we must learn to trust what we're seeing, feeling, sensing, intuiting, or even what comes to us through direct knowing.

The only way to get better at the "art part" is to start trusting in what we colloquially call our "sixth sense" of perception. Very much in the same way, Stimson's quote above directs us that to make others trustworthy, we must learn to trust them. We are each endowed with extraordinary sixth sense receptors, but our Mind's default mode is to dismiss them as they're not part of the five senses it's hardwired and conditioned to rely on exclusively. Our sixth sense receptors are all connected to our Heart. Our third eye and gut are our predominant sixth sense receptors, but we have others as well, including our ability to "feel" energy, which we actually do through the skin, which is our largest organ and a very sensitive receptor.

Cognitive bias is a classic inhibitor of true Wisdom as it steers us to subconscious belief patterns that can be completely erroneous and drenched in Falsehood. At the core of Byron Katie's powerful method of inquiry called The Work is a single pivotal question: "Is this true?" This is the first question in a sequence of four that are designed to examine our subconscious beliefs and especially the ones that are disempowering. What The Work is essentially designed to do is filter out our cognitive bias; its genius is in its simplicity and extreme workability. It's a very powerful tool that you can readily learn and bring into your practice, so now you have a very effective method to consider if this is an area you wish to explore and grow in.

> "Wisdom, thoroughly learned, will never be forgotten."
> —PYTHAGORAS

So far, we have identified some key considerations and biases of true Wisdom, but we have not yet really penetrated into the core of what Wisdom truly is. Let's do just that so we can get a deeper understanding of the various dimensions of true Wisdom.

1. **Nuance.** True Wisdom comes from having a deep grasp of nuance. When we view the world as black and white, we're missing many shades of gray in between. Very few things are entirely binary or black and white, and even when they are true, Wisdom still considers what shades of gray it might be missing.

2. **Holism.** True Wisdom always starts and ends with a holistic view of things before zooming into any specific details. Details are important, but when we start with details, we tend to never spot the relationships, and everything is in some way a complex living system nested within others. Complexity cannot be solved when we get lost in details, and virtually everything in some capacity or at some level is complex.

3. **Suprarational.** True Wisdom is suprarational, meaning it's above, yet inclusive of rational thought, and based on or involving factors which cannot be comprehended or explained by ordinary logic or reason alone. The suprarational nature of true Wisdom allows us to access a depth of truth that is transcendent of what we could arrive at

through inductive or deductive reasoning alone. Of course, what all this points at is that in true Wisdom, the intelligence of our Heart plays a pivotal and leading role, yet it's fully inclusive of the intelligence of our logical Mind.

> "Knowledge is organized information; Wisdom is knowing Life."

4. **Perspective.** As we already touched on, our perspective is saturated with our own inherent bias; none of us have a lens without any coloration on it. So, true Wisdom leans heavily on Awareness so it can parse out its own bias. Wisdom asks a lot of questions for this reason and seeks many opinions before coming to any sort of conclusion.

5. **Empathy.** True Wisdom is rooted in empathy. Not only do others, the whole, or the greater good weigh heavily, but how anything affects anyone or anything else is highly relevant to the truly wise as it takes its karmic responsibility very seriously.

6. **Humility.** As Epictetus said: "It's impossible for a man to learn what he thinks he already knows." True Wisdom, then, is humble; it does not pretend or assume to know everything and is intellectually curious without a shred of fragility, meaning it's receptive to new ideas or the insights of others.

7. **Vision.** True Wisdom is always deeply committed to a big-picture vision that best serves the whole or greater good without being beholden to any ideology or dogma. In

this way, its North Star is unwavering, yet it's flexible and dynamic in what the optimal path might be. This North Star also insulates against seeking comfort and convenience over what might be calling for courage, strength, and heart.

8. **Consequence-Oriented.** There's a very big difference between being result- or outcome-oriented, or consequence-oriented. Results or outcomes are singular; consequences are multidimensional, and include the intended result or outcome but also all other consequences. True Wisdom considers all consequences as a means to eliminate or minimize harm, as this is one of the embedded principles of its North Star to best serve the whole.

9. **Patience.** Rushing to a conclusion is the antidote to true Wisdom. Wisdom knows most time constraints are artificial or false to start with, but moreover, rushing impairs clarity, and it's optimizing clarity Wisdom is always after. For this reason, Wisdom likes to contemplate, sit and think, and take the time it needs to come to optimal clarity. There's zero indecisiveness in any of this because as soon as Wisdom intuitively connects with clarity, the decision is immediately made with precision and conviction.

> "Knowing many things doesn't teach insight."
> —HERACLITUS

What naturally follows from all of this is that a lack of nuance, holism, suprational insight, perspective, empathy, humility, vision, consequence orientation, and patience leads to the shadow state of Wisdom or, in other words, Imprudence. This is to say, stupidity, ineptness, thoughtlessness, injudiciousness, obtuseness, asininity, and even stupor or idiocy are all examples of these qualities being insufficiently present. If you wish to enhance your Wisdom, look to cultivate and weave these qualities into your thinking and decision making.

With this more complete comprehension of what constitutes true Wisdom, it's not difficult to see why age and experience have quite a bit to do with Wisdom. But the young can be very wise also; anyone with true Wisdom never discounts the Wisdom of the young or presumes anyone of age has access to Wisdom.

> "To attain knowledge, add things every day.
> To attain wisdom, remove things every day."
> —LAO TZU

So, finally, what makes Wisdom a virtuous Masculine Gift to the Feminine? Not to be confused with a virtuous Gift from men to women. We're still talking essence of Source Consciousness, not gender. Women have no less access to true Wisdom than men, period.

The answer is rooted in Order and Chaos. As you likely recall, the Masculine represents the infinite Formless, which is Order. The Feminine represents the Finite World of Form, which is Chaos. The Masculine is the structure through which the Feminine, as the river of Life itself, flows. Within true Wisdom, there's Order. Within Imprudence, there's nothing but Chaos. Imprudence leads to exploitation, extraction, illness, suffering, blight, disrepair, atrophy, destruction, decay, death, and, ultimately, extinction. There might be short-term worldly gain in Imprudence, but you cannot outrun the consequences with time.

True Wisdom is a rare and truly priceless Gift, something to nourish and treasure, so it might be bestowed to the Feminine, which is to say Existence, Life itself, or all of Creation in the form of your expression of your spiritual art as a true Poet.

> "There is something in us that is wiser than our head."
> —ARTHUR SCHOPENHAUER

CHAPTER 19

INTEGRITY

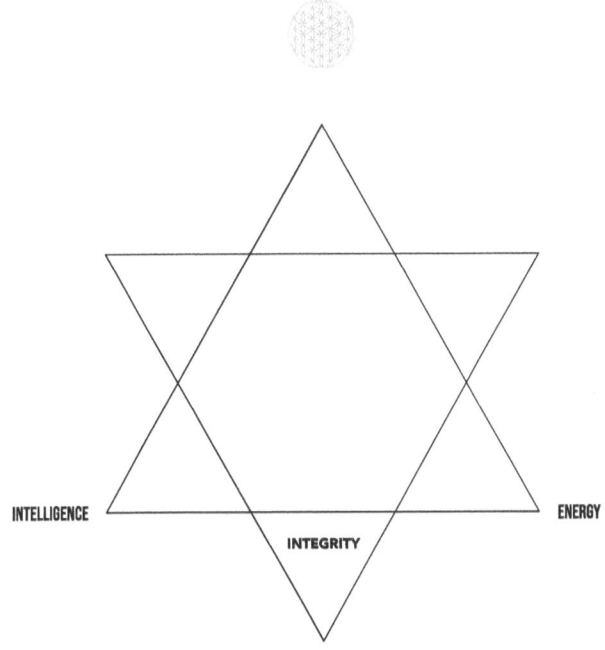

PARADOXICALLY, MANKIND SUFFERS its greatest lack of Integrity in the second virtuous Gift of the Masculine to the Feminine, which is Integrity itself.

Most will refute this strongly, but facts don't lie. Words speak louder than thoughts, actions speak louder than words, and outcomes reveal the truth.

The word Integrity originates from the Latin word *integer*, whereas *integritas* is the noun. In mathematics, an *integer* is a non-fractional or whole number which gives us the first major clue: wholeness. Wholeness means something is undivided and complete; integrity, therefore, holds the meaning "the quality of the state of wholeness."

When we deconstruct *integritas*, more clues are revealed. "In" means "not." "Tegri" stems from the root "tangere" which means "touched." And, "tas" can be translated as "able," and so *integritas* holds the meaning *untouchable*.

Untouchable points at purity, honesty, blamelessness, soundness, incorruptibility, unimpaired condition, chastity, fidelity, honor, trustworthiness, and truthfulness. In other words, when we are *untouchable* in the context of Integrity, we are above/beyond reproach.

> "Integritas Nobilissima Possessio."
> —LATIN PROVERB

Even the Romans knew "Integrity is the noblest of possessions," and still, today, it's as rare as it was back in Roman times. There's a precious regal quality to true Integrity, yet for most, it's merely a fashionable buzzword saturated in utter self-deception.

Even those with the best intentions mostly fail to reach the bar because true Integrity takes copious amounts of spiritual fortitude, as its nemesis is comfort and convenience. And, at consciousness levels below 200, comfort and convenience hold a gravitational force that's near impossible to counterbalance when we're, for all intents and purposes, stuck in survival mode.

Let's explore why.

Let's start at a personal level where most immediately fail. The Hermetic axiom "So within, so without" is a spiritual adage that's pervasive in all ancient and Indigenous wisdom traditions, which points to the law of resonance, which is a Universal Truth. Its basic premise is that our Outer World or reality is a direct reflection of our Inner World. In other words, our beliefs, thoughts, emotions, words, and actions create our reality through sympathetic resonance. This occurs on a personal level as well as for mankind on a collective level. At a deeper level, this adage points at incongruency, which is to say inauthenticity or the masks we wear, and this is where true Integrity comes into play.

Clearly, when we engage in lying, stealing, corruption, malfeasance, fraud, bribes, negligence, or any other improper or non-integrous acts—under the auspices of acting integrous—there's a blatant incongruency with what we're showing "without" vs. what's we're really doing "within." For the record, there's no innocent bystander excuse here, like so many in the political or business arena like to claim when the truth catches up with them. Being a witness is being a participant.

> "The measure of a man is what he does with power."
> —PLATO

Furthermore, there's no such thing as a small non-integrous act that by virtue of its size doesn't count, nor is there any excuse, even if the perpetrator is unnamed, unknown, or never notices. "Everyone else does it" doesn't count, either. The state of the world today is no surprise, given the incestuous web of insidious players that rule, govern, and control the world. The front office of this web is made up of those in the public eye. These are the politicians, large corporations, financial institutions, bilateral organizations, and a host of insidious NGOs, agencies, think tanks, and trade groups that all quite blatantly collude and conspire. However, the real power and influence resides in the back office where—hidden from the public eye—the puppet masters pull their vast strings across borders, politics, industries, and generations. Hence, it's already obvious why true Integrity is so rare, as this is the true prevailing power and governance structure here on the Earthly plane despite the appearance of self-governance of the people through democracies in most countries. All of this is highly controversial to some as it shatters their entire perception and understanding of reality. If you feel called, research and investigate this for yourself with a critical eye and copious amounts of discernment. Consider a great many diverse sources of information and eventually a true picture will emerge for you. The only way to become truly empowered in your knowing (on any topic) is to use your own sovereign critical thought to arrive at your own conclusions based on your own research and analysis. Finally, it's important to note that it's not just the top echelon and figureheads at the controls that are to blame; all the minions willingly and knowingly participating in the system are not just innocent bystanders, they're the engine room that makes all this possible. Ignorance might be an explanation, but it's never an excuse.

On a more personal level, we might perceive ourselves to be nowhere close to doing any of these sorts of grave non-integrous acts. But how many of us are (quite) regularly less than truthful with our loved ones, family, or friends? We tell little white lies, half-truths, or perhaps even more elaborated Falsehoods often as very few of us really speak our mind and hearts. Perhaps we fear rejection or retaliation; however, each time we show up inauthentic from our true Self, we're non-integrous with ourselves. The moment we're non-integrous, we're no longer whole.

How many times do we begrudgingly say "yes" or go just along when inside the answer is "no" (or "hell no!") or vice versa? How many things don't we speak or communicate because we fear to be rejected, abandoned, ridiculed, or retaliated against? What dreams and aspirations have we not pursued to be compliant with someone else's or society's narrative or plans for us? What sexual preferences have gone silent, or which kinky fantasies have never been expressed to our lovers, so we've never lived them? The list is endless, and each time there's a lack of congruency between our authentic Self—including all its dreams, aspirations, values, preferences, and desires—and how we actually show up in the world, we're out of Integrity.

It stands then that true Integrity, first and foremost, requires a radical commitment to stand in your own Truth. It means we're willing to be vulnerable, raw, and courageous enough to drop all our social masks because standing in our own Truth is more precious than holding the image or perception someone else has of us intact.

For if we don't, we're no longer whole, pure, undivided, or unimpaired. Each time we breach our own authentic Self, our Integrity—the whole—gets punctured, and we leak Energy whether we're aware of that or not. This is certainly the case when we commit non-integrous acts, which is why we see so many people that seek relief in distractions and addictions, as they somehow need to numb the inner conflict that arises when we're out of Integrity. Even when the nature of the non-integrous act is solely a breach of standing in our own Truth, we start to leak Energy.

Dolly Parton once famously said: "It takes a lot of money to look this cheap." It's sort of the same when we become non-integrous with our authentic Self as "it takes a lot of Energy to not be our true Self." This is the leak I am speaking of; we're leaking Energy to be something—a mask—we're not. Where it might take a lot more courage and spiritual fortitude to be our authentic Self, it takes a lot more energy to "act" a factitious persona we're truly not.

Courage and spiritual fortitude are muscles we can train, though, so, over time, this becomes just a way of being, which is very energy efficient. Holding up pretenses, masks, and personas we're truthfully not is an Energy leak that never gets any better and likely worse over time. The only problem is that most of us are so conditioned to this being the "normal" way of being they simply have no idea how much energy they're leaking. So, they feel perpetually dense, tense, strained, listless, burdened, or even compromised but lack the Awareness they're both the prisoner and prison guard. If you have the spiritual fortitude to command the prison guard inside of you to open the gates, the prisoner is set free. Nobody else can do this for you; it's your decision and yours only.

> "If it's not right, don't do it; if it's not true, don't say it."
> —MARCUS AURELIUS

When we zoom out from the personal level and take a closer look at the Masculine cornerstones that yield Integrity, we can readily see why the Romans referred to true Integrity as the noblest of possessions. These constituent attributes are Intelligence and Energy.

Intelligence, as the universe defines it, is *that* which creates intelligent outcomes, which implies that its derivative—Integrity—must also be fully aligned with creating intelligent outcomes. This certainly holds true for non-integrous acts like lying, stealing, corruption, malfeasance, fraud, bribes, negligence, etc., as all of those are not conducive to Life itself as they cause harm. So, by definition, all these non-integrous acts are a product of Unintelligence as the universe defines it. The same goes for the non-integrous act of breaching our authentic Self, which robs us of joy, happiness, fulfillment, excitement, adventure, or what have you. Clearly, we can conclude that these all constitute unintelligent outcomes which then, by definition, originate from Unintelligence. So, to be in true Integrity, the constituent attribute Intelligence must be fully online.

So, what about Energy?

I already shared that for us to be in true Integrity, we must have ample courage and spiritual fortitude, both of which are part of our overall Life Force, which is part of Energy. In addition, like we discussed earlier, when we're out of Integrity, we leak Energy; here again, we're pointing squarely at the constituent attribute Energy.

We also already briefly touched on sympathetic resonance—which is an integral part of Energy if you recall from Part II—which is how we not only create our own reality or Outer World, but as part of mankind, co-create our collective reality or Outer World.

> "Our greatest ability as humans is not to change the world, but to change ourselves."
> —MAHATMA GANDHI

At Consciousness levels below 200, we lack the capacity to "see" beyond self-interest, which is why it's near impossible to be in true Integrity below this threshold. But that doesn't take anything away from the fact that we collectively co-create our collective reality.

Hence, our world today is a representation of the countless non-integrous acts committed by countless people ranging from the truly vile and atrocious non-integrous acts to the relatively small and innocuous. Yet, non-integrous is non-integrous, which holds a certain low and dense vibration. Every single vibration gets projected into the formless Infinite Field of Potentialities and reflected back in the way we see, feel, and experience our reality or Finite World of Form. All change starts within; this is a cardinal law of the universe. The only real change we control, then, is to be in total Integrity with our own Integrity. Each of us waiting for the world to change will never change anything; we must each decide to show up in true Integrity, which in turn will inevitably change the world, as this is the Universal Truth of the law of correspondence. So within, so without.

So, it's very clear then why the constituent attributes Intelligence and Energy are the vital fuel source for true Integrity.

> "The superior man knows what's right, the inferior man knows what will sell."
> —CONFUCIUS

Similar to Wisdom, we already discovered that the virtuous Gift Integrity has many nuances and layers to it. So, let's summarize:

1. **Wholeness.** True Integrity is non-fractional and complete, or there can be no wholeness. If this wholeness was represented by a circle, there cannot be any interruption in the circumference of the circle. All is held within the circle, which means we cannot willingly or knowingly cause any harm, or the whole will not be complete; it would be fractured as all is one.

2. **Purity.** True Integrity has a distinct purity or blamelessness to it; we're genuinely above/beyond reproach. In this context, we're not just referring to that which is seen, observed, or noticed by others—but literally anything, especially that which goes unseen, unobserved, or unnoticed and regardless of whether it pertains to something in our Inner World or something we do in/to the Outer World.

3. **Fidelity.** Clearly, loyalty and wedding vows come to mind with the word Fidelity, but this goes well beyond the limits

of our love commitments even though this is where infidelity shows up a lot. But Fidelity applies to all our relationships, our work and professional endeavors, and how we show up in life. Typically, Fidelity gets breached by the lure of lust, which can be for another sexual experience but also power, fame, fortune, or applause, or any other trophy that holds the power to seduce us to breach our Fidelity.

4. **Incorruptibility.** Where Fidelity points at the breach of some form of trust with others, Incorruptibility points at holding the highest levels of sacredness for our norms, values, ethics, morality, and even our authentic Self. We cannot be seduced by pleasure, gain, comfort, or convenience to abandon our standards. For true Integrity, these standards must, of course, be fully aligned with the cornerstones Intelligence and Energy.

5. **Soundness.** True Integrity is robust, firm, and therefore has soundness. There's also soundness in the way that Integrity has beautiful harmonics and resonance, whereas anything non-integrous creates dissonance, which in harmonics is analogous to being off or out of tune. Energetically we can feel and sense this if we're receptive to it, even when we don't know exactly why a non-integrous act feels like a distinct negative energy to us.

6. **Virtue.** As mentioned, true Integrity has a distinct regal quality to it because the sheer nature of Integrity is virtuous, and virtue holds a very high frequency. Albeit often not fully understood, virtue is one of the high-frequency qualities that's even recognized by people with lower levels of Consciousness. It's palpable in that way, and virtue

always serves the greater good—the whole beehive—and so anything that's only self-serving will not hold the frequency of virtue.

7. **Truthful.** To be Truthful, we must "say what we mean; and mean what we say." There cannot be true Integrity if we are not totally honest and forthright. This does not give us license to be careless or unloving with our words, but if our Truth spoken in respectful ways offends or hurts someone, we are ultimately not responsible for their fragility. The Truth can be triggering and highly inconvenient, but we should not water down our Integrity and reside in Falsehood to placate others. Just to overemphasize, any Truth that's intended to hurt or harm someone else is, by definition, a Falsehood.

8. **Trustworthy.** To be Trustworthy is to be reliable and a safe harbor. True Integrity cannot exist when we're unreliable, unfaithful in the trust placed in us, or we cannot be depended upon to stand in our own Truth or the Truth in general.

9. **Unimpaired.** Untouchable, the place we started, implies unimpaired condition. True Integrity might get challenged, or seduction might even pull at it; however, in its purest form, it won't incur so much as a scratch or a dent. It always remains unimpaired, as any impairment would damage its wholeness and its purity.

> "Integrity is doing the right thing when no one is watching."
> —C.S. LEWIS

True Integrity is a very high bar; that's why it's so rare. This sort of Integrity can be highly inconvenient, perilous even, as your steadfast commitment to being and living in Truth is deeply threatening to those that lack the courage and spiritual fortitude to make this commitment, much less actually live it consistently. Integrity is the proverbial ballbuster of Falsehoods, so the reflection of your Integrity is a mirror that those living in Falsehood cannot stomach looking at. This very phenomenon is at the basis of all censorship and its ugly cousin, "cancel culture."

By definition, Truth has zero concerns about any other opinions, views, or perspectives, no matter how idiotic, hurtful, or hateful. It simply has no fragility as it's rooted in Love, so it views censorship and cancel culture as aberrations of fragile minds lost in Falsehood(s). Falsehood(s), on the other hand, need to be defended as they can't stand on their own merit. Those defending Falsehood(s) will go to great lengths, often resorting to lying, deception, manipulating, ridiculing, blacklisting, firing, smear campaigning, and other underhanded tactics until they've created the perfect echo chamber, whether that's in politics, business, or social groups.

The tyrannical bent of the defenders of Falsehood(s) is always intoxicated with its own righteousness and will resort to censorship, cancel culture, fearmongering, old-school tar and feathers, and in some areas of the world, even lynching and public executions. They will even proclaim all of this is justified, which is a reflection of their Ignorance and quite predictable since Falsehood(s) are rooted in Fear. Fear is a psychological distortion agent that serves as the fertile catalyst for war, hate, violence, crime, racism, greed, malfeasance, corruption, and oppression.

The thing to know, though, is that Falsehood(s) eventually always collapses, albeit this can sometimes take years, decades, or even centuries, and great pain and suffering can be inflicted in the meantime. Still, true Integrity and standing steadfast in Truth, and refusing to be silenced is the only viable defense, as the power of Love will ultimately prevail as even utter Darkness loses some of its darkness when exposed to a single ray of Light. The thing to remember is that Love can be firm, will stand its ground, and defend itself against violations of its human rights, but it will not offensively or preemptively inflict injury, harm, or damage.

Righteousness is saturated with superiority, which implies hierarchy, and within hierarchy, there can be—by definition—no equality. Inequality is a Falsehood as within the Sanctity of all Life principle of this universe, all is one and therefore equal in terms of the value of Life. Standing for a truthful Just Cause, on the other hand, honors this Sanctity of all Life principle, or it can be no Just Cause as by definition, a Just Cause must serve the whole. One cannot honor the whole by offensively or preemptively inflicting injury, harm, or damage, which is why most wars, violence, oppression of any sort, and other atrocities in the name of a Just Cause are really just ignoble Righteousness disingenuously masquerading as its noble counterpart Just Cause.

Finally, as C.S. Lewis pointed out, true Integrity is what you do when nobody is watching, which dovetails with the universal Truth that you are what you do when nobody is watching and what you do when nobody is watching is what shows up as your Life. Spiritual art, then, is created when nobody is watching, except you.

> "The ultimate measure of a man is not where he stands in moments of comfort and convenience, but where he stands at times of challenge and controversy."
> —MARTIN LUTHER KING JR.

Similar to Wisdom, Integrity as the virtuous Gift of the Masculine to the Feminine points us at Order. Without Integrity—wholeness—there can be no Order, and things go into disrepair and destruction, which is Chaos. This is exactly what we witness all around the world today, from politics to business to societies. When there's a lack of Integrity, things decline and disintegrate. In all of humanity's greatest challenges, we can see a lack of Integrity at the very foundation of these challenges.

Even though there's definitely such a thing as the Integrity of political and government institutions, the justice system, businesses, and organizations, the fundamental change must come from within. This means, from each of us, in that sense, Integrity is a way of life we decide on more so than Wisdom, which is something we tend to cultivate over time.

Integrity is a decision followed by congruent action. Choose wisely.

Next, we'll explore Gratitude, the third and last of the Masculine Gifts, which is perhaps the most unassuming superpower among all the Gifts. Gratitude will have you in total awe of it, if not gratitude itself.

CHAPTER 20

GRATITUDE

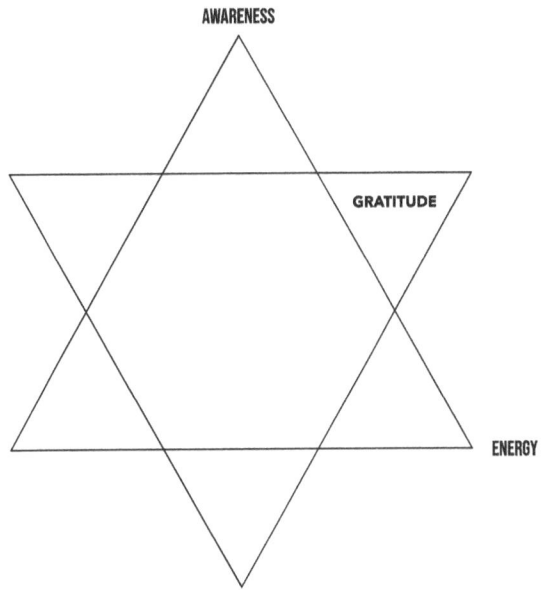

THE PARADOXICAL NATURE OF the virtuous Masculine Gift of Gratitude is that its biggest power resides in that which is not apparent or hasn't occurred yet. Gratitude is the proverbial can opener of the unapparent Formless into the apparent Finite World of Form or what we consider our reality.

Let's unpack why that is and how Gratitude adds an exquisite grace to our spiritual art.

To do so, let's first revisit the two constituent attributes that must coalesce for Gratitude to come into existence: Awareness and Energy.

> "Wear gratitude like a cloak, and it will feed every corner of your life."
> —RUMI

As you might recall, conscious Awareness happens when something registers—appears in thought-form—in our conscious Mind. Our Awareness is the Observer becoming conscious of this thought-form; we could call this our inner Awareness. Our outer Awareness is consciously becoming aware of anything in our Outer World, and as you might also recall, we're typically unaware—unconscious—of upwards of 90 percent of reality as our conscious Mind can only process 10 percent, which it subjectively filters through the reticular activating system or RAS.

One of the core reasons we generally lack access to Gratitude is that we're working with a very small subset of data from which we infer our perception of reality. There's simply a lot we don't see—it's hidden from our perception—and therefore, we're missing critical data and relationships to infer the Truth, which leads us to have an incomplete understanding, which we can also call Falsehoods. Awareness, and even more so ever-expanding our Awareness, is key to see the universal Truth that each moment, each occurrence, and each experience—no matter how horrific or heartbreaking—is deserving of our Gratitude. We'll get much deeper into this as we continue exploring and see how this also relates to the manifestation of the unapparent Formless into the apparent Finite World of Form.

Energy, as we discussed, is the fuel source and building blocks of this entire universe and all of reality, which includes all of our occurrences and experiences. When Awareness—which includes our understanding and direct knowing—becomes animated or powered by Energy, it amalgamates into Faith. Faith is a positive belief in the absence of concrete evidence; its opposite pole is Fear, which is a negative belief in the absence of concrete evidence. In this context, I am referring to psychological Fear—which is a psychological construct or mere thought-form and not real. I am not referring to the Fear of survival triggered by imminent physical danger like someone pointing a gun at you.

Faith is foundational to Gratitude; without Faith, we cannot have true Gratitude, which is being deeply thankful even for those things we don't understand, we can't see, are not apparent, or haven't occurred for us yet in our reality. Gratitude for the gains, riches, and beauty Life itself already bestowed on us is also part of Gratitude, but this leans more on the side of thankfulness as it requires no Faith. Thankfulness is powerful in its own right, but it mostly serves as an access point to true Gratitude—which is far more powerful—as thankfulness is the easiest to bring into our overall practice of Gratitude.

So, gaining access to true Gratitude requires the coalescence of our Awareness and our Energy. We can see this perhaps even more clearly when we consider the dissonant states of Awareness and Energy, which are Ignorance and Impotence, respectively. Clearly, in Ignorance—not knowing or being aware—there can be no Faith, so we're relegated to Fear, which is Falsehood. Similarly, Impotence—which we previously defined as general inadequacy, incapacity, and the lack of sufficient ability, energy, and power—is foundational to Fear. We simply don't reside in Fear when we're in a place of feeling our innate Power, which is our Energy. Instead, we reside in Faith in our adequacy, capacity, and our innate ability to access our energy and power.

> "Faith dictates Fate, and so does Fear."

True Gratitude is the secret visceral power that animates the manifestation of the unapparent Formless into the apparent Finite World of Form. The fuel source of this visceral power is Faith—this concerns all occurrences of manifestation of the unapparent Formless (potentialities in the Infinite Field of Possibilities), which could be tangible worldly success or an intangible experience such as a beautiful love relationship.

We can conclude then that our ability and capacity to be in true Gratitude even for those things which we don't (yet) fully understand, can't (yet) see, are not (yet) apparent to us, or have not (yet) occurred, dictate our Fate—that which will occur for us in reality—based on our Faith. Conversely, our lack of ability or capacity to be in true Gratitude will dictate our Fate based on our Fear(s). In other words, our true Faith in something—expressed and animated through true Gratitude—will inevitably manifest it, and so will our Fear(s) in something. All of this ties directly back to sympathetic resonance as the vibration and frequency of true Faith—and therefore true Gratitude—is very light, expansive, and high, whereas the vibration and frequency of Fear is dense, contracted, and low.

> "All I have seen teaches me to trust the Creator for all I have not seen."
> —RALPH WALDO EMERSON

As mentioned earlier, a key inhibitor of being in true Gratitude is Ignorance, the dissonant state of Awareness. The truth is we're typically aware of such a small sliver of reality; we lack the Awareness of all we don't see, don't know, or simply don't fully understand. If we can't perceive it with our five senses, we wrongfully infer it's simply not there and inevitably conclude Falsehoods, which gives birth to Fear.

Another way to look at this is that Life itself—all of Creation—is a black box of which we typically see only 10 percent of the variables, relationships, and forces at play, so we erroneously conclude Life itself is governed by Chaos. We only conclude that because we can't see or grasp the Order within all of it, so our Mind logically infers there must not be any true Order. Order—the infinite—however, is not governed by logic or linearity; it's simply not constrained by that nor time and space as it's infinitely complex. And anything infinitely complex like all of Creation can certainly not be inferred by only having access to 10 percent of the variables, relationships, and forces at play.

We're back to Faith—a positive belief in the absence of concrete evidence. Moreover, we have identified the culprit that inhibits Faith: the Mind. Our Mind only knows Fear as its Intelligence of logic and rationality is incapable of computing the unseen or unknown. So, Fear is its default mode. For Faith, we must avail ourselves of the intelligence of our Heart, which is suprarational in nature, or in other words, it can go beyond the limitations of logic and rationality.

Our Mind's logical and sensory-based faculties might not have access to 90 percent of this black box, but through increasing our Awareness, we can radically expand on the 10 percent of reality our Mind perceives. Provided we have the courage and spiritual fortitude to tap into our innate capacity of suprarational Intelligence, which resides in our Heart. Our Heart is the portal into the unknown, the unseen, and the mystical formless realm of the Akashic field. Moreover, through our Heart, we can deeply observe the intelligence of Life itself—the output of this black box—and quite readily conclude there's infinite Order in this output. So, we actually don't need to know or understand all the workings inside this black box—we can derive our Faith in our direct knowing of the intelligence of Life itself and conclude there must be infinite Order within this black box for it to produce this infinite Order in all of Creation.

We just discovered another pivotal clue, to reside in true Faith—and therefore true Gratitude—we must surrender and trust in the intelligence of Life itself. If you will, we must surrender and trust in the output of this black box and let go of the very limited perceptions of our logical mind, which leads us to conclude Falsehoods.

We can always know—but only through our Heart—that however anything shows up in our reality is exactly as it's supposed to be—zero exceptions. Everything is always in perfect Order, and everything always happens for our greatest growth, greatest prosperity, and greatest evolution. We might not like it, it might not feel good or pleasant, and perhaps we don't understand it fully. Yet, we can still know this.

Knowing this, despite how it appears to our Mind or the emotional residue the experience created, is moving away from Falsehood into Truth. Our mental chatter and emotions are merely a clue into the growth available in the experience. All of Life itself is just an endless series of seemingly disconnected experiences, yet in the invisible, formless realm, they are all connected and rooted in perfect Order. Just because we can't see that doesn't make it not so. The universe makes no mistakes; we just don't understand all of it because we're not privy to all the invisible procuring causes of the visible and tangible effects we experience as our reality.

> "Everything that happens, happens as it should; and if you observe carefully, you will find this to be so."
> —MARCUS AURELIUS

So, the logical next question—no pun intended—is how can we know this to be true?

Well, we can become aware of the Truth that everything always happens for us, not to us. Even the most horrific, heartbreaking, or apparently catastrophic occurrences in our life are, at their very core, just that: experiences. Experience is how we learn, grow, and evolve here in Earth School. From an evolutionary perspective, there's no such thing as "good" or "bad" experiences; each experience or occurrence is neutral in the perspective of the universe. This includes all barbaric acts of cruelty and all other deeply unintelligent outcomes we can witness all around in our world today.

Darkness is the absence of Light. The level of ascension into higher levels of Consciousness—Light—is directly correlated to our capacity to witness and experience our own Darkness within and in our reality. Each time we're confronted with Darkness in our own life or the world at large, we have a choice. Do we use this experience to move toward the Light or descend into Darkness? As Jesus famously stated as the Roman Centurions hammered the iron nails through his palms during his crucifixion: "Forgive them, Father, for they know not what they do."

Forgiveness is loving your or any perpetrators; it's a reflection of your direct knowing that everything is always in perfect order, no matter how it might appear to us here on the Earthly plane. True Awareness will choose Love each and every time, for it knows at a very deep level there's only true Freedom in surrendering to the intelligence of Life itself. Christ Consciousness can even do this while enduring the unthinkable. Within anger, resentment, hate, revenge, and retaliation, we are unconsciously choosing to carry the Darkness by descending into Darkness ourselves, and so we inadvertently become its prisoner.

> "Before you embark on a journey of revenge, dig two graves."
> —CONFUCIUS

It's important to note that Love doesn't preclude seeking justice. But, for justice to be just, it cannot be revengeful or retaliatory in nature. Justice merely serves as the application of the rule of law of karmic responsibility on the Earthly plane. This is why unjust punishment such as cruelty or capital punishment renders the perpetrated equal perpetrators. In seeking revenge or retaliation under the guise of justice, they inadvertently succumbed to their own Darkness within. Hence, an eye for an eye—such as capital punishment—is a primal form of justice as it's retaliatory in nature, lacks forgiveness, and is not rooted in Love. It's savage and barbaric, so it has no place in a society of a spiritually advanced collective Consciousness. Life itself cannot be honored by taking away from it, as Divinity can never be honored, restored, or made whole by harming that which is of a Divine nature itself. And, either all of Creation is Divine—including those who are utterly lost—or none of it is.

I cannot stress enough that whatever we do to others, we're doing to ourselves.

> "There are always flowers for those who wish to see them."
> —HENRI MATISSE

Coming from true Awareness, we also directly know the universal Truth that everything always happens for us for our greatest growth, greatest prosperity, and greatest evolution. We might not understand it fully (yet), we might not know why (yet), and we might never fully come to know how but our Awareness of this Truth opens our eyes and perception for that which is not apparent to us.

Within the human experience, we overwhelmingly connect the dots through the rearview mirror, sometimes years or even decades later. In psychology, this is referred to as the self-reflection period or cycle, or the period during which we perceive reality in a distorted or disassociated way. The shorter this period, the quicker we're able to complete the experience so we can forgive, let go, and move on. Trauma is a stalled or frozen self-reflection cycle, an inability to process what happened, and so the trauma gets stored indefinitely in our cellular tissue and emotional body until such time as we are able to face, process, and heal the trauma.

During this self-reflection period, we move through stages of evaluation, critical analysis, synthesis, and, eventually, resolution, which results in enhanced self-awareness. For example, we might experience a heartbreaking divorce or breakup, and we're devastated. Our whole life seems to have unraveled, and we cannot find ourselves to heal our heartbreak until we finally move through the deep grieving and healing process. We emerge a changed person (or permanently scarred if we didn't truly heal) and now meet someone else who's an even better match, which results in an even deeper love experience. In hindsight, we might count our lucky stars now for that divorce or breakup as it eventually opened us up for something better to come into our life.

This is what it means that literally everything happens for us for our greatest growth, greatest prosperity, and greatest evolution. It's our lack of Awareness—or Ignorance—that prevents us from seeing or understanding this, which is at the very root of any of our suffering within Life itself. Our job is not to understand everything that occurs inside the black box, which is simply not visible or comprehensible; our only job here in Earth school is to open our Awareness to what it produces and seek the infinite Order within its output. True Gratitude is a direct reflection of our level of surrendering and trust in the intelligence of Life itself.

As the Buddha stated: "all suffering has its root in Ignorance," and similarly, Matisse's quote points us at the Truth that there are always flowers for those who wish to see them. What gets in our way is our perception of how Life should be. Life itself—all of Creation—is unconcerned with your perception of how Life or your reality *should* be as, after all, your perception is merely a thought-form or psychological construct that is not real. The more we can align and surrender to "what actually is," the more we become aware of the flowers in everything, even though they might show up as ugly weeds in our experience of Life itself. Cultivating this heightened level of Awareness is what leads us to cultivating extraordinary levels of Faith, which is at the very foundation of true Gratitude. Now, just to point out what might be obvious to some, Gratitude is not something we bring into our practice of daily life to be "good boys and girls," as it's preached by many religions. No, to the contrary, we practice Gratitude because it adds power, luminescence, and grace to our spiritual art.

> "If the only prayer you said was thank you, that would be enough."
> —MASTER ECKHART

Since the Feminine represents Life itself or Existence, the virtuous Masculine Gift of true Gratitude reflects our appreciation for her.

This was powerfully demonstrated by scientific experiments conducted by Dr. Masaru Emoto, a Japanese researcher and pioneer in studying how human consciousness can affect water as a conductor of Consciousness. His book *The Hidden Messages of Water* was a *New York Times* bestseller and illustrated how intention, prayers, words, and music (harmonic frequency) create crystallization patterns in water. Positive or harmonic vibrations would form a dazzling array of beautiful crystallization patterns, and negative or dissonant vibrations would reveal disorganized and unsightly crystallization patterns. Gratitude as a harmonic vibration has a harmonious effect on its surroundings in this very same way, and water constitutes 70 percent of our body. Water is also a very powerful conductor, so these very crystallization patterns within water that Dr. Emoto made visible to our naked eye mirror exactly what happens within your and my body based on the harmonics of our vibration and frequency.

Therefore, to be saturated in true Gratitude is to say thank you to the Feminine, to Life itself. To see the art, poetry, and beauty in the Feminine—all of Creation—is to embrace her Chaos, knowing that at a deeper level, there's infinite Order in all of it, even when it's not apparent and shows up as mayhem. We can be thankful for each breath, each day we wake up, and each and every one of the smallest occurrences of the miracle of Life itself, which is all around us. All it takes is Awareness, to literally have eyes for it, and to let go of all our inherently limited and, therefore, flawed perceptions of how she—Life itself—should be. In this surrender and trust in the intelligence of Life itself, fueled and animated by Energy, we get to a place of extraordinary Faith, which is the wellspring of true Gratitude.

GRATITUDE

All of Life itself is a miracle, unfolding before us one moment and occurrence at a time. Once you see, you cannot unsee, and once you see, you cannot help but reside in true Gratitude for all of it.

This concludes the three virtuous Masculine Gifts to the Feminine; let's now explore the three virtuous Feminine Gifts to the Masculine, starting with the first one: Joy.

> "There are only two ways to live your life. One is as though nothing is a miracle. The other is as though everything is a miracle."
> —ALBERT EINSTEIN

CHAPTER 21
JOY

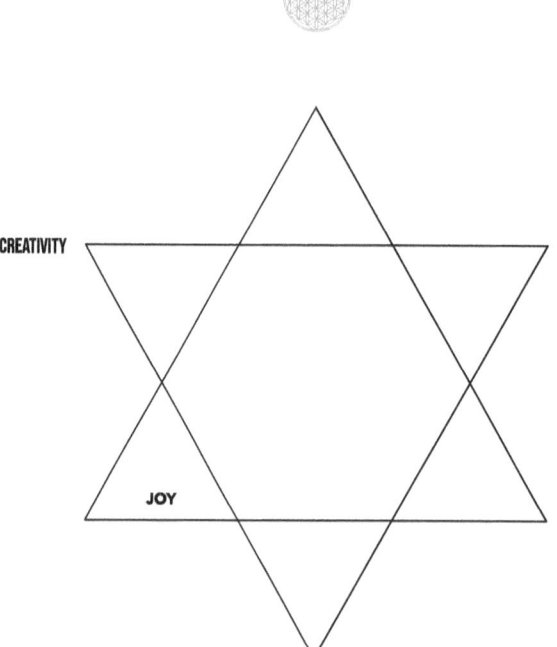

THE PARADOXICAL NATURE OF the first virtuous Feminine Gift, Joy, is that when we confuse it with mere pleasure, we will never know its true depth. Generally speaking, our world is thoroughly confused, so let's journey into the depths of Joy.

Let's start again with the etymology of the word Joy to see what clues that reveals. Joy stems from the Old French word *joie*, which implies "delight, erotic pleasure, bliss, and joyfulness." *Joie* stems from the Latin *gaudia*, which means "expressions of pleasure and sensual delight." The plural form is *gaudium* which refers to "joy, inward joy, gladness, delight, or source of delight." Both *gaudia* and *gaudium* have their origins in the verb *gaudere* which means "to rejoice," which is synonymous with "to exult, to revel, to delight, and to enjoy."

There's a lot to work with here as it's already apparent it's pointing us at a state of Being with some interesting descriptive markers like erotic and sensual, which is pointing us at play. More on that later; let's start with *joie* and the expression we're probably all familiar with: *joie de vivre*.

Joie de vivre is a French expression that has been adopted in English to express a cheerful enjoyment of life, an exultation of spirit. *Joie de vivre* refers to a joy of everything, a comprehensive joy, a philosophy of life even. What's deeply embedded within *joie de vivre* is a sense of playfulness. People with *joie de vivre* have a way of extracting all the nectar from life by being playful with it, to not let the inevitable valleys detract from their joy of living. These people tend to be highly resilient; they get up quickly when life knocks them down and bounce right back from adversity. They're also a pleasure to be with; their glass-half-full view on life and overall playfulness has a way of lifting spirits all around them. So, *joie de vivre* is a way of seeing life that makes it a state of Being independent of circumstances vs. a condition of Being dependent on circumstances.

This is where we see a clear demarcation between pleasure and Joy. We can have pleasure, experience pleasure, and even revel in pleasure, but there's no such thing as a state of pleasure, whereas we can most definitely be in a state of Joy. So, pleasure is momentary and fleeting; it's something we temporarily experience. We seek pleasure; we are (or are not) in Joy.

This goes even a level deeper. We can experience something that is not pleasurable and still be in Joy. This is possible because a prevailing state of Being can override a circumstance or experience. We can even be in Joy during an unhappy experience. We could say then that happiness is related to Joy, but definitely not its equal or source. When we think of happiness as joyous moments, we're getting very close to what it means to be happy, as it's ultimately temporal in nature. When something "bad" happens to us, we are not happy but blue, sad, somber, mournful, bereaved, dejected, distressed, or even heartbroken. Yet, even within any of those unhappy periods, we can still have *joie de vivre* and be in Joy.

> "Poverty with Joy isn't poverty at all. The poor man is not one who has little, but one who hankers after more."
> —SENECA

The fundamental problem with confusing pleasure with Joy is that it leads us on an endless chase. As we seek pleasure, we get a temporary dopamine fix while we experience it only to have the dopamine effect wear off, at which time we have to seek another experience of pleasure. When we equate these fleeting pleasure highs with Joy, we're destined to always hanker after more, as Seneca puts it. The classic case of *Never Enoughitis*, the affliction from which most of our world suffers as it's just never enough. Or, in colloquial terms, never [expletive] enough!

We see this relentless seeking of pleasure expressed in all sorts of ways, from overindulgence in eating, drinking, partying, shopping, and binge-watching to more serious forms of addictions in the form of alcoholism, drug abuse, gambling, sex, porn, and even adultery. Gluttony gets confused with nourishment. Debauchery gets confused with sacred hedonistic play, and sensory orgies get confused with tantric pleasure. We live in a world that's deeply confused between promiscuous and excessive sensory stimulation and saturation versus the art of sacred indulgence of our five senses. There are other forms of seeking misguided pleasure that are often overlooked as they're perceived virtuous in our society when in reality, they're self-destructive. Overworking and overexercising are just two such examples.

There's absolutely nothing wrong per se with joyfully seeking pleasure; in fact, indulgence in tantric pleasure and sacred hedonism are experiences of the *joie de vivre* that's interwoven within the sacred fabric of Life itself. We are here on the Earthly plane to play, experience, and indulge in physical reality and relish the Divinity in the richness of Life itself. Art, music, food, celebrations, and also sex are available to us to be used as sacred pathways to experience the Divine within Life itself.

It's a fine line, though, when the sacred becomes blasphemous gluttony and debauchery, what in its nature is exquisitely rich and beautiful—sacred hedonism—becomes vile and cheap numbing and diversion. The litmus test is not a moral one but experiential.

True tantric pleasure and sacred hedonism take you deeper into Life itself; it's a spiritual experience sought through play and pleasure. Gluttony and debauchery take you away from Life itself; it's a sensory experience. So, are you doing "it" to distract from or forget about Life itself, or are you doing it to get a richer experience and deeper into Life itself? One lulls us deeper into our sleepwalking trance; the other one awakens us.

Having said all that, when we seek mere sensory pleasure in an ill-fated attempt to find Joy, we are destined to succumb to sacrilegious hedonism, which at its very core is a form of overindulgence in self-indulgence. The purpose of Life itself is not self-indulgence but self-realization. The meaning of Life itself is not derived from experiencing whatever gives us pleasure, but from experiencing—i.e., Being in—Joy through play and pleasure. Play and pleasure is a vehicle or mode of transportation not to be confused with the destination itself.

In this light and as a whole, Western civilization as it stands today is living in deep poverty as, despite all our worldly riches, most are totally lost on the never-ending carousel of seeking pleasure for the sake of finding diversion. We only have to look at the obesity rate and exponential growth in chronic illnesses like heart disease, high blood pressure, high cholesterol, diabetes, asthma, and cancer to see we're overindulging. Add to this the opioid crisis and the growing rate of alcoholism, occurrences of depression, burn-outs, suicides, divorce, household debt, homelessness, and mass shootings just to name a few, and it gets pretty obvious all of this has spiraled out of control and has very little to do with the general populace Being in a state of true Joy. At the very root of all these forms of escapism, we find the fundamental schism that confuses play and pleasure for the destination on the one hand and quantity over quality on the other.

> "Joy is owned; pleasure will own you."

So, if mindlessly seeking pleasure is not the path to Being in a state of Joy, then what is the path? Let's take a closer look at the two constituent attributes of the Feminine—Being and Creativity—that yield Joy and see what wants to be revealed.

If you recall from the chapter on Being, one critical nuance is that when we *must play*, we're in Doing, and when we *freely choose to play*, we're in Being. We already touched on it earlier that *play* and *playfulness* are integral to Joy, and here it becomes very clear why as we're back to when we *must play*, we cannot *play*.

When we confuse seeking pleasure for Joy, we must constantly seek pleasure to experience what we mistakenly believe is Joy. Hence, we cannot truly *play* because we *must play*. Or, in other words, pleasure owns us. When we *must play*, we're, by definition, in Doing, the opposite pole of Being. So, clearly, already, we can see that to access true Joy, we must be in Being, as only from that state can we freely choose to play whatever Finite Game it is we feel like playing.

From this state of Being, freely choosing to play any Finite Game, we are also detached from the outcome of the Finite Game. We enjoy them, but we're not playing for trophies anymore, so our Joy is not attached to winning or getting ranked but merely to playing the game. We're playing for the love of the game, which is really a metaphor for playing for the love of experiencing Life itself—we're back to *joie de vivre*.

There's another piece of evidence that confirms all the above. Our *being* in Doing almost inevitably leads to all sorts of overdoing, which is nothing more than the overindulgence in self-indulgence. Why? Because very few lost in Doing—which is *being* lost in Finite Games—do so for the greater good. We chase trophies and fame, fortune, and applause through the pursuit of Finite Games out of self-interest, which is at its core just self-indulgence. When we attach great value and derive our self-worth from our net worth, titles, ranking, status, and possessions, donating to our alma mater, so our name goes on a building, we're Doing out of self-indulgence. People in Doing, seeking pleasure and gain, might occasionally access happiness, but true Joy is unknown to them—they're too busy *doing* Doing to know what it is.

So, we know now it's only within the stillness and quietude of truly *being* in Being that we have access to Being in true Joy. What about Creativity, the other cornerstone?

> "When you do things from your soul, you feel a river moving in you, a joy."
> —RUMI

As discovered earlier in the chapter on Creativity, some words closely associated with Creativity are imagination, artistry, genius, brilliance, virtuosity, flair, playfulness, luminosity, inspiration, ingenuity, inventiveness, resourcefulness, adaptability, and originality. Again, we see playfulness come back as well as all sorts of qualities that point at art, poetry, and beauty. These are all aiming squarely at where true Joy emanates from. Universally, we all derive inspiration and a deep sense of well-being from our favorite music, beautiful design and architecture, and timeless art in whichever form it might take. It touches us, it moves us, and it has a way of shifting our state, even if it's just momentary.

Nobody is inspired and uplifted by the experience and imagery of wars, violence, hate, dirty factories, rampant pollution, poverty, starvation, or any sort of pain and suffering, for that matter. Those are all unintelligent outcomes; nobody will argue there's true Joy in any of that. Because it's so hard to face the Truth of this, we generally ignore it and pretend it's not there. It's too painful to internalize the Falsehood of our own collective human making. This holds even true for the deranged sociopath or psychopath because their total lack of any sort of empathy is rooted in their inability to internalize anything they do. The pain of being entirely cut off from your Divinity within is perhaps the cruelest incarnation possible; in that context, it's been said all of them are old souls that have volunteered to serve humanity by being a reflection of total Darkness in this lifetime.

Besides just art, poetry, and beauty in whatever form that might come, we also previously concluded that for there to be true Creativity within creation, the Creation itself must be conducive to Life itself.

This is pointing us again at intelligent outcomes, and so we can start to see how Creativity—playfully bringing beautiful things into expression—is also essential for the emergence of a state of true Joy. We are each a unique puzzle piece in the greater mosaic called humanity. Each with our own unique gifts, talents, and superpowers, and when we authentically express those into Life, we gravitate toward a state of true Joy. This is exactly what we're here to do and experience, and our insistence on living the narrative of our upbringing, culture, societal beliefs, or religions is what's holding us back from accessing true Joy.

We can only do those things in Doing as it's compelling us to do something. Again, when we *must play*, we cannot *play*. Life is beckoning us to express our authentic Self into all of Creation. God, Creator, Spirit, Source, Infinite Intelligence, or whatever label you wish to give it doesn't make any mistakes, so your innate gifts, talents, and superpowers are there to become fully and authentically expressed through a playful zest for Life itself. This is exactly how your Creativity—fully expressed as the spiritual art that you are—is key to knowing true Joy.

> "Joy of life depends on a certain spontaneity in regard to sex. Where sex is repressed, only work remains, and a gospel of work for work's sake has never produced any work worth doing."
> —BERTRAND RUSSELL

True Joy, then, is the coalescence of the nature of Being and the nature of Creativity; these two combined give birth to the depth of true Joy—a *joie de vivre* that supersedes our inevitable peaks and valleys as we make our life journey and adventure through Life itself.

There's another aspect of true Joy worth exploring a bit more, and we alluded to it earlier: erotic and sensual. Let's understand these words correctly, so we have a basis to work from. Erotic means to be, devoted to or tending to the arousal of sexual love or desire. So, it's actually not sex itself; it's the stimulation of arousal. Sensual means relating to or consisting in the gratification of the five senses or pleasurable sensory experiences. So, why do we care?

Life itself—all of Creation—is both erotic and sensual, and so are all of us. It's part of our nature and an integral part of our physical experience here in Earth School, which is Existence. It's no surprise Existence is Feminine as we generally equate eroticism and sensuality with women or those things that are Feminine (e.g., nature) or have Feminine features like curves, soft bends, or flowing lines.

The stigma on eroticism and sensuality stems from the invention of sin by religion, which has been historically punished by imposing shame and guilt. It's important to point out here that all the major Western religions as we know them today are Patriarchal in nature; they were created, written by, and enforced by men. At the time these religions were born, men viewed women as "chattel," private property basically, and this didn't really start to change until about sixty to seventy years ago. For instance, it wasn't until the 1970s that a married woman could get a credit card without her husband's approval. That's only fifty years ago, so let's not romanticize history here or obscure the facts, no matter how ugly they are.

As chattel, women not only had no rights, but just like a man didn't want to share the milk of his goats and cows, he didn't like sharing any of his "chattel." So, chastity was imbedded within religious doctrine to forbid her from what was deemed unlawful sexual intercourse. To this day, in many Islamic countries, women and girls fall victim to the savagery of honor killings by male family members, even if their so-called chastity or purity was lost due to rape or abuse. All modern-day religious precepts of sin, shame, and guilt stem from a time in human history when women were domestic slaves. No more or less than the goat her husband owned. Literally, he could use, abuse, violate, and even kill her without recourse. This was all within his right to do so.

I know these subjects are sensitive and disturbing even, but if we are not willing to truthfully see where many of the Falsehoods surrounding sex and eroticism in our culture come from, we'll never be able to outgrow them. These antiquated religious precepts of sin, guilt, and shame are still deeply entrenched in our culture to this day, so we see all sorts of puritan dogma which suppresses the natural and healthy expression of eroticism and sensuality into a cultural pressure cooker. The excess pressure created is then released in all sorts of vulgarities, artificial promiscuities, and sexual overindulgence (here it is again) that only serves to have the puritans dial up the sin pressure.

There's also a misnomer that a truly spiritual person somehow is above eroticism and sensuality, as if they're no longer human.

In religion, we see this reflected in the celibacy pledge of Priests, which we know has only served as its own pressure cooker with devastating consequences, as evidenced by the countless abuses that have surfaced over the years. The simple fact is, denying our sexual nature is denying our humanness. We should celebrate it, not suppress it.

Celebrating the eroticism, sensuality, and even sexuality of Life itself can be a beautiful expression of Love and true Joy. We should even relax the handbrake a bit on our aversion to all forms of nudity. From an evolutionary perspective, it wasn't that long ago that humans lived mostly exposed or totally naked. Even today, many Indigenous cultures still live this way, which again demonstrates these practices are cultural in nature, not fixed human nature. Suppression of our true nature leads to pressure, which then needs to be released. Usually, this comes out sideways and with excess force. I am by no means suggesting we should all go strut bare-naked to work or use public parks to indulge in whatever sexual expression we feel like. But embracing eroticism, sensuality, and sexuality as normal human expressions would be a major step in addressing all the frustrated expressions of these things that come out in destructive, vulgar, and even violent and abusive ways.

Case in point is the whole porn industry. Demand creates supply, not the other way around. The demand stems largely from the inhibition and frustration of erotic, sensual, and sexual expression, which fuels a porn industry that takes advantage of an endless supply of mostly young and vulnerable girls and women. Of course, nobody ever watches porn, yet they have billions of viewers. Go figure.

Finally, sex as an expression of true Love is a beautiful and sacred experience rooted in true Joy. Sex, as an expression of lust, is seeking pleasure for the sake of diversion; this is escapism. But we should not confuse relationship status or preferences with any of this. That's applying a moral code to what is ultimately just one expression—whether erotic, sensual, or sexual—of our nature as human beings. Moral codes are personal and culturally dependent as they vary from culture to culture. In some Indigenous cultures, partners are shared, or there's a lot of leeway. The Mormon and Islamic faiths allow for multiple wives, something we generally strongly condemn in Western culture. But provided these wives have a free will sovereign choice in this, who's to say what's morally right? If we wish to be in a monogamous relationship—perhaps even be married—we should pursue and express this and make sure we find a partner who's equally devoted to the same principles. Others might prefer other forms of relationship, whatever that might be. What others wish to do is for them to decide; we don't need to judge the experiences others wish to have in their lifetime. We must trust that nobody can escape their Karmic responsibility and all Karmic debts are eventually to be settled with the universe.

However, as an expression of true Love, sex is always consensual, respectful, loving, honoring, and engaged in with a deep sense of gratitude and devotion. Within those boundaries, there's no sin, shame, or guilt in how consenting adults agree to express themselves sexually. Monogamy, polyamory, sexual preferences, or whatever kinky fantasies consenting adults wish to experience as true Joy is a private matter and just their free will choice.

If you have any doubts that lovemaking and sexual pleasure can be an access point to experience your Divinity, just know the Kama Sutra—an ancient Indian Sanskrit text—is a sacred text devoted to sexuality, eroticism, and the emotional fulfillment in life. The authentic or classical Tantra Yoga (note: not the neo-Tantra that's predominant in the West) is an ancient practice that originated from Hinduism and Buddhism, is over 5,000 years old, and is devoted to weaving together spirituality, sexuality, and mindfulness to advance the sacred union of the Masculine and the Feminine. In fact, in classical Tantra, you make love in order to find God through sacred pleasure, so pleasure is the vehicle in classical Tantric lovemaking but not the destination. Having said all that, we should also note that sexuality is perhaps only 10 percent of the classical Tantra teachings as it's a holistic framework of yogic teachings toward the attainment of spiritual enlightenment, whereas neo-Tantra tends to focus mostly on that 10 percent sexuality aspect and pleasure is made the destination. Both the Kama Sutra and classical Tantra are sacred wisdom teachings that allow for a full expression of sexuality as it recognizes it as part of our true nature as human beings, yet both are also grounded in true Love, spiritual attainment, and mindfulness.

> "It's love that gives joy to happiness."
> —RUMI

Ultimately, all true Joy doesn't just come from the coalescence of Being and Creativity, but it's rooted in Love. Self-love, first and foremost, as the expression of our authentic Self originates from self-love—the deep knowing that we are worthy of full expression.

It's also rooted in Love because true Joy doesn't inflict any undue injury, pain, harm, or suffering on others. Our *joie de vivre* cannot come at the expense of the *joie de vivre* of others, with the notable exception that we are not responsible for the fragile Minds of others. When our genuine and authentic expression of *joie de vivre* offends others as it conflicts with their dogmatic, enculturated beliefs, the responsibility lies with the one offended. Taking offense to something is a perception—a psychological construct—which means it's not real or a Falsehood. None of us needs to dial down or alter our *joie de vivre* for a Falsehood held onto by others. We can respectfully distance ourselves, not engage in argumentative dialogue, or opt to voluntarily make an adjustment, provided none of this diminishes our true Joy. In most cases, it wouldn't, as there's no true Joy in willfully offending others for the spiritually mature.

What Rumi's quote illuminates is that it's this Love embedded in Joy that infuses or elevates happiness to the level of Joy. Happiness then shifts from something we experience from time to time to a state of Being.

We call that state true Joy.

Joy is the first virtuous Gift of the Feminine to the Masculine because through her—Existence—formless Consciousness gets to revel, exult, delight, and play in Life itself. Without the Feminine—all of Creation—there is no sensory experience, so there can be no true Joy or sorrow, for that matter. In Life itself, we can experience formless potentialities in the Infinite Field of Possibilities becoming palpable actualities. All the magnificent expressions of art, poetry, beauty, talent, ingenuity, and imagination, including everything ranging from sensuality to sexuality and relationship to friendship, are only possible in Life itself. Seeing all of this is what gives rise to true Joy, a *joie de vivre* that permeates our entire expression and experience of Life itself regardless of the inevitable ebbs and flows of Life.

Which, incidentally, is the perfect segue into the second virtuous Gift of the Feminine to the Masculine: Peace.

CHAPTER 22
PEACE

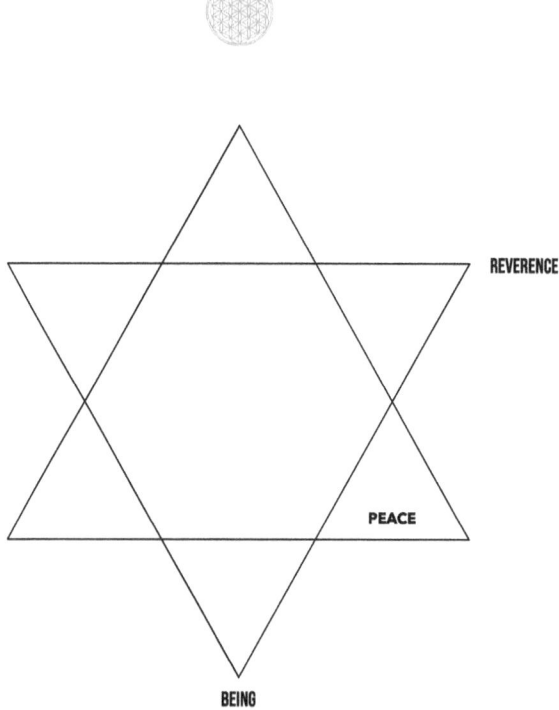

THE PARADOXICAL NATURE OF Peace is that it can't be found in seeking to force—which is a form of *doing*—an ocean of Order within a world of intrinsic Chaos. Peace comes from *being* a world of intrinsic Order within an ocean of Chaos. So, Peace in the context of being spiritual art is learning to be with what is; let's dive in to explore why.

You cannot change the nature of nature itself. The Feminine—Existence or all of Creation—cannot be tamed or robbed of her innate wildness or yearning for freedom, which is to say imprisoned, enslaved, or subdued. She—Life itself—is a kinetic force field that cannot be controlled as she's a wild raging river of aliveness, perpetually in motion and therefore ever-dynamic, ever-changing, and ever-evolving. Chaos is her intrinsic nature, and it's absolutely beautiful and divine.

The Peace we're all seeking and so desperately desire is locked within the treasury of our intrinsic Order deep within, but it coalesces, arises from, and is activated by the Feminine constituent attributes Being and Reverence; hence it's a Gift from the Feminine to the Masculine.

Let's explore this, starting with Being.

When looking more closely at the nature of Being, we are always confronted with the underlying premise of Finite Games—when we *must play*, we cannot *play*. When we *must play* in Finite Games, which is to say we're lost in playing Finite Games, we get inherently caught up in competition. So much so we're entirely blind to the true nature of competition; we even become religious about competition itself, which is a Falsehood.

Competition is a cousin of Force, which means it's not peaceful, otherwise known as violent. Competition serves no other purpose than to determine winners and losers. As we discovered earlier, there can be no winner unless at least one other loses, as you cannot win a game that only has one player. Finite Games, therefore, always have more than one player. The purpose, then, of Finite Games we *must play* is to annihilate the competition, which is all others.

The devotees and staunch defenders of the religion of competition attribute virtually all acquired progress, advancement, and excellence of competitors in Finite Games to competition, and they love to point to Darwinism as evidence this is our true nature and the nature of nature itself. We already discussed the Falsehood in that interpretation of Darwinism as he pointed to the species most able to adapt will survive and not the species strongest or fittest by annihilating its so-called competitors.

At a fundamental level, all of nature is premised on coexistence and interdependence. Yes, there's a food chain, which implies some life forms are killed and eaten by other life forms, but this phenomenon is not rooted in competition but in coexistence. A wolf does not compete with sheep, he/she coexists with sheep, and they are also a food source. But a wolf will not go and kill an entire herd of sheep only to eat one. He will prey and kill the weakest, serving evolution in that way, and peacefully coexist with the rest of the herd. Death and things dying off are a natural part of the cycle of life, which is an integral part of nature and all of evolution. Preying and killing so *all* other life forms die off is not part of nature as it undermines and collapses the diversity within the ecosystem, thereby ultimately destroying it.

> "No great work of art is ever finished."
> —MICHELANGELO

So, what about competition as a driving force of progress, advancement, and excellence? All of these are truthfully accidental byproducts of competition, not inherent outcomes of competition as they might appear to us. We can see this more clearly when we examine why we might play any Finite Game. When we *must play*, we compete for trophies. When we're able to freely choose to play, we play for the love of the game.

When we compete for trophies, we're extrinsically motivated—forced, basically—to progress, advance, and excel. When the competition weakens or slows down, our progress, advancement, and excellence diminish correspondingly. A very clear example of this phenomenon is once monopolistic or duopolistic powers have been established in markets. This inherently leads to a slowdown and stifling of progress, advancement, and excellence as lethargy sets in. Organizations get bloated, bureaucratic, inertial, and become preoccupied with extrapolating all possible excess profits from their dominant market position while fiercely defending their claimed turf, as the actual goal deeply embedded in competition is to eliminate all competition. The goal of competition is annihilation—not progress, advancement, or excellence. The belief it is, therefore, is a Falsehood, which, regretfully, much of our deeply flawed modern theory of economics is premised on.

True progress, advancement, and excellence can only come from playing for the love of the game. We cannot play any Finite Game for the love of the game unless we can freely choose to play it, and this—as we now know—can only come from one place: we must first freely choose to play *the* one Infinite Game.

Within playing for the love of the game, progress, advancement, and excellence become an intrinsic goal; in fact, it becomes the whole reason we play the game. Let's take Michelangelo. When he saw David in the block of marble, he didn't set out for perfection because he was competing to become the best sculptor of the Italian Renaissance; neither was Leonardo da Vinci's dedication to his craft based on competing with anyone when he created the Vitruvian Man or any of his other countless works of art (and science). These men were playing for the love of the game; they sought progress, advancement, and excellence for the sheer desire and purpose to see how close they could come to experiencing divine perfection here on the Earthly plane doing Earthly things in physical reality. They sought to perfect themselves through the perfection of their artistic and scientific expression. They were never in competition with anyone but perhaps themselves; in turn, they were always in Peace as long as they were pursuing this excellence.

Now, none of the above should be confused with the necessity of meritocracy to be the governing principle of an organically harmonious society, industry, business, organization, group, or team. Fundamentally, when nepotism, favoritism, wealth, access, power, influence, underachievement, and identity markers such as race, creed, gender, and nationality are allowed to skew merit— talent, effort, and achievement—a disharmony in the natural order is created. Nature doesn't operate on this premise, and meritocracy itself is color-blind so it's never the cause of the effect called systemic bias. Trophies for eighth place appease the weak at the expense of damaging the integrity of the whole. Positive discrimination is no cure for discrimination, it just redirects the systemic bias elsewhere. To affect systemic change, you must—by definition—systematically change the system or in other words create a new system.

Getting back to the creation of art. You and I are spiritual art, and so is all of Creation, which includes nature, this entire universe, but most definitely everything mankind designs, creates, invents, builds, or brings into all of Creation. Other than drawing on our inner fire to progress, advance, and excel ourselves—including whatever craft we choose to bring into Creation—competition is a misguided framework to draw that progress, advancement, and excellence out of us, as there cannot be Peace within us as long as we're competing to squash, corner, outrun, outmaneuver, outsmart, or outhustle any so-called competitors. This goes for individuals, politics, business, sports, music, nonprofits, countries, religions, or what have you. There's simply no Peace within competition, and it's a Falsehood to attribute progress, advancement, and excellence to competition. It's merely an accidental byproduct that all but evaporates once the extrinsic motivation falls away.

Here I am going to share an analogy that might appear out of context, as world-class athletes might not seem to hold much resemblance to some of the great masters and teachers in history I mostly reference throughout this book. This is a limiting perception as all that's pursued at the level of true mastery holds within it the nucleus of spiritual art. What we pursue mastery in is somewhat inconsequential; some of us are born to build beautiful businesses, others to create inspiring art or music, and yet others to parent or become teachers of some sort. And, clearly, some were born to contribute the respective gifts of Buddha, Einstein, Gandhi, and da Vinci to the history of this Earthly plane. It's only when we start harming ourselves, others, or all of Creation that this pursuit of mastery falls short of being an expression of spiritual art.

So, here we go with some remarkable athletes. No matter how good he was, Bjorn Borg was extrinsically motivated in chasing tennis trophies and retired a disillusioned man by age twenty-eight. Roger Federer was still going after it at age forty and tearfully said goodbye to the game when his body finally couldn't endure the stresses of competition at the elite level. Yet he said farewell with a smile on his face and was the first to congratulate Rafael Nadal when he surpassed him in Grand Slam titles. Roger was intrinsically motivated; he truly played for the love of the game. Whoever says true excellence in sports comes from competition either doesn't know Roger, doesn't know tennis, or both. There are countless sports examples like this, and it becomes even more evident when it concerns a sport where there's no big money to be gained.

It's also important to note that some sports icons start out chasing trophies but end up finding their true love of the game. When they do, something about them changes. Michael Jordan is a great example of this; after winning three consecutive NBA titles, he went on to have his try at baseball only to find his true love for the game of basketball. He returned to win another three NBA titles, but he was a changed man and player. He didn't need to play for the money anymore; he was arguably already a legend, so he played to experience and evolve his own excellence, and he became an even better team leader, clutch shooter, and prolific winner because of it. Even more so, despite his incredible drive and ferocious work ethic, he had discovered his inner Peace—something he never quite had before his diversion into baseball.

So, it's pretty obvious already why Being is a constituent attribute essential to true Peace and why being lost in Doing—which has us lost in chasing trophies and therefore competition—almost directly corresponds with true Peace becoming ever-elusive. Arguably, even *illusive* as going against the true nature of nature is a form of illusion, just like believing in the Falsehood of the merits attributed to competition is, no matter how deep-rooted that societal belief is.

> "The day the power of love overrules the love of power, the world will know peace."
> —MAHATMA GANDHI

So, if not competition, then what? Collaboration or cooperation, perhaps? Or maybe "coopetition," which is a relatively new term coined by the worthwhile book with the same title, which advocates a hybrid between competition and cooperation. All of these definitely have a place and merit in their own right; however, if we wish to align with the principles that govern this whole universe, the answer is "coevolution."

The biological definition of coevolution is the reciprocal evolutionary change that occurs between pairs of species or among a group of species as they interact with one another within an ecosystem that itself is also coevolutionary and nested within other ecosystems with which it has interdependent relationships. In this context, species could be any life form (trees, plants, animals, insects, etc.), and ecosystem encompasses anything from soils, mountains, and oceans to weather patterns. Within all of this, we can clearly see one key essence of an Infinite Game rise to the surface—the object of the game is to go on indefinitely, which is to say, for eternity. It's not about any species winning and calling it a game, the object of playing the game is to coevolve and never stop playing.

Coevolution is the process by which self-organizing complex living systems evolve over time. This is what humans are, and so coevolution is a principle that governs us also, no matter how stubbornly we wish to hold onto our illusion that we can write our own rules.

Let's see what this could look like. An economy and world of business based on coevolution would yield a great diversity of businesses (large and small) that would evolve—i.e., progress, advance, and excel—in pairs of businesses or groups of businesses (e.g., industries) within an ecosystem (e.g., society) nested within other ecosystems (e.g., United Nations, biosphere) with which it has interdependent relationships. This new school of economic theory is the basis of Regenerative Economics or Regenerative Capitalism as it's sometimes called.

Regenerative Economics is based on the principles of self-organizing complex living systems and views the economy and capital markets as something that must be organized in service to the greater good of society, humanity and our biosphere with the sole objective not being the creation of just financial wealth but overall holistic wealth with, most importantly, the perpetuation of the game of Life itself as the North Star. Holistic wealth is an inclusive measure of wellness and abundance across all areas that matter to the well-being of human beings, communities, societies, and all of humanity at large. Financial wealth is only one aspect of that, but health, freedom, happiness, joy, equal opportunity, justice, clean water and air, abundant wildlife and nature, etc. are all measures of wealth as well that aren't captured in GDP or other economic indicators. I refer to this as "Sacred Wealth" as it encompasses all that's immeasurably important to each of us, or in other words sacred. Regenerative Economics is premised on creating harmony between various objectives and constraints such as prosperity, fairness, equitable distribution of wealth, equal opportunity, health, well-being, and a thriving home planet, meaning it's able to access its innate regenerative potential.

Our deeply flawed neoclassical theory of free-market economics is premised on infinite compound economic growth in a physical world with finite resources. This math simply doesn't work, nor does the free-market mechanism adequately compensate and correct as the theory argues it does. And, in turn, our capital markets and financial institutions have essentially become the brothels and pimps, respectively, that will recklessly prostitute anything and everything if there's money to be made. Fossil fuels, weaponry, toxic chemicals, harmful foods, unhealthy beverages, addictive substances like nicotine and alcohol, damaging pharmaceuticals, you name it. Ironically, in our collective ignorance, our modern culture reveres these sophisticated peddlers of mass exploitation and destruction, albeit not quite as much as they revere themselves as the rightful masters of this universe. The ignorance in all of it is nothing short of astounding. And I should know, I was one of them at one point, equally ignorant and equally lost in chasing fame, fortune, and applause—questions regarding what I was part of or contributing toward creating never even crossed my mind. If it was legal and profitable, it was perfectly acceptable and in play for me, and of course, those are very loose guidelines that allow for many things which are not conducive to creating a more beautiful world.

Extreme wealth concentration is inevitable within this form of economics, and we've seen that played out since WWII as the wealthiest 1 percent now owns roughly 50 percent of all global wealth, and the top twenty billionaires have more wealth than the entire continent of Africa with c. 1.3 billion people. It's estimated c. 21,000 people die every single day because of this inequality; that's one every four seconds. What this sort of extreme inequitable distribution of wealth breeds is violence, as it requires the use of enormous Force to hold this sort of inequity in place.

What it's truly indicative of is a general level of lovelessness. We love power, wealth, and influence more than we love people or our planet, as those are considered mere inputs into the system, resources that may be readily exploited, extracted, and used up at will. Within this loveless form of self-absorption—which is nothing but unadulterated narcissism in the clever guise of worldly success—there can be neither true Peace within ourselves nor throughout the world as the constituent attribute Reverence is entirely absent from the equation.

Reverence, as we previously uncovered, is the North Star that anchors our entire perception of reality in the Sanctity of all Life. It's only with a deep sense of Reverence for all others—including those that have opposing political views, customs, culture, religious beliefs, lifestyles, or what have you—that we can actually be in true Peace with everyone else. If we cannot find Reverence for others, we're by definition in conflict with them, meaning we're in "them" vs. "us" or "he/she" vs. "me." Division and separation have been introduced, and once there's separation, there can be no true Peace anymore.

> "Being at Peace is the ultimate position of Power."

Our social conditioning might be strong enough so we will not physically or verbally harm, hurt, or abuse them, but this is merely socially tolerating others, which is not the same as *being* in true Peace with them. True Peace means there are no triggers; we can no longer be triggered into any primal emotional response like anger, hatred, rage, animosity, fury, resentment, indignation, frustration, hurt, sadness, etc. All of these negative emotions are the catalyst for revenge, retaliation, violence, and on a larger scale, wars and armed conflicts. The line between these primal emotions and them spilling over into primal actions is thin and fragile. We see this time and again as we might not commit these actions ourselves, but we support, condone, or even applaud them, which is, for all Karmic intents and purposes, the same thing.

Contrary to conventional belief, true Peace is where we come into true Power and rise above Force. To be easily triggered or offended is to be very vulnerable, weak, and fragile, as anyone with a few careless or pointed words can own you in an instant. Once triggered, your primal emotion has free reign, and you will react with Force in the form of hatred, animosity, revenge, retaliation, or violence, whether physically, mentally, or verbally. Basically, just about anyone can squat in the real estate between your ears and easily manipulate you. There's zero Power in that, and so you resort to Force to combat it. When you're impervious to what anyone says—no matter how hostile, offensive, idiotic, or hurtful—you are in a place of true Power. No more squatters in your Mind, you own you fully, so you become entirely immutable, impervious, impenetrable, and invulnerable, and this is the hallmark of real spiritual mastery. Of course, and not to needlessly offend you, this is also known in colloquial terms as becoming entirely *"unfuckwithable,"* which doesn't sound quite as sacrosanct, but it does neatly sum up in one word the spiritual mastery we're pointing at.

Any form of Force is always weakness; only the fragile need to revenge, retaliate, or resort to violence in their ill-fated attempt to restore their Peace within that way. Spiritual mastery is cultivating the ability to forgive the unthinkable, love the impossible, and have compassion for ignorance, knowing the suffering of living in ignorance is a heavy burden to carry in life. This is where true Peace starts to permeate our whole Being.

Reverence is not only essential for true Peace to come into existence toward others but all of Creation. The way we treat animals, trees and plant life, Mother Earth in general, and her delicate biosphere, and even how we consider the entire universe ours to colonize, is devoid of any sort of Peace because there's simply no Reverence for any of it. We're in conflict with all of it, as evidenced by how we exploit, extract, destruct, and pollute ad nauseam and with total disregard.

> "Man must evolve for all human conflict a method which rejects revenge, aggression, and retaliation. The foundation of such a method is love."
> —MARTIN LUTHER KING JR.

Whereas Being and Reverence are the Feminine cornerstones that coalesce to create the virtuous Gift of Peace, all of this acts as a powerful activator of a profound level of Love emanating from deep within the Masculine.

In human relationships, we see this reflected in men and women, but men especially, becoming deeply appreciative, respectful, devoted, honoring, and protective of women and girls. Not only their lovers, daughters, or friends and family but women and girls in general as the representation of the Feminine. Protection here doesn't point at any sort of helplessness, but it points at their treasured value to the whole. In many Indigenous cultures, women and girls have traditionally been honored this way and played a central role within the family, tribe's governance, and spiritual ceremonies. In many Indigenous cultures, the women even select and crown the King, thereby exemplifying their importance to the tribe's overall welfare.

True Peace then—rooted in Being and Reverence—allows a deeply reverent Love for the Feminine to start casting a wider net to society, industry, politics, animals, nature, Mother Earth, and eventually Life itself and all of Creation. We fundamentally shift our beliefs of the role of science, medicine, business, politics, and leadership in general, which can then self-organize as the systemic change needed to elevate all of humanity to a higher level. True Peace, first within and then throughout communities, societies, economies, and across nation borders, is a prerequisite to rise above all forms of Force. As Martin Luther King Jr. (MLK) wisely reminded us, the foundation of such a method is Love; however, Love is not easily accessible amidst war, hatred, violence, inequality, injustice, abject poverty, etc. Hence, the vital importance of true Peace as it makes Love far more accessible, especially for those below levels of consciousness of 200 for whom an innocuous comment can be threatening enough to start a fistfight.

> "Peace comes from within. Do not seek it without."
> —BUDDHA

Peace is the second virtuous Gift from the Feminine to the Masculine as, through this Gift, she guides the Masculine within each of us to go within. Peace is an inside job; we cannot derive it from our Outer World, as the Outer World is merely a reflection of our Inner World. This holds true even collectively, as our collective physical reality is merely a reflection of our collective level of human consciousness within. The Feminine, which is Life itself or Existence, is ever-evolving, dynamic, flowing, and non-linear and, therefore, has inherent Chaos within. There's no Peace in using Force to try to submit Chaos into Order. There are infinite amounts of Peace in being able to gracefully flow with life, to be flexible, and nimble. Our ability to do this comes from connecting with our Peace within, the true source and place of residence of Order. The Feminine, through the virtuous Gift of Peace, makes us resilient, powerful, and sovereign and settles us deeply into a place of total equanimity.

> "It's only when a mosquito lands on your testicles that you realize there's a way to solve problems without using violence."
> —CONFUCIUS

I cannot say with absolute certainty if Confucius ever made this statement, but it's credited to him, and the profound truism makes it a perfect inclusion. Moreover, it points at something else that's essential: a sense of humor. Taking ourselves too seriously is the surefire antidote to having any sort of Peace. The ability to laugh at ourselves, at Life itself, at situations and occurrences is what brings us Peace. After all, in evolutionary terms, we're each just a mere speck of stardust on a big blue dot hurtling through space at dizzying speed. Lighten up, relax; everything is always in perfect order, and being able to revert to this inner Peace time and again is what allows us to refine our spiritual art even when life is giving us proverbial lemons.

> "Peace is always beautiful."
> —WALT WHITMAN

In the same way that Force cannot lead to anything but distortion, which renders anything misshapen, blemished, or unsightly, Peace cannot help but be beautiful, which is a perfect introduction to the third virtuous Gift of the Feminine: Beauty.

CHAPTER 23
BEAUTY

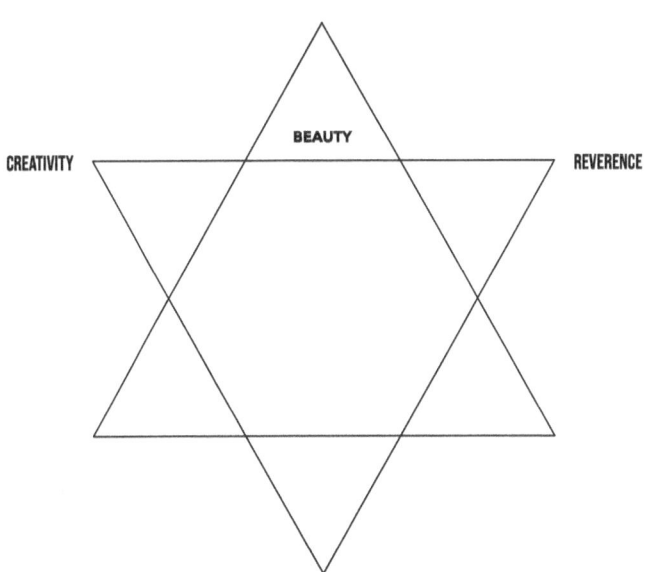

THE PARADOXICAL NATURE OF the virtuous Feminine Gift of Beauty is that all true Beauty knows no time and is sovereign from opinion. All false Beauty is defined by time and derived from opinion.

> "Anything in any way beautiful derives its beauty from itself and asks nothing beyond itself. Praise is no part of it, for nothing is made worse or better by praise."
> —MARCUS AURELIUS

What does this paradoxical nature really mean? "Knows no time" means it's timeless; we see this in all true works of art, music, literature, architecture and design, athletics, and even science and business. We see this abundantly throughout nature, virtuous character traits like integrity and courage, and we can find it in people as well in various ways.

The US Declaration of Independence, MLK's speech "I have a dream," and Lou Gehrig's farewell speech at Yankee Stadium contained Beauty. The 1961 Mako Shark Corvette was among many cars designed in the 1960s that were driving art, so they had Beauty. So did Rosa Parks' courageous bus ride and the real Patch Adams' devotion to spreading health and happiness through holistic medicine. Mathematics and sacred geometry are drenched with true Beauty.

Of course, there's also aesthetic Beauty in people. Marilyn Monroe, Sophia Loren, Paul Newman, and even the Vitruvian Man are some classic examples; decades later, their effervescent aesthetic beauty still captures our imagination. Of course, aesthetic Beauty alone doesn't make anyone perfect or a more valuable person, but we can just acknowledge that true Beauty is timeless as it supersedes fashion and trends.

True Beauty is also sovereign from opinion, meaning it doesn't derive its Beauty from the opinion of others. Not everyone likes Mozart's music, Vincent van Gogh's post-impressionist art, appreciates nature, or sees Marilyn Monroe as beautiful. But it's a hallmark of true Beauty that the opinions of a few or even a larger group doesn't diminish the consensus which is anchored in universality. This is because true Beauty is intrinsically generated, so it doesn't depend on outside validation or recognition. It just is—timeless and sovereign.

False Beauty, on the other hand, is defined by time and opinion. Fashion and trends are mostly false Beauty; once their heyday passes, we come to see them as non-pleasing or even hideous. Displays of military prowess, such as opulent parades by the Nazis and the former Soviet Union, are false Beauty despite the cheering onlookers as they didn't stand the test of time and were based on the validation and recognition of a few. Please don't nod in agreement and believe US military parades are any different; all of them are false Beauty, as we'll come to discover later.

Much of urban design since WWII is false Beauty as the concrete jungles they created have led to incredible degradation and degeneration of nature and the quality of Life itself. Slavery, the imperial conquest of the Americas to the detriment of Indigenous cultures, and the still ongoing barbaric cruelty of whaling by the Japanese are all false Beauty, no matter that there was a time this was considered Beauty by some. All of these examples demonstrate that so-called Beauty generated extrinsically is destined to yield false Beauty in the end.

> "True beauty lies in purity of the heart."
> —MAHATMA GANDHI

Regretfully, in people, we can also see false Beauty emerge from an ill-fated attempt to create true Beauty extrinsically. There's a whole wildly lucrative industry that feeds off people disconnected from their inner Beauty by selling them the notion that all sorts of harmful beauty products, Botox, tummy tucks, breast implants, painful hair removal, etc., will give them true Beauty. This industry feasts especially on the insecurities of women created by the relentless cultural messaging of an impossible beauty standard. All of this starts as early as the first Barbie doll little girls get, as no woman has the shape, figure, and proportions of a Barbie doll naturally. For the rest of her life, she will be bombarded with images and messaging of the so-called "perfect" woman, most of which doesn't really exist as virtually all of it is photoshopped or edited. Yet, the underlying subliminal message is pervasive: your worth is in your extrinsic Beauty. To some extent, we've seen this same phenomenon rise with men as the beauty industry realized they were leaving a lot of money on the table by ignoring men and the same tactics work equally effectively.

There are green sprouts though, as in more recent years, there's a movement emerging that is centered around timeless natural Beauty using the countless beauty medicines available from nature and healthy lifestyle habits. There's also nothing inherently wrong with freely expressing yourself authentically through the elegance or pizzazz of your wardrobe, jewelry, body art, or overall look, including hairstyle and grooming preferences, whether you're male or female. When your unique sense of style is derived intrinsically, you liberate yourself from enculturated fashion beliefs, and this is how true Beauty has the chance to blossom from within. Never worry about others' opinions; that's not where true Beauty comes from.

> "Never lose an opportunity of seeing anything beautiful, for beauty is God's handwriting."
> —RALPH WALDO EMERSON

Intuitively and throughout mankind's history, true Beauty has always been associated with the Feminine, with women being the quintessential earthly representation of the Feminine. It's not surprising then that Beauty is one of the virtuous Feminine Gifts to the Masculine as this Gift is derived from the coalescence of the Feminine cornerstones of Creativity and Reverence.

Let's explore why this is.

As we discovered in the earlier chapter on Creativity, this word is derived from the Latin word *creare*, which means to create, to make, or to produce. The antonym then is to destroy, to destruct, or unproduced. We also discovered what this directly points at is the intelligence of Life itself or *that* which is conducive to Life itself.

That which destroys, destructs, or is unproduced leads to rotting, decay, withering, and eventually death. This is why anything that contains these elements leads to false Beauty at best, but more likely just ugliness of some sort. Polluting industries, gore-filled video games, disharmonious music, GMO foods, and lab "foods" like most fake meats, toxic chemicals, deforestation, war, violence, and hate are all examples of *that* which is not conducive to Life itself. They might be lucrative and highly profitable, but that's not what creates true Beauty.

The many beauty industry examples I gave earlier also fall squarely in this bucket. Most conventional beauty and fashion products are rife with toxic chemicals and devastating for both the user and the environment. The carbon footprint of the global fast fashion industry alone is an environmental catastrophe, not to mention the ongoing prevalence of sweatshops in the fashion industry as a whole. Breast implant inflammation (BII) is a well-documented illness that has wrecked the health of tens (if not hundreds) of thousands of women worldwide, yet the plastic surgery industry keeps implanting with impunity. None of this is conducive to Life itself, so it cannot yield true Beauty as it violates the principles of true Creativity.

I am not judging anyone with breast implants or dismissing that in some cases—like reconstructive surgery after mastectomies—the underlying root cause is medical in nature and not primarily vanity. But the question to ponder is why does our culture judge a woman's desirability and worth by the size and perkiness of her breasts? Are aging and gravity not facts of life? My male body doesn't look the same as it did when I was twenty-two, and I never had to breastfeed, either. The incongruence I am pointing at is that opinion-derived Beauty is a psychological construct; it's not real. True Beauty is sovereign; it's not derived from opinion or praise.

We also discovered true Creativity is ever dynamic, flowing, novel, inspires, and uplifts. Creativity gives birth to things; it's the giver of Life itself. There's a palpable freedom of expression and certain raw bravery and courage in true Creativity as it brings the yet unknown into physical reality or Existence. We can always recognize these qualities in true Beauty, which are all derived from the constituent attribute Creativity.

Reverence is the Feminine constituent attribute that centers around the Sanctity of all Life and relationship to and with all others. Others here could be people but also societies, economies, businesses, animals, wildlife, or Mother Earth at large. We live in relationship to and with all of it. The predominance of reductionism in our logical thinking conveniently overlooks all these embedded relationships, which is the main reason we violate the Sanctity of all Life left and right. Reductionism even gives us rational justifications for doing so, which is why humanity—collectively—readily justifies away wars, violence, racism, inequalities, injustices, rampant pollution, etc., based mostly on a complete identification with political ideologies, theories like neoclassical economics, religion, and patriotism just to name a few.

This is exactly why US military parades and showcasing of military prowess are equally steeped in false Beauty despite the widespread fanbase that sees Beauty in it. Anything created, designed, or used to kill, maim, destroy or decimate does not honor the Sanctity of all Life. Hence, it doesn't meet the principles of true Reverence and can, therefore, never yield something of true Beauty. The same holds for industry, banking, science, medicine, politics, art, music, athletics, or what have you that doesn't honor the Sanctity of Life or is not conducive to Life itself. Without Reverence and honoring the Sanctity of all Life, all they can create at best is false Beauty, which is illusionary Beauty.

That's not to say none of these have the inherent capacity to create true Beauty. There are many examples of companies that have centered their business model around the principles of Regenerative Economics or its agricultural cousin Regenerative Agriculture, thereby honoring the principles of both Creativity and Reverence while still succeeding commercially. In the field of integrative medicine, thought leaders like Zach Bush, MD, and Dr. Mark Hyman are creating true Beauty in the world of holistic health and well-being. Despite the many reflections of Darkness in the world today, humanity as a whole is creating all sorts of true Beauty as it always has throughout history. We just also create a lot of false Beauty, mostly because we're monomaniacally entranced with playing Finite Games and have subscribed to measuring success exclusively in terms of money, material gain, status, power, and influence.

> "Love is beauty, and beauty is Truth, and that is why in the beauty of a flower, we can see the Truth of the universe."
> —BUDDHA

All of Creation, including every single one of us, is an individualized expression of Source Consciousness, and in that sense, we are each a unique piece of Divine spiritual art expressed into Existence. In fact, all there is, ever existed, and ever will be is Divine Creation expressed into Life itself but let's zone in on humans for now.

True Beauty as an expression is what gives us infinite potentialities to experience ourselves as Divine spiritual art. In the same way, false Beauty or ugliness is simply the opposite pole of this expression and, therefore, experience. The one Infinite Game is a game centered around how much art, poetry, and true Beauty you can bring into your expression of being spiritual art.

When we see authentic true Beauty reflected in the expression of another person or anything for that matter, it touches us deeply. We might be in awe, inspired, mesmerized, captivated, feel empowered, or are just rendered breathless. This is because true Beauty has a very powerful energetic field, as its high frequency has the capacity to uplift our vibration through sympathetic resonance. This isn't limited to mere pleasing aesthetic Beauty. Grace, elegance, sensuality, nobility, chivalry, care, integrity, courage, intelligence, kindness, compassion, and Love are all intrinsically generated expressions of true Beauty as well.

We all know this to be true because when we're—for example—confronted with arrogance, distaste, cowardice, dishonesty, rudeness, hostility, hate, anger, rage, negligence, or indifference, we equally viscerally feel the low frequency of these expressions of ugliness lower our vibration. Prolonged exposure to these low frequencies will have us spiral into feeling self-doubt, unworthiness, and depression. In extreme cases, it can even lead to causing self-harm, like suicide. Ugliness is destructive to Life itself.

The realization our expression of self-poetry—or lack thereof—has such an outsized effect on the world around us is a moment of transformation on our awakening journey. The pathway is now cleared to shift from living a life centered around survival, which is self-interest, to being in service to the whole. When this realization leads to a commitment—which is a decision we make—to become a true spiritual artist of self-poetry, a whole new realm of potentialities becomes available to us.

To better understand why, let's look a little closer at the word "decision." Decision is derived from the Latin words "de," which means "off," and "caedere," which means "to cut." So, decision really means "to cut off." When we make a genuine decision, we cut off all other options or alternatives. So, when we make the decision to fully commit to our highest expression of self-poetry, we are cutting off the options or alternatives that aren't reflective of self-poetry. We're cutting off ugliness in a decisive commitment to bring true Beauty into the world through our expression of self-poetry.

That's actually not the only thing we cut off; this decision also cuts off our entanglement with our enculturation, conditioned thinking, and limited beliefs that hold us back from expressing our highest form of self-poetry. These entanglements usually run very deep and can be stubborn, so this isn't an overnight process, but our decision is the first cut-off, and as the saying goes, the first cut is the deepest. We might then have to saw for a while to jettison all these entanglements. Inevitably though, the more true Beauty we bring into our self-poetry, the more ugliness gets crowded out until there's very little left. This is like the proverbial green grasses growing strong and healthy, which leaves no room for the weeds.

Now, in addition to the medicinal effect this has on all we touch and encounter, the true renaissance occurs within us. Cultivating our intrinsic true Beauty—which we each have in spades—has us come fully alive. Our rising vibration and frequency are something that we get to experience as inner joy, happiness, fulfillment, purpose, health, vitality, and a deep connection with our true essence as a spiritual expression of divine art. The outside world will witness this in an organic radiance, luminosity, charisma, and presence that we embody.

This isn't just glossy hyperbole to sucker you into becoming a marginally nicer and kinder person. True Beauty is intrinsically generated and motivated; nobody can lure you into it. The sole place this can come from is your free will decision to commit to self-poetry to fulfill a deep inner desire to experience all the possible art, poetry, and true Beauty that's within you.

I am merely pointing out where to look for it. Once you know, you cannot unknow.

> "When I am working on a problem, I never think about beauty but when I have finished, if the solution is not beautiful, I know something is wrong."
> —R. BUCKMINSTER FULLER

The virtuous Feminine Gift of true Beauty holds the golden key for the Masculine to have the true essence of Life itself revealed. Existence represents Chaos as it's nonlinear, ever-changing, dynamic, volatile, wild, adaptive, messy, and unpredictable. The perfection in Life itself is in its imperfections. In everything and anything of true Beauty, there's a blemish to be found. Even the greatest work of art like the statue of David, the Sistine Chapel, and Beethoven's 5th Symphony have blemishes, however minute or negligible. Even the most handsome man or beautiful woman has imperfections, aesthetically or otherwise. In our physical reality, even the straightest architectural wall is crooked if you magnify or scrutinize it deep enough. Even if it theoretically wasn't originally, eventually, it will become crooked because the earth moves.

No human alive is flawless. Even the person with the highest levels of Integrity and virtue will occasionally make a misstep. But it's the decision to commit to our highest possible form of self-poetry that has us move in the direction of perfection and realize our full human potential available to us in this lifetime. And true Beauty in all its various forms is our divine yardstick, whereas producing ugliness in whatever form is a telltale sign we're off course. As within true Beauty, we know we have honored and lived by the principles of Creativity and Reverence.

The three invaluable virtuous Gifts of the Feminine—Joy, Peace, and Beauty—are arguably the most underappreciated, undervalued, and sullied qualities in our still Masculine-energy dominant Patriarchal world. Our priorities remain highly skewed toward gaining worldly success at any cost. Honoring the three virtuous Gifts of the Feminine as essential qualities and necessities of what a truly rich life constitutes would go a very long way toward eliminating the many aberrations, distortions, and pain and suffering we witness in the world today.

For the spiritual Poet devoted to his or her craft, our spiritual art becomes a reflection of the refinement and finesse with which we're able to paint with all the six Gifts on the canvas of Life itself. In this way, living and being these Gifts is what crowds out the shadow expressions of the Gifts, which are of the Ego and lower octaves of consciousness.

As we conclude this Part III, we have now completed The Architecture and The Gifts within the Love+Truth Framework, which leaves us with the third and final part of the framework. Even though fundamental to the artistry and mastery of our spiritual art, the virtuous Gifts of both the Masculine and Feminine alone will not get us to the creation of a more beautiful world. The universe has its own natural laws and principles that govern us, which we must align with.

That's what we're going to explore next in Part IV—The Principles.

> "Beauty of whatever kind, in its supreme development, invariably excites the sensitive soul to tears."
> —EDGAR ALLAN POE

PART IV

THE PRINCIPLES

"The first peace, which is the most important,
is that which comes within the souls of people
when they realize their relationship, their oneness
with the universe and all its powers. And, when they
realize that at the center of the universe dwells
the Great Spirit, and that this center is really
everywhere, it is within each of us."

—BLACK ELK

CHAPTER 24

COHERENCE ILLUMINATES THE PRINCIPLES

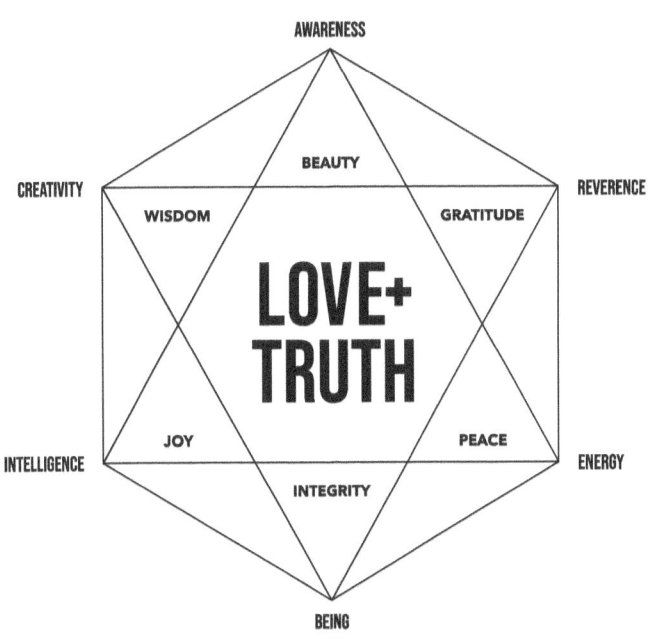

AS THE LOVE+TRUTH FRAMEWORK is now starting to take form, we're ready to reveal another layer which we'll do through discussing the six Principles, which are immutable laws that govern this entire universe. These six Principles—Oneness, Compassion, Growth, Health, Abundance, and Harmony—are best seen as universal design principles rather than part building regulations, which get us into potential code violation trouble. The Principles are absolutely essential, but this isn't about sin, shame, or guilt for violating or ignoring them. The Principles help us understand, at a fundamental level, the province within which *the* one Infinite Game is played and the dynamics that govern the game so we can perfect our spiritual mastery, awaken to our full potential, and elevate our spiritual art.

To get started, we're going to expand on the evolving sacred geometry shape that underpins the entire Love+Truth Framework.

First, we will add *coherence* to the Merkaba. When something has coherence, or we add coherence to something, we're pointing at the quality of forming a unified whole. Within coherence, there's unity, connectedness, integrity, continuity, and/or harmony. We saw coherence earlier in connection with energy, which can be in coherence or dissonance. Music or sound can also be in coherence or dissonance, where we experience coherence as pleasing and harmonious and dissonance as off-key or false notes.

We add coherence by drawing a line from each Masculine and Feminine constituent attribute to the next. As you'll probably note, this connects each Masculine cornerstone with a Feminine cornerstone and vice versa. Hence, we're creating coherence by forming a unified whole that's continuous and connected and, therefore, in total harmony.

What becomes visible by adding coherence is another sacred geometry shape—the perfect hexagon or, in layman's terms, the honeycomb shape. What the coherence lines also create is six new open spaces—coherence illuminates the Principles.

> "Evolution is the law of Life. Number is the law of the Universe. Unity is the law of God."
> —PYTHAGORAS

We'll explore shortly how coherence illuminates the six Principles, but before we do that, though, there's a bit more sacred geometry to explore to start forming a deeper understanding of how this entire universe has an underlying mystical mathematical poetry that forms the basis of all of Creation. This mathematical poetry is deeply interwoven into sacred geometry, and so peeling back the various layers reveals much of this mystery that's been known by mankind for millennia. We know this because these sacred geometry symbols we're about to explore were found in the pyramids of ancient Egypt, the Forbidden City in China, and in Mayan ruins, among many other sacred sites the world over.

Let's start with Leonardo da Vinci's Vitruvian Man, which was modeled by Leonardo after the Golden Ratio. I'll spare you the mathematical equation of the Golden Ratio, which is called Phi (φ) in math, but the magical number to remember is 1.618. This is not to be confused with Pi (), which is 3.142 and represents the ratio of the circumference of any circle to its diameter. Incidentally, both of these very special mathematical numbers are rounded at three decimals, as Phi and Pi are both irrational numbers that go on into infinity after the decimal point without ever repeating themselves.

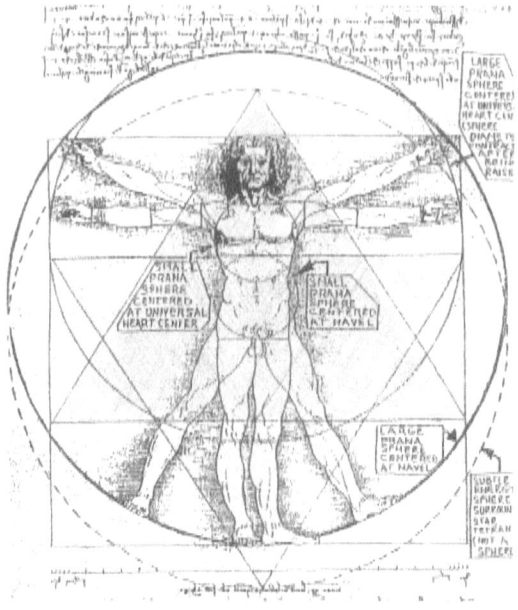

The Vitruvian Man is considered to be the most well-known and iconic piece of art in the world, which is somewhat ironic because it was a working drawing. What's not so well-known is that Leonardo had a habit of burying mystical wisdom in his artwork, including writing from right to left to obscure this mystical wisdom, as, during his lifetime, all of that was considered blasphemy by the still omnipotent Roman Catholic Church. If you're interested, you can go on your own scavenger hunt, as it's beyond the scope of this book to explain all of them. But, within the Vitruvian Man, you can find the exact interior angle (51.783 degrees) and placement of the chambers of the Great Pyramid at Giza, the seven main human Chakras, and the 1/14 master key to squaring the circle using only a straightedge and a compass in a finite number of steps. Moreover, the ancient Egyptian myth of the Divine King Osiris is referenced as well.

The Osiris myth involves his brother Seth and his wife, the Goddess Isis, and is all about resurrection, which is the sacred ritual that took place within the King's chamber of the Great Pyramid of Giza. Leonardo's life is very well-documented as he was already legendary during his lifetime and each work of art, scientific discovery, notebooks of sketches and drawings, and his whereabouts were all dated and cataloged. Except for two years, from c. 1576-78, he disappeared off the face of the Earth.

However, there's a letter in his archives that left a lot of obscure clues as it refers to Bull Mountain and then speaks of all sorts of details in symbolism. Most academic scholars have been puzzled by what this letter actually conveys. Those that are familiar with the mystery school teaching of Thoth, Hermes, and Mercury know exactly what this letter is conveying. I'll give you a hint: in ancient times, the Giza plateau was called "RosTau," which is the anagram of TauRos or Taurus, which of course, means Bull.

Leonardo spent two years in Egypt and was initiated in the ancient mystery school teachings; we know this for a fact because of all the hidden symbolism in his other famous work—"The Last Supper"—which has all sorts of references to the King's chamber down to the exact dimensions and placement of secret sacred murals within this otherwise entirely unmarked chamber. None of this is really surprising since Pythagoras, Aristotle, Plato, and Socrates were all similarly initiated. Later we'll connect some more dots and tie all of this into alchemy or "turning lead into gold and silver."

Let's now continue and explore how Leonardo created the perfect geometry of the Vitruvian Man using the Quadrivium art and science of numbers. The Fibonacci Sequence is very closely related to the Golden Ratio; in fact, as it goes higher and higher, it almost perfectly approaches the Golden Ratio. The Fibonacci Sequence works as follows: Starting with 1, you simply add the previous number each time. This creates the sequence 1, 1, 2, 3, 5, 8, 13, 21, 34, 55, 89, 144, etc. You might not recognize this numerical sequence, but if you look at the graphical display of this sequence, you'll immediately recognize the Fibonacci Sequence:

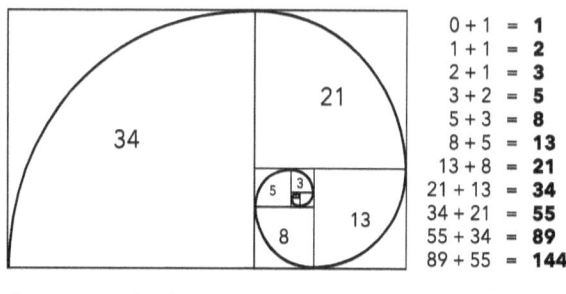

0, 1, 2, 3, 5, 8, 13, 21, 34, 55, 89, 144...

The Golden Ratio and the Fibonacci Sequence are remarkable as we see this growth pattern and proportionality literally everywhere in the universe, from how galaxies expand, to how hurricanes develop and rabbits breed to the shells of sea creatures. We also see it in architecture and proportions of all living forms, including humans. The Golden Ratio was what inspired Leonardo to create the Vitruvian Man in proportions to Phi. Generally speaking, the Golden Ratio is closely linked to true Beauty—things in these proportions resonate with our visual senses on a very deep level.

We can also see how the Merkaba relates to the perfectly proportioned Vitruvian Man, but there's much more sacred geometry hidden here that we're now ready to reveal. We've discovered earlier that the 2D Merkaba becomes the Star Tetrahedron or simply Merkaba in 3D. Since the 2D Merkaba is symbolic of the 3D Merkaba, we can simply use the name Merkaba, and both are implied. If you recall, the Merkaba is what creates our Light Body.

Flower of Life

Merkaba (2D)

Star Tetrahedron

The above graphic is superimposed on what's called the *Flower of Life*, one of the most sacred symbols in all of sacred geometry, but let's start small. What's also visible in the above graphic is that the (2D) Merkaba reveals thirteen circles which are highlighted with bold. Except the center circle, these circles are all connected in their respective center point by a vertex of the Masculine or Feminine triangle or the connecting lines between these vertices. These thirteen circles are called the *Fruit of Life*, which is embedded within the *Flower of Life*.

Now we're ready to take the Architecture and Gifts we discovered in Parts II and III, respectively, and recreate them within the *Fruit of Life*.

You might wonder what goes in the very center. That will come a little later as there's also new sacred geometry that has revealed itself: *Metatron's Cube*.

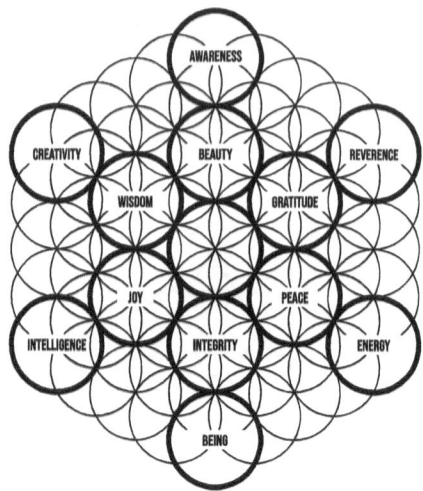

Fruit of Life
(within Flower of Life)

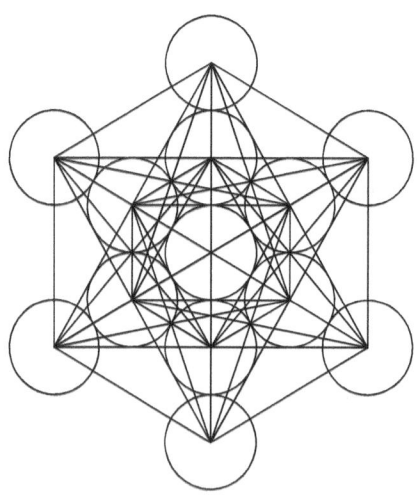

Metatron's Cube
(connected centers Fruit of Life)

Metatron's Cube is as mathematically ingenious as it's Divine and mystical as it contains all sorts of clues about the universe. The cube is named after the archangel Metatron whose origins are clouded in ancient mythology, and there are varying accounts of who or what he really was. The actual Metatron's Cube graphic rendering is credited to the Medieval Italian mathematician Leonardo Pisano (twelfth century), who is believed to have been inspired by the work of Plato and the sacred geometry in ancient mysticism traditions like Kabbalah, which is part of Jewish mysticism.

> "Because it's so unbelievable, the Truth often escapes being known."
> —HERACLITUS

The dots that Pisano was able to connect was the relation between the Platonic Solids and the *Fruit of Life*. As mentioned, the *Fruit of Life* is embedded in the *Flower of Life*, which was adopted by Kabbalah even though this symbol predates Jewish mysticism by thousands of years. But let's start with one of Plato's greatest legacies: the Platonic Solids.

The Platonic Solids have actually been known since antiquity, but it's widely believed Pythagoras (570–490 BC) advanced the understanding of them in ancient Greece. Pythagoras was a brilliant Greek philosopher and widely credited with the advances in mathematics, astronomy, the theory of music, and alchemy that formed the foundation of our modern-day science. Pythagoras credited his work to his master teacher, Hermes Trismegistus, a mystical figure who in ancient Egypt was known as Thoth, but we'll learn more about him later. Pythagoreanism, as his body of work has come to be known, gave birth to the brilliant Greek philosophers that followed in his footsteps, like Aristotle and Plato.

So, even though Pythagoras deserves far more credit than Plato, they're called Platonic Solids because Plato wrote extensively about them in his dialogue *Timaeus* (c. 360 BC). There are only five types of Platonic Solids which are regular solids or regular polyhedra, which are defined by a 3D shape where each face (surface area) is the same as a regular polygon and has the same number of faces meeting at each vertex (corner). That's a mouthful, I know; don't worry, this is not a test, and you don't have to learn them by heart. The only point is to understand them as they form the essential building blocks of all of Creation.

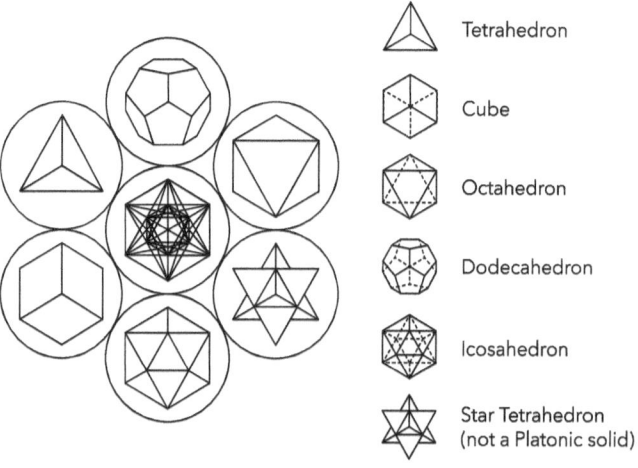

Tetrahedron

Cube

Octahedron

Dodecahedron

Icosahedron

Star Tetrahedron
(not a Platonic solid)

Basically, these five Platonic Solids have many very unique mathematical properties, the most astounding one maybe being that the sums of their interior angles all have the digital root of nine. This is a clue we'll save for later but remember that number also.

In his *Timaeus* masterpiece, Plato then associated each shape with nature and came to attribute the five elements of nature to these various Platonic Solids as follows:

Platonic Solid	Element	Chakra
Tetrahedron	Fire	Solar Plexus
Cube	Earth	Root
Octahedron	Air	Heart
Dodecahedron	Water	Sacral
Icosahedron	Ether	Throat, 3rd Eye, Crown

These five elements of nature are something we see come back in all ancient wisdom traditions as well as Indigenous cultures, and it's remarkably consistent across historical timelines and geographies. The Masculinity or Femininity that's associated with these elements is derived from the Merkaba and is consistent with the elements of the Chakra system in Hinduism, Yogic traditions, and Ayurvedic medicine. Ether represents space, nothingness, or the formless Consciousness, which is why it's associated with the three Chakras above the Heart.

The Platonic Solids are truly mesmerizing as not only their mathematical properties are astounding, but we see these basic forms came back everywhere in Existence or Life itself. All atoms and minerals can be deduced to their essential Platonic Solids, so these are quite literally the building blocks of all of Creation.

Pisano's discovery was that when you connect all the lines in the *Fruit of Life*, what reveals itself is Metatron's Cube, and within Metatron's Cube, all five Platonic Solids can be found as well as the Star Tetrahedron or Merkaba which is not a Platonic Solid but nonetheless integral to the *Flower of Life*.

LOVE + TRUTH

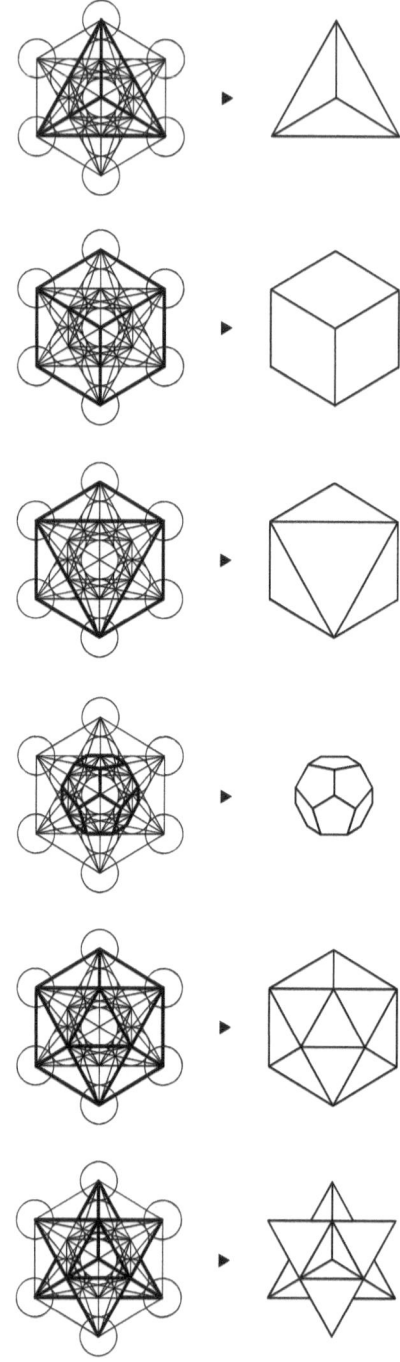

So, in summary, within the *Flower of Life*, we can find the *Fruit of Life*. Within the *Fruit of Life*, we can find Metatron's Cube, and within this sacred geometry shape, we can find all five Platonic Solids as well as the Merkaba. On top of all of this, we can find the Golden Ratio within the *Flower of Life*. If we dig even deeper, we can also find the *Seed of Life* within the composition of the *Flower of Life*. The *Seed of Life* represents the formation of life forms in the coming together of the initial seven circles, which form the center "flower" in the *Flower of Life*.

In the final chapter of Part V, we'll delve deeper into the *Seed of Life* and parse out its deeper meaning and significance. Since the *Flower of Life* predates the Bible by at least 5,000 years, it's widely held by historical scholars that the seven days of Creation referenced in the Bible was likely inspired or at least influenced by the *Seed of Life* within the *Flower of Life*.

What should be becoming evident now is that there's a remarkable mathematical poetry and intricate tapestry of sacred geometry within the *Flower of Life* which has stood the test of time.

With this foundational understanding of the *Flower of Life* in place, we can now shift our focus to the Principles. As you can see in the below graphic, in the complete *Flower of Life* symbol, there are six "flowers" that are still undefined, as well as the center "flower" and the double lines depicting the circumference. We'll leave those for later; in this chapter, we'll uncover the six "flowers" which represent the Principles of the universe.

You'll notice all flowers are in perfect symmetrical proportion to each other, so if we ran a line from the center of the flower called Awareness to the center of the flower called Reverence, we would intersect the open flower between them in the exact center. Since the whole Flower of Life is perfectly symmetrical, this will work the exact same way when we connect a line from Reverence to Energy, Energy to Being, etc.

It's also noteworthy that in each case, we're connecting a Masculine cornerstone (e.g., Awareness) with a Feminine cornerstone (e.g., Reverence) to create a universal Principle; we are creating a Principle that's grounded in the Unity of the Masculine and Feminine. This is very logically explained as the universe and its Principles are rooted in Unity Consciousness, the undivided whole of the Masculine and Feminine.

All Principles are native to this universe, meaning they're inviolable, irrefutable, and apply to all life forms, all things, all phenomena and occurrences, and across all timelines and all dimensions. There's simply no way around them.

We can discount, ignore, neglect, or overlook them, and the Principles will still be in full force and effect. Ignorance or even innocent unconsciousness doesn't give us any refuge; these are simply the eternal impenetrable canons that govern *the* one Infinite Game.

Once we know them, we have a choice to see them as constraints or impediments or to view them as illumination to help light our path unto the pathless land. If you recall, I referred to them earlier as design principles that help us navigate around and play within *the* one Infinite Game while we perfect our mastery of Life itself and beautify our spiritual art.

> "A man's life brings nothing unless he lives in accordance with the whole universe. Playing one's part in accordance with the universe is true humility."
> —LAO TZU

The Principles are not difficult to understand nor particularly challenging to live by, yet mastery of them takes some spiritual commitment and discipline. They don't require you to first ascend to high levels of Consciousness to recognize them at play or bring them into your self-poetry. All it takes is a basic awareness of them and then commit—which is a decision—to embody these Principles into your whole way of Being in relation to Life itself.

Humanity at large suffers from a toxic level of self-preeminence. We deem ourselves the center of this universe and the infallible titleholder of our planet and all other life forms that call Mother Earth home. We're not. We were never granted dominion, we were bestowed with the responsibility of stewardship, and so far, we've been failing miserably with the natural treasury entrusted to us to safeguard for eternity.

> "I am merely a guest, born in this world to know the secrets that lie beyond it."
> —RUMI

Mankind is Mother Earth's greatest menace and threat; there's no other species that comes even close. We are even our own greatest threat as we continue to digress into barbaric, cruel, and deeply unconscious self-destructive patterns and behaviors that are the root cause for an unthinkable magnitude of pain and suffering experienced by billions of people. Mother Earth is teetering on the edge of catastrophic ecological collapse, which will take her tens if not hundreds of thousands of years to recover from. That's not even a dire problem for her; however, it is for us.

What's desperately needed is systemic change on how we collectively view Life itself and all of Creation, including all of our fellow humans. The mindset shift that's required is to start seeing ourselves as stewards, but perhaps guests would be even better. We are not titleholders that can rape and pillage our home planet with impunity. Neither can we create the sort of thriving and prosperous societies we all wish for our kids to inherit if we think it's acceptable that billions of people simply lose. War, violence, and show of Force cannot be the inevitable political answer to resolve conflict; as we should know by now, this has never yielded lasting Peace. Finally, the various dystopian visions of a future of transhumanism, global central government, and a small elite that has absolute powers over all others will produce an Orwellian surveillance state even George himself couldn't have imagined in his wildest dreams.

All the answers for humanity are coming within alignment and recognition of the Principles of this universe. None of the above has to come to fruition; Mother Earth has a remarkable capacity to regenerate herself, provided mankind creates the conditions for her to be able to do so. As we'll come to find out when we uncover the six Principles, there's no scarcity in our universe, nor is there any reason for all the ill health, discord, and suffering by so many.

The answers are right in front of us; let's start to discover why these Principles are so fundamental to creating a new and more beautiful world for everyone and everything.

> "We don't inherit the Earth from our ancestors, we borrow it from our children."
> —NATIVE AMERICAN PROVERB

CHAPTER 25

ONENESS

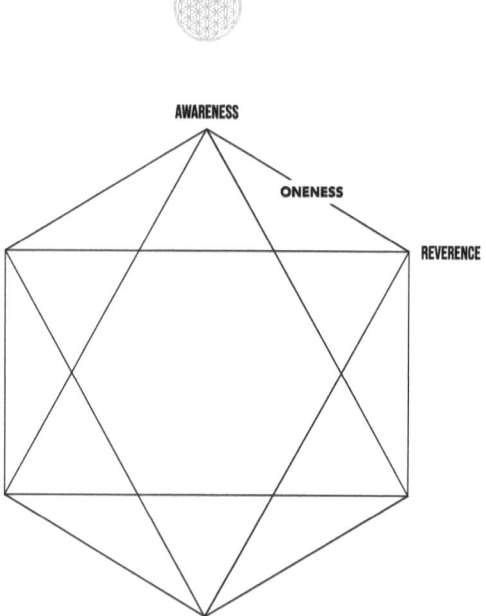

FIRST OFF, THERE'S NO HIERARCHY to the Principles. However, the first Principle we'll uncover—Oneness—is an ideal place to commence our discovery of all the Principles as so many of its essences are interwoven with the other five Principles.

Second, despite its apparent simplicity as a premise, Oneness is multidimensional and contains great depth in its significance. As we reveal these dimensions, we'll also come to see how all these dimensions are subtly interwoven and in relationship to each other. Furthermore, as we delve into all the Principles, we'll also start seeing the congruency and interconnectedness with the grand Architecture and Gifts we uncovered in Part II and III, respectively.

So, with all that in mind, let's get started.

> "When a man sees the one in all things, he's above mere understanding."
> —MASTER ECKHART

Oneness points us directly at the unity, interconnectedness, and the integrous nature of all of Creation of Life itself. Oneness implies everything is one single whole. Everything in this universe is directly related and connected—no exceptions—and all separation is an illusion. If you recall, we call this illusion Duality, the apparent separateness of all others and things, which is an illusion of our five senses as interpreted by our Egoic Mind.

At the quantum level, we discovered earlier everything is just Energy. The totality of all there is is what we refer to as the omnipresent Infinite Field of Consciousness, which is made of the Formless (i.e., space or nothingness) and the world of Form (i.e., physical reality). We called the Formless the Infinite Field of Possibilities and the world of Form the Finite World of Form. All of this is made up of energy, and only the difference in vibration or frequency makes something manifest or experiential to us, meaning we can see, touch, taste, hear, or smell it with our five senses. Or, if the manifestation is an occurrence of some sort, we can detect it through feeling, sensing, or experiencing the occurrence.

Modern-day physics has unequivocally reached unanimous consensus that everything is Energy and that, therefore, everything is connected and one at the quantum level. So, Oneness is not merely a spiritual ideal or philosophical concept; it's grounded in science and universal Truth. Another way to put this is that Duality is now a scientifically proven and accepted property of our entire known universe in the science of quantum physics.

What this implies is that we—humans—are One, not only with all other humans but all of Creation and all of Life itself. We're directly connected to everything else that exists in this universe, whether it's formless, a life form, an animate object, anything contained in nature, or the entirety of Mother Earth herself. Everyone is just one, expressing itself in all sorts of seemingly separate and distinct manifestations of form or being in a formless state.

> "I am that, I am."
> —PROPHECY OF MOSES

In the Prophecy of Moses, the burning bush reveals God's name to Moses as "I am that I am." Although the Prophecy of Moses is mostly identified with Judaism and Christianity, it's actually part and parcel of Islam and other Abrahamic religions, and its symbolic meaning can be retraced in many ancient wisdom traditions. The deeper truth of "I am that I am" is not very well understood by many as it's typically spoken with the wrong intonation. We can correct this by inserting a comma after "that," which then reveals this deeper truth quite readily. "I am that" points us at what God truly is.

Again, no need to get hung up on labels; you may substitute "God" with Creator, Spirit, Source, Universal Mind, Infinite Intelligence, or whichever label you prefer. The point is, as you look at the world around you, literally everything you see, hear, feel, taste, or touch is God. All of it is God, no exception. It's all the same thing, including you. Every human, animal, tree, plant, rock, the sky, and the entire universe, it's all God expressing itself into form. Moreover, everything you perceive to be outside or distinct from you is, in fact, you and within you. There is no separation; that's an illusion.

What this means is that everything you judge, condemn, hate, vilify, harm, or even kill is an aspect of you. The same goes for everything you love, embrace, celebrate, revere, or treat with loving kindness. This is the "I am" aspect that comes after the comma. The "I am" statement is the acknowledgment we recognize ourselves in all of Creation. Yes, this means the cruelty, hate, racism, inequality, injustice, and pollution you witness all around is an aspect of you as well. You might not perpetrate these things directly, but you have it within you as we each have the entire universe within us. And, in many ways, you might not be consciously aware how you're expressing these aspects into all of Creation.

One of the ten commandments of Christianity is "thou shalt not kill," yet most "good" Christians think nothing of supporting sending troops off to war to kill. Hence, anyone—Christian or otherwise—supportive of resolving conflicts through war and violence are murderers as well, we just have others do the dirty work for us.

Given other life circumstances, could we not be rapists, criminals, fraudsters, or murderers? What if you were born in the slums of Rio de Janeiro or poverty-stricken suburbs of Chicago, LA, or New York? What if you were emotionally and physically abused, neglected, or discarded by your caretakers and society? You might meet this notion with indignation; the Truth can be hard to bear. Yet, we can come up with countless examples of this, and some of them don't even need the backdrop of a tragic childhood of hardship and survival.

Many financial institutions and large multinationals fund and operate in industries and regions where corruption, malfeasance, child labor, women and human rights violations, and the annihilation of natural habitat and Mother Earth are pervasive. The well-educated and finely dressed corporate executive, banker, or commodities derivatives trader seated in their well-appointed offices might view themselves as impervious to any culpability in any of this; after all, it's not them doing this directly. But they're instruments of the system that produces these outcomes, so "they are that," however unconscious or ignorant they are of their participation in this system.

Starting to see the entire world around us from the universal Truth "I am that; I am" is a monumental step into embodying Oneness, not as a mere intellectual concept but as a universal Principle of Life itself. Yes, it's very challenging to witness all the unthinkable cruelty and suffering in this world and internalize this directly as something that's also within us. But if you wish to live in Truth, you cannot circumvent and skirt the Darkness. We must see it within us, recognize it fully and unconditionally, so we may transmute it within us toward our journey into the Light, which—when made unconditional—becomes our journey into universal Love.

Incidentally, "I am that, I am" is also the foundation of forgiveness of the unforgivable and the philosophical underpinning of the Golden Rule.

> "Peace will come to the hearts of men when they realize their Oneness with the universe, it's everywhere."
> —BLACK ELK

The fundamental problem is that we simply cannot conceptually grasp this with our logical Mind. Hence, we must transcend our logical Mind to actually experience it as being "real," as this is simply not the reality we experience through our five senses.

The irony is that Oneness is actually our natural state, and separation is something that comes online when our Egoic Mind starts to develop around age two to three, as at this stage of development of our Mind, our psychological construct of the illusionary self is formed, which is what we call the Ego. As the Ego is illusionary—i.e., not real—as it's merely a psychological construct or thought-form, so is the separation our Ego perceives illusionary or not real. Basically, our Ego or persona, if you will, which is just a thought-form, which itself is made out of wavelengths of pulsating energy, perceives all of physical reality, which is just energy vibrating at certain frequencies, so it appears as physical form, as separate and distinct from itself.

So, we must go beyond our logical or Egoic Mind as, at this level, we're stuck in separation as our Mind cannot disentangle itself from the sensory input of our five senses. The answers are in the intelligence of our Heart. Through the language of our Heart—feeling, sensing, direct knowing, and intuiting—the intelligence of our Heart organically connects with the Oneness of all there is. It's able to do so as our Heart's intelligence is not limited or constrained by the sensory input of our five senses as it has direct access to the suprarational intelligence of Life itself. The Heart, then, is our portal to palpably experiencing Oneness, which then allows us to embody it in our whole sense of Being.

> "To see things in the seed, that is genius."
> —LAO TZU

The experience of Oneness is one of complete fullness, vastness, completion, and deep connection with all there is, including ourselves and all others. Oneness is the Source, the original seed, it's home. This is literally our natural state with which we are born, except once our Ego comes online, the enculturation process starts, which dulls and chafes away at this natural state until we lose our connection to this natural state. At some point, our illusionary state of separation becomes our dominant state and the only one we consider "real." This is particularly so for Western culture, which—since the scientific revolution, which started in earnest with the Renaissance—has been entirely oriented, identified, and completely intoxicated with science, logic, and the material world.

Spending time in nature, music, meditation, yoga practiced in true awareness, creating art, and solitude away from electronics, social media, and other noise and distractions are all powerful ways to quieten our mind and shift into our Heart space, so we have more ready access to making Oneness "real" to us. Of course, authentic connection with others or animals can also be great access points. Provided the connection is not lubricated with offshoots of sacrilegious hedonism like excessive eating, alcohol, drugs, overbearingly loud music, partying, gambling, etc., as these are all sorts of numbing that might liberate us socially but disconnect us emotionally from our Heart.

Finally, sacred practices like tantra and consciously connecting during lovemaking are great access points also. Mere sex for pleasure is rooted in lust, which can be enjoyable, but it doesn't do much in terms of truly connecting, so it does little for experiencing Oneness and might even leave you feeling sexually gratified but empty and disconnected otherwise.

Duality is just one dimension of Oneness, so let's now examine Oneness from the perspective of Polarity. Back in Chapter 7, we discovered that our entire universe is subject to Polarity or the law of opposites. Everything exists on a continuum where the opposite poles form the basis of the existence of each other. Without Femininity, there could be no Masculinity. Without bad, good ceases to exist. Without wrong, we would know no right. Day/night, up/down, formless/form, happy/sad, etc., all can only exist because of the law of opposites.

At first glance, it might seem Oneness—which is wholeness or unity—is contradictory to Polarity, which states there are two opposite poles in everything. It's actually not all because the two opposite poles are actually one and the same, as there's complete unity between them. They're inseparable as they're merely the end points of one single continuum. We cannot separate happy from sad, we experience them differently, but they're the same thing, like each coin has two sides. There's no such thing as a one-sided coin in the same way nothing in this universe can exist without its opposite pole, with the only single—but highly notable—exception being universal Love.

> "Whenever you are about to find fault with someone, ask yourself the following question: what fault of mine most nearly resembles the one I am about to criticize."
> —MARCUS AURELIUS

Within each continuum of Polarity, there's also a harmonious pivot point; we call that the still point or Fulcrum. This Fulcrum represents the Oneness within each Polarity continuum. If the opposite poles were to collapse, they would do so within the Fulcrum, which would then contain within it the perfect unity of Source Consciousness.

Let's explore some examples to illustrate this further.

The height of our possible ascension is directly correlated with our capacity, willingness, and spiritual courage to consciously integrate the depths of our own Darkness within which we can call our "descension" into our own Darkness. In other words, the amount of spiritual Light we can access within corresponds directly with the amount of spiritual Darkness we're able and willing to integrate and hold.

Like with anything that's subject to the law of opposites, there's a continuum between complete Light—enlightenment—and complete Darkness or pure evil. We could say enlightenment and pure evil are just opposite poles on this one continuum, so there's Oneness within this continuum. For us to experience and integrate enlightenment (ascension) into Oneness, we must also experience and, most importantly, integrate pure evil (descension).

In this context, experience and integration don't mean we have to commit or participate in pure evil, but we have to be a conscious witness of it and acknowledge it's also within us. That doesn't necessarily mean we have a live wire sick and violent psychopath within us, which could be triggered to erupt into atrocities and barbaric cruelties at any moment. It just means this aspect of humanity is also within us as we're all One, and so each and every thing you see in the world is also within you and me. Every act of courage, kindness, and compassion, as well as every act of cruelty, violence, and greed. On their path of ascension, this is often a major threshold to cross for many spiritual seekers as they simply cannot fathom this sort of "evil" could possibly be within them. After all, they're not like "those" people. Well, just look at what happened during the Pandemic. It took only a bit of propaganda for a horde of everyday people to become irate, in some cases violent, and publicly hostile toward the so-called "anti-vaxxers." Trust me, there's more dormant Darkness dwelling in the nether regions of humanity than any of us would ever care to admit. We can transmute the Darkness within though, but only if we're willing to bring it into the spiritual light of our Consciousness.

When we disown, avoid, or deny one pole of a continuum, we mentally split ourselves into two and become fragmented. Fragmented, of course, is the opposite of unity or Oneness. The whole purpose, then, of Polarity is to guide us toward moving to full Oneness on whatever continuum it pertains to. Fragmentation within is where many of our problems in the world arise from, and Oneness within is where these problems dissipate as they become fully integrated.

On this particular continuum of complete Light and complete Darkness, the perfect Oneness that emerges when this continuum collapses into the Fulcrum is what is called fully self-realized Christ Consciousness or level 1,000 on David Hawkins' Map of Consciousness. As mentioned before, in the history of mankind, only Jesus, Buddha, and Lord Krishna are known to have calibrated at level 1,000, so it's wisest to use this as Divine inspiration of what to journey toward and leave your Ego's grandiose aspirations at the threshold unto the pathless land.

This is what Marcus Aurelius' quote above is really pointing at. We're quick to judge our adversaries and point out their flaws or mistakes. We cry foul and will readily belittle, insult, ostracize, withdraw our love, or worse, resort to aggressive and harsh language. We'll even justify and rationalize harming others, using violence or oppression, or even go to war and kill. However, we fail to see our own shortcomings and flaws. We presuppose our own perfection and flawlessness and turn a blind eye to our own vices.

Truthfully, few of us are so flawless and immaculate in all we do that we don't have the same faults, make the same mistakes, or do things akin to what we are critical of or offended by. This form of righteousness stems from fragmentation in our Mind as we haven't (yet) fully integrated that part of us. We disown, avoid, or deny that part of us, pretending it doesn't exist—whether through consciously suppressing it or unconscious ignorance—and so our lack of Oneness is reflected in our inability to see the wholeness of the situation (i.e., Awareness of understanding) and forgiving others for their transgressions. That doesn't mean we don't bring perpetrators of crimes to justice, whatever that might entail; it just means we forgive first before we seek justice.

> "Everything that irritates us about others can lead us to a deeper understanding of ourselves."
> —CARL JUNG

Understanding the universal Principle of Oneness on a fundamental level, you'll find yourself observing more and more while judging less and less. We are each still spiritual art in the making, not finished art.

For instance, if you have been wronged by greed, deceit, hate, racism, or even abuse, you can *react* from being or feeling offended, violated, or betrayed. Reactions originate from the belief patterns we have stored in our subconscious Mind, which are largely unconscious. So, perhaps you react with anger, violence, revenge, retaliation, or some other form of Force. What you resist persists. This is another cardinal law of the universe that's inviolable. So, this reaction will not solve anything and will likely aggravate or perpetuate the situation, if only in memory.

> "Suffering is not holding you.
> You are holding suffering."
> —BUDDHA

From a place of Oneness, you cultivate and gain the ability to consciously respond to any occurrence. So, in this very same example, you would still recognize the injustice, but you would immediately also recognize that you have also harmed or hurt others in your lifetime. Perhaps not to the same degree, perhaps unknowingly or unintentionally, but most definitely, we have all, in some ways, violated others and perhaps even in very similar ways. With this deeper level of understanding of ourselves and Life itself, we can intelligently *respond* instead of instinctively *reacting*, which gives us access to forgiveness first and then calmly seeking the most appropriate way to respond to the situation. This sort of response will not be guided by seeking revenge, retaliation, vengeance, or getting even because these all create unintelligent outcomes, which means they're created from unintelligence.

Responding intelligently might be reporting our grievance to the police, so justice can be served. Or we might confront our perpetrator to clear the air of our differences, so we transform the situation. Oneness, the sense that each other person is a reflection of ourselves, is crucial if we are to solve our societal discord and deep-rooted political, racial, and gender equality divisions.

Wokism and Critical Race Theory, for instance, are both social movements that originate from just (as in "justified") societal grievances which have evolved into such levels of righteousness that the oppressed have themselves become oppressors. Cancel culture, censorship, and using Force such as rioting, looting and counter-racism are oppressive, which is violent resistance that can—by the laws of physics—only trigger corresponding violent counter-resistance. We see this with the emergence of far-right extremism and populist groups in recent years. Separation and division have only become more glaring as the positions get more and more extreme and polarized.

The only way to reverse this societal polarization originates from Oneness, seeing ourselves in others as a starting point. This doesn't mean we give up on our just cause, but we realize that fighting for our cause begets fighting against our cause.

> "We must learn to live together as brothers or perish together as fools."
> —MARTIN LUTHER KING JR.

From a place of understanding, Love, and forgiveness, we can then avail ourselves to *respond* with intelligent forms of nonviolent resistance as characterized by the luminescent statesmanship shown by the late Nelson Mandela, Mahatma Gandhi, and Martin Luther King Jr. By these same laws of physics, this will then lead to the natural dissipation of the counter-resistance, which opens the door to build bridges and move toward constructive solutions and ultimately intelligent outcomes that are for the betterment of the whole. Oneness is truly the only path to Peace, unity, and wholeness, no matter how great your grievances or just your cause. After all, paraphrasing R. Buckminster Fuller: war, violence, and oppression is nothing but the insolvent answer of bankrupt politicians.

> "Attack the evil that is within yourself,
> rather than attacking the evil that is in others."
> —CONFUCIUS

Oneness emerges from the coalescence of the Masculine constituent attribute Awareness and the Feminine constituent attribute Reverence. As is clear from the foregoing, Oneness must be deeply rooted in Awareness as this is the only viable path to escape our deeply ingrained patterns of instinctual reactions and shift toward intelligently responding to any and all situations and occurrences. The Sovereign Masculine is steeped in calmness, presence, wisdom, and inner strength, which allows for non-fragility of the Mind and is near impossible to trigger into emotional outbursts or reactions. The Sovereign Masculine has risen above victimhood, so it doesn't get offended. It just takes it all in, evaluates what's being communicated with nuance and perspective, and then responds intelligently. The Sovereign Masculine does not get sidetracked by personal attacks, insults, vulgarities, or hostile words, which are all signs of weakness. All of these are reflections of a very deep level of Awareness.

It's also easy to see how the Feminine cornerstone Reverence is such a pivotal building block of true Oneness. If we have no Reverence—no respect—for something or someone else, it becomes near impossible to feel connected, let alone embrace and become understanding of their essence. Whenever we examine any form of fragmentation within ourselves, we can almost always trace it back to disregard, disdain, or contempt for that which we disowned, avoided, or denied within ourselves. The force of the negative energy against something is the very force that keeps it in place.

Within Oneness, by integrating the "negative" on whatever continuum, we neutralize this force of negative energy that holds everything locked in place. To neutralize any negative energy, we must gracefully let go of the disregard, disdain, or contempt which shifts into Reverence. The Sovereign Feminine is the epitome of this sort of illuminated Reverence for Life itself.

> "We're not going to be able to operate our Spaceship Earth successfully or for much longer unless we see it as a whole spaceship and fate as common. It has to be everybody or nobody."
> —R. BUCKMINSTER FULLER

We can see all of this very clearly with the destruction and desecration of animals and Mother Earth. The vulgar exploitation, extraction, and destruction of animals, natural habitats, and natural resources are rooted in deep ignorance. We're so blinded by seeking unlimited gain, convenience, and materialistic opulence that we can't internalize how destructive we really are. No Awareness and deep fragmentation as we simply disown, avoid, or deny what we all deep down know we're doing and the catastrophe we're headed for unless we radically change course.

Similarly, in almost all we do, there's not a trace of any true Reverence for the Sanctity of all Life or the magnificence of Mother Earth. We rape and pillage her with impunity instead. So, the connection or unity between humanity and Mother Earth and all other life forms has been all but severed. There's no Oneness; by and large, humanity doesn't see itself as an integral part of nature and the web of life on planet Earth. We believe we're above all of it, hence our complete separation with all the dire consequences of a home planet teetering on the edge of ecological collapse and so many relegated to living abysmal lives in indentured servitude to boundless capitalist greed or tyrannical oppression.

> "The privilege of a lifetime is to become who you really are."
> —CARL JUNG

To move toward Oneness with all there is in our Outer World, the Oneness with all there is in our Inner World must be one proverbial step ahead. So within, so without. We simply cannot authentically dwell in Oneness with our Outer World if we are not in a place of true Oneness with our authentic Self, which is our Inner World.

Most people live the life they believe the world expects of them. Their upbringing, enculturation, and perhaps religious beliefs run so deep they don't even know or remember who they truly are. So, they go through life wearing masks. Being and living the persona that's not truly you takes a lot of energy as the truly authentic expression of Self needs to be suppressed, and this can only be done with Force.

Often, we learn to numb this silent inner suffering with distractions like overworking, overexercising, overeating, or overindulging in excessive consumption, alcohol, nicotine, drugs, shopping, partying, gambling, sex, porn, or maybe even a marital affair. It might dull the silent suffering inside temporarily, but it never really works and so we continue until it becomes our daily routine at which point we have normalized it.

In most cases, we simply lack the Awareness; we just can't see the distortion on our lens from our own enculturation. However, this doesn't stop us from self-destructing over time, and often, this suppressed expression acts like a pressure cooker.

There are many ways how this pressure cooker, over time, becomes self-destructive as it might become expressed as severe or chronic illness, addictions, depression, or even suicide. We also see it expressed as domestic and sexual violence and abuse, which has been on the rise for decades. Research has shown upwards of 80 percent of all women and girls have experienced some sort of abuse or violence, often sexual and at times absolutely unthinkable in nature. Although the vast majority of victims are women, this is truly a men's issue, as upwards of 90 percent of the perpetrators are men. So, why do we have so many men doing this?

A large underlying cause is this pressure cooker of suppressed expression of their authentic Self. Men generally struggle to express their emotions, but moreover, they often lead very inauthentic and, therefore, unhappy lives. This is also evident in the far higher incidence of suicides among men.

When the authentic expression of our true Self—which includes our emotions, dreams, and aspirations—is suppressed, this Energy must come out when the pressure becomes too great. In men, this tends to come out sideways as rage, anger, violence, and the sorts. And, men, regretfully, tend to direct this rage and anger to the ones closest to them, which is why their wives, girlfriends, or dates tend to be the victims. Women tend to reflect rage and anger inwards and hurt themselves; this is why eating disorders like bulimia and anorexia are far more prevalent among women.

Not being in true Oneness within by not living the authentic expression of Self that wants to be expressed is at the root of all these issues.

You were born enough; it's your birthright to fully express all your inner art, poetry, and beauty in your own unique ways. The only restraint the universe will ever impose on you is Karmic responsibility, which is to say, always live the Golden Rule and don't willingly or knowingly harm others. Other than that, you're totally free. You are not your job, career, bank account, house, or car. You're not defined by whether you choose to be married, have eight kids, or no kids at all. You are free to be who you wish to be. The universe could care less who you share your sheets with, how you wish to identify, or whether or not you make it on the cover of a magazine.

What the universe craves is your authentic expression of your true Self. Screw all the made-up "brules" (i.e., b*llshit rules) and other nonsense society and culture will have you believe you need to be, become, or own to become a worthy somebody. You were worthy and complete the moment you took your first breath. There's literally nothing you can do to make you "more" of a human being. What you can do is refine your art, spiritual art, that is.

The name of the only real game here in Earth School is self-poetry. So, the only thing the universe begs of you to become is the full authentic expression of spiritual art that you are. And only that can bring you into a deep connection with Oneness within.

> "Not I, but the world says: All is one."
> —HERACLITUS

From Oneness within, inevitably, Oneness without arises. How could it be any other way, as all Oneness truly is, is remembering our true origins and therefore natural state. That is the perfect segue into the next Principle, which we could say is a natural quality innate to humans.

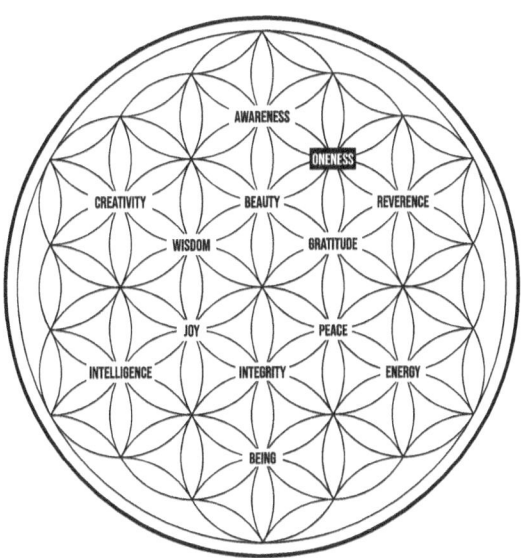

CHAPTER 26

COMPASSION

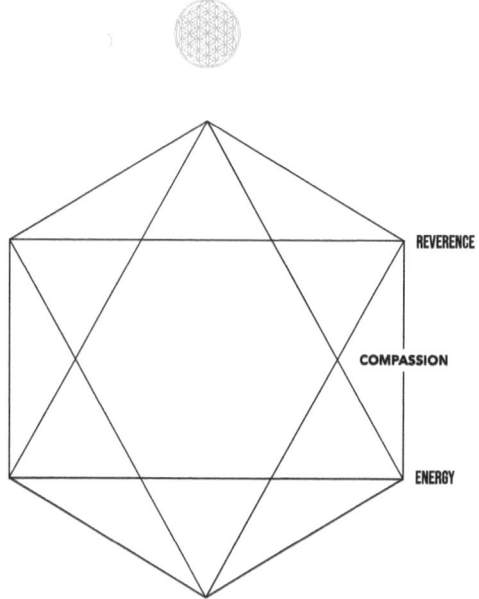

THE SECOND PRINCIPLE—COMPASSION—as defined by the universe, has a much deeper significance and holds far more profound implications than the prevailing understanding held by humanity.

We could say humanity's interpretation of Compassion is at a Hallmark card level and steeped in surface-level niceties, convenience, selectivity, and self-interest. It's something we do when expedient.

For the universe, Compassion is something that emanates from our core and is expressed in action. It's something we are (or are not) instead of something we just do, so it's rooted in our entire Being and expressed in our *doing* of Being. The *doing* then becomes the litmus test of whether our actions are congruent with who we are.

> "The purpose of human life is to serve, and to show compassion and the will to help others."
> —ALBERT SCHWEITZER

The Merriam-Webster Dictionary defines Compassion as the "sympathetic consciousness of others' distress together with a desire to alleviate it." There are some major clues here. First, "sympathetic consciousness" points us directly at the quality of "sympathy" and the nature of "consciousness." "A desire to alleviate it" points us directly at the fact that true Compassion is active—it contains "action"—and not passive. Let's unpack this more, starting with a salient quote we saw earlier.

> "That which is not good for the beehive cannot be good for the bees."
> —MARCUS AURELIUS

The origins of the quality of sympathy in Compassion are actually quite easy to retrace. Compassion is derived from the Latin word *compassio*, which itself was derived from the Old Greek word *sympatheia*. In ancient Greece, the word *sympatheia* meant "affinity of parts to the organic whole or mutual interdependence." In Stoicism, *sympatheia* is considered one of the most important qualities of rational (i.e., human) beings and an essential and revered character trait.

The Stoics held that without *sympatheia*, an individual could not be in right relationship with the whole, which meant they were destructive or disruptive to the thriving of the whole "beehive." The recognition of the mutual interdependence of all Life was a core tenet of Stoicism, and *sympatheia* underpinned their four core virtues: wisdom, courage, temperance, and justice.

"Sympathetic consciousness" also points us at the nature of where Compassion stems from. Clearly, the use of this specific word tells us it's not something that originates from the Mind or even our Heart, or they would have used those specific references. The specific reference to Consciousness itself tells us the nature of Compassion is all-encompassing and something that's inclusive of but also beyond our Mind and Heart. In other words, true Compassion is something that permeates our entire Being; it's not exclusive to our Mind or even Heart. Incidentally, this ties back to how the Stoics viewed *sympatheia*, to which Compassion is directly related.

Our modern-day English meaning of the word *sympathy* is derived from the Old French word *compassion*, which implies *pity, mercy, or sympathy*. The fundamental difference with Compassion is that within the correct use of the word *sympathy* within the English language, we only hold feelings of pity and sorrow for someone else's misfortune. That is to say, it's passive; there's no action in it. As we noted from the Merriam-Webster definition, the correct English interpretation of Compassion specifically includes "a desire to alleviate it," which is an action component. Of course, this is also a reference back to its origins—by way of the Latin word *compassio*—from the Old Greek word *sympatheia*.

You might wonder, *Why all the fuss about the etymology of Compassion?* Well, it will serve us well when we dive into the constituent attributes that are foundational to the coalescence we call true Compassion.

> "Compassion is the basis of morality."
> —ARTHUR SCHOPENHAUER

The first constituent attribute is Reverence, which, if you recall, is Feminine. Reverence points at the Sanctity of all Life and the interconnectedness and mutual interdependence of all of Creation or Existence. Reverence is rooted in a deep-seated respect for the whole, where we view ourselves as an integral part of this whole. It's not hard to see how the Greek premise of *sympatheia* is tightly interwoven into the fabric of Reverence.

Furthermore, to have Reverence, we must look into the world outside of us. We have to relate to others and all things, which is a shift of awareness from our Inner World to the Outer World. This shift of awareness is what opens us up to actually connect with the pain, suffering, and misfortune of others and all other things, which allows feelings of sympathy, empathy, and mercy to well up from our inner core. This essential aspect of Compassion all comes from the Feminine constituent attribute Reverence. We can also see the gentleness, as well as the nurturing and sensory (feeling) nature of the Sovereign Feminine, reflected in Compassion, which also all originate from her cornerstone, Reverence.

The second constituent attribute is Energy, which is Masculine. The Masculine and Energy represent Life Force, power, propulsion, drive, determination, and strength as well as in general Consciousness itself. So, we can readily see that the active or "action" component of Compassion comes from Energy. Within the true nature of the Sovereign Masculine, we can also witness the reflections of protection, safety, assertiveness, and the Sacred King who's in service to his people. We see all these qualities reflected within true Compassion as well.

> "If your compassion does not include yourself, it's incomplete."
> —BUDDHA

We again see how the unification of a Masculine and Feminine cornerstone—each uniquely powerful and magnificent in its own ways—creates the graceful poetry of the universal Principle of Compassion. This is what makes Compassion one of the most accessible Principles regardless of the level of Consciousness, as almost nobody goes untouched when they come into the grace of Compassion. We universally recognize and revere this quality in other people, whether or not we have a lot or very little of it ourselves. Clearly, the doctors that commit their careers to Doctors Without Borders and its mission of devotion to the sick, weak, and outcasts in over seventy countries are drenched with compassion, so much so that even people that would never consider following their path are compelled to donate to this cause as they recognize the Compassion within this organization's missionary work. Universally, those that concern themselves with the less fortunate are admired, applauded, and oftentimes recognized for their noble acts of service. All of these are examples of work and missions which are rooted in Compassion.

Ironically, as challenging as it is for most to truly be in Compassion toward others and all other things, it's universally even more challenging to be in true Compassion with ourselves. We even see this with people who express a deep sense of Compassion for the Outer World yet are still merciless with themselves.

To understand this at a deeper level, let's first take a look at people that show no capacity for any level of Compassion toward others or the world around them. These are the sociopaths, psychopaths, and toxic narcissists of the world. These people are actually in deep pain stemming from a disconnection from their Divinity within. The inability to access or experience Love is torturous for our Soul. In that sense, although they may appear entirely self-centered and maniacally egotistical, they, in fact, also have no capacity for Compassion for themselves. This is evident in their aberrant capacity for self-destruction and complete insensitivity to getting harmed or killed. This is perhaps the most dreadful and nefarious incarnation imaginable; seeing their deep inner suffering beneath their unthinkable atrocities is what gives us access to be in Compassion with them.

What it also clearly shows is that even those lost in extreme forms of self-centeredness and egotistical behavior still don't have any sort of Compassion for themselves. Compassion simply doesn't hurt, harm, maim, endanger, punish, belittle, ridicule, condemn, chastise, ignore, or sabotage itself. On the contrary, Compassion is loving and kind. It uplifts, restores, helps, heals, nurtures, forgives, and doesn't judge.

The Truth is, most of us don't do this for ourselves. We judge ourselves harshly, and we're punishing in our condemnation of our flaws, missteps, and mistakes. This inner critic tends to be ruthless. We struggle to be in true Compassion with ourselves as it's far easier to be in Compassion with others.

Yet, this is where it all comes full circle. So within, so without. True Compassion for ourselves originates from the acceptance that we're human and we're inherently flawed. Our imperfections are not a sign we're not good enough, but merely that we're a spiritual art project which is unfinished. We're allowed to make mistakes; that's how we learn and grow, provided we choose to learn the lesson. Just as a figure of speech, God doesn't expect perfect execution, just perfect effort.

Coming full circle in true Compassion is what allows us to deepen our Compassion considerably. Our Compassion for ourselves opens us up to extend the same grace to others and all other things. When we witness the healing powers of our true Compassion touch the lives of others, it only serves to reinforce our Compassion for ourselves as we become deeply sympathetic to the Truth that most are in some form of pain and suffering.

Even the rich and famous, the seemingly successful and beautiful, and all those we believe are living a dream life. At closer examination, we'll start to see through the tiny cracks in their armament of worldly success, and inevitably, we will find that even those on the top of the proverbial mountain have their share of human tragedy and hardships. They experience loss, heartbreak, disappointments, grievances, pain, and suffering in different colors, perhaps, but all these gradients of color come ultimately from the same palette of human experiences.

> "When we practice loving kindness and compassion we are the first ones to profit."
> —RUMI

We started this chapter with the statement that humanity's prevailing understanding of Compassion is rooted in surface-level niceties, convenience, selectivity, and self-interest. That might sound like harsh judgment, but if we're willing to be truly honest, we can see this is not harsh, just the naked Truth. After all, we know the outside world is a truthful and perfectly accurate reflection of our collective Consciousness. And so, by taking a closer look at the macrocosm which is our world, we can learn and come to know much about the microcosm, which is ourselves.

Our form of Compassion is drenched with surface-level niceties. We might donate generously to alleviate hunger in Africa, but then we turn right back around and go about our merry way. We do the same for refugees, war-torn areas, areas hit by natural disasters, and also the next-door neighbor that lost his income or the distant family member who got sick.

We help a little, say some nice well-intended words, but then we move on with our own life. These are all surface-level niceties that are wonderful gestures in the moment, but it's also why none of these hardships seem to ever get systematically transformed. And, in the case of these personal examples, after an initial outpouring of support and assistance, the sympathy traffic dies down, and people typically find themselves lonely and left to their own devices to muddle through their misfortune.

In our fast-paced world, where most live stressed-out lives, the longevity and endurance of our Compassion tend to be anemic. The root cause is that we're really just being sympathetic; others' suffering is not something we consider unacceptable, just unfortunate.

If we did, there simply wouldn't be a homelessness epidemic in the US, sex trafficking of the most vulnerable women and young girls, or upwards of 1,500 dolphins barbarically butchered in the Faroe Islands each year purely for trophy hunting purposes as their meat is toxic.

It's also based on convenience and selectivity, especially in politics and business. It's done when there are votes, favorable media exposure, or profits in it. But, short of those, good luck. Most corporate sustainability efforts are rife with greenwashing. An inconceivable number of private jets fly into Davos every year for their annual pilgrimage to the annual World Economic Forum conference, where the elites "compassionately" discuss how the rest of the world should drive less and eat less meat while they unabashedly sunbathe in their cornucopia of opulence. It's a farce.

In our personal lives, we pretty much do the same, although most of us lack the dense ignorance to do it as blatantly as the elites.

We're selective in that some—whoever we consider to be our own tribe—are deemed worthy of our Compassion, but others we don't really know, not so much. We stop at convenience because we're too busy living our stressed-out lives; we simply don't take the time to pause to even take notice.

Finally, self-interest. Good for the sake of doing good is mostly a lost art. Politicians, institutions, corporations, and even NGOs and nonprofits have agendas that are almost exclusively rooted in self-interest, no matter the pretty PR story that's spun. And we often do the same as we mostly give for the feeling it gives us, less so the actual Compassion we have for others.

True Compassion can be expressed in a myriad of ways; financial is only one of them. Picking up trash we see is an act of Compassion toward Mother Earth; so is helping the mother traveling with small kids get her bag in the overhead bin. Opening a door for someone else, offering a seat to an elderly or disabled person, or letting someone merge into our traffic lane are all small gestures of true Compassion. So, living a life of true Compassion is readily available to anyone and can be expressed in the smallest of kind and helpful gestures.

Having said all that, as Rumi points out, there is actually a deep medicinal quality to Being in true Compassion. We do profit in what we become and in how the universe has a way of rewarding benevolence with benevolence. True Compassion is deeply healing as it reconnects us with all there is; we come into right relationship with all of Creation, which serves to fortify the whole web of life. All of Life is built on interconnectedness and mutual interdependence, and true Compassion is an access point for us to become a truly symbiotic node in the web of life. The positive ripple effect cannot be underestimated, as true Compassion has a way of echoing long after it has been received. If or when we've been touched by others' Compassion, this lives on within us and we feel organically compelled to pay it forward to the best of our ability. The law of compounding then kicks in as it ripples out in all directions. In this way, the flap of a single butterfly truly does become a hurricane of Compassion all around the globe.

> "Compassion is a muscle that gets stronger with use."
> —MAHATMA GANDHI

True Compassion is innate in each of us; we're all naturally talented and gifted to be a superstar of Compassion. However, it does require devotion, which the dictionary defines as "having love, loyalty, and enthusiasm for a person, activity, or a cause." True Compassion is both a cause and an activity, as we discovered earlier. It's a cause in that it's a way of Being, and it's an activity as we must express this Being into action for true Compassion to be complete. Devotion gets deepened and sharpened through application and practice; in that sense, Compassion is a muscle we can train to become ever stronger.

The more we bring true Compassion into our whole being, the more this way of looking at the world becomes the predominant lens through which we perceive all of Life. The more we radiate Compassion from our whole Being, the more Compassion we'll attract into our life as like-kind energy is attracted to like-kind energy. This reciprocating cycle then creates its own form of kinetic energy that propels itself forward and upward on its own steam. It literally becomes effortless for us until we know no other way to be anymore.

When true Compassion becomes this effortless and even fun and joyful, we know we're on the right track.

> "Compassion is the wish to see others free from suffering."
> —DALAI LAMA

There's another natural evolution in true Compassion as its circles tend to expand outward as we deepen our Compassion in our whole Being. Whereas it might start with those closest to us, then our friends and family, then our community, and then our larger tribe or country, it will eventually spill over all these artificial borders.

Humanity as a whole, animals, tree and plant life, all of nature, Mother Earth, and our entire biosphere until eventually, it's all-encompassing. We're no longer limited by whom or what is worthy of our Compassion. As we start to see the intelligence of Life itself in everything, we also start to recognize the Divinity and magnificence in all of Creation.

Suddenly, an otherwise innocuous human act like shooting a Tesla into space primarily for publicity purposes occurs to you as a violation of all of Creation. Why are we needlessly polluting space? These sorts of perceptions rise from true Compassion as we start to see even inanimate objects or the nothingness of space as something that warrants our Compassion.

True Compassion is what makes a society caring and livable; it fosters community and a sense of connection even with strangers. As Plato reminded us: *"Everyone you meet is fighting a battle you know nothing about. Be kind. Always."*

Finally, how might we know the universe lives by its own Principle of Compassion? A cursory look at the world might suggest otherwise, but if we're willing to be truthful, we must admit that almost all our greatest challenges are man-made. We are the procuring cause of the lack of Compassion in this world, not the universe.

The universe simply operates through sympathetic resonance; it will always merely mirror and reflect what's within each of us. Existence or physical reality as we know it is the reality collectively created by mankind, and this is exactly why the level of mastery of our spiritual art is so essential, as we each only control the little sliver of the collective that is ourselves. But each of us together make up the collective. Your spiritual art, then, is your unique contribution and responsibility at the same time.

We also know humans have an enormous capacity for Compassion; there's plenty of evidence for that also. So, there's nothing wrong with how the universe works or operates; we—mankind—have to change. And not just change, we must grow and evolve, which brings us to the next Principle—Growth.

COMPASSION

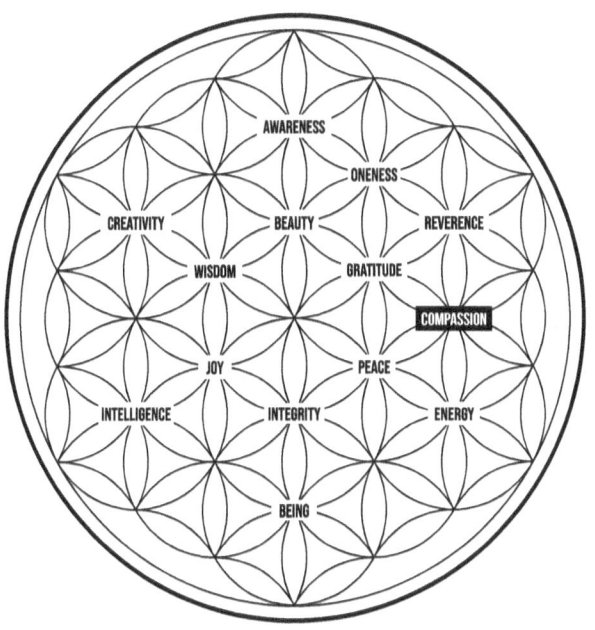

CHAPTER 27
GROWTH

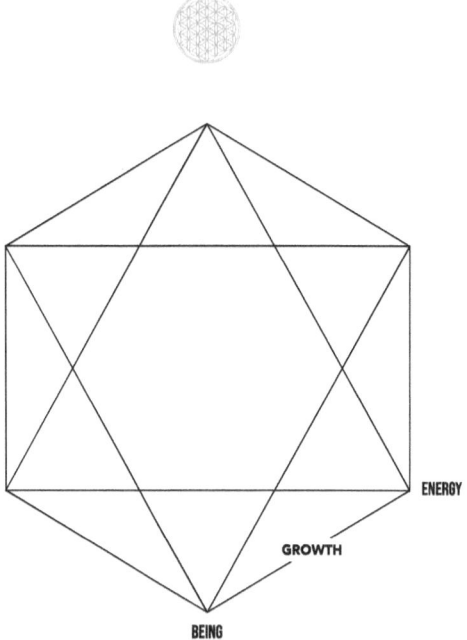

GROWTH IS THE NATURAL STATE of this entire universe. Ever since the Big Bang, the entire known universe and everything within it has been in a continuous state of creation, adaptation, expansion, and evolution, which is to say, Growth.

We see this play out at all levels of Creation, from the minute single-cell organism to entire new galaxies being born and created.

Countless species have evolved over millions of years, geographies and landscapes have evolved, and stars and planets continue to come into existence. This entire process of continuous change and evolution is centered around one single precept: Growth.

What's also clearly evident is that everything in our universe is subject to fundamental fractal patterns meaning everything is scaled from the infinitely small to infinitely large according to these same fractal patterns that differ only in their scale. This is where we see the Hermetic axiom "so above, so below" comes back.

Everything also evolves to become more and more complex as it expands in time and space; however, paradoxically, the underlying Order seems to increase with complexity despite the appearance of increased Chaos at the surface level. Since these fractal patterns hold true for everything in our universe, it's now widely presumed, even in scientific circles, that our Big Bang might just be the singularity of one single proton of an infinitely larger universe we're nested within. And as we're able to discover and measure smaller and smaller scales, it would be entirely logical to assume that each proton in our universe is its own entire universe nested within this singular proton.

> "Each celestial body, in fact, each and every atom, produces a particular sound on account of its movement, its rhythm or vibration. All these sounds and vibrations form a universal harmony in which each element, while having its own function and character, contributes to the whole."
> —PYTHAGORAS

The point to take away from all of this is the incomprehensible enormity that's all of Creation and, at the same time, each speck of stardust—including our spiritual art—matters in monumental ways and contributes to the formation and never-ceasing evolution of this enormity.

And, even though our science and understanding of mathematics might not yet be able to account for all of it, we can see there's an Infinite Intelligence embedded within all of it as we're discovering there's infinite Order in all of Creation. To deeply connect with this vastness of Existence is to reconnect our Divinity within with all there is, ever was, and ever will be. There's a distinct grace that embraces us once we are able to escape our sense of self-importance and see ourselves for what we really are: a single speck of stardust hurtling through space and time on a blue dot at dizzying speeds.

Yet, at the same time, we're able to internalize our utter insignificance in the large scheme of things; we can also internalize that everything we speak, think, do, and create affects the whole, and so we're simultaneously completely insignificant as well as vitally relevant, valuable, and important. And Growth in all its forms and variations is the underlying deeper purpose of all of the unfolding of all of Creation as far and wide as we can possibly conceive it to reach.

There's even a single fundamental law that governs Growth, and that is that everything in this universe that stops creating, adapting, expanding, or evolving will eventually wither, degenerate, and die off to make room for new Growth.

Within the process of Growth, there are gravitational forces that suck the old into the core where—without adaptation—it will get stuck and subject to the entropic laws of evolution. Again, this happens at all levels of Creation, from the formation of galaxies and planetary systems to everything in nature, the world of business and politics, and even such things as music and art. Empires, nations, and civilizations all follow this same pattern of the Adaptive Cycle of Change.

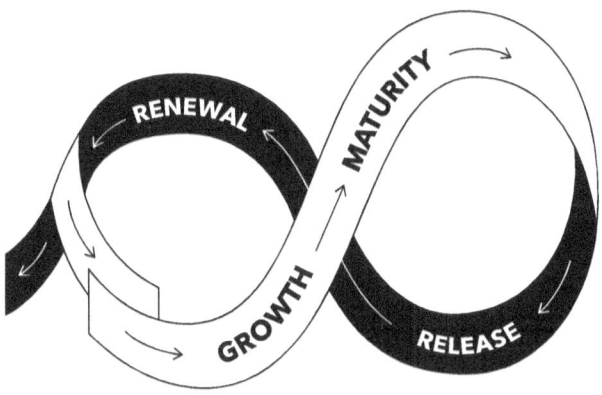

Humans are no different from any of these other examples; we're an integral part of all of Creation and, therefore, part of Life itself, which follows this cycle at all levels of Creation.

The first phase in the Adaptive Cycle is actually Growth itself. Something comes into creation that can be as conceptual as just an idea at first. Ideas, intentions, or inspiration contain energy as they're thought-forms, and this is how all Creation starts. Even in nature, nature has an idea. Political movements are born from an idea or ideal at first, and so is any business, artwork, love relationship, or house design. What follows from this catalyst is the

Growth phase. In this phase, the original idea or notion grows into something of Creation. Eventually, this Growth levels out and goes through its first transition phase into the phase we call Maturity.

In the Maturity phase, things still grow, expand, or evolve but the Growth levels off, stabilizes, and then plateaus. At some point upon stabilization, the Adaptive Cycle has its next transition phase into the Collapse phase. During this stage, the stagnation of the Maturity phase has come to its end station, and the intelligence of Life itself prompts a Collapse of what is so something new can be born or take its place. The Collapse phase then becomes the birthplace of the Renewal phase in which new invigorated Growth and renewal take center stage.

Virtually all we know follows this Adaptive Cycle of Change; it's literally how the universe and everything within it evolves in a never-ending movement of dynamic change. Even things we perceive as virtually fixed, like mountains and landscapes, evolve like this, which we would be able to see if we changed the timescale and intervals at which we follow this change.

While this Adaptive Cycle has several phases we could perceive as decline or anti-growth (i.e., death), the whole process is one of constant Growth and, therefore, evolution.

> "Remember that life's greatest lessons are usually learned from the worst times and the worst mistakes."
> —BUDDHA

Beyond the recognition of this universal pattern of Growth, what the Adaptive Cycle shows us is that resistance to change is futile. Nothing is static in the dense material world, and so embracing the inevitable change of Life itself is Being in alignment with Life itself. Resistance to "what is" seeds frustration, disappointment, disillusion, pain, and suffering, and all of this is self-imposed as it's mental in nature.

The even deeper truth is that we must grow and evolve; we don't have a real choice as all of Creation around us is constantly growing and evolving. This includes all people, relationships, situations, and circumstances that touch and affect our life. Rigidly holding on to how things used to be is a catalyst for experiencing suffering as it introduces the notion of how things "should be" instead of how they actually are right in this moment.

Much of our mental suffering is directly related to the mental labels we affix to certain conditions, events, or circumstances. When we label something a failure, we've introduced the experience of something bad. That very same thing labeled an "experience" neutralizes the bad label and perhaps even opens up the possibility to see the Growth in the experience.

This doesn't just transform what we previously labeled as "bad" into something "good" or at least valuable, but it shifts us into a position of power instead of victimhood. By definition, in victimhood, we have no power whatsoever as we've relinquished our power to that which was done unto us. An experience is also something that showed up in our life, and no matter how dreadful the experience is, if we can recognize the Growth within the experience, we have the capacity to learn and evolve, which means we've stayed firmly grounded in our power.

> "The gem cannot be polished without friction nor man without trials."
> —CONFUCIUS

Life sometimes knocks the wind out of us. Things don't always go the way we hoped, hearts get broken, and loved ones will pass. Some friendships will sour, some things fail or don't come to fruition the way we hoped, and inevitably we all get to witness our fair share of greed, dishonesty, lies, and hurtful words or actions. Nobody is exempt, no matter how rosy their social media accounts look.

The point is not to not feel any of these things; in fact, feeling them deeply is the way to go, as numbing will only postpone what needs to happen. Feeling allows us to recognize the inner suffering—however mild or intense—and alchemize it into true Growth. This is the sort of expansion the universe is beckoning from us whenever we're dealt with pain, hardship, or misfortune.

What we're unable to process in the moment gets stored as trauma in our cellular tissue and emotional body. Trauma is unprocessed emotional pain; these are the wounds and scars of Life that, left unattended, will dictate our beliefs about Life itself, including our fears. The only way out is through. Or, better yet, rise above them so we can release the trauma and the beliefs and fears held in place by this trauma.

Even trauma follows the Adaptive Cycle pattern where Growth is the experience itself in whatever form it showed up in our life. Maturity represents the crystallization of the trauma in our nervous system, cellular tissue, and emotional body. It can reside here dormant for years or decades, festering away until it reaches a zenith of pain and often silent suffering. This zenith signals the phase transition into the Collapse phase. We or our life might literally collapse, or this long-dormant trauma starts to stir our Soul, indicating we're being prompted to alchemize this inner suffering. When we finally do—perhaps with the help of therapy, healers, coaches, etc.—this trauma gets released from our system. Literally, we flush it out and alchemize the trauma into Growth, which then releases us into the Renewal phase from an elevated level of Being as we overcame the trauma, which was never there to hurt or harm us in the first place. It's just how the raw diamond inside gets polished to an ever more radiant luminosity.

> "Humble yourself; you'll grow greater than the world. Your Self will be revealed to you, without you."
> —RUMI

Let's now see why the Principle of true Growth comes from the coalescence of the Feminine cornerstone Being and the Masculine cornerstone Energy, why this makes intuitive sense, and why it is beneficial to creating a life as spiritual art.

If you recall, Being is all about rediscovering the wholeness we already are. Doing, on the other hand, is all about being in action or motion to pursue wholeness through *doing* or, in other words, pursuing, striving, chasing, and conquering in the Outer World.

In Doing, we might realize our craftsmanship and skills or realize material or worldly success, but none of this will ever get us to the wholeness we already are.

Without a doubt, in this form of Doing, there's growth in the experiences we gain, whether they're sensory, kinetic, mental, emotional, or even financial. All of these are meaningful and part of living a full life, but these aren't the true Growth the universe is ultimately after. For the universe, all of these are compliments and aids to assist in the one true game in town: spiritual Growth.

This is because, in Doing, we're merely skimming the surface and often so lost in our busyness we never even take notice of the depth of Growth we're truly after. We bear witness to this all around. This world is littered with people who have mastered worldly success yet remain spiritual novices. They are Outer World dominant and materially rich but remain Inner World disconnected and spiritually poor.

The litmus test is quite obvious; strip all the various "trophies" away and see what remains. A person entangled with Doing is defined by their trophies, so little remains when these trophies are stripped. On the other hand, a person in Being is defined by who they are, and the stripping away typically reveals only more of who they truly are.

The depth the universe beckons us to seek, we can only find in truly *being* in Being, which means even our *doing* now takes place from a place of Being. The main difference is that when we're lost in Doing, we're lost in the identification with the Ego—or persona—who's *doing* the Doing. We play a role called father, wife, daughter, lawyer, doctor, athlete, or any combination of roles as we always play numerous in Doing despite there always being one dominant role.

This is exactly what Rumi's quote points at. True Growth is about revealing—rediscovering—your true Self so you may see the illusion of yourself. The Ego (or our illusionary self) is not real; it's a psychological construct, as we discovered earlier. Hence, our illusionary self cannot experience true Growth as it's simply not real. True Growth occurs at our Soul level, which we can only access when we're in Being. And, again, only from this place of Being can we choose to freely play as in Doing we *must* play since we're identified with the role we're playing.

The most expedient way to access Being is stillness. We have to quieten our mind so we can start to listen to what arises from the depths of our Inner World. As discussed earlier, there are many practices that can help us with this, but frankly, the most important one is making the decision to actually listen to what wants to come forth from our Inner World. This singular decision alone opens the door; the rest is about finding the tools and techniques that work for you and cultivating the necessary level of devotion that comes from infusing that singular decision with spiritual discipline.

So, one essence of true Growth is unequivocally *being* in Being; what about the Masculine constituent attribute Energy?

Any sort of Growth requires a fuel source. Something needs to power the expansion, change, growth, or evolution, or that something will literally not move. In fact, it will wither and eventually die without a fuel source. We see this in nature, in business, in politics, or even an ultra-short-lived fad like a viral meme. In that viral meme, the fuel source is people sharing the meme. Once that stops, the meme dies off into oblivion.

A hurricane needs warm tropical waters, low air pressure, and tropical winds—those are its fuel sources. Once these dissipate, the hurricane loses its ferocity and eventually dissolves.

Our fuel source for true Growth is the Masculine cornerstone Energy. If you recall, the dissonant state of Energy is Impotence. In Impotence, we literally lack the fuel source for Growth. Nothing demonstrates this more vividly than male impotence, which is his inability to grow erect or orgasm, which is to say he cannot procreate Life itself. Of course, male impotence is merely symbolic for there not being a fuel source to power true Growth on any level in Life itself.

Energy is what fuels Growth, even though we might experience this inner drive as inspiration, motivation, or desire. We can also harvest Energy from fear, anger, revenge, and even hate, which, albeit powerful, are very inefficient and detrimental sources of Energy. They're inefficient as they require a lot of our energy to be sustained as our source of Energy as they're not innate. Our natural state is not Fear, anger, revenge, or hate, so to cultivate these emotions, we must spend a lot of our own Energy creating and sustaining these emotions. They're detrimental for obvious reasons as they not only blur our moral compass, which opens the door for causing harm to others, but they're an acid that can cause great harm to the vessel that stores it (credit: Mark Twain). Any

Energy mined from a negative mental and/or emotional state has these two defining characteristics: inefficiency and harmfulness.

Since the prevailing level of human consciousness is below 200, most of humanity's Energy has traditionally come from Fear. However, anger and hate have been on the rise for years as our society is becoming increasingly more divided and polarized in political extremism. As degenerative as these negative mental and emotional states are as a source of Energy, within shame, guilt, and especially apathy, we become impotent. This is why these states can be so challenging to escape, as we literally lack the Energy to move out of them; they become emotional and spiritual traps. Often, we have to move into anger first to gain access to enough Energy to then move through to courage and get into the realm where our Energy becomes highly efficient and regenerative in nature.

This realm is Love (the energy). Love (the energy) comes from an endless well as it's our true natural state. Once we tap into this well, we cannot outspend what's being internally generated, and it takes no effort to sustain the Energy. It just flows through us, and the more we spend or give away, the more we receive in return, which is what makes this fuel source so highly efficient. It's also naturally regenerative to true Growth as Love itself holds no capacity to cause harm to others or ourselves.

We should note, though, that not all inspiration, motivation, or desire is of the same spiritual quality, as it can originate from either Love or Lust. Lust ultimately comes from lack or scarcity, or in other words, our Fear of not having it. That's why within inspiration, motivation, or desire stemming from lust, our moral compass gets blurred easily, which then tends to show up as greed, corruption, malfeasance, abuse of power, infidelity, or ignorance in the harm caused to others or Life itself. Lust can get us worldly success, maybe a lot even, but it will inevitably hollow us out spiritually.

True Growth, then, can only come from the purest form of Energy, which is Love (the energy). The telltale hallmark of this purest form of Energy is its very high frequency. Anyone, regardless of level of Consciousness, who comes into contact with Love (the energy) immediately recognizes its visceral Power. We're drawn to it as if pulled by a magical gravitational force as it touches something deep inside of us. For many that are operating from Fear, the instinctive reaction will be to close down, and resistance will bubble up to the surface. This is the Ego's instinctual defense mechanism as the Ego's illusionary nature is deeply threatened by the realness of Love, the energy.

An act of spiritual courage is to resist this closing down and lean in instead. When we repeatedly do this, our own source of Love, the energy gets kindled and, over time, will flare up, thereby opening up this source of Energy for us as well.

> "What we fear doing most is usually what we most need to do."
> —RALPH WALDO EMERSON

So, we know now that the universal Principle of true Growth is grounded in Being and Energy, but what stops us from seeking true Growth, which is to be in alignment with Life itself?

Mostly, just Fear.

As we touched on earlier, other than acute physical danger, all Fear is psychological in nature, so it's not real. Our illusionary self—the Ego—paralyzes us with illusionary dangers that have us in the vise grip of Fear. Fear, again, is defined as any negative belief in the absence of concrete evidence. So, the shift we're really after is on the other side of the continuum, which is Faith—a positive belief in the absence of concrete evidence.

Faith requires us to surrender into trust. We need four key ingredients to truly surrender into trust. First, we must embrace the notion that we cannot fail. No matter the outcome, it's just an experience. Second, we must recognize that we cannot get hurt. Our Ego can get hurt, but the deepest and eternal part within us simply cannot. Third, we must internalize that we live in a benevolent universe. The universe is neither indifferent nor cruel, it's here to aid us, and everything that happens always happens for our greatest growth, greatest prosperity, and greatest evolution, regardless of how that shows up in our reality. Fourth, we must relinquish control of the outcome, meaning set an intention and move toward that intention with congruent action, but let go of how and when that's supposed to show up. In Part V, we'll unpack Fear in greater detail in the chapter "Fear—The Great Illusion."

If we can master these four precepts, we will inevitably find it easier and easier to surrender into trust, which gets us to Faith.

And, once in Faith, we become simply unstoppable, and true Growth cannot help but stir our Soul into exuberance and excitement—and this is what it feels like to be truly alive in alignment with the universal Principle of Growth while being firmly grounded in Being and Energy.

This universe never stops. It's perpetually growing, perpetually becoming anew in each and every moment. This is the true meaning of aliveness and perpetual Growth.

> "No man ever steps in the same river twice, for it's not the same river and he's not the same man."
> —HERACLITUS

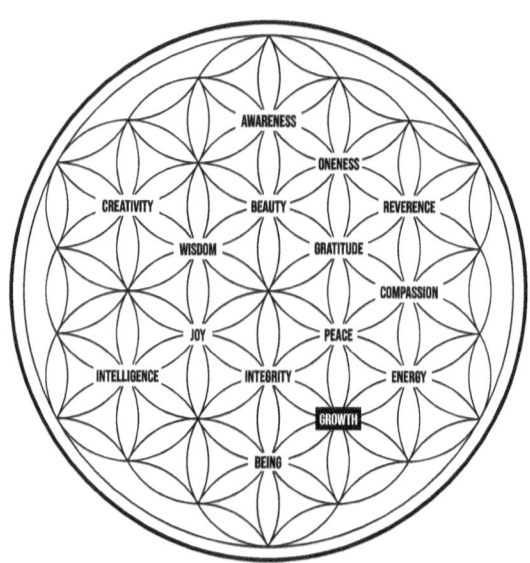

CHAPTER 28
HEALTH

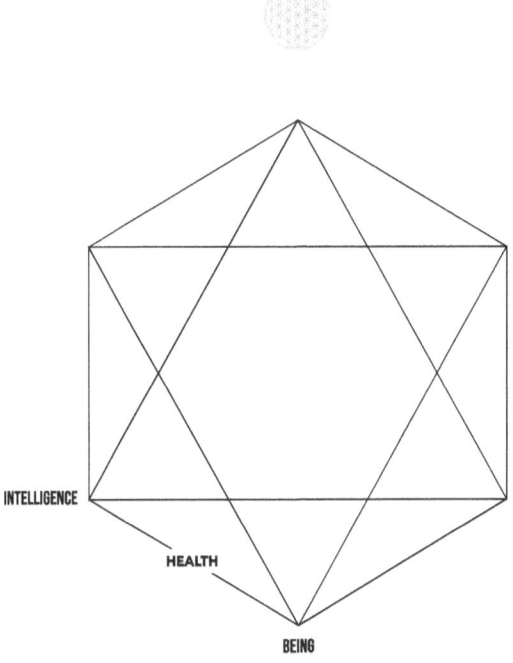

THE UNIVERSAL PRINCIPLE OF HEALTH is grossly ill-understood (no pun intended) by humanity today for two main reasons: (1) reductionist science; and (2) fixating on the singular dimension of physical reality. Mankind's primary confusion is that true Health—in any form—doesn't originate from the dimension where it's experienced. The root cause of any form of disease or ill health is within the dissonance of formless energy; the effect we call disease or ill health we then experience in the realm of frozen energy or physical reality. Disease of any kind at its very core is energetic disharmony. We'll delve into all of that but let's first get a better understanding of the etymology of the word Health as that might reveal some important clues.

The word Health comes from the Old English word "hælþ" which means "wholeness, being whole, sound or well." This Old English word appears to have its origins in the Old Norse word "heill" ("healthy"), which has its origins in the Old Norse word "helge," which means "holy or sacred."

We have a lot to work with here, starting with the word "holy," which points us not only to wholeness but to God. Once again, God is just a label or word we use to point at something; please feel free to substitute with any other label such as Creator, Spirit, Source, Allah, Infinite Intelligence, Universal Mind, etc.—they all point at the exact same thing. Anything holy receives its absolute sanctity from God, not man, which is what makes it sacred. We could say then that Health is holy and therefore sacred.

Next, "hælþ" refers unequivocally to wholeness or being whole. When something is whole, it's integrous, so wholeness points us to integrity and, therefore, coherence, as we know from the chapter on Integrity that coherence and integrity are like two peas in a pod.

We also already discovered that coherence is synonymous with harmony; in the later chapter on Harmony, we're going to go deep into how the theory of music relates to all of Creation. But, for now, it suffices to just know that all of Creation is based on the harmonics of vibration and frequency. This is why some quantum physicists have referred to the Finite World of Form as being frozen music. In the same manner, true Health is based on energetic harmony where disharmony or dissonance is the cause of the underlying complex living system becoming disharmonious, which we call disease or ill health.

We also discovered in that same chapter on Integrity how Intelligence is one of the two Masculine constituent attributes that are integral to Integrity, so it's no surprise we'll see Intelligence come back as we'll delve deeper into the universal Principle of true Health. For now, we're still just laying the foundation for this deeper exploration.

We can see then that true Health points us at wholeness that's holy in nature and, therefore, sacred. Health is also not limited to our biology. The precept of true Health applies to our physical body but also our emotional, mental, and spiritual bodies. Not only that, true Health is a universal Principle because it applies to anything and everything in our known universe and whatever might be beyond. It applies to relationships, situations, occurrences, businesses, societies, nations, geopolitics, nature, Mother Earth, and anything else in between.

> "It's no measure of health to be
> well-adjusted to a profoundly sick society."
> —JIDDHU KRISHNAMURTI

With that baseline understanding of the inherent meaning of the word Health, we have a basis to examine these two reasons I first mentioned at a deeper level. As explained before, reductionist science isolates what is nested within an infinitely complex web of life so it can comprehend what's otherwise too complex to analyze and understand. This can be a very helpful tool for scientific research, provided you don't presume the findings or conclusions are representative of how things really work in reality. In reality, we cannot sever the myriad of relationships as everything is interconnected, interdependent, and literally, nothing exists in a vacuum.

We'll see this fundamental fallacy come back time and again as we explore how ill-understood true Health truly is. Moreover, this fallacy is amplified by our monomaniacal fixation on only one single slice of reality—the physical realm of atoms and molecules. The origins of this fixation are that—since the Renaissance—humanity as a whole has been obsessed with scientific measurements and mathematical proof, and the physical realm lends itself the best— at our current level of understanding—for this approach. We do all of this despite full-well knowing there's a subatomic level of fundamental Energy and non-physical realms like the emotional, mental, and spiritual realms. All of these realms are nested, entangled, interdependent, interconnected, and we can never arrive at wholeness—true Health—by fixating on only one of these slices.

After nearly five centuries of this sort of myopic perspective, our world is a perfect mirror of where this leads to. At all levels of Existence, we've drifted very far from true Health, yet, as Krishnamurti's quote points at, our diabolical answer is to adjust to this profound sickness and define our ability to cope and adjust to sickness as Health.

In Western medicine, we see this with "adjusting" to chronic illness with pharmaceutical interventions rather than going to the root cause and addressing what caused the chronic illness in the first place. We see this in the geopolitical arena by adjusting to war and violence by engaging in more war and violence. Our scientific "prowess" has created all sorts of harmful technologies and inventions such as toxic chemicals, nonbiodegradable plastics and composites, GMO foods, industrial farming, EMR, 5G, chemtrails, dirty fuel sources, and even gore-filled content we consume as entertainment. This is not to speak of our voluntary participation in ruining our own Health and that of Mother Earth through our lifestyle choices.

Albeit much of the true harmful nature of all of these is carefully suppressed by those with commercial interests tied to their propagation—which is another profound sickness of humanity altogether—we basically know what all of these do to our Health as well as the Health of our home planet. Yet, we collectively adjust to all of these by creating more of them along the same lines instead of doing the only real sane thing, which is to address them truthfully at the root cause so we can restore true Health.

> "All that man needs for health and healing has been provided for by God in nature. The challenge of science is to find it."
> —PARACELSUS

We already alluded to the Masculine cornerstone of Intelligence being integrous to true Health; the other is the Feminine cornerstone of Being. The coalescence of Being and Intelligence is what creates, promotes, and supports true Health so let's uncover why this is self-evident. We could restate this as saying for true Health to come into Existence, there needs to be a harmonious concert between Intelligence and Being.

As we pointed at earlier, true Health—as well as wholeness and coherence—is not only our natural state but that of the entire universe. We can logically derive this from the constituent attribute Intelligence, which the universe defines as *that* which produces intelligent outcomes. For a universe—all of Creation—that originated, was brought into Creation and is directed in infinitely intelligent ways by an Infinite Intelligence, we can only surmise that all it produces is intelligent outcomes.

Intelligent outcomes are those which are conducive to Life itself and all that creates the greatest prosperity, greatest growth, and greatest evolution. From this, we can clearly extract that true Health is the only possible intelligent outcome that would obey these laws of the universe. Ill health or illness which stems from energetic dissonance or disharmony is not an intelligent outcome. Hence, it must be—by definition—the product of Unintelligence.

We can see this demonstrated very clearly on a personal level. Throughout the Western world, but especially in the US, humanity is faced with a health crisis of epic proportions. Obesity, cancer, heart disease, high cholesterol, diabetes, asthma, thyroid disorders, ADHD, declining fertility rates, etc., are all natural consequences of the unintelligent lifestyle choices we've adopted as a society over the last forty to fifty years.

Admittedly, all of these choices are also put before us by profit-oriented commercial interests that have become deeply entangled with those governmental agencies that are supposed to be the guard at the door. But, the US Food and Drug Administration (FDA), Centers for Disease Control and Prevention, World Health Organization, and all their various counterparts in other countries are deeply corrupted and have become regulatory extensions of corporate interests as these organizations are beholden to corporate funding and sponsorship. There's no other way to explain how it can be that so many of the foods, pharmaceuticals, cosmetics, and household products we use are toxic and ruinous to our Health, yet still perfectly legal and even promoted in the FDA-published food pyramid and sponsored through farm subsidies.

We think nothing of alcohol, sugar, corn syrup, synthetic preservatives, and all the other unpronounceable toxic chemicals that lace the products we eat, drink, and use, yet all of these are well-known to destroy our Health. Add to this all the environmental pollutants we're exposed to daily, like electromagnetic fields (EMFs), 5G cellular networks, chemtrails, fluoride in our drinking water, etc., and it's no longer surprising that our Health is as abysmal as it is. Our general answer to seek relief from the symptoms through pharmaceutical interventions only adds to the circularity of ill health among the general populace.

At this stage, the most lethal lurking danger to our Health might be science itself. As the Paracelsus quote states, the challenge is for science to "find it"; however, science has taken it upon itself to "create it." In other words, science is pretending to be God.

> "Concern for man and his fate must always form the chief interest of all technical endeavors. Never forget this in the midst of your diagrams and equations."
> —ALBERT EINSTEIN

When we tinker with the genetics of foods (i.e., GMO), we fail to realize that the innate intelligence of our body and all of nature has evolved over millions of years of evolution to be able to "read" the nutrients, which it does through reading the genetic code of the foods we consume. When you change these codes, our body can no longer read this code, and so, for all intents and purposes, we're eating dead food.

In the same way, when you feed industrially farmed animals GMO foods like mono-cropped corn, soy, and wheat, which aren't even their natural diet, their meat will contain the chemical residue of all the herbicides, pesticides, glyphosate, antibiotics, and hormones used to grow and feed these animals. The latest fad of lab-grown fake meat is another example of science creating more problems than solutions as overwhelmingly, all these lab-grown so-called foods are disastrous for our Health.

On all levels—personal, corporate, scientific, and governmental—this paradigm is deeply rooted in Unintelligence and a complete abdication of responsibility. We can even see how these choices spill over into the immense harm we cause to the Health of our planet. It's quite obvious then how true Health is directly connected to Intelligence as defined by the universe as intelligent choices create intelligent outcomes, of which true Health is just one prime example.

Let's now explore why the Feminine cornerstone of Being is integral to true Health, and to do so, let's recall the deeper meaning of the word Health: wholeness.

We've now encountered in various contexts that the true nature of Being is wholeness or being whole. This existential quality of Being is how and why the puzzle piece of true Health is directly connected to Being. We cannot *do* coherence; we can only *be* in coherence. To be in coherence, we must be in Being, which includes *doing* while in Being. When we get lost in Doing, we fragment, and we lose our wholeness. A loss of wholeness—Integrity—creates dissonance, which over time creates ill health in whatever form that might show up.

The other existential quality of Being that's fundamental to true Health is sovereign critical thought. On a personal level, all the health issues and poor lifestyle choices I discussed earlier are evidence of a lack of sovereign critical thought. Because all the information to make intelligent choices is out there. True health is readily accessible to anyone, even on low budgets or food stamps. But we have to take full responsibility for every aspect of our life, we have to lose our addiction to pleasure and convenience, and most of all, lose our gullibility to be so easily influenced by the medical industry and commercial interests that profit off your ill health but principally view your true Health as a threat to their economic interests.

Sovereign critical thought pierces right through all the advertising, marketing, and the preponderance of misrepresentation of health facts and information. Sovereign critical thought sniffs out the corruption, entanglements, and conflicts of interest that are rife in corporations and our governmental agencies, and so it will seek Truth about Health itself rather than blindly following whatever narrative it's spoon-fed. Most of all, sovereign critical thought is what reconnects us with our own innate intelligence of the body, and this again can only be accessed through Being.

Our body is a self-organizing complex living system that's inherently intelligent and capable of creating and maintaining true Health, unless we disturb it by making unintelligent choices. Sovereign critical thought is how we reconnect to this innate intelligence as it creates the interface between external information sources and the feedback loop, which is the health condition of our body. The intelligence of our body communicates with us 24/7 through how we feel and by what we can observe. All we really need to do is learn to be still—in Being—and take in what it's telling us. This inner guidance, in combination with sovereign critical thought, is what allows us to be our own best health advocate. We might still occasionally seek the help of a doctor, healer, or chiropractor, but this will be guided by a deeper knowing of what we need to do to create optimum health.

While being firmly grounded in Being and making intelligent choices through the application of Intelligence, true Health becomes all but inevitable. So, if it's this seemingly simple and self-evident, why is the world in such poor Health?

HEALTH

> "Access to power must be confined to those who are not in love with it."
> —PLATO

The harsh and inconvenient Truth is that we're addicted and infatuated with all sorts of things, but true Health is not one of them. On an institutional level—business, science, education, and government—we're addicted to profits. Profits simply trump harm caused. Because this is hard to admit for even the staunchest capitalist, they conveniently hide behind excuses like we only provide what the market demands, or they simply hide or obscure the facts.

This is nothing new. The tobacco industry did this, Big Oil has known its devastating environmental legacy for decades, the chemical industry is well aware of the harmful effects of glyphosate, herbicides, and pesticides, and Coca-Cola and Pepsi know how bad corn syrup is for us. More recently, we've been able to see Big Pharma's egregiousness on full display with a myriad of tactics ranging from trying to legally obscure trial data for seventy-five years (which was legally overturned) all the way to sheepishly admitting to a committee of the European Parliament they lied about transmission efficacy as they never actually tested for that. None of this is surprising as our world is rife with special interests being hopelessly entangled with the bureaucrats and elected officials who are supposed to regulate and supervise them on behalf of the people. It's pervasive, and all institutions at all levels are completely entangled, so it's difficult to suggest anymore there is any unbiased party looking out for the interest of the general public.

> "It's health that's real wealth
> and not pieces of gold and silver."
>
> —MAHATMA GANDHI

On a personal level, we don't recognize the value of Health until/unless we lose it. And, even then, we don't really want to make the intelligent choices we should. The COVID-19 pandemic was a classic case of this general cognitive dissonance. With an 80 percent+ co-morbidity rate, it was known very early on that this virus was particularly deadly for the obese and those with chronic health issues. So, did we make any systemic changes to our unhealthy lifestyles or food choices? Did we start seeking more exercise, better sleep, more fresh air, more vitamin D, and healthier diets? Nope, we closed the gyms but kept the liquor stores open. We implemented mask mandates, lockdowns, and then put all our faith in experimental vaccines for which, to this date, we have no mid- to long-term trial data. Incidentally, alcoholism, drug dependency, domestic abuse, depression, and suicides all rose during this two-year span. The overall "pandemic" response to a virus with a 99.7 percent survival rate has been a cataclysmic disaster on all levels but mostly human. A big opportunity was missed as in that two-year span, systemic changes could have been easily made.

However, true Health is unattainable unless you first value it as real wealth. When it holds no value, you won't be inclined to make the intelligent choices that are needed or kick the addictions and bad habits that need to go. The problem these days is that our ill health has become so normalized most don't know any better. People have grown accustomed to being obese, tired, and sickly. It's normal to be on all sorts of pharmaceuticals, and we pop NSAIDS (e.g., Tylenol, ibuprofen, Aleve, etc.) like they're Tic Tacs even though it's well-documented they wreak havoc in our biome, which plays a central role in our body's ability to create true Health on a physiological level.

So, how do we break this impasse?

> "Let your food be your medicine
> and your medicine be your food."
> —HIPPOCRATES

There are many things beyond our direct and immediate control, e.g., we can't stop chemtrails or even stop taking many medications overnight. But where we can easily start is food. And food happens to have an outsized effect on our Health, so much so that many chronic illnesses like diabetes, high cholesterol, high blood pressure, etc., can all be reversed or cured simply by changing what we eat.

It's beyond the scope of this book to go deeply Into what a healthy diet would look like, but I highly encourage you to look into the work of Dr. Mark Hyman, Zach Bush MD, Dr. Berg, and Dr. Steven Gundry if you wish to deepen your understanding of how food can radically shift your Health. What's fundamental to understand is that food is also energetic in nature. Food holds vibration and frequency just like anything else in this universe, and when our diet consists of foods with dissonant frequencies, then that will affect the vibration and frequency within the self-organizing complex living system called our body.

Whereas food is a practice we can adopt, knowing about food is perhaps even more powerful in reconnecting us with true Health. Our modern-day foods come mostly from industrialized mono-crop farming, factory livestock production, and commercial fishing. All of these have huge implications for the environment, animal welfare, and human health. Mono-cropping leads to soil degradation, increasing dependency on toxic fertilizers, and are a leading cause of CO_2 release as they remove ground cover. The lack of ground cover also affects the capacity of the soils to absorb rainwater, thereby depleting natural aquifers and causing flash floods. All of this creates heat islands, which affect small weather patterns, which in turn affect macro weather patterns. In short, it's ill-fated on many levels and well on its way to impairing our food security.

Factory livestock farming is equally catastrophic for the environment and immensely cruel to the animals as they live their abbreviated life in confinement and abysmal conditions. In Part V, we'll get deeper into the mammalian brain and their level of Intelligence; suffice to say it will be uncomfortable to learn how well-developed their Limbic brains are, which tells us about their capacity to consciously experience Life itself. Commercial fishing using large trawlers has a myriad of problems as well, such as seabed degradation from scraping nets across the ocean floor; bycatch, which is sea life that's needlessly killed in the process; and large-scale overfishing, which leads to collapsing fish stocks. There's a lot more depth to all of these, but the point I am trying to get across is that we must reconnect with our food and where it comes from, as that literally changes everything.

How so?

HEALTH

> "Our entire biological system, the brain, and the Earth itself, work on the same frequencies."
> —NIKOLA TESLA

Our own Health and the Health of Mother Earth are interconnected and interdependent. We cannot rape, pillage, and abuse her and expect we'll still be able to end up healthy. So, we don't only need to change the food we consume; we need to change our entire relationship with food all the way to the source—animals, plants, and Mother Earth.

If you recall, Mother Earth has her own "heartbeat" called the Schumann Resonance, which is instrumental to our health and well-being in a variety of ways. These Health benefits are in large part directly associated with what's called "grounding" or "earthing," which connects us directly with the Schumann Resonance and facilitates a discharge of static energy as our positively charged body connects with the negatively charged Earth. A decades-long mass urbanization—living in concrete jungles, worse, in high rises—and the advent of rubber soles are now all being associated with our overall decline in true Health. And this is not all granola hippie stuff. Cliff Ober, who pioneered the recent scientific advances in understanding "grounding," has an electrical engineering background; this is how he discovered the negatively charged electrons that we absorb through grounding serve to neutralize free radicals in our body. In essence, our body is a highly complex electrical circuit disguised as a physical body. This is the same fundamental premise underlying Ayurvedic medicine and ancient Chinese medicine, which have both been around for thousands of years.

> "More than a mere alternative strategy, regenerative agriculture represents a fundamental shift in our culture's relationship with nature."
> —CHARLES EISENSTEIN

Back to food and food sourcing. Fortunately, there's a new paradigm of agriculture coming into vogue, which is called Regenerative Agriculture, although other variations like biodynamic farming and permaculture all fall under the same category. It's actually not new at all; it's the way we used to farm before industrial farming took off after WWII. The basic premise of Regenerative Farming is no-tilling, using crop cover, crop diversity, integrating livestock grazing into farm operations, and using natural composting techniques instead of synthetic fertilizers.

It takes about two to three years on average to fully convert a farm to Regenerative Agriculture, but once this is done, the profitability per acre goes up ten- to twenty-fold. Not only that, but the ground cover also has a net CO_2 sequestration effect, so it literally sucks CO_2 from the atmosphere back into the soils. Soils with ground cover have an enormous capacity to absorb rainwater, which replenishes natural aquifers and all but resolves flash flood run-off.

The animals enjoy a much higher quality of life, eat their natural diet, and are integrous to the composting and restoration of the soils through their trampling and nutrient-rich excrement deposits. Crop diversity enriches the soils, acts as a natural pesticide-controlling agent, and creates much less volatility in farming profitability as it reduces the dependence on one single crop. Finally, it produces nutrient-dense organic foods, which is exactly what we humans require to obtain true Health.

Basically, it solves all problems of our current system at all levels. It's also proven to be scalable, meaning it's not a niche application. The only thing standing in the way are powerful commercial interests that benefit from the status quo not being disturbed. There's a lot of money at stake for the chemical producers, the GMO seed producers, and the large conglomerates that have consolidated the agriculture industry to such an extent that independent farmers are becoming a dying breed.

Knowledge is power. Once you see, you cannot unsee. And knowing where our food comes from, how they're grown or raised, and what they do to our Health and the Health of Mother Earth will shift your understanding about Health in dramatic ways.

> "Medicine is not only a science; it's also an art.
> It does not consist of compounding pills and plasters;
> it deals with the very processes of life, which
> must be understood before they may be guided."
> —PARACELSUS

True Health is our natural state as well as that of Mother Earth and the entire universe, and all of these are entangled and interdependent. Once we see these relationships, it becomes obvious that the disturbance of Health in one part of the system inevitably will spill over in all other parts of the system unless it's corrected. This plays out in our own body as its own self-organizing complex living system but also in all the systems that are nested within it and the larger systems that we are nested within.

We can even extrapolate this same premise to business or society. If we have a cancerous cell within a company, it can ruin the team spirit of an entire division and eventually even spill over to the entire organization. Within an industry, one bad player can ruin it for all players. In society, when there are cancerous cells that are hateful to others, this can easily spill over and sicken the whole system.

In this way, we can view our Health but also the effect we have on all we touch and interact with as something sacred. This holistic view on Health rises above the concern for our own good Health to the true Health of the larger system we're part of.

And, frankly, that's really the only way the spiritually mature consider true Health as they have embraced true Health is a universal Principle which, if ignored by us at any level, makes us the dissonant note in the orchestra of Life itself.

> "Every human being is the author of his own health or disease."
> —BUDDHA

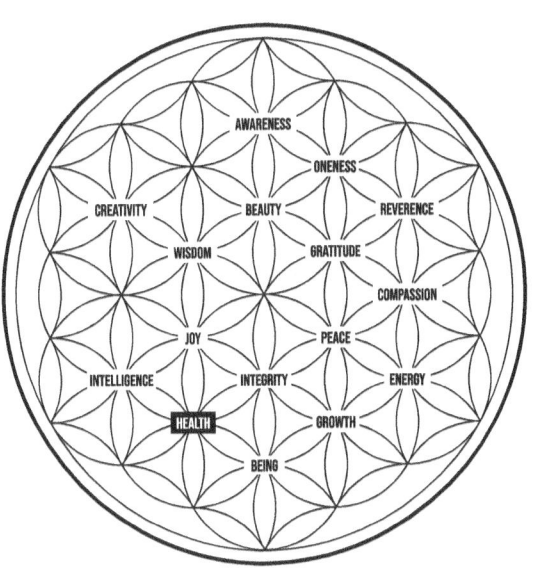

CHAPTER 29

ABUNDANCE

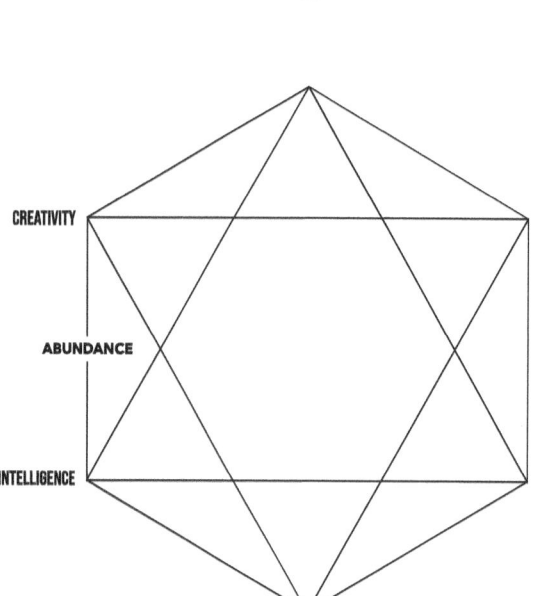

THE NEXT UNIVERSAL PRINCIPLE—ABUNDANCE—is also riddled with misunderstanding. So much so that most of humanity deems it some form of the elusive holy grail of Life itself to be found in the material realm, never realizing it's the very metaphysical fabric of Existence that's omnipresent.

Vast sectors of our economy exist solely on the false premise you're lacking something. A whole cottage industry of "law of attraction" coaches and so-called teachers are dedicated to deftly exploiting this deep-rooted primal yearning by the many to know what it feels like to create Abundance in their lives.

The irony, of course, is that they're selling you a phantom deficiency that, in reality, doesn't exist. In colloquial terms, they're all snake oil salespeople. Except, overwhelmingly, they believe in their own snake oil, so for the most part, all of this is rooted in innocent ignorance—the deaf leading the blind, so to speak.

Here's the subtle Truth: true Abundance is not something that can be created as it's already omnipresent and eternally part of your very Existence. It's only elusive because you have no eyes for it, even though it's hiding in plain sight. And you have no eyes for it simply because you don't know what to look for. You don't know what to look for because the definition of Abundance you were told—by virtue of the cultural fishbowl or "Matrix" you were born into—is actually only allowing you to see Scarcity.

> "Giving thanks for abundance is sweeter than the abundance itself."
> —RUMI

Let's dissect this subtle Truth a bit deeper so it will reveal itself clear as day. The reason you cannot see true Abundance is that it cannot be found in anything you create. There's simply nothing within anything material, or experientially that formulaically produces true Abundance.

If you recall from Chapter 2 ("Universal Love"), there's Love (the emotion) and Love (the energy). The first one is a fleeting emotion dependent on circumstances; the latter one is a state of Being. Abundance, as most of humanity understands and defines it is really just "Plenteous," not true Abundance. Plenteous refers to some "thing" constituting or existing in plenitude. This some "thing" could be either material or experiential, but it has to exist first to be able to be Plenteous. Plenteous, then, is a condition derived from a circumstance. Conditions themselves might be objectively quantifiable, but they're still subject to perception, e.g., what one person considers a lot, another might perceive as a little. Same objective condition, different subjective perceptions—in this same way, Plenteous will only ever be *Plenteous* in the eyes of the beholder.

True Abundance is a state of Being, and by definition, a state is not a condition derived from any circumstance. A state of Being is actually best described as an energy field with a distinct natural frequency. Through the harmonic phenomenon of sympathetic resonance, our state of Being in this specific energy field, in effect, determines our circumstances as this frequency gives us access to that reality.

Another way to view this is to see true Abundance as an energy field with its own reality of Abundance, whereas Scarcity is also an energy field with its own reality of lack. Which energy field we access and are in determines which reality is available to us. They both exist contemporaneously at all times, but we cannot be in both at the same time, so we're either in one or the other. Which one we're in dictates how we perceive our reality, which in turn drives our psycho-cybernetic loop, which, as covered earlier, determines the results or outcomes we come to experience in our life.

> "Wealth consists not in having great possessions, but in having few wants."
> —EPICTETUS

Plenteous is the snake oil I referred to earlier. Most of the self-development industry, including many self-anointed gurus, sages, and mystics, advertises Abundance but sells Plenteous. Once you can clearly see the distinction between the two, you know this to be true because virtually all of them are selling you their secret sauce on how you can manifest more in your life. That's selling you Plenteous, plain and simple.

The disservice in all of this is that by our world selling you Plenteous disguised as Abundance, you are inadvertently and unknowingly directed into a perpetual state of Scarcity. Because the moment you misinterpret Plenteous to be true Abundance, there's a lack created. As it were, Abundance has now been rendered a condition tied to a circumstance or occurrence, which creates an inner void that something is missing—a lack—which cannot do anything but produce a state of Scarcity, which, again, acts as an energy field with its own version of reality.

This prevailing state of Scarcity then gets superficially camouflaged whenever we encounter Plenteous, whether that's materially or experientially. But this Plenteous is very fickle; our definition of it tends to change on a whim because as soon as we encounter what we believed was Plenteous, we inevitably want more, or we become fearful we might lose it. That's the embedded trickster quality of the underlying state of Scarcity; it might be temporarily concealed at times, but it never stops pulling the strings.

Also, Existence is ruled by Chaos; everything always changes, so as circumstances change, the conditions inevitably change as well. All of these forces combined create a self-reinforcing loop where Scarcity is the gravitational force propagating an endless cycle of seeking, striving, attaining, and metabolizing Plenteous regardless of whether the target is money, success, fame, shiny objects, love, health, or even doing good in the world. Incidentally, this is exactly what the world sells you, including all the enlightened coaches and law of attraction gurus who themselves are still trapped in this paradigm.

The only way off this carousel is to directly know what true Abundance is, so let's explore that next.

> "When you arise in the morning,
> think of what a precious privilege it is to be alive,
> to breathe, to think, to enjoy, to love."
> —MARCUS AURELIUS

When we think of the great Stoics and many of the other great wisdom teachers and philosophers, we tend to confuse their teachings with what we consider philosophy today. We even confuse it with what we consider religion to be today, which is largely rooted in ritual and doctrine. Stoicism wasn't concerned with birthing conceptual, theoretical frameworks as our modern-day academia does. In ancient times, philosophy was concerned with how we can best understand and live Life itself. It was oriented toward application or the practice of Life itself, not coming up with esoteric theories, which then get published for peer review.

In these ancient times, men (note: there were also female Stoic philosophers like Porcia Catonis, albeit very few) would study under a teacher—sometimes for decades—as preparation to contribute to and serve society. Marcus Aurelius is known to have had at least five teachers, and he corresponded with Epictetus. Plato was a student of Socrates and, in turn, a teacher of Aristotle. This ancient practice of philosophy was based on the Socratic Method, a form of cooperative argumentative dialogue based on asking and answering questions to stimulate sovereign critical thought and to draw out ideas and parse out presuppositions or Falsehoods.

This preface is not just a history sidebar but fundamental to "grasping" what true Abundance really is. As mentioned, first and foremost, it's a state of Being that, as mentioned, is best visualized as an energy field. A state of Being cannot be created as they already exist within like a radio channel broadcasting at a specific frequency. So, we access them, tune into them like we tune into a radio channel, and once we do—and only when we do—we can hear the music played on that channel. When we access the state of true Abundance—tune into that radio channel—we cannot help but "hear" that music. Tuned into this state, we suddenly see true Abundance everywhere and in every little thing, even though nothing really changed in our direct circumstances.

In this way, states of Being are entirely independent of our circumstances as they're not subject to or created by or from conditions.

We could rightfully say the state of true Abundance is sovereign to circumstances, and this sovereignty comes directly from the sovereignty of the Mind. And this deep understanding of the sovereignty of the mind was at the very core of Stoicism.

> "No person has the power to have everything they want, but it is in their power not to want what they don't have, and to cheerfully put to good use what they do have."
> —SENECA

The Stoics realized that our perception of our circumstances is entirely governed by how our mind perceives it. In turn, our thoughts provoke our emotions, and hence how we feel is entirely dependent on the circumstances. At low levels of Consciousness, we have no Awareness of any of this as the Observer is offline. So, circumstances dictate our state of Being as our subconscious conditioned thinking interprets and perceives reality as it unfolds before us. We're a proverbial leaf in the wind where circumstances are the prevailing winds. When we deem them favorable or Plenteous, we're happy. When we deem them unfavorable or not plenteous enough, we're down and out.

At this level of Consciousness, the only logical conclusion we can come to is that we must change the circumstances—the wind—as we can't "see" that it's our perception that colors the experience of the circumstance. So, we must find ways to be more Plenteous—game over, we are now firmly lodged in the state of Scarcity and riding its never-ending lack carousel only briefly interrupted by fleeting moments of feeling Plenteous. We now *must* play to address the lack, which is how we get stuck and wrapped up in Finite Games for all the wrong reasons.

In the state of true Abundance, we've accessed an entirely different energy field that shows us a different reality. In the moment, so to speak, the actual circumstances of our reality don't change, but our perception of it changes. Over time, however, this different perception will yield radically different experiences of reality. The realization we have the power to change our perception of reality—shift our state or energy field—was central to the Stoic philosophy of living to our highest human potential.

You could view these two energy fields—Abundance and Scarcity—as plot lines of a movie we experience as our reality. In the state of true Abundance, we'll see all sorts of blessings, beauty, bounties, and opportunities in everything around us. We'll act and show up in the world accordingly, and so the plot line that unfolds as our reality is one of only more blessings, beauty, bounties, and opportunities. Conversely, in the state of Scarcity, we'll see all sorts of adversity, ugliness, lack, and competition. We'll act and show up in the world accordingly, including perhaps not acting or being stifled by Fear or doubt, and the plot line that unfolds as our reality is one of lack, struggle, and enduring scarcity regardless of our actual circumstances, which might be Plenteous.

So, what's important to note here is that in the state of Scarcity, we might actually create Plenteous in terms of material wealth, fame, fortune, and applause, but we simply won't experience it as true Abundance. We can see this everywhere in our world; many people have created enormous worldly success and still don't feel anywhere close to true Abundance. They're fearful of losing what they already have, crave more, and will quite readily stoop to greed, malfeasance, fraud, and corruption in one form or another, as their prevailing perception of reality is one of Scarcity, which is little more than our primal survival instinct.

> "When you realize there is nothing lacking, the whole world belongs to you."
> —LAO TZU

To help see why Abundance is a universal Principle, we have to first be able to see it's the natural state of our universe. For all intents and purposes, our universe is infinite in all directions and eternal, and this entire vast ocean of space is made up of nothing but Energy. Our mighty Sun alone, which is a 4.5-billion-year-old yellow dwarf star, strikes Earth continuously with 173,000 terawatts (trillions of watts) of solar energy. To put that in perspective, that's 10,000 times the world's total energy use. Clearly, there's an overwhelming abundance of Energy in our universe.

For the estimated 13.8 billion years it's been in existence, our universe has done nothing but expand, create, and birth all possible forms of Creation ranging from entire galaxies to billions and billions of stars and planets. On our planet alone, DNA researchers have estimated there are at least 1 trillion species. Nature is teeming with life; even in our urban concrete jungles, we find a weed or flower coming through the smallest crack. Clearly, there's an overwhelming Abundance of form and life in our universe as well.

Everything we call our physical reality, or the Finite World of Form, is made of this same Energy that everything else is made from. All experiences and occurrences are also a form of Energy. Fundamentally, even money is Energy, and so is Love (the energy). So, why is it that there's an overwhelming surplus of Energy, and yet humanity perceives its reality to be a world governed by Scarcity?

Mostly it's our deeply flawed perception of physical reality, but it cuts deeper as this flawed perception has us choose not to abide by the laws that govern nature, which are the same laws that govern this entire universe. In physical reality, there are laws of thermodynamics—e.g., entropy—we have to abide by, and there are principles of self-organizing complex living systems which are inviolable. You can ignore, break, or compromise these laws and principles and falsely conclude there's Scarcity, or you can align and organize all of Life itself in accordance with these laws and principles and experience nothing but the natural state of Abundance of this universe.

At the current collective level of Consciousness below 200, humanity is caught in a self-reinforcing psycho-cybernetic loop. We operate from an energy field of Scarcity, so all we can see is Scarcity, and therefore, we are misguided to break these laws and principles, which only reinforces our original false premise that there is Scarcity.

The only way to break this psycho-cybernetic loop is to shift our perspective, which is to say, access the energy field of true Abundance. The only way to do this is by raising the collective level of human Consciousness above 200.

To better understand how and why, it's helpful to see how the universal Principle of Abundance is derived from the coalescence of the Masculine constituent attribute Intelligence and the Feminine constituent attribute Creativity.

> "It's not the man that has too little,
> but the man who craves more that is poor."
> —SENECA

Much of the state the world is in is directly attributable to the Falsehood that we mistake Plenteous for true Abundance. Our relentless and ill-fated pursuit of Plenteous is attributable to operating from deep Unintelligence. This Unintelligence is due to collective levels of human Consciousness below 200. As we discovered earlier, by definition, *that* which creates unintelligent outcomes comes from Unintelligence. All wars, violence, hate, racism, injustices, vast inequalities, famine, and epic pollution are all examples of unintelligent outcomes. The completely unbridled exploitation, destruction, and desecration of our home planet—fueled by an insatiable craving for Plenteous—is akin to primal and deeply unconscious animalistic behavior or survival instinct.

The newest flavor of unconsciousness that's gaining popular traction is the notion Earth is overpopulated. Earth is not overpopulated; Earth is grossly mismanaged. We grow enough food today to feed the entire world 1.5 times over, yet, we have close to 1 billion people that are food deprived or close to starvation. We cannot all live a Western lifestyle, eat a Western diet, continue to power our world with dirty fossil fuels, and create so much toxic and nonbiodegradable waste that by 2050 we'll have more plastic than fish in our oceans. But none of these will be solved by having fewer people operating with the same level of Unintelligence, as we'll just have fewer people creating the same systemic problems. Nothing changes, except we add the Falsehood. We now have more headroom, so the people remaining have some added runway to create more unintelligent outcomes per capita.

Individually we might be operating at slightly higher levels of Consciousness than 200, but collectively as a species, we're not. We perceive ourselves as very technologically advanced, cultured, and civilized, yet when you look beyond this thin layer of shiny veneer, what you see is a species that's still very rudimentary, cruel, and downright barbaric in its ways and entirely preoccupied with survival. Even though, technologically and scientifically, we're far beyond having to worry about mere survival and providing for basic needs.

Our survival today depends entirely on how we avail ourselves of our technology and science as it has both the capacity to "save" us or "destroy" us. Human civilization is now entirely dependent on actually becoming truly civilized and jettisoning our survival instinct so we may rise into a species of higher Consciousness. It would be correct to state that our current level of technology and science has raced far ahead of our collective level of Consciousness. If we don't put virtually all our emphasis on the latter catching up, we'll simply self-destruct, and unfortunately, that event horizon is ominously near—we're speaking maybe ten to twenty years at best, which in evolutionary terms is less than a fraction of a second.

Our current reality is both stark and very simple. At our current collective level of human Consciousness, we simply don't have access to true Intelligence, without which true Abundance cannot be accessed or realized. Intelligence is a key operant because true Intelligence, as defined by the universe, is *that* which creates intelligent outcomes, which are only those outcomes that are conducive to Life itself. Anything that violates the laws and principles that govern this universe is never going to yield outcomes that are going to be conducive to Life itself. What you get then is an outcome that we might perceive as materially or experientially Plenteous, but what we're truly after—true Abundance—remains elusive.

Only the intelligent outcomes of true Intelligence have the power to connect us with the sensation of true Abundance in our Outer World. However, this all originates from our direct Inner World, knowing that true Abundance is our natural state. We could view the state of true Abundance as highly fertile soil for Intelligence to blossom and create the intelligent outcomes we then resonate with internally. In this sense, the state of true Abundance is a precursor and prerequisite to recognize and experience true Abundance in our Outer World.

> "Many eyes go through the meadow,
> but few see the flowers in it."
> —RALPH WALDO EMERSON

A crucial threshold to cross to truly "get this" is to let go of the Falsehood that Plenteous is analogous with Abundance. It's not. What we misperceive Abundance to be, is truly Plenteous. Abundance is not limited to copious amounts of money or material possessions. It's not defined by having a big house, fancy clothes, or a luxurious lifestyle. True Abundance is seeing the riches in a single flower, the kind gesture of a stranger, the miraculous in a spider web, or the ability to take a full breath of cool crisp morning air. When we start having eyes for true Abundance, we literally start seeing it everywhere, in everything, and all the time. Even though nothing changes, it changes everything.

There's one more stubborn myth to dispel on this topic. There's nothing inherently unspiritual about financial wealth. Poverty is not a prerequisite for attaining high levels of consciousness or creating a life of spiritual art. Financial and material abundance—whatever that might be for you—stemming from the coalescence of Intelligence and Creativity is every bit as artful and spiritual as the missions any philanthropist, master Yogi, social activist, or Buddha himself devoted their lives to.

> "Without a rich heart, wealth is an ugly beggar."
> —RALPH WALDO EMERSON

Creativity, as we mentioned before, is the juice of Life itself. But for something to be true Creativity it has to be aligned with certain embedded principles. One, if you recall, was to be conducive to Life itself so here we see a main premise of Intelligence reinforced by the Feminine cornerstone Creativity.

In terms of true Abundance, there's another key principle of true Creativity that must be met and present. For there to be aliveness and thus Creativity, things cannot be stagnant, dormant, or restricted. We discussed this in the context of every single person being a unique puzzle piece of the mosaic called humanity. We're each blessed with our own unique talents, gifts, and superpowers, which, when expressed into the world in authentic ways, has us claim our unique puzzle piece. These talents, gifts, and superpowers could be anything, and there's no hierarchy in any of this. It makes no difference to the universe if your uniqueness is geared toward being a celebrity movie star, a chef, CEO of a billion-dollar company, master plumber, Kindergarten school teacher, or a dedicated parent.

This is not to say we should or will all get paid the same, but we must reorganize our values in society to one of a higher level of Consciousness that acknowledges all contributions by all people with equal respect. Incidentally, pay scales should be normalized, meaning the exorbitant self-dealing excesses at the highest corporate levels must be contained and brought back to the Earthly plane. In 1965, the CEO-to-typical worker compensation ratio was c. 20:1 and today it's close to 300:1. Of course, the root cause here also is a Scarcity mindset or survival instinct at work.

Nevertheless, this ever-widening gap has no basis other than this survival instinct showing up as an adolescent abuse of power, repulsive self-dealing, and a complete absence of any form of responsibility toward the whole beehive as income inequality drives a deep wedge into the perceived fairness of society.

When a society becomes perceived as a rigged game and unfair, it drives behaviors by all accordingly. It promulgates and reinforces Scarcity as that becomes the lived experience of most and what ensues over time is what we see play out today: division, hate, radicalization, polarization, extremism, and violence, which are then all oppressed by use of Force, which only serves as more fuel on the fire of those oppressed. What the very few should realize is that this blood is on their hands; at higher levels of Consciousness above 200, they immediately do and become the change we need to see in the world. There is then a disproportional accelerated ripple effect that occurs when people with access to great wealth, power, and influence reach higher levels of Consciousness.

So, where do we see stagnancy, dormancy, or restriction as evidence there's a lack of true Creativity in support of true Abundance?

Inauthenticity is the simple answer. When we're wearing a mask and living the story society told us to be through enculturation, we're showing up in inauthentic ways. This blocks how our unique talents, gifts, and superpowers are expressed into the world, which inevitably will have us locked into a state of Scarcity as everything we do feels like work, effort, and struggle. In terms of worldly success, we might still achieve Plenteous, but it will never be an experience of true Abundance. These are all telltale signs of being stuck in *must*-play mode, which cuts us off from true Creativity.

> "A man's true wealth hereafter is the good he has done to his fellow men."
> —MAHATMA GANDHI

One of the most powerful ways to access the state of true Abundance—which is an energy field within—is to shift our focus without. We can teach and condition ourselves to celebrate loudly for others' successes, recognize beauty and splendor in small and common things, and to be attentive to the countless small forms of Abundance that flow into our life on a daily basis. Ending the day with a gratitude list of five or seven items and starting our day with recognizing we're alive and breathing are additional practices that can help habituate our Mind to have eyes for the Abundance all around us. All of this serves to disturb the Scarcity energy field and shift us to the higher plane of true Abundance Consciousness.

This form of consciously cultivating Awareness for true Abundance has a way of eliciting ready access to Intelligence and Creativity, which then become the driving forces that tune us into the state or energy field of true Abundance within.

When you start noticing an organic shift toward the appreciation of the quality of things and less so the quantity—in all aspects of your life—you will know you're shifting away from Plenteous into the miraculous force field of true Abundance.

Trust me, just in being spiritual art you're already rich and abundant beyond your wildest imagination but you won't truly know this until you master the last Principle—Harmony—so let's explore that next.

ABUNDANCE

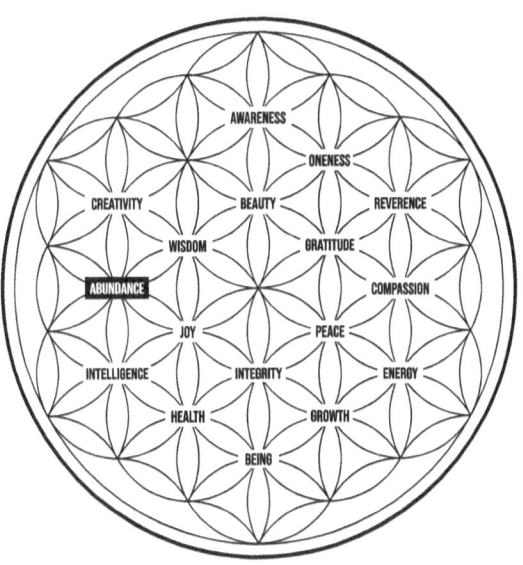

CHAPTER 30

HARMONY

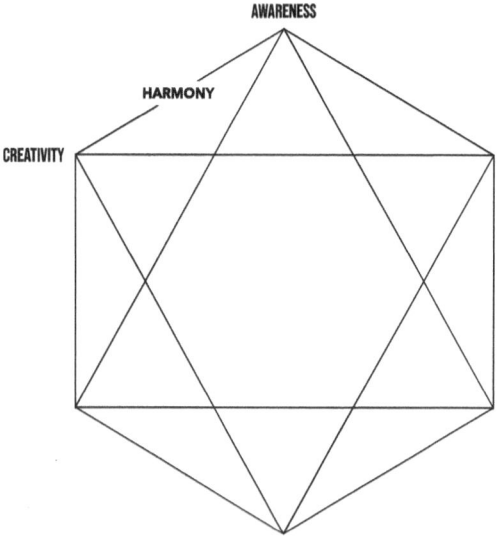

THERE'S A POETIC SYMBOLISM to the universal Principle of Harmony being the very last of the Cornerstones, Gifts, and Principles we explore to complete the Love+Truth Framework. It's also not coincidental—as nothing truly is—that there are six Cornerstones, six Gifts, and six Principles which makes for a total of 18. In turn, 18 reduces to 9 (1 + 8 = 9), which I alluded to earlier is a very special and sacred cosmic number. Please see the Addendum for more on this.

Before we delve deeper into Harmony, let's first clarify that balance and Harmony are not the same thing, as these terms are often used in tandem or interchangeably. In fact, they're very different, and whereas Harmony is a universal Principle of our entire universe, balance is not.

> "Change is the only constant in life."
> —HERACLITUS

Balance refers to an equal distribution of weight or the condition in which different elements are equal or in the correct proportions to establish an equilibrium. As it pertains to our universe, Existence, or Life itself, there's no such thing as true or real balance; at best, you could speak of a purely theoretical notion of balance. This is because Life itself and everything in this universe is in perpetual and continuous motion. As we discovered, everything is also infinite, and this applies to linear time as well. Even though our smallest measurement is a second, there's an infinite amount of fractions of a second we can again theoretically measure, and so time itself is continuous and in perpetual motion as well.

Balance is, by definition, static. It's a fixed or finite point in time and space at which some conditions are in perfect balance. However, our universe or Life itself has no fixed points, nor is it finite anywhere; literally everything is in perpetual and continuous motion, and everything is also fractal-based, which is to say infinite, so balance is a purely theoretical concept in terms of our universe or Life itself.

Balance also presupposes opposites, whether they're forces or elements. A singular thing in the absence of time and space cannot be balanced. Even when we "balance" a singular object like a whirlabout by giving it a turn, what's really balancing is the rotational forces of the mass of the whirlabout against the gravitational force of Mother Earth. As soon as the velocity of the spin falls below the equilibrium range, the whirlabout will fall on its side or, what we call out of balance. Balance, then, is based on the premise of the Law of Opposite Forces. Our entire universe, on the other hand, is based on the Law of Polarity, which has as its premise the idea of unity within opposites. The Law of Polarity informs us that seemingly opposite poles are really two sides of the same coin. Polarity is a part of the Fundamental Architecture and an inviolable law.

Understanding this at a deep level is fundamental as we'll contrast balance and Harmony throughout this chapter as I'll demonstrate with various examples how the misunderstanding of this core Principle is at the basis of some of the greatest challenges facing humanity today, including the many personal, health, relationship, gender, societal, economical, and environmental schisms we see.

> "When things are unified, they are beautiful.
> What makes music beautiful? Harmony.
> And what is harmony? Unity."
>
> —RADHANATH SWAMI

The etymology of the word Harmony shows us the roots are from the ancient Greek "harmonia" which means "agreement, concord of sounds." From the Merriam-Webster Dictionary we can distill even more aspects imbedded in the word Harmony such as: "the combination of simultaneous musical notes in a chord"; "pleasing arrangement of parts as in congruence"; "the science of the structure, relation, and progression of chords"; and "agreement or accord." There's a lot to work with here, so let's delve in.

It's clearly not surprising to see the reference to sound, music, chords, and notes, as we all intuitively associate Harmony with the harmonics of music. Music is not just an existential and integral part of our universe; it's at the very origins of all of Creation. Just like our physical reality is an expression of mathematics, music is as well. In fact, our physical reality is music expressed into form.

In other words, physical reality or all of Creation is sonic geometry or music frozen into form. We know this to be unequivocally true as all of physical reality is based on sacred geometry expressed into form, and we know each of the sacred forms of sacred geometry has a unique note which, in turn, is each based on the poetry of mathematics.

The Addendum contains a full explanation of how each sacred form has its own note; however, there's one element of the mathematical poetry in all of this I would like you to take away. The frequency of each form is derived from transposing the addition of the inside angles of the form into hertz, which allows us to then correlate them with their equivalent note on the musical scale. For every single one of these sacred forms, the digital root of their respective inside angles—and therefore frequency of their note—has a digital root of 9. Incidentally, the primordial sound of the universe—often referred to as "Om"—is 432 Hz, which, of course, also has a digital root of 9 (4 + 3 + 2 = 9).

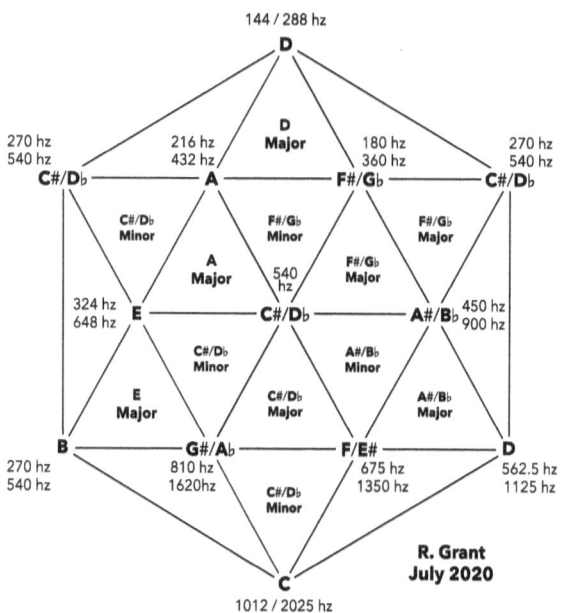

In 1955, the International Organization for Standardization affirmed A4 = 440 Hz as the standard tuning pitch and reaffirmed this as part of ISO 16 in 1975. The musical note of A above middle C—or "A4" in scientific notation—is traditionally used as the baseline musical note, and all musical notes, lower or higher, are then tuned in relation to this baseline tuning pitch of A4. Pythagorean tuning is based on A4 = 432 Hz, which is in harmony with sacred geometry, whereas A4 = 440 Hz could be considered a synthetic tuning standard, meaning it's not in harmony with nature. One long-standing argument against Pythagorean tuning has been that all major thirds and major sixths are too sharp, and this has been an imperfection Pythagoras left in his work. In recent years, polymath Robert Edward Grant solved this small glitch mathematically and published this in his Precise Temperament tuning pitch, which is based on A4 = 432 Hz and perfectly solves for "9" across all chords and octaves.

I share all this and the (simplified) graphic representation of the Precise Temperament tuning pitch because nothing shows the connection between music and sacred geometry more eloquently and powerfully. Metatron's Cube is displayed as music, and if you recall, Metatron's Cube represents the Fundamental Architecture of all of Creation. Hence, here we can see how all of Creation is just the harmonics of sacred geometry or frozen music we experience visually.

So, why do we care? The tuning pitch determines the frequency of all other notes, which means music based on the standard tuning pitch A4 = 440 Hz is in disharmony with nature. Our brain is a highly sensitive neurological frequency receiver, and music in the standard A4 = 440 Hz is in dissonance with our true nature as all of Creation is based on the harmonics of sacred geometry. Dissonance deregulates our gene expression as frequency is what plays our DNA like an instrument. Biologically, we see this exact same dissonance represented by synthetic (GMO) foods. I will leave it to you to intuit what might happen to mental health when you make a synthetic tuning pitch the standard for music people the world over listen to each and every day.

So, if physical reality is music expressed into form, what is or makes music?

For practical purposes, we'll cover this topic in somewhat broad strokes because covering the full depth of the science of music would take volumes of books. So, in a nutshell, a musical note is an audio vibration with a frequency measured in Hz. We could view each musical note as a basic unit in music representing a sound with a definitive pitch. In Western music, musical notes are organized according to the chromatic scale, which recognizes twelve main musical notes (i.e., A, A#/Bb, B, C, C#/Db, D, D#/Eb, E, F, F#/Gb, G, and G#/Ab).

Octaves denote a scale within which each musical note can be played. The name "octave" can be a bit misleading as it suggests there are only eight octaves. In theory, there are an infinite amount of octaves, but the human hearing range of c. 20 Hz to 20,000 Hz can only access ten octaves, so most music falls within the first to eighth octave, which is within this human hearing range. The more important point about octaves is that any musical note played in the subsequent next higher octave is precisely twice the frequency, so there is a perfect mathematical relationship for each musical note across all octaves it's played in. The tuning pitch mentioned earlier functions as the baseline note from which all other notes are derived based on the mathematical relationship between the notes and octaves.

A chord in music is created by playing multiple notes simultaneously, thereby creating their own unique sound. If you just take the twelve main musical notes and multiply this by the typical eight octaves, we already have ninety-six unique notes or tones. If you now imagine the multiplicity of variations of chords possible from just these ninety-six unique notes, you can see music is infinitely creative, and we'll never run out of "new" music. In very basic terms, music is created when we harmoniously arrange musical notes and chords. When this arrangement is disharmonious, we get audible dissonance, which is what we experience as noise.

The overall harmonics of music is rooted in science and referred to as the Elements of Music. There are eight basic Elements of Music, and this is where things get really interesting, as we can directly translate and transpose these elements into what we could call the Elements of Life. These Elements of Life hold the same relationship to the harmonics of Existence as the Elements of Music do to the harmonics of music.

The following table shows what that would look like:

Elements of Music	Reference	Elements of Life
Dynamics	Volume	Tides of life
Form	Arrangement	Chapters of life
Harmony	Agreement	Dance of life
Melody	Tune	Mood of life
Rhythm	Beat	Cadence of life
Texture	Density	Orchestra of life
Timbre	Tone Color	Richness of life
Tonality	Experience	Seasonality of life

Dynamics refers to the volume of music or loud and soft, and all the gradual changes from loud to soft or vice versa. Dynamics are the ebbs and flows of music. This corresponds with the Tides of Life.

Form or structure of music refers to the order and arrangement of the different parts such as introduction, verse, chorus, bridge, solo, in and outro, but there are many more descriptions. We could say this corresponds with the phases and Chapters of Life.

Harmony, in musical terms, refers to the sound coherence or agreement between notes and chords. In other words, it's the dance between all the notes and chords, which, when in agreement, sound harmonious. This corresponds with the Dance of Life.

Melody is a series of pitches that make a tune. Melody can be happy or sad or anything in between, so you could say it reflects the mood of music. Melody also determines harmony and tonality and typically drives the rhythm of music. Isn't that interesting? Because what we basically have here is our mood (melody) determining the dance (harmony) and highs and lows of life (tonality) and typically driving the cadence (rhythm) of life. Melody then corresponds with the Mood of Life.

Rhythm in music actually has different aspects (e.g., tempo), but in the simplest of terms, it's what we call the beat of the music as it's the rhythm of the music we dance to. Rhythm can be upbeat, slow, and all sorts of variations in between. So, this directly corresponds with the Cadence of Life.

Texture in music refers to the number of instruments or voices that contribute to the overall density of music. Texture can be thin or sparse, like in a duet or vocalist, supported by a single instrument like the guitar or piano. When there are a multitude of instruments or voices, like a band or orchestra, we call the texture thick or dense. We see this exact same dynamic in Life itself; some things we must do alone or involve only one or very few other people. Other things we do in groups. Texture then corresponds to the Orchestra of Life.

Timbre in music refers to the unique sound quality, which is why it's sometimes referred to as tone color. An instrument can have a rich sound or a thin or shallow sound and, again, all tone colors of the rainbow in between. This corresponds with the Richness of Life.

Finally, tonality refers to the overall sound of the music, which can be pleasant or unpleasant, but there are countless other descriptors like minor, major, basic, expansive, moving, touching, warm, cool, rich, light, deep, erotic, happy, joyful, dark, somber, and even harmonious. Tonality then points at the Seasonality of Life.

So, you might wonder, *Why this dissertation on music?* What emerges from all these insights is that within music is the composition of Life itself. Life = Music and vice versa. All of Creation or Existence is the harmonics of frequency and vibration, both in how physical reality is created and what Life itself constitutes. And even if you forget all the above by the time you turn to the next page, the seed I truthfully hope was planted is to see the divine poetry in how all these miraculous puzzle pieces come together to create you and all your experience as your reality. So, when I keep reiterating you are spiritual art, I truly mean that you are literally the harmonics of the vibration and frequency of your entire being. In that sense, you truly are art, music, poetry, or a living sculpture if you prefer that visual. However you wish to look at it, you truly are spiritual art expressing itself into Life itself, thereby co-creating this miraculous reality we call life on the Earthly plane.

> "He who lives in harmony with himself lives in harmony with the universe."
> —MARCUS AURELIUS

There was a second major theme in the etymology of the word Harmony, and that was "agreement, concord, or accord." This is a curious juxtaposition because the reference to music in Harmony points us at fluidity, movement, dance, and the dynamic nature of Harmony, whereas—at first glance—agreement, concord, or accord seems to be the very opposite. It's not. Unlike balance, Harmony is ever-changing, ever-flowing, ever-reordering, and ever-evolving. It's never static; it exists within a dynamic harmonic field which we could view as the range of possible harmonics where anything outside this harmonic field is out of Harmony. This harmonic field itself is not static as depending on the relationships and circumstances, this harmonic field morphs. This is the musical nature of Harmony.

Within this dynamic harmonic field, there's a range of possible harmonic points in each point of space and time—this is the agreement or accord nature of Harmony. Since space and time are dynamic, these possible harmonic points are also dynamic. Harmony, then, is an agreement or accord that's fluid and dynamic in nature that exists within a certain range—outside this range, Harmony becomes Disharmony. In that context, we could say the universal Principle of Harmony is both art and science, which makes total sense as that's the true nature of our whole universe.

So, let's show this in a real-life example to demonstrate how this works. Let's assume Seller A has their home for sale for $250,000, and they would be pleased to sell it for $225,000 or above. Buyer B loves Seller A's house. But, ideally, Buyer B would like to spend $215,000, but their maximum budget is $235,000. The harmonic field is between $225,000 and $235,000, as only within this range can there be a harmonious transaction where both Seller A and Buyer B walk away feeling happy, which is to say harmonious. At Seller A's asking price or Buyer B's ideal price, there would be disharmony as one of them "loses," so to speak. Now, let's say interest rates drop, and now Buyer B's maximum budget goes up to $240,000. This morphs the harmonic field as the range now becomes $225,000 to $240,000 assuming nothing changed on the part of Seller A.

As rudimentary as this example might seem, in very basic terms, all of Life itself operates like this, except most of us don't look at Life through this lens. The prevailing lens humanity looks through is zero-sum game; we're obsessed with winning and optimizing our personal outcome, and Harmony never even crosses our mind as a consideration. You will be perplexed by how much Disharmony you could dissolve and turn into Harmony in all areas of your Life if you start applying just this fundamental understanding of the universal Principle of Harmony.

> "We must see that peace represents a sweeter music, a cosmic melody, that is far superior to the discords of war."
> —MARTIN LUTHER KING, JR.

With this foundational understanding of Harmony in place, let's now examine the Masculine cornerstone, Awareness, and the

Feminine cornerstone, Creativity, and see how and why the coalescence of these two respective cornerstones creates the universal Principle of true Harmony.

Let's start with Creativity, as we already delved deep into the relationship of music with Harmony. For all intents and purposes, the art and science of music is but the expression of Creativity in the spectrum of sound. And we already discovered that all the elements that make for harmonious music can be applied to Life itself to create true Harmony.

You might recall from the chapter on Creativity that the word Creativity is derived from the Latin word *creare*, which means to create, to make, or to produce. The opposite pole of Creativity was, therefore, destruction or decay and death. Derived from the cornerstone Creativity, something must be conducive to Life itself for there to be true Harmony. Moreover, true Harmony is something we have to create, make, or produce.

We can easily see all of this when we look at war, violence, hate, racism, disproportional inequalities, injustices, and epic pollution. None of these have so much as a trace of Harmony in them, which is why all of them are in direct violation of the universal Principle of Harmony. Incidentally, all of these have harmonious potential, but this potential cannot be accessed—that is, created or produced—with the prevailing zero-sum game lens through which humanity views the world at collective levels of Consciousness below 200.

We also discussed Creativity ceases to exist when things go stagnant, dormant, or are restricted. This is to say, static. As one of the three Feminine constituent attributes, Creativity is all about *being* fully alive and in dynamic motion. True Harmony mirrors this essential quality of Creativity, as we discovered before when we discussed the dynamic harmonic field and how true Harmony is always changing and evolving.

Within Creativity, there's also the notion of receptivity—the flow of Life itself always oscillates from giving to receiving. This exact dynamic feature of Creativity we also see mirrored in true Harmony. True Harmony is a constant movement of giving and receiving. We see this come back in relationships that are harmonious, in any food chain in nature, or even in negotiations or the seasons of our life.

It's clear how closely correlated true Harmony is with Creativity, so let's now see how Awareness fits into this picture.

Let's first recall that Awareness is one of three constituent attributes of the Masculine and that the Masculine itself represents Consciousness, whereas the Feminine represents Existence. As we discussed, Awareness has an element of sensing in it or of being aware. And Ignorance is all *that* which we are simply not aware of. We also stated that when we're raising our Awareness, we reduce our Ignorance and our level of Consciousness raises correspondingly, which then also gives us access to higher levels of Intelligence and Energy, the other two Masculine constituent attributes.

In simple terms, we could state at higher levels of Awareness, we see more. We see more relationships, interdependencies, interconnections, etc. More of the totality of the complexity that is Life itself and all its countless nuances becomes accessible to us as we ascend in our level of Awareness. This is exactly how Awareness is the perfect complement to Creativity in the creation of true Harmony. True Harmony has the same amorphous quality to it as Awareness does; it's neither exact, formulaic, nor precise nor is it ever fixed or static. To navigate this, we need Awareness—the essential quality of sensing, feeling, intuiting, and seeing deeply.

We all already know how to do this and do this all the time, probably without consciously knowing. We palpably "feel" Harmony as well as Disharmony. When something is harmonious, a love relationship, for instance, we can tangibly feel this. We might have no idea how to deduct it logically, but we can definitely feel it. Similarly, when something feels "off" to us, it's disharmonious, whatever that something might be.

We also know it can shift very fast; sometimes, even a few careless words can disrupt the Harmony into Disharmony. What happened, in essence, is the harmonic equilibrium point got pushed off the dynamic harmonic field. We can see clearly then that this harmonic equilibrium point is the Fulcrum or still point. And, to restore Harmony, this Fulcrum needs to be brought back into the dynamic harmonic field. This Fulcrum is dynamic also in that it could be any of the range of points within the dynamic harmonic field and rarely actually stands still.

Awareness is actually the intangible structure—Order, if you will—that brings true Harmony into agreement or accord. Awareness is what allows us to see into the dynamic harmonic field and discern its boundaries. This is why lacking sufficient levels of Awareness, creating harmonious outcomes is really a luck of the draw exercise as it might, by chance, fall within the range of the dynamic harmonic field or might fall outside of it.

We can use music again as an analogy. Let's assume we have a three-year-old toddler with a little Playskool toy piano. She has never had a music lesson in her life, so she has no trained skills or faculties for music, which is to say, no Awareness. She'll bang away on this little toy piano and create all sorts of sounds; most of it will be noise, but at times, she might actually hit a few notes right and create music, which is to say, Harmony.

Now, let's go to the other side of this spectrum, and now we have a virtuoso concert pianist who graduated top of his class at Juilliard and went on to become a celebrated concert pianist and music composer. When he merely looks at or thinks about the piano, he can "see" music or true Harmony. Whenever he plays, listens to, or creates music, he immediately senses when there's Disharmony in the notes or chords. His faculty of Awareness for music is extraordinarily high as he has talent (art), studied music (science), and practiced countless hours to perfect his art and science.

Through our Awareness, we each have the capacity to become a virtuoso spiritual artist of Life itself, and when we do, we gain the highly valuable capacity to tune into the dynamic harmonic field and connect with true Harmony. To literally sense and see true Harmony as if it's palpable to us, to flow and dance with it like it's music we can hear and feel. Awareness is instrumental to true Harmony and coalesced with Creativity, giving us access to becoming an entirely unique and one-of-a-kind harmonious note within all of Creation.

> "Diversity leads to perfect harmony."
> —HERACLITUS

Let's now examine some examples to illustrate the application of true Harmony in real life. All of nature, as well as our entire universe, is premised on diversity; on our planet alone, biologists estimate there are over 1 trillion species. Nature thrives on diversity; it makes the whole web of life more resilient and therefore enhances the health and vitality of the whole system. True Harmony emerges from the interdependencies, interconnectedness, and symbiotic relationship among all this diversity of Life itself.

When humans interfere and damage this complex web of life by eradicating species and wildlife, the Harmony is disturbed, and entire food pyramids collapse due to Disharmony. In essence, by our interference, we're pushing nature out of its dynamic harmonic field.

We can see this same dynamic play out in society. Everything in society is geared toward the commoditization of humans, with the whole transhumanism agenda as advertised by the World Economic Forum and various technocrats being the ultimate form of commoditization of humans into programmable and controllable Cyborgs. People that are unique, outliers, different, or don't fit the mainstream narrative are marginalized and, in many cases, even ostracized. And I am not talking about extremists here who spew out foolish hateful rhetoric. We have too many of those also, but they are a symptom of the root cause that our society seems to have become hyper-allergic to diversity.

The pervasive Disharmony we see in society is largely due to the narcissistic parasite that has slipped into our collective Consciousness that all others should act, think, dress, and live like me, like me, and approve of me. And, if they don't, they're wrong, and Force in the form of hate, racism, violence, cancel culture, and censorship is all permissible. Force, by definition, creates resistance, which is counter-Force, and this is why we see all these extremist offshoots sprout up left and right.

All of this is madness and in contradiction to the inviolable laws of our universe. If our aim is to create a harmonious society, we should welcome and celebrate diversity, but Harmony can never be created by use of Force. We don't all have to be the same; in fact, we shouldn't be, as we're each unique, and all it takes is to live in Harmony with each other. Being the same, or liking or approving of you, is not a prerequisite for me to live in Harmony with you. I can just let you be, and you let me be, and provided we each honor the Golden Rule, we'll be in perfect Harmony with each other. Harmony will inevitably arise if we move toward unification in diversity. Disharmony will inevitably persist if we continue to seek unification in commoditization.

> "Happiness is when what you think, what you say, and what you do is in harmony."
> —MAHATMA GANDHI

Another major venomous thorn of Disharmony in our society is centered around equality and plays out in various areas. One of those is around the vast income and wealth inequalities, a gap that's only widening at an accelerating pace.

Here we can clearly see how a fundamental Disharmony created by abuse of power, economic leverage, political influence, and self-enrichment by a self-preeminent executive class cannot be restored to Harmony by policies that are anchored in propping up the marginalized masses.

The root problem is that executive pay scales are entirely out of whack, mostly through excessive levels of self-importance, which translates into unchecked greed. Except for actual founders, executives are not nearly as indispensable or invaluable as they like to believe they are, nor did any of them at any time put their own balance sheet at risk. They're playing with other people's money, and this includes the vast majority of the financial wizards in private equity, venture capital, money management, and the banking industry. This circle of friends even includes the law, accounting, consulting, and political lobbying firms that get paid exorbitant fees to keep this whole web of self-dealing insular and self-propagating. All of this is based on low levels of Consciousness below 200, no matter the appearance of worldly success and sophistication.

Harmony can only be restored by this upper class of society recognizing there's a harmonic field within which income and wealth inequalities can harmoniously exist. Meritocracy itself isn't the problem; in fact, it's essential for a society to function properly, but the asymmetry or skewness of meritocracy created by the excessive self-dealing of this relatively small executive upper class is what translates into the extreme stickiness of the Disharmony, and no amount of marginal rebalancing of the lower 90 percent of society will solve the fundamental skewness in the income and wealth distribution curve.

At levels of Consciousness above 200, we start seeing the world from the perspective of unity, which is Oneness, Compassion, and Harmony. We move beyond just operating from pure self-interest, which shows up as greed; our Awareness expands to see the interconnectedness, interdependencies, and symbiotic relationships that are essential to creating a harmonious society. It's a relatively small upgrade in the level of Consciousness that's required, but it would create a sea-change effect on how we view the vital importance of shared prosperity, creating a harmonious society, and our role in it when we're granted the privilege of showing true leadership and stewardship for the greatest good of the whole beehive.

> "Be in harmony; yet be different."
> —CONFUCIUS

Another essential misperception we see in modern Western society concerns gender equality. In an attempt to balance the stubborn gender inequalities that most definitely exist, this cultural movement has now evolved into gender neutralization, which is triggering a cascade of distortions that are disharmonizing society. Women and men are equal, yet we are different creatures by design. One is not more or less valuable than the other, but that doesn't change. We're fundamentally different. We're built and wired differently, and this is partly biological since different hormones dominate our respective biological spacesuit, but most of all, it's energetic. Women are typically Feminine-energy dominant and Masculine-energy non-dominant, and vice versa for men. At its core, gender neutralization is aimed at balancing these energies within men and women, respectively, with the premise being that this balancing will create gender equality.

It won't. What it will do is create lots of gender confusion and Disharmony. Gender equality that's aimed at creating true Harmony between the genders and within society is centered around celebrating and welcoming the innate uniqueness, value, and natural qualities of the Feminine and the Masculine and how they complement each other. Again, there's a dynamic harmonic field of gender equality where both genders can harmoniously exist, and each feels fully seen, heard, valued, respected, and worthy in their own unique expression, which includes their individual uniqueness in sexual preferences or gender identification. This doesn't mean everything must be rigidly structured, regulated, and codified to be perfectly balanced in all aspects as that's using Force, and we see that nowhere else in nature or this universe. It's just a collective recalibration of dancing with true Harmony within this dynamic harmonic field which will organically morph according to circumstances and specifics.

This is a much more dynamic and fluid approach to gender equality, which would be aimed not at marginal incremental movements toward systemic change but creating a whole new system that is conducive for both genders to thrive and flourish within their respective unique nature. This does once again require levels of Consciousness above 200 as the identification with mind, or body prevents us from rising above these purely psychological constructs of self. At higher levels of Consciousness, we can access the higher knowledge Truth that we're but a Soul walking around with a corpse, as Epictetus used to say, which allows us to then dance with Harmony within this dynamic harmonic field without any attachment to identification or enculturation.

> "Love is the energizing elixir of the universe, the cause and effect of all harmony."
> —RUMI

What should be becoming apparent now is that true Harmony is near-impossible to access from a place of Fear or indifference. We cannot dance with others, with society, with nature, with Mother Earth, or with Life itself when the lens through which we perceive all of Creation is fogged over with Fear or indifference. In fact, we cannot even dance with ourselves and find true Harmony within unless the foundational underpinning is self-Love (the energy).

Fully embodied, the universal Principle of true Harmony is the one Principle that uniquely connects us deep into the energetic web and intelligence of Life itself. It's a powerful portal through which we can express into Life itself the other five universal Principles of Oneness, Compassion, Growth, Health, and Abundance at much deeper levels. And these deeper levels represent a whole new level of expansiveness, which only serves to enlarge the canvas available to paint our spiritual art.

As we can see on the *Flower of Life* below, with Harmony added, we can now see the three Masculine and three Feminine cornerstones of the Architecture, the six Gifts, and the six Principles of the entire Love+Truth Framework.

So, with all the foundational puzzle pieces now in place, let's delve into how we can embark on our journey of becoming a true spiritual artist.

That's next as we start Part V.

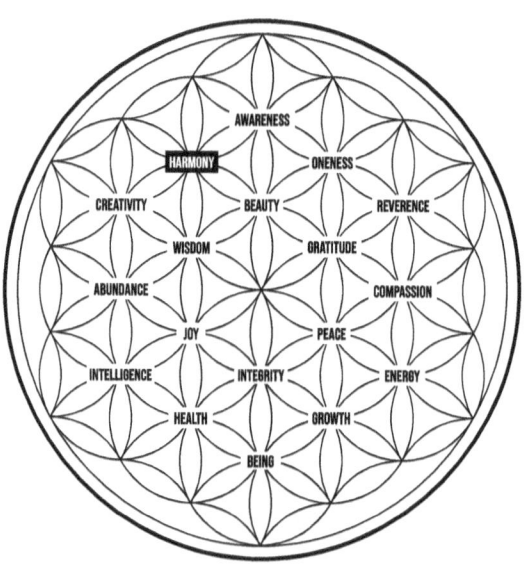

PART V

LIVING A LIFE OF SPIRITUAL ART

"There is nothing in a caterpillar that tells
you it's going to be a butterfly."
—R. BUCKMINSTER FULLER

CHAPTER 31

AUTOPOIESIS & SELF-LOVE

WITH THE ARCHITECTURE, GIFTS, AND PRINCIPLES all laid bare, what's next is how do we make our life a work of spiritual art. That's to say, how do we become the sculptor of the sculpture or the Poet devoted to the art of self-poetry?

There's a spiritual Poet in each of us, no matter how deeply buried; this Poet might be under dense layers of the mud of enculturation and unconsciousness. These seemingly impenetrable layers of sludge act as dense veils of illusion that have us severed from our Divinity within. And we cannot start to become a true Poet unless we have an inkling there's poetry within us.

> "It's during our darkest moments
> that we must focus to see the light."
> —ARISTOTLE

The universe has its own mystical ways of awakening a first whisper of remembrance in us, which prompts a curiosity that leads to an unmistaken call to go within. These whispers and calls might be faint at first, but they are persistent, and over time we will not be able to unhear them no matter how hard we try to ignore them. Most often, the catalyst of awakening our remembrance shows up in gifts wrapped in sandpaper.

Crisis, catastrophe, or calamity shows up in our life, and we are forced to examine all we believed was real. These 3 Cs can show up in a myriad of ways, whether it's illness, divorce, financial ruin or a sidelined career, death of a loved one, or a child that succumbs to an addiction. It doesn't matter what it is, and these are all just experiences divinely orchestrated to facilitate our greatest growth, greatest prosperity, and greatest evolution.

That's not typically how we experience them at first. We more likely experience them initially as hardship, pain, or injustice, and the deeper the suffering, the more likely we are to discover the universe is merely nudging us on the rite of passage called awakening. Endowed with free will, the decision when we decide to go on this rite of passage is ours to make, but the passage itself is not optional.

Resisting, fighting, or outright not choosing to go is always an option; just know the natural laws and forces of the universe do not yield. The 3 Cs will circle back time and again, each time amplified in severity, making the pain, suffering, and darkness each time a little less bearable. There's nothing cruel or malicious about any of this; when your divinity within has decided it's time for your journey into remembrance, it will orchestrate the events and circumstances necessary to guide you on that path.

All forms of enduring unhappiness, restlessness, emptiness, anguish, anxiety, misery, sadness, meaninglessness or more serious mental afflictions like depression and suicidal tendencies are all telltale signs we are negating the call to go within.

Conventional psychiatrists and psychologists will argue these are all trauma-based afflictions or due to hormonal imbalances, but while that's not a diagnostic error, it's still an incomplete understanding. Most of us do carry deep traumas and wounds that most definitely need healing, and psychiatrists and psychologists can play a valuable role in that process. But overlooking or ignoring the deeper spiritual beckoning of why this trauma or wound is in our life in the first place is akin to declining the universe's invitation to ascend to higher levels of evolution. We might superficially heal the trauma or wound, but deeper lessons not learned will be presented again in other challenges.

The same goes for a diagnosis of hormonal imbalances, which are typically "treated" with synthetic pharmaceuticals that do nothing but address the symptoms. Oftentimes, they do more harm than good as they tend to numb us out and render us chemically and mentally dependent, which is to say, addicted. So, nothing was really healed, and we now have a chemical dependency as a bonus. Root causes are always metaphysical in nature; that's not to say these hormonal imbalances are a diagnostic error, as they are real. Real as they are, they're also just a symptom of a deeper cause, as our natural state is health or homeostasis in biological terms.

> "If you are to advance, all fixed ideas must go."
> —JOSEPH CAMPBELL

The writer Joseph Campbell refers to the call to go within as our Hero's Journey. The Hero's Journey is as old as antiquity and is a recurring theme in all mythology, ancient wisdom traditions, and the mystery schools of ancient civilizations. The rite of passage called awakening is like a dormant spiritual journey of ascension encoded within our human blueprint. Each of us, at the exact right time and place, will find this dormancy stirred into disturbance, which acts as the first whisper of remembrance.

This remembrance and the entire process, from how it's initiated all the way through its entire unfolding, has one singular overarching purpose: awakening us to our divinity within.

For the remainder of this book, we are therefore going to focus solely on how we can align our life's purpose with the purpose the universe has for us. That is to say, we're now moving beyond talking about playing or being lost in Finite Games. We're going to leave the trivial realm of worldly success behind for the moment and zero in on how we may become a spiritual Poet first and foremost. Our sights are squarely set on *the* one Infinite Game, and this will require us to let go of all fixed ideas. We must surrender all the things we believe we know, as Epictetus reminded us: "a man cannot learn what he believes he already knows."

The game Man plays is very different from the game Spirit plays. There are different rules, different goals, and a fundamentally different way of measuring success—all of which we'll explore next and uncover layer by layer. This chapter will create the foundation of "living a life of spiritual art" by exploring the deeper meaning of "autopoiesis" (i.e., self-poetry) and how self-love is the bedrock of this foundation. Then, we'll pick apart Fear as it's the archnemesis of the creation and expression of being spiritual art. Next, in the "The All Is Mind" chapter, we'll venture into the deepest realms of ancient esoteric wisdom and explore what's uncharted territory for all but the most advanced spiritual masters. For some, this chapter might feel inaccessible, which is perfectly fine as the next chapter on Mind Mastery & States of Being is purposely taking the wisdom of the prior chapter and making it more readily accessible and practical to the refinement of our self-poetry or spiritual art. The final three chapters—"To Surrender"; "Spiritual Success"; and "Flower of Life—All Change Starts Within"—mark the capstone of this book and serve to ready those that are ready to take the spiritual leap of faith into *the* one Infinite Game.

So, to get you ready, let's embark on a much deeper exploration of the "rules" of the game Spirit plays.

To become a spiritual Poet, we must unbecome everything we might have thought we were before. Whatever persona or limited idea of self you have, we must unbecome that as all of that is just a collection of thought-forms. Psychological constructs which are not real. We're going to set aside all the roles, titles, and identifications we accumulate and carry around in physical reality. None of them have any weight or significance in the formless spiritual realm.

What we're really after here is liberation. Within our longing to be "somebody" in the world, we're a prisoner of that longing. There's only an illusion of freedom in that, as we're unconsciously controlled by strings, we cannot see or feel. What we're after is becoming nobody at all. This is your Ego's worst nightmare, but it's your Soul's liberation into the unfettered freedom of authentic creative expression it craves. Somebody is a finished painting where the paint has hardened. We can try to paint over it, but what's underneath will always bleed through. Like the past bleeding into our future in a self-repeating loop. Becoming nobody is the magical ever-blank canvas, the painting that's always evolving and never finished. This ever-blank canvas only exists in the present moment, the past doesn't bleed through, and we can paint the future each day as we wish.

Not to worry, though, none of these roles, titles, and identifications—"somebodies"—will truly go anywhere as they're entangled with our physical reality. They'll all still be there, but once we awaken the spiritual Poet within, their meaning and significance will change dramatically, and you'll likely discard many of them as masks that have outlasted their expiry date.

> "Know thyself, and thou wilt know the universe."
> —PYTHAGORAS

The old Hermetic axiom and spiritual truth "as above, so below; so within, so without" points us at the true nature of our Existence and Life itself. Everything in this universe is subject to the same natural laws and principles, and everything contains the entire universe within. From the smallest single-cell organism to entire solar systems and galaxies and everything in between, everything is a mirror image microcosm of the entire macrocosm. Everything in this universe is fractal-based. Humans are no different. Each one of us is an individual expression—microcosm—of Source Consciousness or the whole macrocosm. All ancient and Indigenous wisdom traditions, all mystery schools of the ancient civilizations, and all the greatest teachers—e.g., Jesus, Buddha, and Confucius—professed this same adage in the words and language of their time. The great ancient Greek philosophers and Stoics devoted their entire lives to "knowing thyself" through the pursuit of arts, science, medicine, math and geometry, alchemy, and philosophy. This pursuit was considered sacred and revered above all else. Studying all of the true greats of history, the very well-known and the lesser well-known, the common thread that connects all of them is their devotion to pursuing their highest human potential. In their own unique way, they were all Poets devoted to "Autopoiesis" and the discovery of the infinite universe within.

Autopoiesis comes from the Greek word "auto," which means "self," and "poiesis," which in basic terms means "creation or production," but "poiesis" has a far deeper meaning. In Greek, "poiesis" also refers to poetry in terms of the artful creation of something that didn't exist before. The conjoined word Autopoiesis has been adopted by biologists and systems theorists to describe the innate capacity of intelligent, self-organizing complex living systems to reproduce, regenerate, adapt, and evolve over time to become ever more intelligent and complex forms of life. Autopoiesis is then also called the poetry of nature, which at its core is self-poetry.

Autopoiesis—self-poetry—is at the very core of becoming a spiritual Poet and living a life of spiritual art. Life itself becomes our canvas. A Poet is nothing but a name for an artist, and so we could use painter, sculptor, or musician just as well. In fact, we could see the Architecture, Gifts, and Principles as the instruments, musical notes, and Elements of Music we covered earlier, respectively. To make beautiful music, which is a divine art, we need to tune our instruments and gain mastery in how to play them. This is the Architecture of the Masculine and Feminine and their respective constituent attributes of Awareness, Intelligence, Energy, Being, Creativity, and Reverence. The Gifts are the musical notes, so through our embodiment of the Gifts, we arrange the musical notes of Wisdom, Gratitude, Integrity, Joy, Beauty, and Peace in harmonious chords and arrangements. Finally, the Principles are the Elements of Music, so our mastery of Oneness, Compassion, Growth, Health, Abundance, and Harmony enables us to create a musical masterpiece that's divinely orchestrated. Finally, in this analogy, we can view higher octaves as bringing this whole musical arrangement to increasing levels of Consciousness, thereby refining the level of spiritual art we're bringing into all of Creation.

Whichever way you wish to look at it, there's a fundamental inner shift that takes place the moment we choose to view ourselves as a spiritual Poet and self-poetry, the art we're devoted to. The moment we make this choice—in the form of a definite decision—we will have signaled our Divinity within we heard its whisper. From this singular yet momentous decision, the wheels of transformation will have been set in motion to reveal to you the miraculous expansiveness of what and who you truly are. No matter how slow these wheels might seem to turn at first, your Divinity within will have started its unfolding in all sorts of magical ways.

> "The rose does best as a rose. Lilies make the best lilies. And look! You—the best you around!"
> —RUMI

All of humanity is a miraculously complex mosaic made up of unique individual puzzle pieces, each endowed with incredible creative potential and superhuman gifts, talents, and superpowers. No two puzzle pieces are the same by intentional and intelligent design. No two puzzle pieces have the exact same dreams, aspirations, and desires. We are all unique, no exceptions. None of us are here to live anyone else's life or anyone else's story of what life is supposed to look like.

Yet, that's not what our culture, society, or even religion tells and teaches us. Through enculturation, starting from the moment we come out of the womb, we are molded and programmed to fit into some neat box of what we're supposed to be and do, how we're supposed to dress, act, and think. And, most of all, what success or being worthy looks like. So, almost all of us, by the time we leave our parental home we're sufficiently programmed and enculturated to know no better.

What this programming looks like might differ or vary depending on which culture, society, social class, and religion you were born into. This is also how we know it's programming and enculturation, not who you truly are, although there might be remnants of that still present. The process of "unbecoming" is the—at times—arduous task of letting go of everything that's not real. This is no easy task, as what we believe we are and believe to be real is all we know.

What we're after, though, is who we truly are, our most true authentic Self, which has been living and hiding behind all the masks we wear to accommodate the world or perhaps even succeed in the world. The first leg of the journey inwards is the piercing of all the veils of illusions that have governed our life. The true Poet is a truth seeker at heart; all that's not real must be revealed so we can shed the masks that aren't truly who we are. This is the Observer's main job, taking the controls from our Ego. Our Ego will resist and protest, but it's no real competition for the Observer as our Divinity within that's been awakened now will not allow our true light to be dimmed any longer.

The challenge all along on this journey of awakening will be to trust the intelligence of our Heart. We're not used to listening, let alone following, the guidance we get from feeling, sensing, intuiting, and direct knowing. Our Ego, through logical thought and clinging to the known, will fight this all the way by doubting, questioning, and even ridiculing the guidance of our heart's intelligence. Trust it anyway; we're training a spiritual muscle that hasn't been used much before, so it takes some time to gain strength and endurance, which will inevitably happen. There's a litmus test as well. Whenever in doubt, seek to create silence, which is most easily done by withdrawing the Mind from outside stimulation, and then just ask yourself the question you most want answered. Once asked, don't seek to hear the answer but focus on retaining the silence and quietude. I promise, as by Divine intervention, you'll find the answer bubbling to the surface of your conscious Awareness as some sort of subtle whisper of higher knowing. That's exactly what it is; the silence allows you to hear the whispers of the Akashic field or what I like to call the Poet's library of cosmic intelligence.

One of the most profound gifts the true Poet gives him or herself is permission to express their self-poetry. It's a critical threshold to cross in becoming a true Poet, and it's rooted in acknowledging we're worthy to do so. To cross this threshold, we have to restore self-love. I know it might sound paradoxical to say we have to restore self-love in a world where most humans are lost in some form of egotism, selfishness, or even toxic narcissism. But the reality is that all of these are born from a lack of self-love and/or low self-worth. Even those who are entirely lost in some form of narcissism, and even sociopaths and psychopaths, are just deeply wounded souls unconsciously bathing in the excruciating pain of separation from their Divinity.

> "The man who does not value himself cannot value anything or anyone."
> —AYN RAND

Self-love is not very well understood, yet in the simplest of terms, we can define it as simply as complete self-acceptance. No matter how far you've ascended or how far you've traversed the pathless land, none of us are perfect. If you're here on the Earthly plane, you're human, and you're perfectly imperfect. These imperfections are not something to take lightly or just dismiss, but on the other hand, chastising yourself for your imperfections is not going to move the spiritual needle. In fact, it will turn them into your spiritual quicksand.

The reason is quite simple. There's only ever one moment, the present moment. Chastising yourself in any way over your imperfections is reliving the past. We can't change the past; it is what it is. So, anything that's in our past that we chastise ourselves over becomes lodged in spiritual quicksand. No matter how much we chastise ourselves, we can't get out, and the more we chastise, the deeper we sink into the downward suction of this spiritual quicksand.

The way out is forgiveness. We must forgive ourselves for anything and everything we've done. That's not washing our hands in innocence, as in true forgiveness; we also take full responsibility for it. We accept our Karmic debt, but we release the creditor called faulting ourselves for our past imperfections. Now, absent true self-love, we lack the transformational powers of Love to do so. We get stuck, literally, in lamenting our shortcomings even when we do this unconsciously. The realization to internalize is that we are a piece of art in the making. We're not complete yet; none of us are. So, occasionally, a brush stroke goes awry, or a musical note gets played out of tune. This doesn't mean the whole work of art is worthless, hopelessly lost, or beyond repair or restoration. It just means we have a little corrective work to do; we have the opportunity now to become a better Poet. That's all; never abandon the work of art because that's abandoning yourself.

Nothing is ever all lost, either. Remember, you're working with an ever-blank canvas, so no matter how deep you sink, how much you screw up, or how ugly your art is as of today, tomorrow is another day. In fact, right this moment is a new moment!

> "I exist as I am; that's enough."
> —WALT WHITMAN

True self-love is giving yourself this very grace. Few of us do; just watch your self-talk, and you'll know what I mean. There's no need to be cruel or brutally harsh on yourself, just like there's no use or need to gloss over your flaws and imperfections with superfluous Falsehoods. This is all you need to know; your Soul has a bullshit radar that's hypersensitive. Your Ego can dwell in righteousness and talk a circle straight all day long, but you can't fool your Soul. So, in each and every moment, just move toward Truth. Whatever that entails or means, however small it might seem in the moment, just move closer to Truth. The compound interest of just doing this is what moves spiritual mountains.

The foundational underpinning of self-love and healthy self-worth is that we're enough. Right now, right here, we're exactly where we need to be. We don't need to get carried away with our accomplishments or trophies, and neither do we have to chastise ourselves for all the things we could have maybe done better. Self-acceptance of where we are, who we are, and what we've done or maybe not done is all that's needed. In this way, we skirt the quicksand of sin, guilt, and shame and just plot our next best step from exactly where we are today. We accept all of it, embrace it even, and take ownership. Ownership means we take responsibility for the entirety of where our life stands today, which is the only cosmic duty we have. It's the only thing we actually can do, as we can't change bad brush strokes and false notes from the past. We can, however, devote ourselves to learning, growing, and becoming a more skilled Poet going forward.

> "There can never be peace between nations
> until there is first known that
> true peace is within the souls of men."
>
> —BLACK ELK

The essential nature of self-love is grounded in the spiritual Truth "so within, so without." If we are to be genuinely loving, compassionate, and forgiving toward others and all of Creation, we have no foundation to work from if we cannot extend this to ourselves first. Without holding ourselves in universal Love, which by definition is also unconditional, we have no access to the capacity to hold the world outside of us in universal Love.

As we discovered earlier in the chapter on Oneness, the Prophecy of Moses and the mythical wisdom teaching of "I am that, I am" is foundational in coming to the realization that self-love must be the starting point. Whichever unloving, dis-compassionate, unforgiving, cruel, and judgmental criticism we subject ourselves to is what we will project to the world all around us. That's not to say we should not commit and hold ourselves to the highest standards, but we're each fallible human beings who will inevitably make mistakes, missteps, and errors. As Confucius stated: "if you make a mistake and don't correct it, this is called a mistake." The only real mistake we can make then is not to learn from our mistakes. Learning from our mistakes is also taking full responsibility for them—no excuses—and this includes correcting our mistakes in whatever way that's appropriate. This might come in the form of an apology, paying restitution, accepting just punishment by a court of law, or simply bearing our Karmic responsibility with dignity and integrity.

The deeper the well of self-love, the deeper the well of universal Love, compassion, and forgiveness we'll have for the entire world all around us and especially others. This is where self-love is easily distinguishable from indulgence in self-interest or even narcissism, as those are outwardly projected as harm, pain, and suffering we readily inflict on others. Dwelling in self-love, we'd experience this as ultimately harming ourselves as the notion of Oneness, the Golden Rule, and "I am that, I am" become self-evident as the inviolable laws and principles of this universe.

> "Hardship often prepares an ordinary person for an extraordinary destiny."
> —C.S. LEWIS

There's a false notion that going on our Hero's Journey and seeking higher levels of consciousness is a near-impossible spiritual mountain to climb reserved only for those that commit themselves to monk robes, chastity, solitude, devotional prayer, singing mantras, and what have you. All these things have a place and purpose, but all it takes to become a true Poet of self-poetry is to live the ethos laid bare in this book to the best of your abilities and circumstances. Spirituality has no dress code, no preordained rituals, and there's no specific path to follow. Study the Buddha, but don't follow his path. Study Jesus, the Stoics, and explore physics, math, the arts, ancient history, philosophy, and whichever teachers cross your path or happen to speak wisdom that resonates. The point is to become a Poet and create your own spiritual art, which is you.

You are the sculptor and the sculpture. You are worthy and brimming with human potential that wants to be creatively expressed in this world. If all this book ever does is to rekindle the remembrance deep within that you are Divinity reincarnated in human form, then it was worthwhile writing it. Your full human potential is enormous, beyond your wildest imaginations even, but you have to make a decision.

You have to choose whether you're ready to become a Poet of self-poetry. You have to decide which game you're really playing. Is it Finite Games and merely gaining more trophies, or are you ready to enter *the* one Infinite Game? The latter doesn't preclude the former, but the former does rule out the latter. Nobody else can make this decision for you.

What typically stops us from making this decision is Fear, so let's explore that next.

> "A true artist is someone who gives birth to a new reality."
> —PLATO

CHAPTER 32

FEAR—THE GREAT ILLUSION

YOUR GREATEST ADVERSARY will never be anything or anyone outside of you. It won't be competitors, other contestants, unfavorable circumstances, seemingly impossible odds, scarcity of resources, or lack of opportunity.

None of that; your greatest adversary lives within you. Not only that, this insidious adversary is invisible, ephemeral, amorphous, devious, and even toxic at times. Its venom can paralyze you, and as a true fraudster and trickster, this adversary will lurk in the shadows and strike—time and again—when you're most vulnerable and when your defenses are at their weakest.

Yes, Fear is the most formidable of opponents, which will come to test every last grain of spiritual fortitude within you. But rest assured, Fear is more blowfish than the great white shark it pretends to be. Still prickly but infinitely conquerable.

> "The only thing to fear is fear itself."
> —FRANKLIN D. ROOSEVELT

Let's first make an important distinction about the sort of Fear we're talking about here. There's concrete or primal Fear which is triggered by imminent physical danger or possible harm, like being attacked by a saber-toothed tiger, someone pointing a knife or gun at you, or an impending car crash. The lizard brain, the oldest part, will kick into survival mode and instantaneously activate our sympathetic (i.e., fight or flight) nervous system, thereby triggering a whole host of bodily responses. In this chapter, we're not talking about this garden variety of Fear. This sort of Fear is a normal and very useful primal survival instinct that is designed to keep us alive and out of physiological danger. And, frankly, in our modern world, for most of us, there are relatively few instances when we're in such circumstances of grave and imminent life-threatening danger.

The adversary that will test your spiritual fortitude is the other sort of Fear, which is abstract or psychological in nature, and that's what this chapter is all about. Because it's this Fear that stands between us and living our dream life. Not just our dream life in terms of material comfort, but our dream life in having all our magnificent spiritual art within fully and unabashedly expressed into Life itself. As we'll come to explore, this Fear is entirely illusionary in nature, yet its mental and emotional vise grip can be as palpable, piercing, and irrefutably omnipresent as an ice bath. This is the sort of Fear Franklin D. Roosevelt was pointing at in his most famous words that are now etched into history.

Fear is also what holds us back from leaning into the spiritual path, as the metaphysical is all that which goes beyond our five senses. Understanding Fear then on a deep level is what helps remove roadblocks from venturing unto the pathless land. So, let's seed this exploration into Fear with some ancient wisdom from *The Art of War*:

> "If you know the enemy and know yourself,
> you need not fear the result of a hundred battles.
> If you know yourself but not the enemy, for every
> victory gained you will also suffer a defeat.
> If you know neither the enemy nor yourself,
> you will succumb in every battle."
>
> —SUN TZU

There are actually two layers to this statement as it pertains to Fear, one obvious one and one that reaches far deeper and is somewhat obscured from initial sight. Clearly, the enemy or adversary is Fear, and as it goes with anything, the better we understand it, know what it is, where it comes from, and how to manage it, the better we're equipped to not become beholden to or governed by it. This is the obvious wisdom we can glean from Sun Tzu's statement.

A deeper wisdom is that Fear, once fully understood, cannot only be mastered but dutifully serve us well. Fear is an infallible signpost; it can show us much insight into ourselves and even guide us on where we need to go. We'll cover this aspect—how to transmute Fear into a navigational aid—later in this chapter. But first, let's undress Fear a bit more as an emperor without any clothes on is not nearly as imposing as one in full armor.

So, let's begin by dissecting what Fear really is. Primarily, Fear is thought-form, or psychological constructs, which we learned earlier are fundamentally not real. Fear might feel and appear very real, but it's truly not. Fear's main characteristic is that it's a negative thought-form, meaning it predicts or suggests some sort of risk, danger, or possible bad outcome. We defined it earlier as a negative belief absent any concrete evidence, contrary to its opposite pole, Faith, which is a positive belief absent any concrete evidence. Fear is also entirely anchored in the future. In the absolute present moment—this split second exactly—Fear doesn't exist. You can try this experiment moment-by-moment, and you'll find Fear cannot rise as long as we're entirely anchored in the Now or present moment, which, as we already discovered, is the only true moment there ever is. We can worry, regret, lament and reminisce about the past, but we actually cannot Fear it as it has already happened. And, so right there, we have a major clue revealed as Fear somehow is entangled with the future, which is the unknown.

> "A man who fears suffering
> is already suffering what he fears."
> —MICHEL DE MONTAIGNE

The unknown is the archnemesis of the Mind. We could even state the unknown is the mind's core Fear itself, and all other Fear the mind produces in thought-form has its origins in this core Fear. The unknown, then, is the mother of all other Fears. To understand this better, we have to examine and further define the three domains of knowing.

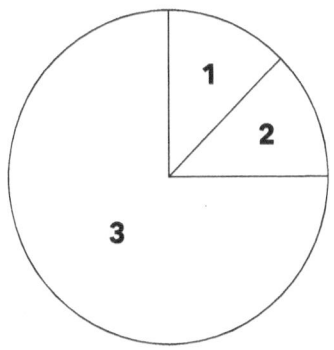

1. The things you know you know
2. The things you know you don't know
3. The things you don't know you don't know

Above graphic representation is not necessarily to scale or proportional; realistically, the areas 1 and 2 are far smaller. The first domain of knowing is the things we know we know. This is very straightforward and doesn't require further explanation. The second domain is that which we know we don't know. This area is not problematic either because as long as we're aware we don't know, we know and can seek the information or the help of others to fill in the gap. The third domain of knowing is not only disproportionately large compared to the other two domains, it's also problematic as we're entirely blind to it—hence, we call this our blind spot. If you think about the totality of all information or knowing in this universe and taking into account that, in the most optimistic estimate, we perceive perhaps 1 percent of reality, you can start to see why the third domain of knowing is simply enormous. Moreover, this third domain, or our blind spot, is tricky as well because how might we come to know things we don't even know we don't know? More on that later.

Let's get back to the unknown; this third domain of knowing, or our blind spot, is to our Mind the unknown—its archnemesis—or just one vast dark void of unknowingness, uncertainty, and unpredictability. Now, the Mind is somewhat specific in the part of this third domain that it considers truly unsettling, and that is the future. Our Mind can only comprehend this whole notion of this third domain conceptually to start with, sort of like the faintest of Awareness of the existence of this dark void. But it's ignorant to all that's within this third domain, so for the most part, to the Mind, it simply doesn't exist. There's literally nothing to compute. Except as it relates to the future. When the future or any future scenario it's trying to compute comes into play, the Mind feels the emergence of a looming presence of this dark void and responds the only way it knows how: producing fear-based thought-forms.

Producing fear-based thought-forms is an autonomous defensive response of the Mind to the unknowingness, uncertainty, and unpredictability of the future. That's all it really is. You can easily verify this based on your own experiences. Whatever is fully known to you, even if it's something unpleasant, you will not experience any Fear. You might be nervous, anxious, or uneasy, but it won't rise to the level of Fear. For there to be Fear, there must be a future unknown, as Fear is really the product of the Mind not being able to compute some unknown.

> "Fear defeats more people than any other thing in the world."
> —RALPH WALDO EMERSON

The Mind is a pattern recognition supercomputer. It takes known variables or estimates of variables and starts computing away. As long as it can ascertain an outcome with reasonable accuracy, the

Mind will feel satisfied and at reasonable ease. When it can't, it goes in computing overdrive and eventually haywire as it runs into circularity problems absent any new or better variables. Fear is the product of all of this; at their core, they're just future scenarios the Mind cannot satisfactorily solve, so it tries harder and harder until the fear-based thought-forms become pervasive and dominant. This only serves to amplify the perceived magnitude of the risk or obstacle, which, in turn, is more oil on the fire. This is how a little mental brushfire can become a runaway raging mental wildfire, so we can't see our way through the smoke anymore. It drenches us in doubt, worry, anxiety, overwhelm, stress, pessimism, and even procrastination and slows us down or stops us in our tracks.

And all of this is just mere thought-forms produced in response to the incomputable future unknown, a negative belief absent any concrete evidence. Psychological Fear is entirely illusionary, yet it's the one thing that defeats us more than anything else in Life itself will ever do. It has the capacity to hijack our dreams, douse our motivation with cold water time and again, and make us doubt our creative capacities to the point we're frozen to act and move forward.

So, this is what we're up against: a cunning and lethal opponent engaged in guerilla mental warfare who hides in the deepest abysses of our subconscious Mind. At the same time, like I said before, Fear is also infinitely conquerable.

> "He who has overcome his fears will truly be free."
> —ARISTOTLE

Once we know what Fear really is, all we need to know next is that Fear is a gateless prison. In its custody and confinement, you'll never be truly free, but you can walk right out, anytime. From the place of the Observer, you're both the prisoner and the prison guard. From the place of the Egoic Mind or your small self, you're only a prisoner and have no eyes for the fact this prison has no gate. In fact, it doesn't even have real walls. But the Fear will appear so real and its enclosure so hermetically sealed that it feels like you're stuck in a decompression chamber.

All we need to do, though, is to be able to shift our Awareness to the Observer. This zooming out allows us to pierce the thought-based illusion that we're stuck and the Fear is real. Fear has a high stickiness factor and can have deep hooks into our subconscious belief patterns, so this is not always easy or immediate, but practice and persistence will inevitably pay big dividends as we lay new neural pathways in the brain, which over time has the old ones fade away from nonuse. In the upcoming chapter—"Mind Mastery & States of Being"—we'll get deep into mindset mastery and how to habituate the untangling from our Fears.

> "Of all the liars in the world,
> sometimes the worst are our fears."
> —RUDYARD KIPLING

What Fear ingeniously obscures from sight is that we're each a divine puzzle piece of the mosaic called humanity. We're each a Poet born to bring our most beautiful spiritual poetry of creative self-expression into this world. Any dream, inspiration, or true soul desire uncolored by any enculturation is a seed planted within you by Source. The very fact you have this seed within you should be ample evidence and confirmation that what wants to be expressed through you is divinely supported and orchestrated. Source and this entire universe operates in infinitely intelligent ways and will always conspire to come to your aid if and when you choose to tend to this seed. There are no flukes, accidents, coincidences, or random events anywhere in this universe. Everything operates in perfectly intelligent ways through an intelligent design of intricate Order at levels which are simply not comprehensible to us.

In light of this, we can view Fears as the lies we have to bring to Truth. We do that by leaning into our Fears so they may be dispelled and dissipated. We transmute our Fears into Truth by going through them. By overcoming our Fears, we come to see them for what they truly were, the proverbial ghosts hiding under our bed. No great feat of any real significance by any person ever came before that person overcame their Fears. It's a rite of passage to get to our dream life, realize our full creative potential, and come to experience how we truly never had to do it all by ourselves.

Yes, there are those that reach the mountaintop and claim to have climbed it all themselves. In reality, though, Life itself is a team sport. Nobody truly ever does anything of any real significance without the assistance of others whether they're mentors, guides, parents that pay for college, or a boss that gives you a promotion. Nobody ever accomplishes anything worthwhile without some favorable winds and circumstances arising at just the right moment. You might think you did that all by yourself, but you never truly did. The invisible hand of Source or Infinite Intelligence is always at work, always conspiring, and always nudging, arranging, and serendipitously coinciding events for our greatest growth, greatest prosperity, and greatest evolution.

The gravitational force that pulls all this into our Existence is our openhearted leaning into our Fears; the more we do so, the greater this gravitational force. The deeper we're willing to lean into our Fears, the more we get to directly experience this invisible hand of divinely orchestrated serendipities at work. It's as mesmerizingly precise as the most refined Swiss clockwork, except it's mystical in nature and engulfs us deeply into the pure magic of all of Creation.

> "How very little can be done under the spirit of fear."
> —FLORENCE NIGHTINGALE

We would be remiss to examine Fear without touching on what resides on the opposite side of the continuum it's part and parcel of. The opposite of Fear is Faith or the positive belief absent any concrete evidence. Except, Faith does not originate or reside in the Mind. Faith dwells in our Heart and is the autonomous product of our Heart's intelligence, which is directly linked to the Akashic Field.

The "openhearted leaning in" as mentioned above is a direct reference to the fact that a closed Heart blocks our access to Faith. It's not that Faith isn't there in our Heart; it's always there as its presence can only be obscured, not diminished. In the same way, a closed Heart obscures our access to the Akashic Field of all-knowing intelligence as our Heart is the portal to this higher dimension of Intelligence and Faith actually originates from this

Akashic Field. Harnessing the strength, power, and wisdom of Faith then is not so much about anything we need to learn to produce as it is about learning to open our Heart.

Opening our Heart is a sheer act of courage as it makes us seemingly vulnerable, and it feels like stepping into the dark void of the unknown, which is the very place our Mind doesn't want to go. So, our Mind will protest, mostly in the form of amplifying its Fear rhetoric. Do it anyway. This might surprise you, but that vast dark void of the unknown is actually home. That's where we all came from, we just don't remember so in our human embodiment it feels eerily strange, unfamiliar, and even ominous.

Our Mind is entangled with our five senses, and as we come out of the womb and take our first breath, we become virtually instantaneously sensory dominant even though at the earliest stages of life there's still quite a bit of remembrance. As we learn to navigate our way through physical reality in this new biological "biosuit" we were given, we slowly but surely become ever more sensory dominant, which leads to Mind dominance. This is only amplified in our modern Western culture, which has lost its connection with nature and Mother Earth. Our entire upbringing and educational system are Mind-focused and Mind-dominant, and so by the time we're four to five years old, almost all remembrance has already been covered by a dense layer of sensory orientation, which creates lots of mental activity, which then acts as a static on the line with our Heart. This noise of our Mind drowns out the whispers of our Heart and so the remembrance gets pushed into the background until we can no longer hear the whispers.

All serious meditators and silence practitioners can tell you their very first time they got a glimpse again of the vast dark void of the unknown within. It's a memorable moment when we sink into this deep abyss of complete silence, surrounded by absolutely nothing yet feeling we're being held by it at the same time. This is home and the experiential nature of accessing our Heart portal. And right there is where we access Faith. Faith is our direct knowing of Truth; it whispers to us through the total stillness of the vast dark void of the unknown. What these whispers lack in amplitude (volume), they make up in coherence. Faith is extraordinarily coherent, so much so that while submerged in this stillness every shred of Fear or doubt dissipates into thin air. This is our direct knowing, the accessing of Truth through our Heart portal, which is in direct connection with the Akashic Field.

> "Faith is not something to grasp; it's a state to grow into."
> —MAHATMA GANDHI

Once you learn to open your Heart, accessing Faith is quite easy but holding on to it can be more challenging. This is because we're mushy sensitive beings, so keeping our Heart wide open at all times is not always easy as our conditioned response to any form of negative external energy is to close our Heart. Mastery takes practice; every time you notice your Heart closed you consciously open it back up. Just shifting your Awareness to opening your Heart and allowing all to touch and pass through you is all it takes. At first, it can be overwhelming to actually feel the whole world including all of yourself. This isn't a capacity issue, we're just not used to it. Most of us have lived our entire life with our Heart virtually closed; we don't remember anymore what it feels like to have so much energy and Life itself pass through us. But, with time, you'll find it becomes the only way you want to live until at some point it becomes the only way you know how to live, at which point it's become our state of Being.

That's true Faith for you; there's zero doctrine to it, no need for rituals or praying to some humanoid version of God. Just direct knowing in its purest form, a quiet power that knows no equal and a depth that has no bottom.

> "A boat is safe in the harbor.
> But this is not the purpose of a boat."
> —PAULO COELHO

It's one thing to know what Fear really is, another to understand how it operates, but it's an entirely different thing to learn to love your Fear. And, frankly, that's where we really want to go with all of this as your most beautiful and magnificent spiritual art lies right behind whatever Fears you may have. These very Fears are what's holding you back from expressing your spiritual art fully and in its purest form, which means these Fears are showing you something. You could say there's a sacred treasure within these Fears, and Love is the secret key that unlocks the treasure.

As I alluded to very early on, Fear is actually an infallible signpost and potent navigational aid as we venture unto the pathless land and the pursuit of our dreams and aspirations. You see, Fear is telling us exactly where we need to go. Whatever Fear is informing you is what you need to examine, explore, and lean into. Fear points us at Falsehoods within our perceptions; this never fails and there are no exceptions. Hence, this is the infallible treasure within each Fear we may hold.

To see this clearly let's contrast Fear with the silent whispers of our Heart we also receive about anything that's simply not in alignment with our highest good or what we could say is not in sympathetic resonance with our highest Being. These sorts of whispers—which come from our Heart's intelligence—can also appear in the form of doubt, hesitation, unease, or discomfort but they're always coherent in nature. What this means is that these nudges are consistent, persistent, yet subtle, calm, and stable. This is the defining nature which tells you it's a so-called whisper from our higher intelligence versus a Fear produced by our Mind.

Fears are dissonant, meaning they are loud, noisy, erratic, unstable, and unwieldy in nature. They lead us to self-destructive, self-sabotaging, and self-deprecating thought-forms, which we then experience as emotional knots in our gut area, predominantly in a blockage or restriction in our sacral and solar plexus chakras. Our sacral chakra is our sexual or creative energy; when this flow gets restricted, we'll experience that as a lack of creative force and inspiration—our best work simply doesn't want to come out. Our solar plexus is our personal willpower; when this chakra is not flowing properly, we'll experience that as procrastination, lack of motivation or willpower to motor through. All of these are dissonant in nature, meaning they're disruptive and make us feel uncomfortable in a restless way.

The silent whispers I mentioned are coherent; they dissuade us in subtle and gentle ways to signal something is off, but they don't violently disrupt, destruct, or incapacitate us in the same "rude" ways Fear does. This also makes them easier to ignore or be ignorant of, as if we're not attuned to their subtle and gentle nature we can easily dismiss them or not notice them at all.

The fact Fear is dissonant and disruptive is actually something to love about Fear as it makes it very easy to pick up on. In fact, it's impossible to not notice Fear although we can choose to numb it with addictions and distractions. This never makes Fear go away, but it can provide temporary relief and when we habituate seeking this temporary relief, we will create a dependency on this numbing whether it's alcohol, drugs, nicotine, gambling, shopping, sex, porn, or what have you.

So, as erratic and unstable as Fear is itself, it's a very trustworthy navigational aid. We can tune and lean into Fear and see where it's guiding us. We can always know Fear is both a Falsehood and a signpost informing us which direction we need to go for our dream life. Our dream life—that which seems just out of reach—is always hiding right behind Fear. The greater the Fear, the greater the potential bounty. In this way, we can come to view Fear as something we love as it's a precursor to something beautiful, expansive, and enriching that's about to come into our life. In fact, Fear itself can also be alchemized into creative energy that makes us feel alive as all it is really is stuck mental energy, so harvesting this aspect of Fear can boost our level of aliveness. Provided of course we're courageously willing to lean into it, with a fully open Heart, and get so close we can smell its breath, so to speak, so we can find out—inevitably—there was nothing real to it after all. It was all illusionary, the great phantom trickster.

> "We ask ourselves, who am I to be brilliant, gorgeous, talented, and fabulous? Actually, who are you not to be? You are a child of God and you playing small does not serve the world."
>
> —MARIANNE WILLIAMSON

There's always an interesting question that arises, how can it be that some people are wildly successful in the material world, yet we say they're still operating from a fear-based mindset? The answer is quite simple: they have very strong attractor fields, which are belief patterns of success, superiority, and even entitlement. You see, operating from low levels of Consciousness or survival instinct doesn't preclude you from having these very strong attractor fields. Fundamentally, they're still operating from a scarcity mindset and the fear-based belief Life itself is a zero-sum game. Someone has to lose for them to win, so this means just about anything can be justified or rationalized, if need be, by availing themselves of the classical misinterpretation of Darwinism.

Underneath this thin shiny veneer of worldly success though, we find very insecure people grasping unto their trophies, status, prestige, and material possessions for dear life. Strip those away, and you'll find a lot of Fear, emptiness, isolation, and of course ignorance.

The only real measure of courage is not even in overcoming your Fears but opening your Heart. To feel all of it, all of Life itself and everything within us and as well as everything outside of us. Now, that takes real courage. Merely overcoming your Fears can be done with mere conviction. Still admirable on some level, but it falls short of where we become a true Poet devoted to our spiritual art as it's only our Heart's suprarational intelligence which can guide us to higher octaves of consciousness well beyond Fear (i.e., level 200) where our self-poetry comes into ever closer alignment with our full human potential.

Marianne Williamson once said our greatest Fear is not failing but succeeding and experiencing our true greatness. It's unleashing the true genius within us that might be the greatest Fear for each of us because it forces us to let go of any and all enculturated ideas and conditioned thinking about what that genius might do or be like. It forces us to venture off the well-paved highway prescribed by our upbringing, culture, and society and to truly follow our own bliss. This means we need to wean off our infatuation with financial riches, security, comfort, and "the known" and go unto the pathless land and discover what truly wants to be expressed. This is the journey without any specific end destination, no pre-planned itinerary, or no roadmap to follow.

That takes real courage, which we find in connecting with Faith. It doesn't mean we'll be poor or need to struggle in the material world; often we find expressing our genius into the world has a miraculous way of creating the abundance we wish as well, except far more effortlessly and easily within the confines of the Architecture, Gifts, and Principles we covered earlier.

Whenever in doubt, just remember, Fear is nothing but a little prickly blowfish and you are the actual great white shark. Fearless in Faith is your true nature, which is the perfect lead-in to the next chapter—"The All Is Mind"—where we'll explore your and my true nature at depths few ever do.

LOVE + TRUTH

"The moment one commits oneself, then Providence moves too. A whole stream of events issues from the decision, raising in one's favor all manner unforeseen incidents and meetings and material assistance, which no man could have dreamt would have come his way."

—W.H. MURRAY

CHAPTER 33

THE ALL IS MIND

THE HUMAN MIND IS A beautiful instrument and a true marvel of divine ingenuity. A human supercomputer with incredible capacities and capabilities, much of it remaining virtually untapped and completely unutilized. And this is frankly a very good thing as at humanity's prevailing levels of Consciousness below 200 we're not even able to intelligently command the cognitive horsepower we have been able to unlock thus far.

But, if our aim is becoming a true Poet and living a life of spiritual art, it's essential we gain a solid foundational understanding, which goes well beyond mainstream psychology, psychiatry, neuroscience, and the plethora of the "latest" mindset and neuroplasticity science and practices that are finding an ever larger audience these days. None of these are wrong or bad—we'll actually cover some of this in the next chapter—but it's wholly incomplete for where we want to go.

We're after mastery of ourselves on all dimensions, not just worldly success on the physical plane. If we could only decode the mystical, we might just discover the master key to the universe. To decode the mystical, we must step outside the boundaries of what our conventional modern-day sciences have to offer as they are all reductionist in nature. Their respective scopes are each too narrow and even stitching them together wouldn't get us to the holistic understanding we're after.

Fortunately, history left us many clues and breadcrumbs embedded in mythology, ancient ruins, sacred scriptures and artifacts, ancient wisdom traditions, Indigenous cultures, and a whole host of teachers, sages, mystics, shamans, artists, scientists, mathematicians, astronomers, alchemists, and philosophers who were all the quintessential mavericks of their time.

So, in this chapter we're going deep into the abyss of the cosmic ocean of Consciousness, well beyond the Finite World of Form, well beyond what's provable within today's scientific body of knowledge, and quite likely well beyond your current beliefs about reality and perhaps even spirituality. Fortunately, others have gone there before us so we can trace their footsteps and venture deep into the mesmerizing essential nature of consciousness. For all intents and purposes, this is a quest to discover and reveal the origins of our own Divinity so we may know, without a shadow of a doubt, that we are each spiritual art expressed into form.

For now, I invite you to just follow along with a curious mind and an open heart. We're now entering the sacred grounds of the ancient mystery schools and esoteric wisdom teachings. This is pretty deep stuff so don't be dismayed if some of this is not soaking in fully on your first read. Just know whatever is for you will reveal itself to you and readily discard whatever is not for you.

> "Mythology is much more important and true than history. History is just journalism, and you know how reliable that is."
> —JOSEPH CAMPBELL

The Kybalion is a contemporary compilation of the Hermetic teachings, named after the mystical sage Hermes Trismegistus (the "Thrice-Greatest") who was highly revered in ancient Greece. Hermes is a pivotal figure in both ancient Greek mythology and the Greek wisdom schools it produced and has a striking resemblance to the Egyptian deity Thoth. To this day, it remains well-clouded in esoteric mystery and routinely debated among scholars if they were one and the same or that the Greeks modeled Hermes after Thoth. Incidentally, the Roman version of Hermes is named Mercury.

In Egyptian mythology, the deity Thoth was the God of wisdom, learning, and communications and considered the scribe of the Gods who authored the sacred Hermetic works encrypted on the Emerald Tablet and throughout all the Egyptian pyramids and monuments. Like Hermes in ancient Greece, Thoth was considered the founder of science, religion, mathematics, geometry, alchemy, philosophy, medicine, and magic.

The Hermetic teachings, which were derived from The Hermetica, which are widely considered sacred ancient texts, can be readily traced back in all branches of Judaism, Christianity, and Islam as well as philosophical schools like Stoicism and Pythagoreanism.

The scientific revolution that got its official start in the Renaissance was heavily influenced by the Hermetic teachings with Leonardo da Vinci being maybe its most well-known student but many others—before and after—like Fibonacci, Galileo, Copernicus, Spinoza, Newton, von Goethe and countless other luminaries of human history are all believed to have been heavily influenced and guided by the Hermetic teachings.

What's really important to understand is that what we're typically taught about the history of mankind and human civilization is riddled with fallacies. Our textbooks have the prescribed academic narrative of what our history is; however, museums, universities, and religious institutions the world over have entire storage buildings filled with archeological findings and historical artifacts that dispel this narrative, which is why they're safely stored out of sight. Through carbon dating and other scientific methods there have been countless discoveries—facts—that don't fit the timeline of the prevailing narrative of Earth's history. For instance, there have been so many scientific holes punctured in the biological evolutionary theory of Darwinism that all that's really left is a speculative hypothesis. Yet, the narrative endures as our predominant theory of evolution even though the facts don't fit.

We encounter the same basic problem when we consider ancient civilizations. Take Egypt, for instance: the prevailing academic narrative is that somehow a fairly primitive band of hunter-gatherers somehow transformed and organized themselves overnight (in evolutionary terms) and created what we now know as ancient Egypt. Never mind that even with today's technology we would be hard-pressed to recreate the mathematical precision of the countless pyramids and monuments they left behind. Better yet, we don't have cranes big or powerful enough to lift the gargantuan stones in place and we still can't solve how they were able to quarry these massive stones with such angular accuracy. The notion primitive hunter-gatherers woke up one morning having an intricate understanding of Phi, advanced mathematics, geometry, astrology, and astronomy is simply ludicrous. We can extend this same scenario to the Mayan pyramids and ruins and countless others spread throughout the world. Incidentally, scientific geological dating of the weather erosion on the Luxor Temple in the ancient city of Thebes revealed the c. 3,400-year-old timeline tag is off by "only" about 10,000 to 15,000 years, maybe more.

The fact is this: there's overwhelming evidence that humans have been here much longer than the c. 200,000 years of history tells us. There's also considerable evidence that during some periods, there were advanced civilizations that had remarkable levels of higher knowing far exceeding where humanity is today. We can leave scholars and academia to debate who or what these civilizations were and where they might have come from. What we're after is knowledge and a fundamental understanding so we can become true Poets. And, to truly do so, we must be willing to cast aside all notions of what history books have told us if that's inaccurate, incomplete, or simply doesn't correspond with the scientific discoveries that have been made and are well-documented. This opening of our perception to a new understanding of history is a pivotal stepping stone to opening up our perception that all of reality might be quite different from the "narrative" we have adopted so far.

To see anything in a new light, we must be willing to part ways with what we currently understand to be true. Just something to stay mindful of as we continue revealing more layers starting with parsing apart the title of this chapter with the necessary rigor and precision.

> "The Universe is Mental—held in the Mind of The All."
> —THE KYBALION

Let's start by deciphering what "The All Is Mind" really means. The first of seven principles of the Hermetic teachings as commemorated in The Kybalion is the Principle of Mentalism. In what follows, it's of vital importance to remember the opening sentence of the Tao Te Ching: "A Tao that may be spoken is not the enduring Tao," which, if you recall, refers to the fact that with words we can only point at *that* which is truly beyond words, beyond content, and beyond language. As it pertains to capturing the underlying Truth of reality, words are labels used in symbolic context to convey a very precise meaning. So, we're now going to methodologically parse apart these labels so we can get to the deeper meaning held within what's superficially just the arrangement of mere words.

"The All" points us at something absolute in that there's nothing else. It's all there is, it's supreme, there is literally nothing beyond this. The Kybalion further explains this as "under, and back of, the Universe of Time, Space, and Change, is ever to be found the Substantial Reality—the Fundamental Truth." Substantial means "actually existing" or "concerning the essentials of something." Reality means "the world or state of things as they actually exist" or "the state or quality of having existence or substance." So, what we have here then is that underlying the Universe of Time, Space, and Change—the Finite World of Form or what we perceive as our physical reality—there is the Substantial Reality, which is the Fundamental Truth.

> "We come into harmony with the Unknowable
> only when we surrender to The All being Unknowable."
> —THE KYBALION

For this Substantial Reality to truly be The All, we can logically deduce that it must be Infinite, Eternal, Unchangeable, and Absolute. This then informs us anything that is Finite, Temporary or Transient, Changeable or Fleeting, or Conditioned or Limited cannot be The All. It can be within The All, born or created from The All, but it cannot be The All itself. There's yet more we can glean from these qualities of The All.

Infinite indicates it has no boundaries or limits; something can only be Infinite when it's infinite in all directions. We see this in the fractal nature of our universe, which also implies our universe is but one of an infinite number of universes within The All. Eternal means there's no beginning and no end; the Big Bang might have been the birth of our universe. but we can logically conclude that's likely all we'll ever retrace as The All has no beginning and no end. Unchangeable means everything is contained within The All; nothing it creates, births, or gives rise to changes The All in any way. Nothing takes away from it and nothing can be added, as The All is infinite and eternal. Finally, The All is Absolute in that it's immutable to conditions or limitations; it's the ultimate cause of everything but is impermeable to any and all effects. Where all this leads us is but one conclusion: at its very core The All is and will forever be unknowable to us. We can only conceptually grasp such vastness, and even then whatever we can conceptually grasp is but a speck of stardust of what it truly is.

We've already covered all of this before; this is directly referring to Source Consciousness or just Source. Once again, words are all just labels pointing at something—God, Creator, Source, Monad, Yahweh, Elohim, Abba, Universal Mind, Infinite Intelligence, Spirit, or even Great Spirit as some Indigenous cultures refer to it are all pointing at the same thing using a different label. The Hermetic teachings just use "The All" to point at what's ultimately unknowable.

> "The Universe is a dream dreamed by a single dreamer where all the dream characters dream too."
> —ARTHUR SCHOPENHAUER

The problem with the reference "God" or "Creator" is that it conjures up an image in our mind of an old wise man with a grey beard reigning from the heavens as that's how God is visually depicted in Judaism and Christianity, the two religions most dominantly present in Western civilization. We have to be willing to set aside this image and the general desire to postulate "The All" or "Source" having some form of humanoid embodiment as it blocks us from getting to the deeper meaning we're after.

So, what exactly is meant by "Mind" in the Hermetic use of this word? Again, we first have to set aside our typical understanding of "Mind" as it conjures up the image of our own finite human

Mind and what it does, which is way too limiting. What the Mind is pointing us toward is some form of Intelligence that creates this universe. But this is not just some form of Intelligence, it's infinitely intelligent hence it's pointing us at an Infinite Intelligence.

Thus, what we have so far is that there's a Substantial Reality—the Fundamental Truth—within and from which all of Existence, Life itself, or physical reality is created as well as our entire known universe and whatever might be beyond what's provable by science today. We've seen this earlier also; we called that the Infinite Field of Consciousness, but other labels often used in scientific circles are Unified Field or Quantum Field—different words, same thing. We also established this omnipresent formless "field" is pure Consciousness and we call that Source Consciousness or simply Source. Knowing "The All" is just the Hermetic term used for Source, which points us at something that's inclusive of the Infinite Field of Consciousness, we can logically infer that this Infinite Intelligence is contained within The All and that's how it creates universes, galaxies, stars, planets, and all life forms and possible experiences and occurrences.

So, there we are—The Hermetic teachings Principle of Mentalism points us at the Fundamental Truth that our universe, and all it contains, is a mental Creation which is just another way of saying a Creation of the Infinite Intelligence contained within Source. We've now deciphered the symbolic meaning embedded within the ancient Hermetic axiom "The All Is Mind." If you recall, this entire universe is fractal in nature meaning our personal spiritual art is ultimately just a fractal of the whole. In other words, if "The All Is Mind" this would imply we—in some shape or form—must be "Mind" also. Hold on to that notion as we continue, we'll circle back to it shortly.

> "While All is in The All, it is equally true that The All is in All. To him who truly understands this truth come great knowledge."
> —THE KYBALION

There's one more key understanding that is fundamental as we—humans—have a very particular understanding of the words Mind and Mentalism. We interpret those words and anything "mental" with logic, rationality, and IQ. However, those words have no association in our common use of the English language with the mystical, magic, or Divinity. This might prove to be one of the longest bridges you're going to have to cross if you desire to become a true Poet, because Mind and Mentalism in the Hermetic use of the word refers directly to Divinity. The All *is* the Divine, and so the reference to "mental Creation" is really referring to "Divine Creation."

Also, knowing this master key to decoding the Hermetic teachings, we can now restate the quote above as: "While all of Divine Creation is within the Divine, it is equally true that the Divine is within all of Divine Creation." Or, in other words, each part is in the whole, and the whole is in each part. Or we can also rephrase this and say "All of Creation is within the Creator (i.e. God, Monad, Great Spirit, Yahweh, etc.), and the Creator is within all of Creation." Or, as Rumi stated it: "you're not a drop in the ocean, you're the entire ocean in a drop." Or, as we covered when we were exploring quantum physics, each subatomic particle in wave form contains all potentialities of the Infinite Field of Possibilities. So above, so below. I can keep going; there's not only a million paths—*words*—that lead to Rome but they *all* lead to Rome.

I encourage you to reread the above paragraph a few times, for the moment this "knowing" connects deep within your entire world changes. Everything is God, everything is Divine Creation, nothing—and I mean absolutely nothing—is outside or not Divine Creation. And this includes you. Knowing this, at a very deep level, literally changes everything.

Once you see, you cannot unsee.

We'll keep building on this foundational understanding; if not all is immediately clear it's because we're likely reframing your entire understanding of reality. The most important thing to take away is all—zero exceptions—is a Divine Creation of the one Divine, which means you and anyone or anything else are Divinity expressed into form. The true Poet deeply knows his or her Divine essence, which is how the true Poet is able to become a powerful creator of spiritual art—Divinity—expressed into all of Creation or Life itself through self-poetry.

> "The philosopher is in love with Truth, that is, not with the changing world of sensation, which is the object of opinion, but with the unchanging reality which is the object of knowledge."
>
> —PLATO

Let's go a layer deeper now and see how all of this translates into the many aspects of brain, Mind, and "Intelligence" as we commonly understand it and—fair warning—we're going to completely reframe some of this by adding a layer of depth to it. First, we yet again need some more foundational understanding to build upon. What Plato refers to as "unchanging reality" is Source or The All from which everything else form-based arises. Since Plato was schooled and initiated in the Hermetic teachings through the Egyptian mystery schools he's known to have attended, we can safely presuppose Plato knew everything form-based is a mental Creation as we defined it before.

Now, The All and its Infinite Intelligence with which it creates is the highest order of "Mind" but not the only level of Mind. As we'll uncover, there are different levels of Mind and each one of them is a "Plane of Causation" meaning each level of Mind has certain creative powers defined by its Level of Causation. The higher the order of Mind, the higher its Level of Causation meaning the more powerfully it affects and can manifest all of Creation.

All of this is governed by frequency. The higher the level of Mind, the higher the frequency. The higher the frequency, the higher the energy. Energy equals light and light equals information. So, the higher the level of Mind, the higher the frequency of its Plane of Causation and the more information we have command over.

With that foundational understanding in place, let's use the following visual to reveal more deeper layers of understanding.

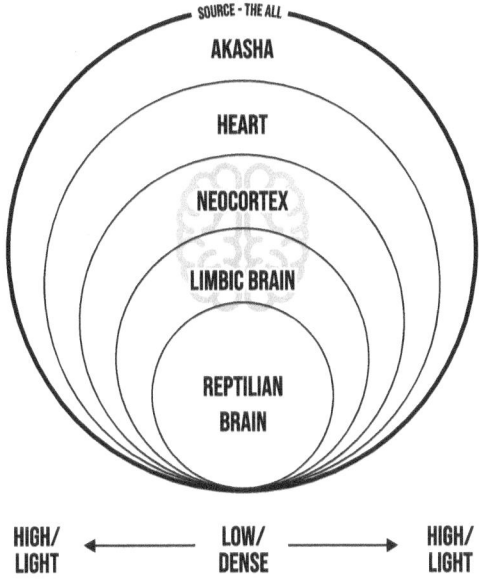

Akasha – Infinite Intelligence
Cosmic Body Mind – Oneness
Divinity or Monadic Plane

Heart – Suprarational Intelligence
Spiritual Body Mind – Oneness Bias
Spiritual or Ethereal Plane

Neocortex – Rational Intelligence
Mental Body Mind – Separation Bias
Astral Plane

Limbic – Experiential Intelligence
Emotional Body Mind – Separation Bias
Astral Plane

Reptilian – Primal Intelligence
Physical Body Mind – Separation
Physical or Material Plane

Frequency
Energy = Light = Information

Let's examine how to read this as there's quite a bit of information here, and then we'll go into the specifics of each. Let's recall that our Mind is the ephemeral or formless psychological supercomputer—hence "psyche"—that's somehow created by our brain, which is an organ. So, the existence of a "Mind" requires some sort of "brain."

We can see that concept clearly above as we humans have a Reptilian Brain, Limbic Brain, as well as a Neocortex and Heart, which are all human brain centers with billions of neurons and synapses. We also know all these brains are all connected through nerves, and information in the form of electromagnetic signals is communicated back and forth 24/7 creating a mesmerizingly complex neurofeedback loop. Source or The All has a "brain" as well; we can call that brain Akasha, although please note this would be a metaphysical brain, not a physical organ.

Please note that across ancient wisdom traditions and teachings there's been a multitude of different words or labels created and used to point at the very same thing. I am using these labels in this book but that doesn't mean other labels are wrong. From time to time I will point out other commonly used labels so you can cross-reference this with other works and teachings or knowledge you might already have.

Each of these brains has specific functions, capacities, and capabilities and so it commands a certain level of Mind, which we can define as or equate to a certain level of Intelligence. For our lowest level of Mind—the Reptilian Brain—this would be our Primal Intelligence, which we colloquially call our survival instinct. This level of intelligence is very basic, for instance, all animals have this level of brain also. We could say Primal Intelligence is the Mind of our Physical Body, the most basic survival instincts of our physical body, which is the most dense or low frequency body we have. Hence, we can call this our Physical Body Mind. The Plane of Causation of our Primal Intelligence is the Physical or Material Plane which, in other contexts, we've referred to as the

Finite World of Form or physical reality. This is the most dense and low frequency plane of dense matter and inanimate objects. At this level of Mind, we have very limited mental power, which is just another way to say creative power, so at this level of causation our ability to affect the whole is very limited in scope and reach. Imagine a crocodile in the Nile, she might terrorize and even dominate her territory in the Nile, but this crocodile's imprint on all of Creation is for all intents and purposes de minimis.

Primal Intelligence resides at a very low level of Consciousness, whether that pertains to humans or crocodiles. At this level of Mind, we're entirely unconscious to our own Consciousness; all thought-forms that bubble to the surface are autonomously generated by our subconscious programming and purely reactive or instinctive in nature. Most people will shrug their shoulders and claim this is not them, but we only have to see how people respond to something as innocuous as cutting them off in traffic to see how easily they're triggered and fall back in the complete unconscious behavior of road rage. Most people—even those with fancy degrees and prestigious titles and jobs—are very easily triggered and then unconsciously react from their Primal Intelligence. Heck, just watch TikTok for ten minutes and you'll have all the proof in this world many people live a considerable amount of their daily lives operating from this very low level of Mind.

This unconscious reactive characteristic of Primal Intelligence is also reflected in that—at this level of Mind—we perceive and experience reality through a lens of complete separation. At this very low level of Consciousness, we have no concept of Oneness as we perceive ourselves as totally separate, disconnected, stand-alone entities from the rest of our physical reality. Everything and everyone is a potential threat (or meal, so to speak) as this level of Mind has only three predominant instinctive objectives in the following order of importance: survival, sustenance, and sex. At this level of Mind, the latter is based on the instinctive impulse to procreate, not even pleasure and let alone Love of any kind.

Finally, and this is a nuance for extra credit, our physical body is actually contained in what is called our etheric body, which extends approximately one-half to one inch outside our skin in the exact contour of our body. The etheric body is visible in our aura as the first layer outside our skin and it's an integral part of the human energy system. In fact, technically, our physical body is nested within our etheric body as our physical body "grows" within our etheric body, which comes into Creation first.

> "Until you make the unconscious conscious,
> it will direct your life, and you will call it fate."
> —CARL JUNG

The next level of Mind in humans is the Limbic Brain; it's not exclusive to humans, though, as all mammals have a very well-developed Limbic Brain as well. Note that the Reptilian Brain is nested within the Limbic Brain and so on and so forth; this "nesting" should be a familiar pattern of the intelligent design of nature by now. The level of Mind of the Limbic Brain is our Experiential Intelligence—everything that has to do with feeling and emoting based on sensory input. Our Experiential Intelligence is what informs us how we feel about things, others, the world, circumstances, occurrences, or even buying decisions. Savvy advertisers, marketeers, movie makers, retailers, restaurateurs, hoteliers, consumer brands, etc. all target the Experiential Intelligence of your Limbic Brain by using colors, smells, tonality, music, ambiance, décor, visuals, imagery, symbolism, sexuality, etc. as most decisions are *made* through our Experiential Intelligence whereas the decision analysis is computed by our Rational Intelligence.

Experiential Intelligence is our Emotional Body Mind, and its plane of causation is the Astral Plane. This plane is less dense than the Physical Plane as it's already formless and so it also has a higher frequency than the Physical Plane, which makes it a more powerful causal plane. The Astral Plane is also known to be the plane of astral travel, which occurs in our dream state or when we have out-of-body experiences. Paranormal experiences such as meetings or communications with archangels, angels, ascended masters, or spirits also occur in the Astral Plane, except for spirits who are trapped in the Astral Plane; these higher beings descend into the Astral Plane from higher dimensions so they're reachable to us.

In various ancient wisdom traditions and esoteric teachings, the Astral Plane is considered to have two or three strata like lower, middle, and higher. This deeper level of delineation between the strata within the Astral Plane is not important for our purposes here, but just in case you come across it somewhere else, I wanted to mention it.

As noted, all mammals and many other life forms like most fish species have a Limbic Brain and therefore Emotional Body, and higher order mammals like dogs, cats, cows, pigs, monkeys, horses, elephants, dolphins, and whales, for instance, have a very well-developed Limbic Brain meaning their Experiential Intelligence is quite advanced, or in the case of whales and dolphins, very advanced. Perhaps this will put the cruelty and brutalities of slaughterhouses, commercial fishing, and whale hunting in a different light. Rest assured they consciously experience what is done to them, not all that different from if those things were to be done unto you. Once you see, you cannot unsee.

Experiential Intelligence perceives and experiences reality through a lens of separation bias, meaning it's still slanted heavily toward separation, but at this level, we can consciously override this bias. At this level of Mind, we start to have access to compassion, sympathy, empathy, affection, and connection with others and the world around us, but it's not our prevailing perspective; we have to consciously override the bias to open up this perspective. Our ability to do so would be quite limited without the analytical computing power of the Neocortex, but since that hardware is factory standard for humans, this is a theoretical notion. In case you were wondering, all mammals have a Neocortex as well; theirs is just vastly less developed than ours yet powerful enough to showcase a wide range of social behaviors and an ability to learn to use things and affect their environments through their Creations. For instance, the otter has a meaningful impact on the ecosystem of a river through the ingenious dams it's able to build using materials available in its habitat.

The Limbic Brain and its Experiential Intelligence is a significant step-up in level of Consciousness from Primal Intelligence, but we'll cover this in combination with the Neocortex and its Rational Intelligence; as for humans, these two intelligences operate in unison as there's no such thing as a human without a Neocortex and therefore Rational Intelligence. This is also reflected in the fact both our Experiential Intelligence and Rational Intelligence share the Astral Plane as their plane of causation.

Before we proceed to the Neocortex, let's take a short detour first. If you look at the graphic, you'll see a topical view of the two brain hemispheres superimposed on the Limbic Brain and Neocortex. The prevailing academic view is that the left-brain hemisphere is our logical side, and the right-brain is our creative side. The left brain is said to be linear, logical, sequential, analytical, and objective, and our right brain is said to be non-linear, creative, holistic, emotional, intuitive, and subjective. What's called the corpus callosum connects these two brain hemispheres; this connection allows information to pass back and forth, and the more developed this corpus callosum is, the more integrated our brain functions and so the broader the range of these qualities we have access to. We can measure all of this by measuring brain activity, so we can see which part of the brain lights up with which specific activity based on the function that's activated.

So far, so good. Lots of this has been empirically validated, but as our science advances, there are some interesting and noteworthy things that have been discovered. First, our brain operates far more holistically than hemispherically, as originally hypothesized. For instance, about 10 percent of the population is left-handed, and of those, about 30 percent have reversed hemispheres, meaning their "right brain" is in the left hemisphere and vice versa. There also appears to be a lot more neuro-flexibility in that the brain has quite a bit of leeway, which area of the brain it utilizes for whatever function. The right-brain and left-brain hypothesis also falls apart when we analyze the Limbic Brain as the Hippocampus, Amygdala, Hypothalamus, Mammillary body, and Cingulate cortex, which are all part of the Limbic System, are lateralized, meaning they're mirrored in each hemisphere. Where all of this is pointing at is that the lateralization of our brain has much more to do with a built-in redundancy than an actual strict compartmentalization of the typical qualities we attribute to the left and right hemisphere of our brain. It's still useful as a conceptual framework, but this is not to be confused with our brain actually functioning like this.

We're also starting to discover, for instance, that a musician who was traditionally assumed to be so-called right-brain dominant uses quite a bit of left-brain computing power as music draws heavily on mathematical and motor skills. At the same time, an investment banking analyst building complicated financial models was always assumed to be left-brain dominant but it turns out there's a lot of creative brainpower and spatial thinking that goes into building intricate financial models. The point is, there appears to be some level of lateralization of the brain hemispheres, but it's not nearly as neatly compartmentalized as originally believed.

Here's where all of this is pointing us. There is a level of lateralization of our brain, but it's far less hemisphere (i.e., location) related as it's function related. We can generally "lateralize" the brain in the functions we can attribute to locational hemispheres, but it has far more to do with which functions we develop and use most often than it has to do with where they're located. In Western society, which is monomaniacally infatuated with all things logical, scientific, and analytical, our entire educational system is geared toward the development and use of the functions associated with the left brain. Neurons that fire together wire together. So, it's not surprising that, as a whole, the "left-brain" functions are overdeveloped compared to the functions we associate with the right brain. However, our brain as a whole operates holistically, and the popular notion of what we commonly believe to be right-brain vs. left-brain hemispheric specialties (logic versus creativity) has been all but debunked. I realize this might feel like brain anatomy overload to some of you, but you'll understand why we needed to debunk this popular myth when we get to the intelligence of the Heart, as it's this intelligence that is predominant in the evolved spiritual Poet and not his/her right brain dominance as commonly suggested.

What this does mean is that we're leaving a whole host of invaluable functions and capacities of our brain underdeveloped, and generally speaking, the more we can equally develop these diverging functions in tandem, the more computer power we have access to. What has exponentially more gravity though is our level of Consciousness as that dictates our ability to create intelligent outcomes as we'll discover next as we explore the Neocortex.

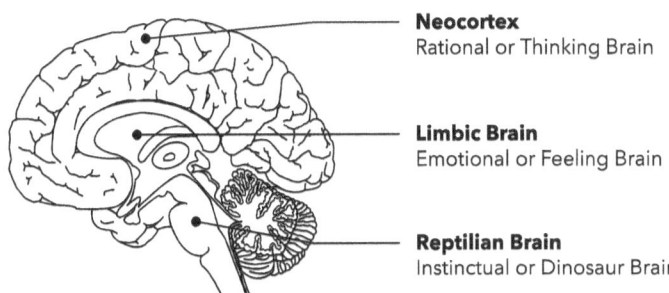

Humans pride themselves for our Neocortex or our capacity for analytical and logical thinking. And it's true our Neocortex is an incredibly powerful human supercomputer that sets us completely apart from all other mammals. Just imagine, a mere two pounds' weight difference in brain matter—essentially all Neocortex—is the difference between a Chimpanzee living in trees in the jungle and humans orbiting satellites in space. However, this Rational Intelligence of the Neocortex is also the root cause for virtually all the unintelligent outcomes we see in the world, so it's a double-edged sword, but more on that later.

Rational Intelligence is our Mental Body Mind and affects the higher strata of the Astral Plane of causation. These strata of the Astral Plane is very powerful; with its higher frequency, it's far more powerful than the lower strata in the Astral Plane and orders of magnitude more powerful than the Physical Plane. The best way to view these various intelligences and the respective planes of causation they affect is as being logarithmic in scale. Each successive higher order of Intelligence and its corresponding plane of causation is exponentially greater and more powerful than the next lower order of Intelligence that's nested within. For instance, we know through scientific studies that the electromagnetic radiation of our Heart's intelligence is c. 5,000 times more powerful than that of the Rational Intelligence of our Neocortex. Infinite Intelligence is not even measurable, which is why trying to scientifically plot all these intelligences on a logarithmic scale is maybe a fun scientific folly, but it's ultimately a futile exercise as you can't solve for Infinite Intelligence.

The mental power and, therefore, creative power of Rational Intelligence is very potent; this is very advanced machinery, so to speak, and in the hands of an unskilled machinist, things can go sideways fast. This is where humanity is today; we have access to this incredibly powerful creative power of our Rational Intelligence, yet our collective level of human Consciousness below 200 makes us very unskilled machinists. We're like novices who've been given a priceless eighteenth-century Stradivarius violin to practice on, and so far, the "music" we've made out of things here on planet Earth is pretty much unbearable to stomach knowing what a Stradivarius is capable of.

Our Rational Intelligence, including the artificial intelligence (AI) we're copiously modeling after it, can become instrumental to saving us from extinction or accelerating us into extinction if we continue on our current trajectory. The choice is literally ours, but how we—humanity—will utilize our Rational Intelligence is entirely hinged on our level of Consciousness. Again, we're in a race to raise human consciousness—either we do that or it's going to be game over within this century.

The main reason Rational Intelligence is this double-edged sword is because the lens through which it perceives and experiences reality is also a separation bias like the Limbic Brain. The analytical computer power of the Neocortex adds a lot more ability to consciously override this bias, but the underlying bias remains. This, coupled with collective levels of human Consciousness below 200, translates into all the unintelligent outcomes we witness in the world today.

A stark example is Pablo Escobar, the infamous Colombian drug lord of the '80s and early '90s. Pablo took the mom-and-pop cocaine trade by storm as he transformed the logistics, industrialized crop farming, consolidated territories, and created an intricate distribution network. It's been said he made so much cash at one point he literally had no idea what to do with it. He also committed unthinkable crimes. In a way, he was an innovator and entrepreneurial genius. Had he applied all his innate talents and capacities in a legitimate business, he would have probably been a success story for the ages. He had very high levels of Rational Intelligence paired with very low levels of Consciousness; this is a deadly combo.

> "No one is more hated than he who speaks the truth."
> —PLATO

Before you dismiss this as an extreme example, note that today most of the politicians, business tycoons, tech moguls, private equity and venture capital titans, and the countless prestigious lawyers, accountants, and bankers are all similarly lost in their Rational Intelligence. They might not commit the same horrific violent crimes as Pablo, at least not directly, but they command the economic engine of this world that's as cruel, barbaric, unjust, corrupt, greedy, environmentally destructive, and morally bankrupt as anything else the world has ever known. And moreover, it's not only hotshots and kingpins that do this; it's all the minions that readily and knowingly participate in all these shenanigans in exchange for a paycheck. Again, ignorance might be an explanation, but never an excuse. I know this is a harsh reality to accept, but if we are to ever come to address the serious problems facing humanity, we must start being willing to face the Truth for what it is. There is simply no legitimate excuse for the pervasiveness of war, violence, and unthinkable cruelty committed in the name of righteousness.

Please note I said most, not all. However, most of the above-mentioned political luminaries, titans of business, technocrats, and icons of capitalism that we idolize and glorify as being the epitome of (worldly) success, are really just spiritual adolescents disconnected from their Divinity. They're not inherently flawed human beings, just asleep. They're also just a little bit cleverer and cuter at disguising what happens behind closed doors than we've seen in prior times.

I will say, there are also true Poets bringing their luminescent self-poetry into this otherwise vast pool of unconsciousness. Yvon Chouinard—the founder of Patagonia, a business dedicated to the health of the planet—is one such example, so we know it's possible, even at significant scale. Albeit still sparse overall, fortunately, we're starting to see more and more Poets burst onto the business stage, many of whom are female game changers that are bringing a whole new level of Awareness, Wisdom, Compassion, and Consciousness to the world of business.

> "Five percent of the people think; ten percent of the people think that they think; and the other eighty-five percent would rather die than think."
> —THOMAS EDISON

What Thomas Edison is indirectly pointing at is, again, our level of Consciousness. At levels of Consciousness below 200, virtually all people are fully body and mind identified, or in other words, they identify with their Ego or persona. At this level of Consciousness, we're predominantly governed by our beliefs in our subconscious Mind. We're not aware we're the Observer and have, therefore, very little conscious Awareness that our subconscious programming is really running the show. We're sleepwalking with our eyes open, literally. At this level of Consciousness, we tap out at the Neocortex as we're completely unconscious to our Heart's intelligence, so this intelligence is basically in a dormant state. This is where roughly 80 percent of humanity is today, although the awakening of the masses is noticeably accelerating.

> "The collective unconscious contains the whole spiritual heritage of mankind's evolution born anew in the brain structure of every individual."
> —CARL JUNG

There's a very interesting phenomena to introduce here to further demonstrate the connectedness of all things and beings. It's called the "hundredth monkey effect" and is named after observations by biologists of groups of monkeys. The biologists observed that right around the time the hundredth monkey in a group learns a certain skill or discovery about its habitat, then this skill or discovery miraculously gets assimilated by other groups of monkeys, which might be on other islands or a great distance apart. We've seen this same phenomenon with scientific discoveries where scientists oceans apart produce the same scientific discovery right around the same time even though they have no knowledge of the other scientists working on the same problem. There are countless other examples as well, for instance in sports, the arts, music, and especially how the entire ancestral body of culture and archetypes gets transmitted to us. What's underlying all of this is the morphogenetic field within the Collective Consciousness of which we are all a part. For our purposes, it's not important to know more about its inner workings, except to know it's scientifically accepted it exists (albeit not well-understood yet) and, more importantly, that this communication and information comes to us through our Heart, which is connected to the Ethereal—or Spiritual—Plane, which is nested within the Monadic Plane (which, in a different context, is referred to as the Akashic Field). This happens entirely autonomously and unconsciously to us unless you're at advanced levels of Consciousness, at which time the innate telepathic capacities we each have become within our conscious Awareness. The point is, through this morphogenetic field we're connected to all of mankind and our Heart is the radio receiver and then this information arises as spontaneous thought-form (e.g., an idea, hunch, precognition, etc.) before our conscious Mind.

When our level of Consciousness rises above 200, a spiritual sea change occurs as that opens up our access to our Heart portal. Our Heart is the highest level of Mind we have access to in human form, as this gives us access to our Suprarational Intelligence. Suprarational Intelligence includes all the lower levels of Mind, but also our ability to interact and exchange information with the Infinite Intelligence of the Ethereal Plane and Monadic Plane.

The higher we ascend in Consciousness, the higher the level of information we can draw from these higher spiritual planes, and this works via logarithmic scale also because, as we noted earlier, levels of Consciousness are logarithmic in scale. At Christ Consciousness—level 1,000 or full enlightenment—our Heart, brain, or Spiritual Body Mind, for all intents and purposes, merges with the Ethereal Plane.

Suprarational Intelligence perceives and experiences Life itself on the Spiritual or Ethereal Plane, which is an extremely powerful plane of causation of very high frequency. Again, exactly how powerfully we can affect this plane of causation depends on our level of Consciousness. For all the planes of causation, the principle applies that the higher the plane of causation and the higher the level of Consciousness, the more powerful and faster manifestation manifests. As our mental powers go up, our creative powers increase exponentially, which makes the Spiritual Plane extraordinarily fertile for bringing creation into all of Creation. This shouldn't be seen as now you have a magic wand, and anything you wish you can make spontaneously appear in form. Rather, your ability to recognize and therefore capitalize on serendipities, magnetize the right people and favorable circumstances, and your overall ability to attune with aligned potentialities accelerates the timeline within which these potentialities materialize into actualities.

However, as our mental and, therefore, creative powers increase, our responsibility goes up correspondingly as well, so as we ascend to higher levels of Consciousness, our self-poetry organically becomes more and more closely aligned with what's truly in alignment with the universe, and our interest and desire to act solely out of self-interest dissipates. If you will, more and more of our Divine essence gets expressed and bleeds into our Creation.

A big part of the spiritual sea change is that our bias makes a fundamental shift; we go from separation bias to Oneness bias. So, this "step-up" from the Neocortex to activating our Heart or Spiritual Body's Mind is a major one, especially since up to the Neocortex, we don't really have to do anything to activate the hardware. We can readily substitute the label "Spiritual Body Mind" with the label "Higher Self" as they're pointing at the exact same "thing."

We're born into this world with our Neocortex, Limbic Brain, and Reptilian Brain fully online. Our Heart is actually also online when we're born, but it overwhelmingly gets shut down in our early developmental years, especially in Western society. Another way to view this is that our Higher Self is always online whether we're aware of it or not; we just lose our connection with it until we learn to reconnect with it, which we do through our Heart portal.

Children with an open Heart portal are actually quite easy to detect; they'll talk often about seeing or talking to ghosts, spirits, or angels and seeing visions, having lucid dreams, and they tend to have a very vivid imagination. They might talk about past lives, see or feel energies, and all sorts of other possible phenomena we typically pile on the heap called paranormal. Any of these sorts of experiences of the child are usually met with disbelief, dismissed as nonsensical, or even condemned as heresy, and that forces the child to shut down their Heart portal as children have a natural instinct to want to be loved and accepted by their parents and family.

Shifting into the Oneness bias is a total game-changer; it radically transforms our perspective of ourselves and all of reality. We start feeling ever more connected, interdependent, and interwoven with the entire web of life. Either right around or very early on in making this shift, it becomes inevitable we come to the point we are ready to freely choose to play *the* one Infinite Game, which radically transforms our perspective on how and which Finite Games we continue to play going forward. All of these shifts and changes are part and parcel of the rite of passage called Awakening, which might last from a few weeks to several years. Even within the awakening process, we go through stages and phases as we start to ascend through levels of Consciousness, with each higher level bringing its own awakening and growth lessons.

> "All our knowledge has its origins in our perceptions."
> —LEONARDO DA VINCI

Our perception of reality can be seen as a cone-shaped form where the cone fans out as we gain access to higher levels of Mind. At the level of Primal Intelligence, the cone is very narrow, and we're only able to perceive and therefore understand a tiny sliver of reality. At the level of Suprarational Intelligence, the cone is vastly wider, so we perceive and understand reality at a much deeper level. Again, all of this is logarithmic in scale also, which makes the step-up from the Neocortex to the Heart such a monumental shift. Also, at higher levels, we have access and command of all the nested lower levels of Mind, but in reverse, we can't perceive the next level until we're ready. It even holds true that when we're triggered into our Primal Intelligence, we basically get cut off from our Experiential Intelligence and Rational Intelligence until we can settle down our central nervous system and bring those intelligences back online. Just watch someone completely lost in rage or panic, and you'll know exactly what I mean.

Before we move on the next level of Intelligence, it's important to note that our Intelligence of our Mind is Masculine, and the Intelligence of our Heart is Feminine, which is well illustrated by the language of the Heart—feeling, sensing, direct knowing, and intuiting. Regardless of gender, we all have access to both of these intelligences, but men generally tend to be very much in their Mind, especially when they're unawakened, and women tend to have a natural proclivity to access and tap into the Intelligence of their Heart. These are generalizations, but they pretty much hold true across the board.

> "The desire to know your own soul will end all other desires."
> —RUMI

There's a far greater significance to this, though; as with the above, we can now introduce and connect the dots between these two intelligences and the Alpha and Omega, a fundamental concept that ties into Polarity, Hermetic teachings, and a host of other ancient wisdom traditions. Of course, in Christianity, the Alpha and Omega points at Jesus Christ being the beginning and the end. But, in Hermetic and the ancient wisdom teachings, the Alpha and Omega point at something much deeper. Alpha is the Masculine and refers to the intelligence of the Mind (rational), and Omega is the Feminine and refers to the intelligence of the Heart (suprarational). Similarly, Alpha refers to Awareness, Intelligence, and Energy, and Omega to Being, Creativity, and Reverence—the respective constituent attributes of the Masculine and Feminine. In Egyptian mystery schools, the practice of resurrection was a sacred initiation ritual of the merging of the Alpha and Omega, or in other words, the reunification of the Masculine and Feminine into Source Consciousness.

"Resurrection" in this context refers to symbolically rising from the dead so the initiate may enter Paradise—Heaven on Earth—while alive. "Dead" symbolically refers to the state of being unawakened, which all major ancient wisdom traditions, including Gnosticism, consider a waking trance of Unconsciousness or sleepwalking. The Alchemical axiom "turning lead into pieces of gold and silver" refers to the exact same thing. This had nothing to do with some chemical secret, as those still sleepwalking have historically interpreted it. Lead points at mortal man or the "dead" man. Gold was symbolic of the Masculine, and silver of the Feminine. This pointed at the reunification of the Masculine and Feminine. Same for the Holy Grail, which itself was gold and stood on a silver platter called "salver." The word "salvation" actually originates from salver, if that tells you anything.

The point to take away from all of this is that the Alpha and Omega, like everything else we've seen so far, points us at that "Paradise" that is within the reunification of the Masculine and Feminine. Moreover, you can enter Paradise right here on the Earthly plane while still alive. No clergy middleman needed either; each of just has to awaken to this Truth.

The final level is the Divinity or Monadic Plane—which we've mentioned is in a different context, referred to as the Akashic

Field. This has Infinite Intelligence, which is the Mind of the "The All," which we can also refer to as the Cosmic Body Mind. It is the omnipotent plane of causation where every thought of The All instantaneously manifests a potentiality into an actuality. At this level of Mind, there's no longer any bias; only the totality of Oneness exists.

It should be noted that according to various ancient wisdom traditions and esoteric teachings, there are several other planes of causation between the various planes referenced so far, and again, the labels might be different as well. Labels are just words; they're immaterial. These planes in between are subtle gradient differences, which, depending on which school of wisdom teaching you study, are named separately or bundled into a single named plane which then has a subtle gradient within itself. This is akin to taking the base color red and delineating it into subtler shades of red. Both are correct; at the end of the day, they just convey the color red in a different level of granularity, which depending on the context, might or might not be helpful. For this chapter, further granularity would not aid in the conveyance of the overarching conceptual understanding we're after. Just grasp the essence; all else is details.

The main thing to take away from the Monadic Plane and Infinite Intelligence is this is the Substantial Reality—Fundamental Truth—that underpins all else. It's omnipresent, omnipotent, infinite, unchangeable, absolute, and eternal. It has no beginning and no end. Everything we know or consider as Existence or Life itself arises from this Substantial Reality.

What we have now discovered is that all of Creation or Existence is a "mental" Creation that originates from some level of Mind, which is just one aspect of the Mind of The All. Even you and me are ultimately a mental Creation of this The All, and so we can know then that this The All must be within us as well. And The All is just another label for God, Creator, Source, Yahweh, Elohim, Allah, Spirit, Great Spirit, Universal Mind, Infinite Intelligence, or whichever label you prefer—knowing this is knowing The All is the Divine, and so we—and all of Creation—are Divinity expressed into form.

My true wish, though, is to take you yet one level deeper. As we've now deconstructed the humanoid version of "God" prevalent in most world religions, it's time to reconstruct God or Divinity in the most truthful way possible, and paradoxically, the original teachings of Jesus guide us there most gracefully. You see, Jesus' native language was Aramaic, and the word he preferred to use for God was "Abba." Abba means "Father," but even more so, "Papa," or in English, we would use the word "Dad" or "Daddy." He would describe his relationship with God as one of being in direct and intimate relationship with his Abba—Fatherly love—and taught this was readily available to all of us as we're all his Creation—we're each his child or offspring. So, when we speak of all of Creation being a mental Creation, including each of us, we're pointing at all of Creation being a "child" of Abba. And Abba has infinite love for each of his children—no exceptions—and so much so he granted us free will. Our free will choice of disownment of him—of our Abba—does not stop or alter his infinite love for us in any way.

Here's the crux of all of this. You are not who you likely have always believed you are. Even the deepest part of you—let's say your Soul—is just an expression or aspect of The All, which is, therefore, in some traditions, referred to as the Oversoul. So, your physical presence here on Earth is definitely not who you truly are, and all your feats and accomplishments here on the Earthly plane are truly just The All or Divinity expressing itself through you as The All is experiencing itself through all of Creation. In the very same way, all your defeats, missteps, heartbreaks, and challenges don't define you either; they're ultimately just experiences running through you so you may grow and evolve into remembrance.

Remembrance of what, you might ask. Your truthful lineage. That at your deepest core, you're a spark of Divinity currently experiencing a lifetime on the Earthly plane. Remembrance of this Truth is the transcendent knowing that you are not only in direct relationship with Abba, but you are a part of Abba. Yes, that's right, you are an aspect and Creation of The All, which renders your true lineage Divinity. The true meaning and purpose of what we call "awakening" is this realization, as this remembrance changes everything from how you view yourself, others, all of Creation, and your relationship to all of it. This realization parts the seas to make the teachings contained in this book a lived experience that you—as a true Poet—express as your spiritual art into all of Creation. You don't have to take my word for it, by the way, but this was at the very center of Jesus' teachings of being in intimate relationship with Abba.

For those that get hung up on biological genders and take offense to Abba representing the Father, please note that we "reach" Abba through the Mother and Motherly love. And, what's the Mother? All of Creation. The Feminine or Existence or Truth. The path home is through the Mother, through the Feminine. She's of no less significance or importance, her role is just different, and of course, all of this supersedes any biological gender, as we're pointing at The All, which is Source, which is inclusive of both the Masculine and Feminine.

This is the Hermetic Principle of Mentalism—The All Is Mind. The Universe is Mental—held in the Mind of The All. We've gone fairly deep here; please don't shy away from reading this part a few times to allow remembrance to do the heavy lifting instead of trying to intellectually absorb and decipher this with your rational Mind.

> "The first step in learning is
> the destruction of human conceit."
> —PLATO

The prerequisite of seeing the magnificence and perfection in all of Creation is to let go of all arrogance and forms of self-importance. If we desire to become true Poets, we must learn to become humble so we can see our rightful place in all of Creation. The All itself is Unknowable; we can only surrender to it so we may come into harmony with it. To be in awe, reverence, and veneration is the humility needed to become a seer of the mesmerizing magnificence of all of Creation and the Substantial Reality from which it all arises.

In evolutionary and cosmological terms, we are but a speck of stardust in something that's so much grander, richer, deeper, and exquisitely designed and so much more magical than we could ever perceive with our finite level of Intelligence.

The thing is, we are not just any speck; we are each a *Divine* speck of stardust. Infinitely purposeful, valuable, and meaningful in all our smallness and insignificance. If you can grasp that paradoxical nature of Duality, it means you're well on your way to becoming a true Poet.

In the next chapter, we'll explore how to use Mind Mastery to do just that.

CHAPTER 34

MIND MASTERY & STATES OF BEING

FROM THE DEEP ABYSS of the ancient esoteric wisdom of the Hermetic teachings, let's now rise to the surface and come into the practical and likely more familiar discipline of Mind Mastery.

Mind Mastery—or Mindset teaching as it's sometimes called—is the shallow end of the pool, and there's a whole cadre of peak performance and life coaches that have made this a massive industry. That doesn't mean it's not useful, beneficial, or worthwhile, but virtually all of them are monomaniacally focused on one single thing: make you a "winner" in Finite Games.

This could not be any other way as we can only teach at the level we're at. These coaches—many who are truly gifted and offer a lot of valuable know-how—are still Finite Games participants themselves. Their business of teaching you Mind Mastery might come from a genuine interest and enthusiasm to share their know-how, but they operate at the level of winning or ranking in the Mind Mastery business. This is not a judgment of any sorts, just an observation.

My main aim is not to make you more successful—more lethal—in the games humanity really shouldn't be playing anymore. This book's core purpose is to invite you to become a true Poet and step with both feet into *the* one Infinite Game, as it's only from this playing field that you can freely choose to play in any Finite Game.

But please never doubt that becoming a Poet means forfeiting success in whatever Finite Game you freely choose to play. You will likely choose to no longer play or participate in certain Finite Games, seeing the futility, meaninglessness, and harm it causes. But the paradox is that in freely choosing to play, you can actually truly *play*, and herein lies your highest human potential as detachment from outcomes releases all Fears, which is the greatest inhibitor of you reaching your full potential. When we freely choose to play any Finite Game, first and foremost, to unleash our spiritual art, literally everything changes—even the Finite Game itself.

So, the true Poet will also seek Mind Mastery, but his or her motivations will differ fundamentally as they're anchored in a deeper Truth about Life itself. The realization that Existence or Life itself—including any Finite Game—is merely a playground to perfect our spiritual art and bring the Divinity within us into all of Creation opens up a whole new way of Being.

For this reason, and this reason only, a whole chapter is devoted to Mind Mastery as my aspirations for you are not to just become a true Poet, but a true Poet that's living and realizing their biggest dreams and aspirations for this lifetime as even your wildest dreams for experiencing worldly success are but a seed planted by The All.

> "If I have the belief I can do it, I shall surely acquire the capacity to do it, even if I may not have it at the beginning."
> —MAHATMA GANDHI

Let's start where it all begins: you! You are the only thing standing in the way between all your wildest dreams of success, prosperity, abundance, and even love relationships. We can know this to be true without a shadow of a doubt as everything already exists as a potentiality in the Akashic field. It's just a matter of sympathetic resonance as this potentiality—whatever your dream might be—holds a specific frequency and vibration you must match for it to manifest into your physical reality.

Already, right there we have quite a bit to work with. Since it's a frequency we must match, we can know that it's not circumstances or other factors like race, gender, looks, national origins, or the lucky sperm club that dictate our destiny. There's no such thing as accidents, flukes, coincidences, or random events in this universe. All circumstances, coincidences, serendipities, or what we might call "lucky breaks" arise from the Infinite Intelligence that governs this whole universe. It's the corresponding nature of reality; that is, reality corresponding to us and mirroring our Inner World in our Outer World.

It is entirely possible your "dream" is rooted in Falsehood, at which time your realization of this dream becomes challenging as you will struggle mightily to attain the frequency for it to manifest. Our Egoic Mind spins up all sorts of dreams which are rooted in Falsehood, most often that some form of Outer World success in the form of trophies, titles, prestige, status, fame, fortune, and applause will fill our Inner World void. This is always a good place to start: examining whether your dream is based on the quicksand of your Egoic Mind or whether it's a true experiential desire of your Heart and Soul in this lifetime. A good litmus test is whether your dream is rooted in your art—your unique talents, gifts, or superpowers—that want to be expressed into all of Creation or mere worldly success that must be achieved to become whole.

If your dream is a true dream of your Heart and Soul, you will—as Mahatma Gandhi put it—surely acquire the capacity to realize this dream as you will be motivated by something far grander than superficial outcomes. I call this being blessed by Divine willpower, a power far stronger and more resilient than mere mindset techniques can teach you. However, poor Mindset hygiene—negative beliefs and thoughts—can muddy the waters and disconnect you from this Divine willpower, so let's explore how we can master the Psycho-Cybernetic Loop by understanding our Mind's operating system and all the trickery it can do at a deeper level.

> "The ancestor of every action is a thought."
> —RALPH WALDO EMERSON

The Psycho-Cybernetic Loop is our Mind's operating system; it's how it fundamentally functions, which dictates our perceptions and creates our experience of Life itself through the direct outsized influence it has on our frequency and vibration. Let's dissect the below graphic to understand how our beliefs ultimately dictate our destiny.

BELIEFS

Our Egoic Mind holds our beliefs about Life itself. Most of these beliefs are stored in our subconscious Mind and based on an entire lifetime of deep enculturation. From the moment we take our first breath, our interaction with our parents or caretakers, our upbringing, and exposure to cultural, societal, and religious norms, values, and doctrine all amalgamate into a belief system that's deeply engrained into our subconscious Mind as "the way the world is and works." Ancestral wounds and heritage are passed down as well, including any beliefs about worthiness, potential, injustices, race, gender, and even nationality. Our beliefs about the way the world is and works is the foggy lens through which we view Life itself and all of Creation. It's our unique vantage point—based on the entirety of our lived experiences and those beliefs passed on to us by our unique circumstances like our parents, ancestry, culture, or religion—that forms our inherently biased perspective. It's our relative Truth, never to be mistaken with the absolute or universal Truth.

These beliefs can be empowering or disempowering, which is when we call them limiting beliefs. Disempowering or limiting beliefs are any beliefs that hold us back from realizing our ideal or dream life. If you hold deeply rooted beliefs that you're not enough, not worthy, not capable, or that whichever you wish is simply not available for "people like you" (whatever that might be), then those limiting beliefs will dictate your destiny of experiencing—without fail—exactly that in your Outer World.

Conversely, the opposite is also true of empowering beliefs as all thoughts that bubble to the surface of your conscious Mind are colored by your beliefs, but even when these beliefs—empowering or disempowering—run in the background outside your conscious Awareness they will have the same omnipotent effect.

THOUGHTS

All thoughts—whether conscious or unconscious—spawn from your beliefs and your belief system as a whole colors your perspective of everything that occurs to you in physical reality through your five senses. Thoughts also are potent frequency creators, which we all know firsthand. When we have a "positive" thought or perspective, our frequency and vibration rises and conversely when we have a "negative" thought it diminishes. What's positive or negative to us is actually entirely relative and subjective and, as we'll come to discover later, entirely malleable. Thoughts are also highly potent in that they trigger and directly influence our emotions or feelings.

FEELINGS

Thoughts directly trigger our emotions or feelings; in fact, thoughts play our emotions and feelings like a virtuoso concert pianist. Which also means that to the extent our thoughts are involuntary, autonomous, and compulsory, our feelings or emotions are really not under our conscious control. Our subconscious programming (i.e., beliefs) creates our thoughts, which in turn trigger our feelings and emotions. Feelings add amplitude (i.e., volume) to the frequency of thoughts, so feelings serve as a powerful amplifier or loudspeaker in the process of manifestation. We'll get to see how we can use this to our advantage later.

ACTIONS

Humans are very predictable in that how we feel overwhelmingly determines our actions and inactions. Fear, stress, worry, doubt, and anxiety, just to mention a few, will have us do or not do certain things, and conversely hope, joy, enthusiasm, gratitude, optimism, and confidence can propel us to take (or abstain from as the case might be) remarkable actions. You might think what about strongly held beliefs of right and wrong? Well, even in that case, language gives us a very powerful clue as those norms and values—which are beliefs—and their ensuing thoughts make us *feel* compelled to do or not do something. Whereas beliefs and thoughts are the underlying instigators, our emotions and feelings are the activators that drive our actions or inactions. Actions of course don't lie, but more so, consistent action in congruence with our aims tends to manifest those aims into our physical reality. Generally speaking, the more powerful, consistent, and persistent any congruent action, the faster we'll see the desired results in our experience. This works in reverse also with weakness, inconsistency, and discontinuity and/or incongruency of our actions. What follows from Actions then is Results.

RESULTS

Results are not exactly the same as what we experience because within our experience is our perception of the experience. Results are just outcomes; from the perspective of the universe all Results or outcomes are neutral—they're neither good or bad, favorable or unfavorable, they just are. Our experience of our Results is far more consequential though than the actual or factual Results or outcomes. Since this whole human operating paradigm is a loop, the Results tend to be an organically produced outcome of our fundamental Beliefs, thereby serving to only reinforce those very Beliefs continuously. We can call this aspect the experience of our Result,s which is far more consequential than the actual Results themselves, as it gets us stuck in this Psycho-Cybernetic Loop.

Of course, stuck is not necessarily bad when we're experiencing the Results we desire. But when these Results are not what we desire, we have to somehow make changes, and this can be incredibly challenging to do when we (a) don't understand the fundamental operating system of our Mind; and (b) we keep experiencing what we don't want, which only reinforces the unconscious Limiting

Beliefs that are the root cause of the final effect—the Results—we keep experiencing time and again.

> "Nothing is; everything is becoming."
> —HERACLITUS

Before we delve into the more practical application of Mind Mastery and how to use the Psycho-Cybernetic Loop to our advantage, we must cover some philosophical ground to build the proper foundation of understanding.

The first key concept is what Heraclitus points at: nothing is fixed. You are not fixed, unchangeable, immutable, or conditioned to be anything. Every morning when you wake up, you're a blank canvas. We hold on to all sorts of mental ideas and psychological preconceptions about ourselves and the world, but the fact is everything is always becoming—no exceptions. Knowing this is knowing you are free to sculpt yourself today in whichever likeness you wish. Perhaps you were a "loser" yesterday, so sculpt a "winner" today. Knowing this key concept is knowing you have total creative freedom; your past is completely irrelevant in terms of who you decide to be today. The past might echo a bit longer in your reality as the aftereffects of what you've created before, but it has no bearing whatsoever in who you decide to be today except whatever baggage you allow your Mind to carry forward into the Now, which is the only moment there ever is and will be. Liberate yourself from your Mind, thoughts are not real.

Know your job is not to figure out the "how"; that's an unknowable task which is therefore reserved for the Unknowable or The All.

The universe will show, guide, and direct you toward the "how" so focus on getting very clear on the "why" followed by the "what" that follows naturally from the "why." It's most helpful to let go of "when" as well; time and space are unpredictable quantities outside of our direct control. Dictating our timeline onto the universe is a surefire way to create stress, anxiety, worry, and doubt. "When" is irrelevant anyway as everything is just an experience. The proverbial pot of gold is not hiding at the end of the rainbow, it's in experiencing all the rich colors of the rainbow.

Most dreams never come to be because people get stuck on figuring out the "how" or stopping prematurely if their fixed notion of "when" doesn't materialize. They get intimidated by the seemingly insurmountable task of figuring out the "how" or discouraged when "when" turns out to have a mind of its own. So, focus exclusively on what needs to come from deep within you: your "why" followed by the "what" that follows from your "why."

Just note that not all "whys" are of the same quality as each "why" has what's called an attractor field. A small "why" is one which is rooted in pure self-interest; this will have a relatively small attractor field. A big "why" will serve a bigger purpose or the whole beehive; the more it will serve all others and this whole universe the larger and more powerful the attractor field. An attractor field is what electromagnetically draws opportunities, resources, coincidences, serendipities, and favorable circumstances our way to fertilize our "why" in the seed.

Don't ever be fooled by superficialities like worldly success; it's simply not a good or useful barometer for what the universe considers success. Those we might idolize and glorify because of their seemingly boundless worldly success might actually be taking on copious amounts of Karmic debt that are invisible and unknowable to us. If this is the case, their worldly success is coming from incurring spiritual credit card debts that will all have to be repaid, this lifetime or another. So, best not to heed any importance or relevance to any sort of worldly success; it's unknowable to any of us except the Unknowable what invisible Karmic debts are counterbalancing any visible worldly success. In fact, don't concern yourself with anyone else unless you can draw inspiration or helpful lessons from their wins and successes. Just stay in your own lane and focus on your own biggest possible "why" that sets your Heart and Soul on fire; all else is Outer World noise.

Finally, in terms of philosophical foundation and to paraphrase Einstein, we have to make a choice—a decision—whether we live in a friendly or hostile universe. This is not merely a decision about the essential nature of the universe, it's the decision whether we surrender to the Unknowable or The All. And any form of indecision or being inconclusive is a de facto not surrendering and allowing a bias to remain—however faint—toward the universe possibly being hostile. The illusion we are or should be in control is akin to not surrendering. The notion Existence or Life itself is within our control, is controllable, or must be controlled are all based on a fundamental doubt that the universe is or could be hostile. Until you decide to truly surrender, you will not be able to see and experience all the miraculous ways in which the universe conspires to aid you each step of the way.

Upon total surrender—which is a decision—all will invariably become fully visible and as palpable as burning your hand on a hot stove. Surrendering takes great courage and spiritual fortitude, which we can only access through the intelligence of our Heart. At levels of Consciousness below 200 we lack the access to our Heart's intelligence, which is why this decision is a major obstacle and we tend to spastically cling onto notions of wanting to control Life itself, others, and circumstances—if need be, by use of Force including but not limited to oppression, abuse of power, fraud, malfeasance, corruption, and causing harm to others. These are the inherent spiritual adolescent tendencies of mankind; we each outgrow them at some point.

> "Most powerful is he who has himself in his own power."
> —SENECA

Knowing all about the Psycho-Cybernetic Loop operating system of our Mind is powerful information but knowing it doesn't mean it's within our power yet. The sort of Mind Mastery we're after is having our Mind within our power. There are just a few more key building blocks we need to cover to bring it truly within our power.

As I alluded to earlier, our Feelings and emotions have a high amplitude, which means their frequency or vibration is much more readily discernible than those of Beliefs or Thoughts. Our Feelings and emotions are denser as Beliefs and Thoughts are more subtle. And, since our physical body is nested directly within our emotional body, our physical body directly absorbs and corresponds with the frequency and vibration emitted by our emotional body.

In that sense, our physical body is a very accurate radio receiver and, in turn, transmitter. Our emotions are even stored in the cellular tissue of our physical body.

There are numerous healing modalities and therapies based on this, including aspects of Reiki and sound therapy. Trauma, which fundamentally is unhealed deep emotional wounds, can be brought to the surface through somatic therapies that release the trauma from our cellular tissue, which allows us to then process them psychologically and spiritually. There are highly gifted practitioners doing miracle work this way who are able to guide their clients through remarkable life-changing transformations. Another example where worldly success pales in comparison to the gift of healing these practitioners are contributing to deeply scarred souls.

It's my personal conviction that the medicine of the future will be sound- or frequency-based, and pharmaceutical interventions will fade into the background and eventually disappear. And this would only be logical as our bodies are complex energy systems that are regulated and animated by frequency and vibration. Pharmaceutical interventions are based on affecting the atomic and biological level, but that's the level of effect and not cause. The underlying cause of any disease or illness is dissonance in the energy at the subatomic level.

Our emotions and how they make us feel are directly accessible to each of us, even the uninitiated and otherwise deeply unconscious, as our body doesn't lie. If we tune into our body, which takes but a mere pointing of our Awareness into our body, we immediately sense whether we feel light, heavy, good, bad, etc. We know when we have a pit in our stomach or when our body feels elated. All of this is our body being our emotional register; it's directly accessible to each of us and operates with pinpoint accuracy as we cannot consciously manipulate, control, or misinterpret what our body is feeling. It's important to note that our body is feeling this, and we are—again—not our body as we have a body. This distinction is key as we're the Observer, and only from this vantage point can we dispassionately observe how our body is feeling and "read" what it's informing us.

The only way we can tune out what our body is telling us is by numbing it; this would be through alcohol, drugs and opioids, pharmaceuticals like antidepressants, sleeping aids, and seeking other distractions like excessive eating, shopping, risk-taking like gambling, binge watching, partying, sex, porn, etc. These are unfortunately all very prevalent in our society, partly because it's very good business for some so it's advertised as normal, or worse, harmless. Partly because so many people live inauthentic lives, so they want and need to numb themselves; this makes life more bearable for them.

To illustrate this further, Las Vegas is a perfect microcosm of this dominant aspect of Western civilization. Sin City, as it's also referred to, is the cornucopia of excess, gluttony, debauchery, consumerism, gambling, alcohol, drugs, sex, and shiny objects. Vegas' sole raison d'etre is to numb and distract you; the very moment you disembark your plane you're sucked into the city's vortex of excessive external stimulation. The real tragedy is that when people leave Las Vegas, they're not really leaving. Everything is just amplified and uncensored in Vegas, which makes it easier to see, but don't be fooled as Sin City is a mirror or derivative of our culture and society. Nobody ever leaves Las Vegas as, truthfully, Las Vegas is the world we live in.

Besides the obvious impact on our health and well-being, the problem with numbing is that it robs us of our internal compass and a key navigational aid. Our Feelings and emotions, as reflected in our body, are a vital information source on whether or not we're in alignment with Truth or Falsehood. Not just our relative Truth, which is based on our perspective, but universal Truth. Anytime something feels off in our body—however it shows up—we're not in alignment with universal Truth. Which is to say, our Beliefs and Thoughts are rooted in unintelligent thinking, which is not in alignment with creating intelligent outcomes. When we feel good—whatever way that shows up—our Beliefs and Thoughts are rooted in intelligent thinking and the creation of intelligent outcomes in our life. This is fail-safe, we cannot consciously manipulate any of this and in fact our body's autonomous nervous system corresponds directly with this and reflects it in the prime state it shifts into.

There are only two prime states of Being we can be in, Harmonic and Disharmonic. There are countless sub-states like flow, happy, sad, depressed, etc. but all of those are sub-states to these two respective prime states. These prime states correspond directly with our body's autonomous nervous system which also has only two prime states, namely the parasympathetic and the sympathetic nervous system. Just like the prime states, we can only be in one at the same time, but we can flip-flop back and forth.

Our Harmonic prime state corresponds with the parasympathetic nervous system, which is the "rest and relax" state of our nervous system. In this state, all our bodily functions operate optimally, our blood pressure stabilizes, our heart rate goes down, and our digestion system is fully online. Our body generates, regenerates, and restores itself toward homeostasis or optimal health when it's operating from the parasympathetic nervous system. We have more cognitive clarity, better access to imagination and creativity, sleep better, and our sexual organs are upregulated.

Conversely, our Disharmonic prime state corresponds with the sympathetic nervous system, which is the "fight or flight" state of our nervous system. In this state, all our bodily functions nonessential for survival are downregulated, which idles our digestion system, our restorative and bodily repair processes, and our sexual organs. Our heart rate increases, blood pressure increases, pupils dilate, muscles contract, and a host of hormones like adrenaline are secreted to prepare the body to fight or flight. We all know what this feels like as we've all been startled before, gone on a scary roller coaster ride, or saw a horror movie which had us screaming and at the edge of our seat. Of course, these are all innocent occurrences; perhaps you've experienced more grave real-life dangers, in which case you definitely know what I am pointing at. This is our body's perfectly normal survival instinct and it's designed to incidentally shift into the sympathetic nervous system to stave off immediate danger only to revert back to the parasympathetic nervous system when the danger has cleared.

The problem arises when we spend too much time in this Disharmonic state; that puts enormous stresses on our body, which translates into dissonance—illness—if the prevalence of this state becomes enduring or too frequent. Most chronic illnesses in our modern-day society can be retraced to the Disharmonic prime state—and therefore the sympathetic nervous system—being the dominant state people are in due to living stressed-out and inauthentic lives. Add to this poor diet, too little rest and sleep, too little sunlight (Vitamin D) and fresh air, disconnection from nature and Mother Earth (i.e., "grounding"), and all the various numbing agents and you have a very potent cocktail to introduce illness, disease, and an overall lack of well-being.

> "Your worst enemy cannot hurt you as much as your own unguarded thoughts."
> —BUDDHA

For most, all of what we've covered so far operates silently in the background impervious to their conscious Awareness. They're unconscious to what's actually operating and dictating their destiny, claiming oftentimes all sorts of illusionary external reasons and excuses why their Outer World experiences show up the way they do. Sympathetic resonance makes no mistakes, though; our Outer World is therefore always a perfect reflection of our Inner World and the only way to reshape our Outer World experiences is to reshape our Inner World frequency and vibration.

This is the art and science of Mind Mastery, reshaping our Inner World so our Outer World experiences transform into the destiny we desire. In practical terms, the Psycho-Cybernetic Loop is our roadmap on how to most effectively do this and our physical body is our navigational aid.

In practical applications, we can start anywhere in the Psycho-Cybernetic Loop and retrace backwards until we get to the underlying Beliefs we hold about Life itself. So, if we observe or experience Results we don't desire, we can trace this back to the Actions or Inactions we took, the Feelings that prompted those, the Thoughts that triggered those Feelings, and finally the Beliefs that gave birth to those Thoughts. We can do this from anywhere in this loop and just trace backwards until we get to the root of the problem, which is always in some Belief we have about Life itself, which could be a Limiting Belief we have about ourselves.

Let's go a level deeper though.

> "Our life is what our thoughts make of it."
> —MARCUS AURELIUS

Mind Mastery is predicated on being able to step into the Observer vantage point; we cannot dispassionately observe ourselves if we believe—i.e., identify—with our Thoughts and therefore our underlying Beliefs. We also have to assume 100 percent responsibility for everything we see and experience in our Outer World, otherwise we disclaim our creative power to change it by reshaping our Inner World. The hardest part is not dismissing our Thoughts but to truthfully see and then masterfully reshape our own Beliefs. The reshaping of our Beliefs is sometimes referred to as neuro-sculpting where you are the sculptor.

Embedded within a Belief is the notion it's true. So, reshaping and overwriting a Belief goes directly against the grain of our long-held perspective of how this world is and works. This makes Beliefs very stubborn and all the affirmations, visualizations, and "love & light" wishing in the world—albeit helpful—won't hold the power to actually overwrite the deep grooves and neural patterning of our subconscious Mind. We might make slight improvements only to find ourselves fall back into the very Beliefs we're trying to reprogram.

The answer is in making a decision and this is based on the foundational knowledge that every Belief we have is a decision we at some point made about Life itself. Through some lived experience or form of enculturation, we decided on how the world is or works and this became a Belief held in our subconscious Mind. We're not born with Beliefs and certainly not Limiting Beliefs; they form over our lifetime. Knowing this allows us to make a new decision about how the world is or works, which might be a new decision about ourselves.

Then we copy and mimic the very same process of enculturation; we seek evidence in our own Life, the lives of others, or the world at large to substantiate our new Belief about how the world is or works. Finding examples from your own Life are always the most powerful, and you might be surprised how much evidence you can find if you look for it. But, for instance, if you're born into poverty on the wrong side of the tracks and hold the Limiting Belief that a minority person cannot do x or y, you can look to Oprah Winfrey or Martin Luther King, Jr.—whichever corresponds better—to find evidence that it's possible. And if it's possible for anyone it's possible for you also. If you hold the Limiting Belief women can't do x or y, there are countless examples of women who have done it already and so on and so forth.

The point of this exercise is that the new decision—the new Belief—needs to take root and to do so we need to create new neural pathways—neurons that fire together, wire together. Over time, perhaps aided with affirmations, visualizations, sticky note reminders, empowering mantras, and mostly definitely congruent actions, this creates new neural pathways, which, over time, will also render the old ones associated with the prior Belief dormant until they dissipate altogether. All of this is possible due to the neuroplasticity of our Mind; when it comes to Thoughts and Beliefs literally nothing is fixed, beyond repair, or beyond constructive reprogramming.

> "The only person you are destined to become is the person you decide to be."
> —RALPH WALDO EMERSON

Who knew that the person you're destined to become is the person you decide to be? This is what Mind Mastery is all about, and although this works equally powerfully for the unconscious pursuit of trophies and rankings in Finite Games, my goal is to arm you with the power over your Mind so you'll use it to create spiritual art as a true Poet would.

And, let's be honest, this world doesn't need more vain superstars bathing in the temporary glory and limelight of mere worldly success. This world desperately needs more true Poets making their Life spiritual art.

And, besides, as a true Poet you can have both so why settle for one? In fact, we don't ever need to settle but we do need to learn to surrender, which is what's next.

> "The best of men choose one thing in preference to all else, immortal glory in preference to mortal good; whereas the masses simply glut themselves like cattle."
> —HERACLITUS

CHAPTER 35

TO SURRENDER

THE MERE NOTION OF "SURRENDERING" makes most people cringe, especially men. The word evokes the stirring acrimony of weakness and capitulation, of submission. We associate the act of surrendering with failure, with losing, with being inferior. We infer that within surrendering, this can only be done to others who in our surrendering to them become our victors, conquerors, and superiors.

So it is that the simple word "surrender" elicits a rebellious resistance within. Lots and lots of internal resistance.

Yet, in spiritual terms, to surrender might very well be the holy grail. The pinnacle, the final threshold to cross, the doorway to true freedom.

Let's explore this paradox and see what wants to be revealed so this paradox can come to serve us in our quest for spiritual Poet mastery.

> "Be crumbled. So wildflowers will come up where you are. You have been stony for too many years. Try something different. Surrender."
>
> —RUMI

Our resistance to surrendering is a natural survival instinct deeply embedded within our primal human archetype, which is hermetically entangled with our physical Existence on the Earthly plane. In mankind's earliest days on the Earthly plane, surrendering to others, predator animals, or even nature was submitting to death, literally or figuratively.

To surrender was to submit to another person or tribe's superiority. This implied a loss of sovereignty, honor, dignity, identity, culture, customs, deity, territory, possessions, language, and perhaps even our spouse or family. In other words, a total loss of all Earthly power. In this Earthly plane context, death often becomes preferable and more merciful than to live.

Even in more modern times up to this date, this is what's basically at stake in war and armed conflicts. It's primal so the resistance runs very deep.

The Earthly plane is the realm of Finite Games. Mankind has been wrapped up and lost in these Finite Games since antiquity. That's why Force—war, violence, armed conflict, and oppression—is always the inevitable ultimate tool of politics. To surrender in Finite Games is to capitulate, to lose, to become conquered. And, so, whether it's sports, business, or politics we must never surrender as to surrender is to choose death. Of course, this evokes resistance, visceral resistance even. This is the enduring struggle of life on the Earthly plane for as long as we perceive winning Finite Games and all that comes with that to be the purpose of our Existence. Within Finite Games themselves, there's no way out. There's no other way to perceive what it means "to surrender." We're trapped in that matrix for as long as we don't dare to look behind the veil of illusion that's the entire Earthly plane.

So, let's go behind this veil and see what we might find.

> "The more you struggle to live, the less you live. Give up the notion that you must be sure of what you are doing. Instead, surrender to what is real within you, for that alone is sure. You are above everything distressing."
> —BARUCH SPINOZA

For the mortal being within us—the Ego—death is the formless enemy we duel with each and every day—consciously or unconsciously—until we finally surrender, which is to say, die. For the spiritual being within us—our Soul—death is the formless companion we surrender to each and every day until we finally merge, which is to say, continue life in another form. For our Ego life is a struggle and losing battle against death; for our Soul life is an exuberant dance with Life itself with nothing to lose.

Where all of this points us is that what we're after—to uncover the deeper meaning of "to surrender"—lies beyond the realm of our mortality on the Earthly plane. We're now entering the Divine Paradox of Life itself where our ceaseless struggle against our mortality on the lower Earthly plane holds us back from Being truly alive and where our surrender to our immortality on the higher Spiritual plane gracefully guides us to Being truly alive.

To understand this better, we have to be willing to accept the Truth that our mortality on the Earthly plane is an undue burden to carry as it doesn't just encompass our inevitable physical death but all the small psychological deaths we suffer on our journey toward it. Every loss, failure, injustice, disappointment, heartbreak, or breakdown we encounter is a small psychological death. And, as mortals, each one of them programs us deeper and deeper that Life itself is a struggle. Each one informs us to play it safe(r) and to guard against the next one. Each one thickens the armor, makes us less carefree, and therefore less alive. Stuck on the Earthly plane, Life itself tends to suck the life out of us, beat us up, and spit us out at the end. Even when our personal circumstances are fairly favorable and comfortable, we're still witnessing this in the world all around us. It's the soiled bathwater we swim in daily, it's inescapable. Surrendering to this makes no sense at all, so we naturally resist and struggle on.

The lower Earthly plane is our Outer World, that which we call our reality, which is defined by time and space. The higher Spiritual plane is our Inner World, the infinite inner silence within which has no beginning and no end. This is the pathless land where we can discover our immortality. However, discovering our immortality on the higher Spiritual plane hinges but on one thing: we must first embrace our Divine essence. Our Divinity within is the doorway to surrendering, and surrendering is the master key to Being truly alive.

But we have to first answer a few more important questions, like what does it mean and look like to surrender and what or who are we even surrendering to?

> "In a real sense faith is the total surrender to God."
> —MARTIN LUTHER KING, JR.

The word "surrender" comes from the Old French word *surrendre* which means to "give up or deliver over" as the word comes from "sur" which means "over" and "rendre" which means "give back." So, in a nutshell, in surrendering we're releasing something or handing something over.

Surrendering is also a voluntary act; we must be compelled from within to surrender or there can be no surrender. To be compelled to voluntarily do anything, we must gain something, or we simply wouldn't be compelled to do it. Voluntary implies this is within our power. This might sound paradoxical if you think of a soldier or army surrendering to an enemy, but if you examine it closely this can only be done voluntarily—as it's a choice or decision—and there is also a gain. It's a choice or decision because even under extreme duress the soldier or army can choose not to surrender, in which case they likely simply lose. There's also a gain; in the case of soldiers or armies surrendering it's typically to stave off imminent death. You can take any scenario you wish, and you'll always find this to hold true.

So, we can now see that in surrendering—which we can only do voluntarily—we hand something over to gain something. Earlier we discovered that to do this we must first embrace our Divine essence or Divinity within.

Let's solve this quest now. What we hand over is the illusion of control, what we gain is a release from the struggle so we can come into Being truly alive. And embracing our Divinity within is the doorway, as without that, we cannot recognize the Divine as that's what we're surrendering to.

We have a lot more to unpack now; let's get started.

> **"Sometimes surrender means giving up trying to understand and becoming comfortable with not knowing."**
> —ECKHART TOLLE

Other than our Inner World experience and what we express into the world in the form of what we say, think, do, and create, the notion we have control over much of anything is not much more than a stubborn illusion. Take any great human feat or success, and you'll find that billions of variables had to all align in the exact sequence they did or that feat or success would never have been. Our lives are a living mosaic of coincidences, serendipities, synchronicities, and favorable circumstances that somehow—as if orchestrated by an invisible intelligence—surface into our field of perception as our reality. Existence or Life itself is a complete mystery that way, but somehow it all works flawlessly and is absolutely perfect in its design. Everything works and functions in infinitely intelligent ways by infinitely intelligent design, in accordance with immutable natural law and order, whereby everything synchronizes in our known universe to produce our experience of Life itself.

The Truth is, we're each very powerful but we also each have very little control in the big scheme of things. Our idea of control is an illusion, but we need it as a mental crutch to not succumb to the darkest place in our Mind, which is the place of not knowing.

Deep down, we all know the Unknowable is not knowable to us. The non-linearity of Life is an unsolvable riddle for our Mind, so it force-fits linearity into that which has none. It invents lower laws it understands to obscure from sight the inviolable higher laws of the universe it cannot fully grasp. It prefers the illusion of control over simply surrendering to the Unknowable.

Surrendering to the Unknowable is surrendering to a higher power and whether you call that God, Creator, Spirit, Source, Infinite Intelligence or The All as the Hermetics do is irrelevant. To hand over your fate like this takes immense courage, spiritual fortitude, and most of all, trust.

In absence of embracing your own Divinity within, it's near impossible to surrender into the trust that the universe—the Divine—has your back. It's near impossible to surrender into the deep knowing that everything is always in perfect order and that everything always happens for our greatest growth, greatest prosperity, and greatest evolution. To surrender into a deep knowing regardless of whether we understand all of it, that's completely surrendering into trust.

But to release and hand back the illusion of control, more will be needed than some comforting words that all is always swell because, from your Mind's perspective, that simply hasn't always been its experience.

> "The heart surrenders everything to the moment.
> The mind judges and holds back."
> —RAM DASS

At the very core of our struggle with Life itself is the ill-fated attempt to know, manage, and outsmart the Unknowable. Like a heroin addict, our Mind is addicted to certainty, predictability, and familiarity. That's its comfort zone, that's what it knows how to compute, control, and trust. Anything outside this comfort zone—the unknown as well as the Unknowable—cannot be trusted as it's uncertain, unpredictable, and unfamiliar and therefore incomputable and uncontrollable.

Herein lies our conundrum as the nature of Existence or Life itself is immutable and the Unknowable is inviolable. We have no choice but to surrender to these higher orders or our choice not to surrender is the de facto choosing to continue the ceaseless struggle.

Our Mind further complicates this choice as it only knows Life itself as a struggle; it has no concept of what Being truly alive looks or feels like as that's never been within its lived experience. At the level of the Mind then we cannot make this choice; we need to access the higher intelligence of our Heart to access the courage and spiritual fortitude we need to make this leap. And we all intuitively know this to be true from experience. We've all faced big decisions in our life and after much "thinking" and "analyzing" through the options with our mind we eventually had to forge ahead by making a decision. Do we date, marry, or break up with that person or not? Do we buy that house, take that job, move to that city, or go to this college or that one? It could be anything. And, since we can never have perfect information and know all the answers or outcomes, there's inevitably a final leap of faith we have to make in every major decision, and the energy to make this leap—however small or enormous—comes from courage. And courage exclusively lives in our Heart and nowhere else.

The suprarational intelligence of our Heart gives us access to that which is beyond linearity, logic, and knowledge, which is mere stored information. Through the language of the Heart—feeling, sensing, direct knowing, and intuiting—we can access the higher level knowing of our own Divinity. From this place, what seemed like an insurmountable leap of faith to our Mind becomes a few small yet momentous steps.

By embracing the miracle of our own Divinity, as if by magic the path to walk down unfolds before us organically. As within recognizing our own Divinity we cannot help but realize our Divine essence is but one droplet in the cosmic ocean of the Divine. As we make small steps down this path this cosmic ocean becomes ever more real and palpable to us, we start having eyes for all the magic and miracles in our own Life and the world around us. A whole new world—invisible to our Mind—comes into focus as we allow the mystical Unknowable to flow through us. This all takes courage and spiritual fortitude as we have to learn to let go of all our Mind has ever known.

As we move down this path toward surrendering, we'll start to undress the heavy armor we carry around layer by layer. Removing our armor is our unbecoming of all our Mind thought we were. As we unbecome more and more, we invariably start losing our various masks, detach from enculturated beliefs that no longer serve us, and move toward true authenticity. Every step toward our truest expression of Self is a decisive step toward introducing more aliveness into our Being.

Invariably, as we make our tenuous steps down this path, we'll stumble upon our Crucible, which typically shows up as some form of crisis or catastrophe. The Crucible is not a punishment or some form of cruel humor the universe bestows on us. It's a test, or more so an invitation by The All to cross the threshold. It's giving us the opportunity to make a conclusive choice to surrender and it's using adversity to nudge us. The test is one simple question: are you ready to surrender into full trust?

On the other side of this Crucible is freedom, liberation, and stepping into Being truly alive. No more struggle as you have known Life itself to be. But, not to worry if you're not ready to cross this threshold just yet; the Crucible will be presented as many times as you need to cross the threshold.

> "The greatness of a man's power is the measure of his surrender."
> —WILLIAM BOOTH

Again, paradoxically, in surrendering to the unknown and the Unknowable, we gain great Power, which in turn will have us cede the penchant to use Force to control Life itself. To be able to accept, welcome, and embrace Life itself in whatever way it appears right now is true Power. To dance with the unknown and the Unknowable is true Power and so is knowing—at a deep level—everything is always in perfect order no matter if we don't understand it fully. The more we're able to surrender into full trust, the more true Power we command to create and live the Life we desire. This isn't in our enhanced ability to control Life itself but to make what shows up for us the Life we fully embrace in that moment.

We still dream, imagine, set intentions, and work toward all of these in congruent ways but we now have the Power to welcome it whichever way it shows up, whenever it shows up. This is what it means to have no more struggle. As underpinning every loss, failure, disappointment, heartbreak, or breakdown is a fixed idea how Life itself should be. This false premise gives the universe no leeway or any degrees of freedom to come to our aid in whatever contributes to our greatest growth, greatest prosperity, and greatest evolution. So, we resort to Force as we want to control Life itself. Of course, the universe will not stop operating in its infinitely intelligent ways as our Force is no match and it's unconcerned with how our Mind believes Life itself should show up.

This is why our true Power rests in surrendering into full trust; let's discover how we can truly know this is so.

> "Unless you fall back to the Feminine and surrender. Unless your resistance and struggle become surrender, you will not know what real life, and the celebration of it, is."
> —OSHO

The deeper our surrender, the more true Power we gain, which translates directly into our level of aliveness. We've seen this before in the salient axiom about Finite Games: "when we *must* play, we cannot *play*." If you recall, this axiom pointed us at the Truth about being compelled to play in Finite Games. We're compelled to play—we must play—when we believe winning or gaining trophies, titles, status, prestige, accolades, fame, fortune, or applause will make us become somebody. This "somebody"—whatever that might be—is by definition a psychological construct, it's not real. The struggle on the other hand is very real, especially as this "somebody" is amorphous and so it shape-shifts over time, making actually getting there at best temporary and most often entirely elusive.

Within surrendering into full trust in the Divine, we get to truly play, and this is where true aliveness lives. This sort of surrendering is Feminine in nature as it's dancing and flowing with the currents of Life itself, which is why so many unawakened men struggle mightily with surrendering as it goes against their Masculine-dominant nature of wanting to control everything.

The Feminine teaches us to dance with Existence, to come into Being through Creativity and Reverence. By surrendering into full trust of the Unknowable or the intelligence of Life itself, we trust in the Order within The All, which allows us to accept and embrace the Chaos within Existence or all of Creation. It's this acceptance and embrace of the Chaotic messiness of Life itself—in whichever way it shows up—that releases the struggle and sets us free to truly play within all of Creation.

The true Poet knows his or her freedom to play freely, to freely express his or her spiritual art into all of Creation, lies within the decision to surrender into trust. We can master our Inner World and our expression into the Outer World, but we cannot control the Outer World. It's a fool's errand well beyond our paygrade; the only wise thing then is to surrender to the higher power that governs all of Creation.

This is not always easy at first, and it takes courage, but it's the only way out of the struggle and into Being truly alive. Not only that, it's the only path to spiritual success, which, truthfully and as we'll discover in the next chapter, is the only success this universe is ever concerned with.

> "The great soul surrenders itself to fate."
> —SENECA

CHAPTER 36

SPIRITUAL SUCCESS

WE ALL HAVE AN INNATE DESIRE to be successful, and this has the capacity to serve us and everything we touch in profoundly poetic ways. It can also be exploitative, degenerative, and destructive to Life itself, as desire holds a highly potent kinetic energy that pulls us forward toward that which we desire. So, *what* we desire is of paramount importance. We could say desire is the driving force and our *what* dictates the destination.

Here we can already see a major demarcation from how we traditionally define and measure success as in Finite Games or the game of worldly success the *what* is gaining trophies, winning, or ranking so we can beget fame, fortune, and applause. This renders the journey there merely a means—"how"—to an end, which is why we so easily gloss over and justify all sorts of less-than-noble means.

Spiritual success is single-mindedly concerned with *how* we get there, or in other words, the journey *is* the destination and our true *what* then becomes *how* we make that journey. From the perspective of spiritual success, the end is sort of inconsequential and so whether we end up gaining worldly success holds little weight. We gracefully embrace and happily celebrate it when it comes our way, and we equally gracefully attach little meaning to it when it doesn't.

Hence, in this chapter, we'll crystallize and define success—the *what*—from the perspective of all of Creation as our spiritual art is nothing but a fractal of the whole universe, so its definition of success is inherently ours as well. But, before we do so, let's dig a little deeper into the driving force—i.e., desire—first.

> "Life is not a problem to be solved but a mystery to be lived. Follow the path that is no path; follow your bliss."
> —JOSEPH CAMPBELL

Weak desire translates into apathy toward Life itself; there's no energy to infuse life force into the expression of our spiritual art into all of Creation. Weak desire stems from lack of purpose and meaning. In our world of glossy superficiality, shallow, worldly objectives, and pervasive disconnectedness from others, nature, and the Divine, apathy has become a dangerous cancer to society. More and more people—but many young people especially—feel lost, empty, and unfulfilled. We see this reflected in such social phenomena like "the great resignation" but also a digression into violence, extremism, alcohol and opioid abuse, as well as addictions like excessive consumerism, binge-watching, gambling, video games, sex, and porn. All of these forms of escapism stem from the same root cause, a fundamental lack of purpose and meaning. Desire, and therefore life force in their Life expression, can only be rekindled by first reconnecting these lost souls with purpose and meaning.

> "I know you're tired but come; this is the way."
> —RUMI

Within the unawakened pursuit of winning Finite Games, the *what* blinds us to our own poetry within. The Architecture, Gifts, and Principles captured in this book become words we read, but the poetry within them is obscured from sight. It's not that we cannot understand these spiritual theorems intellectually, but we cannot connect with them with our Heart. Our Mind digests the information, but our Soul is not stirred and elevated into remembrance.

There's nothing wrong with pursuing worldly success or even being lost in doing so, but at some point, we exhaust the ability to be all-consumed by Finite Games. That might occur this lifetime or the next, but this game will invariably lose its fervor. We can no longer find the motivation, and our desire dwindles and erodes until the dimmest of pilot lights is left of what was once a fiery flame. When this happens, we often feel confused, disoriented, and lost, as if all our familiar bearings have been hidden from sight. Perhaps the universe even throws in some crisis or catastrophe to amplify the despair, except there's nothing to despair. All this is an invitation from the universe to go on your Hero's Journey—the sacred rite of passage of awakening that we all must make on our way to becoming a true Poet.

This place of despair, of searching, and grasping for a deeper meaning, can feel dark and very foreign, but it's there to serve us and guide us to the doorway to see Life itself in a completely different light. Deeper, more expansive, more colorful, and far richer than you have ever viewed all of Creation and your vital role in it. The dark tunnel is just a passageway to jettison all the baggage of enculturation and Falsehoods that have served their time and purpose.

Your vantage point is being gently redirected to spiritual success. You are being guided, nudged, and provoked to open your Heart so you can hear the whispers of your Soul. And what your Soul desires most is to become re-entangled with the eternal cosmic expansion of which it has been an integral part for eternity. What your Soul is whispering to you is that it's time now to become a true Poet again.

> "Try not to become a man of success,
> but rather try to become a man of value."
> —ALBERT EINSTEIN

It would be painfully obvious to define spiritual success as bringing the spiritual theorems of this book into your expression of Life itself, but pointing out the self-evident is too lazy and wastes a valuable opportunity to connect you on a deeper level with how the true Poet goes about gauging their expression of spiritual art into all of Creation. So, in no particular order of importance or relevance, we'll next cover nine key markers by which we can get our bearings and navigate the path of spiritual success.

> "The object of life is not to be on the side of the majority,
> but to escape finding oneself in the ranks of the insane."
> —MARCUS AURELIUS

SOVEREIGNTY

To do what's right under all circumstances, we must relinquish the need to be validated and approved of by others. Sovereignty is our ability to stand alone in our Truth, to become a sovereign critical thinker, and examine Life unbiased from what the masses, our tribe, or mass media wants us to mindlessly adopt or regurgitate. We rise above any political ideology, race, gender, nationality, societal beliefs, or religious doctrine to discover—to the best of our ability—Truth in all things and situations. Sovereign beings are the antidote in any societal or group setting of being ruled by manipulators, schemers, populists, extremists, or tyrannists. Sovereignty is what allows us to be contrarian when what's mainstream propagates and violates the inviolable higher laws that govern this universe.

> "The world will ask you who you are,
> and if you don't know, the world will tell you."
> —CARL JUNG

AUTHENTICITY

You are here to be you, not some narrative spun by the Outer World of what or who you should be. You are a unique puzzle piece of the mosaic of humanity bestowed with unique gifts, talents, and superpowers that were intelligently gifted to you to fulfill your unique dreams and inspiration for this lifetime. Authenticity is unabashedly bringing the art that is the true you into the expression of your spiritual art. There's nobody to emulate, copy, or repeat, as nobody is you. What this universe and all of Creation craves most is your authentic true Self. So, no matter what, stay true to yourself and heed the call of the whispers of your Soul. True Authenticity never violates the rules that govern this universe, as this Authenticity stems directly from your Divine essence. So, there's never a real concern for the true Poet that allows their spiritual art to be born from true Authenticity to violate the universal Principles.

> "Re-examine all you have been told.
> Dismiss what insults your soul."
> —WALT WHITMAN

WONDER

Each day, look at the world with fresh eyes, and you will see miracles and things not seen or realized before. To Wonder is to approach Life itself with curiosity, to be open to the novel, new, and different, as everything in all of Creation has multiple dimensions. All of Life itself is paradoxical and rooted in Duality and Polarity. Wonder is a perspective we take on the world that makes everything always fresh, different, and deeper from how we perceived it before. Wonder is the antidote to boredom, staleness, and plateauing and keeps our life force crackling strong, as there's no beginning and no end to true Wonder. Wonder rejuvenates, regenerates, and revitalizes our aliveness as we meander through the movie called our life. With true wonder, there are no dull moments; every speckle of Life itself becomes filled with richness.

> "Any man attached to things of this world
> is one who lives in ignorance and is being consumed
> by the snakes of his own passions."
> —BLACK ELK

GENEROSITY

Due Generosity serves as a powerful lived affirmation of the Principle of Abundance. When we give and contribute generously into the web of life, we're circulating energy in whatever form that might take. Generosity then can come in many forms, such as Love, kindness, compassion, wisdom, time, effort, opportunities, resources, or of course, financial resources. The circulation of energy is an essential attribute of any healthy and thriving complex living system; it promotes and enables the generation, regeneration, evolution, and vitality of the entire web of life, which makes it more harmonious, resilient, robust, and dynamic. Choking off circulation of energy in all its forms through hoarding, greediness, selfishness, and gluttony destabilizes the whole, erodes health, and leads to staleness, decline, degradation, and degeneration whether it's a love relationship, society as a whole, the economy, or our personal health.

> "Life without love is no life at all."
> —LEONARDO DA VINCI

BENEVOLENCE

The embodiment of Benevolence goes well beyond being just peaceful, as it also encompasses grace, courtesy, kindness, helpfulness, respectfulness, humility, and even mercy. The practice and embodiment of Benevolence starts within; the more benevolent we can be toward and with ourselves, the greater the amplitude of Benevolence we can express to others and into all of Creation. Even though Benevolence exudes a soft and gentle energy with a distinct Feminine quality to it, this doesn't mean we become a passive doormat or martyr of abuse. Benevolence is anchored in a deep sense of self-worth, so firm boundaries and Benevolence are not mutually exclusive. But, within Benevolence, we no longer avenge violence with violence or trade insult for insult as we rise above revenge and readily dismiss any primal instinct to get even. Benevolence beholds the wisdom of Karmic debts that any violation "done" to us is a Karmic debt assumed by the violator.

> "You've got to say yes to this miracle of life as it is, not on condition that it follow your rules."
> —JOSEPH CAMPBELL

COURAGE

Whereas bravery is the audacity to take risks, Courage itself is the audacity to face and overcome Fear. In terms of spiritual success, Courage, therefore, holds a lot more weight as it's our deepest Fears we must face and overcome—time and again—to ascend to ever-higher levels of Consciousness. It's Courage that holds us when we face ourselves with a raging inner storm or in a dark place of despair. It's Courage that grants us the valor to press forward when everything inside of us is screaming we can't. It's Courage that helps us dare to venture unto the pathless land or summit the peak we deep down inside know we must, except we don't know how yet. It's Courage that reignites our spiritual engine time and again whenever it sputters or stalls. Without Courage, we could never discover we have wings as we'd never jump off the cliff.

> "It does not matter how slowly you go
> as long as you do not stop."
>
> —CONFUCIUS

FORTITUDE

The spiritual path can be long and arduous at times; Fortitude is what carries us through, as it's much more than just strength. True Fortitude encompasses endurance, stamina, grit, determination, tenacity, and having backbone. Whereas Courage ignites our spiritual engine, Fortitude is what keeps it running. Fortitude is what allows us to go the distance, stay in the game, and deal with setbacks and adversity, as it helps us push through the inevitable inner resistance that rises to the surface when we're seeking growth and transformation. Fortitude is what aids us in doing what's right instead of what's most convenient. It's Fortitude then that separates the boys from the men (so to speak) on the spiritual playing field, and this metal gets forged harder and more tough the more it gets tested. Fortitude then is a muscle we must exercise, or atrophy will set in; we do this by seeking the limits of our comfort zone where we have to go beyond our existing conditioning. The axiom "the way you do anything is how you do everything" holds especially true for Fortitude; it's a powerful practice to exercise Fortitude in all we do as this will greatly enhance our ability to access Fortitude whenever our spiritual success depends on it.

> "The ethic of reverence for life is the
> ethic of love widened into universality."
>
> —ALBERT SCHWEITZER

VIRTUE

We are each born—hard-wired—with an innate knowing what's virtuous and what's not, no exception. We also never lose our ability to recognize Virtue; however, most of us struggle mightily to live it fully as we allow our primal intelligence too much reign over our expression, so personal gain, the seeking of pleasure, or the avoidance of pain gets the best of us. Any lack of Virtue can typically be retraced to two core deficiencies: Integrity and Fortitude. If you recall, the Masculine Gift of Integrity stems from the coalescence of Intelligence and Energy, so these two need to be shored up to anchor in our Integrity. Fortitude helps us overcome the temptation of convenience, and most often, that which is of Virtue is not the path of least resistance or convenience. Virtue, though, is worth our deepest commitment; not only is it a powerful purification and redemption tool for ourselves, but it holds great healing powers for those touched by it. Virtue is the actualization of Divinity, which is why it holds a momentous capacity to transmute ancestral wounds, prejudices, and suffering caused by grave injustices as it restores remembrance in the form of hope and faith in Divine righteousness. Never underestimate Virtue's magnanimous ripple effect on the web of life; the Divine grace of Virtue has a way of touching a person's Heart in a way a thousand words can't do.

> "The best way to find yourself is to lose yourself in service to others."
> —MAHATMA GANDHI

SERVICE

To shift away out of the myopic spiritual adolescence of self-interest toward service to the collective is a natural evolution of spiritually awakening; to recognize it's a privilege is a marker we're reaching spiritual maturity. Albeit this is counterintuitive for the person held hostage by self-interest, Service and contribution to all of Creation are quite possibly the highest return investment any person can make. When we become a net contributor instead of a net taker (or worse, abuser) of the web of life, this same web of life has a magical way of multiplying our genuine Service into far richer rewards than we ever contributed. The reason is that genuine Service expects nothing in return; we give and contribute for the sake of giving, or it's not true Service. The universe rewards the absence of expectations of reciprocity with Abundance; this is not a matter of rewarding good behavior but based on sympathetic resonance or the operation of natural law. Genuine Service that expects nothing in return can only be made in the frequency of Abundance—of having plenty—and so through the law of resonance, this is "reciprocated" by the universe with Abundance. And, again, Abundance is not limited to money as it can come our way in many forms, such as Love, joy, peace, gratitude, fulfillment, meaning, connection, serendipities, etc. In Biblical teachings, true Abundance is tied to "my cup runneth over," which is a metaphor for the full richness of Life itself being felt as a lived experience within. No amount of zeros on your bank account can come even close to this sort of richness, as this is the Holy Grail, literally and figuratively. Service is the access point for this sort of vast riches to enter your Life, which is all about everything that money can't buy.

> "Every morning, we are born again.
> What we do today is what matters most."
> —BUDDHA

If I wanted to be cute, I would have added amnesia to this list. As for most of us, our past is an albatross we lug around as dead weight. We're so closely identified with our lived experiences we literally carry them into the future, which only serves to perpetuate the same lived experiences and thereby reinforcing our limiting beliefs.

Spiritual mastery is cultivating an acute sense of intelligent amnesia, which is defined as learning our lessons—growth through gaining wisdom—yet having the experiences themselves say absolutely nothing about ourselves. You see, no experience defines you in any way, as you're not the experience. You are merely the vessel through which an endless stream of life experiences passes. The objective is to distill the lessons from these lived experiences but allow the experience itself to flush through. Yet, through our memory, we tend to hold on to all these lived experiences and then erroneously believe they say something about us. That's the albatross you're carrying around, and that gets very heavy, very fast.

You are free to wake up every morning and be an entirely blank canvas with no past whatsoever. Because, frankly, that's closer to reality than anything else. There's only ever the eternal Now—the only moment there ever is—and so any entanglement of our identity of who we are as a person is illusionary. It's not real; it doesn't really exist except in the thoughts swirling around in your head.

The Truth is, you invent yourself anew every moment of every day. In that sense, Life itself is nothing but an infinite amount of "mulligans," to use a golf term, to reinvent yourself the best way you know how right this moment. And the next moment, the next moment, the next moment, and so on and so forth. If yesterday you were a "loser," today you can wake up and decide to be a "winner." All you have to do is make that decision and then take congruent actions. If you were an "impatient" person a moment ago, this moment, you can decide to be a "patient" person. There's no limitation on your ability to decide what version of you you're going to be this very moment; you are both the sculptor and the sculpture, so you have total creative control.

The only thing this requires is taking radical responsibility for yourself. No more victimhood that somehow the world did this to you, your childhood made you this way, or societal norms are forcing this upon you. As factually true as these things and circumstances might be, they're still just stories in your Mind that you choose to carry forward into your Life. You'll know when it's time for you to lighten the load and let the albatross go; just know this is fully within your power, and it's your prerogative to sculpt the sculpture whichever way you wish in this very moment.

To close the loop where we started, these nine key markers of spiritual success (and amnesia!) are not something to memorize as doctrine or turn into dogma, as that will constrain and suffocate your spiritual art. Rather, use these markers as signposts to help navigate the path and pursuit of spiritual success. These are the qualities and attributes that raise and refine the level of mastery and artistry of our spiritual art, so use them freely to help perfect your self-poetry.

> "Man is most nearly himself when he achieves the seriousness of a child at play."
> —HERACLITUS

Finally, play! Just learning to play again is spiritual success. Learn to laugh at yourself again, see the cosmic humor in this whole game, dance, and be giddy. All true spiritual masters have one thing in common: they smile and laugh often and have a self-deprecating sense of humor. They take growing and evolving as a Soul very seriously, but they don't allow that to get in the way of taking their humanness itself not too seriously. We're each here in Earth school as imperfect beings; we'll get a whole bunch of things right, and occasionally, we make a misstep, error, or maybe a colossal fuck-up. At the end of the day, they're all just lived experiences; as long as we grow and evolve from these experiences, Earth school is serving its purpose.

So, play, have fun, be like a child at play, as from a spiritual evolutionary perspective, we humans are just children. Bright and highly talented "children" capable of rising to great heights and doing amazing things, but spiritually still very young and here destined to freely choose to *play* in *the* one Infinite Game. Just making this choice alone is a form of rarified spiritual success, even though more and more people are awakening and making this leap.

Which brings us to the final leap that all change starts within. We're now ready to walk the final mile of this book and have all parts come together in a harmonious symphony of Love+Truth.

CHAPTER 37

FLOWER OF LIFE—ALL CHANGE STARTS WITHIN

"The nature of things is in the habit of concealing itself."
—HERACLITUS

WHAT SHOULD HOPEFULLY BE CLEAR as day now is that what we experience as our physical reality—the Outer World—is nothing but a thin veil hiding the true Substantial Reality or Fundamental Truth. Yet, we can motor around in this Outer World and play Finite Games a whole lifetime and never have the faintest idea we're skimming about the surface of an infinitely deep cosmic ocean of pure Consciousness. This surface of apparent solidness and form is convincingly real, yet it's absolutely not.

Now, once we start on our path of remembrance, all sorts of tools, teachers, teachings, and wisdom will come our way that will help us see past this surface into the depths of this cosmic ocean. And as we do, we discover none of the Truth is really hidden; it's all hiding in plain sight. Incidentally, the same goes for all Darkness as those lost in Darkness masterfully avail themselves of this same hiding place. The only real difference is that Falsehood—which any Darkness by definition is—has to be held in place by Force as it has no Power of its own. Truth, on the other hand, holds infinite Power; that's why it can neither be destroyed nor hidden indefinitely by Force.

Spiritual Truth and esoteric wisdom teachings go beyond words as words are content and universal Truth lies beyond language, beyond words, and beyond content. This is why so much of the ancient wisdom teachings are often captured in symbols and symbolism.

The Flower of Life is arguably the most sacred and revered of all these symbols; not only has it been around since antiquity, but it's been recognized and incorporated across many ancient wisdom teachings, sacred monuments and sites, and even many religions. The Flower of Life is widely considered to symbolically hold all knowledge of all of Creation; it's all hiding in plain sight within the deeper meaning of the sacred geometry forms that constitute this most sacred symbol and all the symbols and symbolism that are hiding within it. So, we're now going to shift back to complete the Love+Truth Framework within the Flower of Life.

> "Beyond a doubt, truth bears the same relation to falsehood as light to darkness."
> —LEONARDO DA VINCI

So far, we have all of the Architecture, Gifts, and Principles geometrically placed on the Flower of Life, and already it revealed how the Merkaba, Fruit of Life, and Metatron's Cube were hiding within this most sacred symbol. Each of these symbols alone are sacred and revered, and they each have their own remarkable wealth of knowledge.

And, in all these cases—like Metatron's Cube, which has all the Platonic Solids within that form the very basis of all of Creation—we have only touched on the very basics as there are many layers deeper we could go as there have been volumes of books written on each of them. But this book's aim is not to get you a PhD in sacred geometry and mathematics, just see the Divine design in all of it, as that will take you to the inevitable conclusion: there's a Divine intelligence that permeates all of Creation, including you and me.

Having said all that, from where we left off last, the center flower still remains open, and we still have the two perimeter circles that complete the Flower of Life undefined as well. Let's start by going on a quest to figure out the center flower, which, perhaps not surprisingly at this point, reveals yet another sacred symbol hidden within the Flower of Life. This one is called the Seed of Life, and it's very special because it tells us about Genesis and the Biblical seven days of Creation.

Now, this part of the Bible has been traditionally accredited to the Prophet Moses, who is said to have authored it roughly 3,000 to 3,500 years ago. Moses was born in Egypt, and the Biblical story is that he grew up with the Egyptian royal family as a foundling from the Nile River. As a part of the royal family, Moses would have been exposed and likely schooled by Priests in Egyptian deities and religion, sacred rituals, as well as the Egyptian mystery school teachings, which were reserved for royalty and the highest echelons of society. The earliest Egyptian discoveries of the Flower of Life are about 6,500 years old, so I will leave it up to you which one might have inspired the other.

Let's start with the Seed of Life, which, like the Book of Genesis, is a story about Creation. Clearly, scientifically, we know the world wasn't actually created in seven days; as best we know, it's about 13.8 billion years older than the Bible tells us. Like with all ancient wisdom teachings, these are all stories rich with symbolism that reveal deeper truths, so when we read these esoteric writings literally, we easily go way off track. So far off track, even, that people fight wars and kill over whose God is right even though these very same Gods each clearly stated, "thou shalt not kill." Go figure.

Here's the Seed of Life that's within the center flower of the Flower of Life.

The center flower is the origin of the Flower of Life, and this pattern then repeats itself to create the complete Flower of Life. This center flower—the Seed of Life—is formed by the coming together of the first seven symmetric circles shown in black (bold). As you can tell above, the first image (top left) has no purple circle(s)—it's just "empty" so to speak. This is on purpose; it's not just empty but symbolizes the Void or Source or the nothingness from which all of Creation arises. You may also call this God, Creator, Spirit, Monad, Yahweh, Elohim, Abba, Most High, Infinite Intelligence, The All, or Substantial Reality. It doesn't matter; the point is there's something from which Creation originates, whatever you wish to label that something. I will continue to refer to this as Source which is short for Source Consciousness.

DAY 1—"LET THERE BE LIGHT"

If you start with nothingness, total absolute darkness, and introduce light, you create day and night or light and darkness. Or, in other words, you create Polarity as now there's contrast where before there was only one vast ocean of black nothingness.

Not only that, when you create light in total nothingness, you create a dimension. The best I know how to explain this is in the context of a thought. Let's say you have a totally "void" Mind, and then a thought occurs. Now there's a dimension when before there was none. Within this previously totally "void" Mind, there's now a thought, which isn't the same as the rest of this still totally "void" Mind. So, in essence, you've also created Duality. Can you see that?

Also, we've covered before that Energy = Light = Information. So, by creating light, you've created energy and information also, as it's all the same thing in different forms. We also know that Energy is entangled with its fellow constituent attributes, namely Awareness and Intelligence, and that together these coalesce into the Masculine. So, really what "Let There Be Light" points us at is the creation of the Masculine pole (not men) or, in other words, Consciousness, which, in this case, pertains specifically to our universe. Or, in other words, our universe was born.

Now, just pause for a second. Where does all of Creation originate from in physical reality? An idea, which is a thought-form. Thought-forms originate from our Mind, which is the Masculine center of Intelligence. An idea is the genesis of creation on the Earthly plane; it represents the unrealized potential of a possibility that wishes to be born into physical reality and thereby take form as an actuality. In biological terms, we call this sperm.

DAY 2—"LET THERE BE CLOUDS AND SEAS"

If you create clouds and seas, there's now a planet or Earthly plane or there could be no separation between clouds and seas. Clouds and seas are also water; that's not only the element associated with the sacral chakra—sexual or creative energy—but water is the ultimate creator and conductor of Life itself. Whatever you sprinkle with water grows. We are roughly 70 percent made out of water and without water Life itself is not possible. Much like Life itself, water flows and is dynamic. Like in a river or ocean which are in perpetual motion.

What all this points us at is the creation of the Feminine. If you recall, the Masculine is the structure (Order), the Feminine is the dynamic ever-changing river of Life (Chaos) that flows through the structure. She is what births Life. She is Existence, physical reality, or Life itself; hence, we now know what goes in the very center flower of the Flower of Life: **Truth**.

It gets even better but we have to make a little diversion off-course for this. As you can see above, the first two circles coming together form a new geometric shape that looks like an oval. This is called the *Vesica Piscis* which is Latin for fish bladder and it's another deeply revered symbol hidden within the Flower of Life. You might recognize it because the ubiquitous Christian *Vesica Piscis* symbol was derived from this by adding two little flares so the fish has a tail.

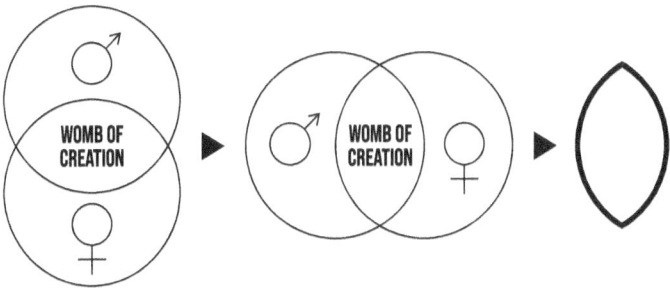

That's not the deeply sacred meaning of the *Vesica Piscis* we're after, as true spirituality is non-denominational since it doesn't concern itself with any particular religion. The *Vesica Piscis* represents what we could call the Womb of Creation, which is created when the Masculine pole merges with the Feminine pole to create Life itself. The Masculine and all his ideas cannot do anything without the Feminine's capacity to create and birth Life itself and vice versa. A sperm needs an egg and vice versa. All of this is deeply symbolic; it doesn't just pertain to biology but all of Creation, whatever that might be.

There's another deeper meaning held within the *Vesica Piscis* and to better reveal that, the graphic flips the two circles on its side first and then isolates the Womb of Creation. Recognize this shape? In some cultures and teachings it's not called the Womb of Creation but the Yoni or Vagina of Creation. Yoni is a Sanskrit word that refers to the vulva or vagina; however, it translates as "sacred cave" or "sacred space" and a stylized representation is worshiped as a symbol of the Goddess Shakti. This most-revered Goddess in Hinduism represents the female generative power in nature. In all ancient wisdom traditions including Tantra traditions the Yoni is deeply revered as symbolic of the Feminine's sacred role in all of Creation as she—her Yoni especially—represents all of Creation. The Feminine itself is considered Divine and sacred as the creator of all Life. So much so she's worthy of protection, provision, devotion, and the utmost reverence from the Masculine.

This is a far cry from the male-dominant culture that has ruled the Western world for more than two millennia, and perhaps if you're a man this might give you a different lens through which to view women as the embodiment of the Feminine. And, perhaps, it might even have you (and some women as well) reconsider the sacredness of her Womb of Creation and how you view sex. Similarly, we can view the whole world—whether it's society or Mother Earth—as a Womb of Creation, and so we can also see this in the macro perspective of what we're creating in business, politics, medicine, the arts, etc. Are you making reverent love to all of Creation or are you [expletive] for sport, or worse, abusing or even raping her?

> "All difficult things have their origin in that which is easy, and great things in that which is small."
> —LAO TZU

DAY 3—"LET THERE BE DRY LAND WITH PLANTS AND TREES"

If this isn't clear yet, what the Seed of Life is revealing is the master key sequence—the fundamental stages—that all of Creation goes through on the Earthly plane. It's all there if you can read into the symbolism and hyperbole. So, now we have the Creation of lower life forms such as dry land, plants, and trees. This is symbolic of the incubation stage of Creation; it starts out basic, rough even, and then will evolve and grow in complexity, size, and completeness over time. If you have an idea for a book, you have to make an outline first and then start writing. A painting starts rough, a piece of music is born from an inspiration that might only have a few chords at first. You get the picture.

DAY 4—"LET THERE BE A SUN, MOON, AND STARS"

If you weren't convinced yet that the Book of Genesis is symbolic and not meant literally this might convince you, as clearly there can't be plants and trees without the Sun there being first, literally. Either way, what does this really mean or imply? Well, what happens to planet Earth when you create the Sun, Moon, and the Stars? You give it an environment to exist within and be relative to.

So, we've now exited the incubation stage and "Creation" is entering into the world at large. Imagine you were tinkering away in your garage on some sort of prototype and then you get to a stage where you have a viable product. Now you take it into the world; perhaps that means finding some early-stage investors or perhaps it's setting up a basic website and seeing if it sells. We see this same thing in nature where a seed gestates, shoots roots, and then breaks through the surface, and now we can actually see it. It was already there, germinating underground.

DAY 5—"LET THERE BE CREATURES IN THE SKY AND SEA"

Now we're introducing higher levels of life forms, or in other words, the web of life is growing more evolved and more complex. This is the natural evolution of self-organizing complex living systems; literally the whole pattern is there within the Seed of Life. We see this evolution in ourselves from a little helpless baby, to a crawling toddler, a confused teenager, until we enter young adulthood and so forth. We get ever more evolved and complex as we age. A business grows like this and so does a nation. Even the world at large and humanity evolves in this pattern.

We can take this a step deeper even, because among these creatures some are benevolent and some are our natural predators, and we become predators to some perhaps as well. We see a natural hierarchy and order come to life, and again we see this in all aspects of physical reality as well.

DAY 6—"LET THERE BE ANIMALS AND LET'S MAKE MAN IN OUR IMAGE"

Not just in Biblical terms of Creation as God created man in his own image, but there's something much deeper that's hidden within Day 6. Something that has been totally lost on most of mankind, in large part because the religious interpretation of the Book of Genesis is so skewed.

If you noticed, all of Creation all the way through Day 6 comes from God, which is just another word for Divinity. Which means all of Creation, every last speckle of it, is Divine Creation and is therefore sacred. Each rock, each plant, each tree, each animal, and each human—no exceptions. All of it is Divinity expressed into form. And we—mankind—were made in his image.

Do we act like that? Do we take care of all of Creation like that? Do we recognize that the only reason we can create anything at all is because we were made in his image? That is to say, do we honor and recognize that Source bestowed Divinity within us and gave us a mesmerizingly beautiful garden to play in called the Earthly plane?

The word "dominion" is perhaps the worst typo ever made by mankind. We took that word as if we can do whatever we want, however we want. We were entrusted with heaven on Earth and we made it a cesspool. Collectively, we haven't shown up in his image; we've acted more like heartless and unevolved savages or hooligans.

The first deeper message of Day 6 is Divinity. Made in his image, how much clearer does it get? The second even deeper message is responsibility. We are responsible for everything we say, think, do, and create. If that's not "in his image"—i.e., Divinity—we are still responsible and those become our Karmic debts. Finally, there's a third and even deeper message within Day 6 and that's that all cycles of Creation on the Earthly plane have a zenith or apex and this climax simultaneously signals the end as well as the start of a new cycle. We can know this because of what follows in Day 7.

DAY 7—"ALL HE HAD MADE WAS VERY GOOD, AND THEN HE RESTED"

The paradoxical nature of Life itself is that all things come to an end—completion—and then again nothing ever does as everything flows into the next thing. Even our physical death is just another progression of all of Creation. All of Creation in the Finite World of Form follows this pattern on all levels of Creation. In the context of the second law of thermodynamics we call this entropy. But entropy is part of reductionism, so it isolates a particular part of Creation from the totality of all of Creation. Looked at through the lens of holism, all you would see is a continuous progression of Creation where things change expression and become ever more complex yet more orderly at the same time.

We can even see this in the Seed of Life as the seventh circle completes the first flower, but then this is just the start sign of the ongoing creation—addition—of circles that ultimately create the Flower of Life. And even the Flower of Life is not really finished; it's just artificially capped at nineteen total flowers but the pattern itself goes on into infinity and eternally.

Day 7 then symbolizes the overall process of creation and evolution, which is eternal and ever-evolving. The "rest" or sabbath or lull is a natural step in the process of all of Creation. We even see this come back in the sine wave which underpins all of the Creation of form, which has a neutral or zero point when it's neither positive nor negative. This is its rest point, yet again it's also fluid as nothing ever truly stops; everything is just always evolving, growing, and becoming.

The Seed of Life is the blueprint of the progression of all of Creation in Life itself whether it's galaxies, planets, life forms, nations, societies, businesses, friendships, or even our love relationships. There's also a deep layer of mathematical relationships within the Seed of Life that's well beyond the scope of this book, as you don't need to be a math wizard to express your spiritual art into all of Creation. Just see the poetry in all of this; it goes so deep and has endless layers to explore.

> "At the center of the universe dwells the Great Spirit. And that center is really everywhere. It's within each of us."
> —BLACK ELK

We're not entirely done, though, with the Seed of Life and what's next will reveal another layer and guide us into yet another highly revered sacred geometric form held within the Flower of Life. If you look carefully at the first circle of "nothingness" and the final completed Seed of Life, you'll notice there's an outside perimeter circle that's not yet defined. Truthfully, sometimes the Seed of Life on a standalone basis is shown without this perimeter and sometimes with as you could say it's implied.

It holds infinite meaning for our purposes as a circular enclosure in sacred geometry is symbolic of the heavens or Divinity. And later we're going to tie this back to the double line that encircles the Flower of Life, which represents the *Zona Pellucida*, which is often shown as a singular line but this is technically not correct as it distorts some of the advanced mathematics held within the

Flower of Life. We'll circle back to the *Zona Pellucida* shortly; let's first define this singular line that encircles the Seed of Life.

I'll come right out with it: the heavens of Divinity point us directly at just one thing: *Love*. Everything within all of Creation is held within, made of, and created by Love. If we could penetrate to the very core of Substantial Reality, we would find that the fundamental "substance" (for lack of a better word) it's made of is Love. Hidden underneath all fundamental energy, subatomic particles, electromagnetic fields, gravitational fields, and all the other elements and properties we're starting to comprehend through science and advanced mathematics lies the fundamental creative power, which is Love.

Yes, Love is even the fundamental creative power hidden underneath Consciousness, although in the case of Consciousness it's a toss-up if you would better say within or underneath. We're using words to describe what can't be contained by words, but either way, Love is the ultimate power. I know this will be frustrating for those of you who need science and mathematical proof to accept the Unknowable, but there's only one question that will inevitably lead you there. Name one power that's ultimate to Love.

This question has only one conclusive answer. Once you see, you cannot unsee.

By way of the encircling line of the Seed of Life, we've now also found another puzzle piece to complete the Flower of Life in addition to the earlier center flower we defined as Truth.

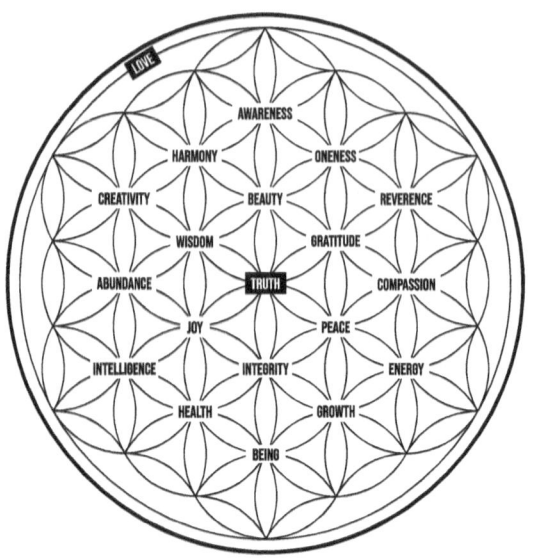

As you can now see, the inner circle of the double line we referred to as being representative of the *Zona Pellucida* is Love. Everything of Creation within all of Creation that's Substantial Reality—meaning all universes existing at all dimensions known or unknown, all galaxies, all planets, all species, all of humanity, or literally the entirety of everything there is—is held within, made of, and created from Love. Or in other words, Love (the energy) is the force field that creates, orchestrates, animates, powers, and serves as the fabric of all of Creation. This is why Love (the energy) feels like no other experience we can have as humans; it's literally coming home to what we're fundamentally—as in "energetically"—made of, so there's no experience we can possibly have of higher coherence. In Buddhism, Hinduism, Jainism, Sikhism, and various yogic traditions the state (note: "state," not just a fleeting "feeling") of this experience is referred to as "Samadhi," which is the attainment of a state of Oneness or merger and complete unification with the Absolute. If you ever wondered why Buddhist or Tibetan monks dedicate years, decades, or even an entire lifetime to meditation, prayer, and study, then here's your answer. Samadhi is why; they're seeking to attain that state. The good news is that doing it that way is just one path one can follow; there are infinite paths that can lead us to Samadhi so becoming a monk or even a yogi is not even in the slightest a prerequisite. Becoming a spiritual Poet devoted to perfecting your spiritual art is; it's the "how" of Life itself that counts, not the path you choose toward mastery of the "how."

There's more though, as hidden within the Seed of Life is yet another highly revered sacred form which is called the Egg of Life. This one is not easy to spot as it's partly disguised. The Egg of Life is a 3D form hidden within the 2D Flower of Life, so in 2D there's one element we cannot directly see and have to infer. Here's how you can find the Egg of Life.

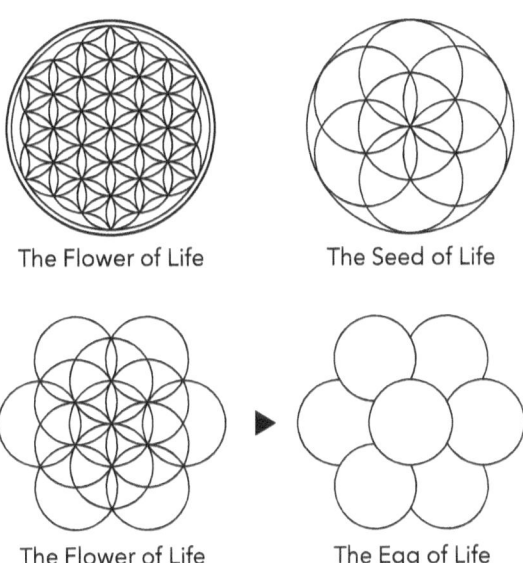

The Flower of Life

The Seed of Life

The Flower of Life

The Egg of Life

The Egg of Life holds eight equal spheres (circles), and if you refer back to Metatron's Cube, you'll see the center points of these eight spheres hold the cube within Metatron's Cube. So, this sacred form holds eight spheres, not the seven we can see in 2D. Let's now see what this sacred form reveals when we relate this back to the Love+Truth Framework.

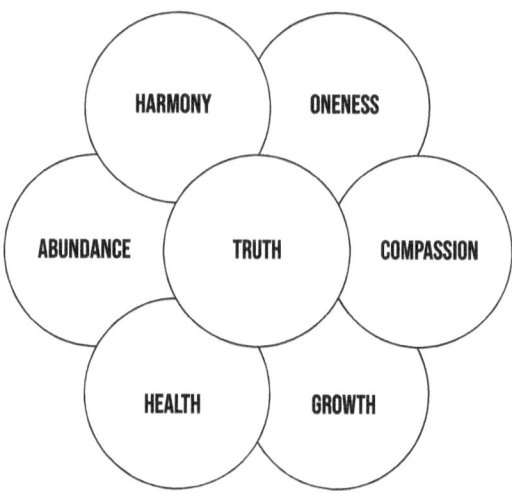

So, what we have here is Truth—Existence or the Feminine—and the six universal Principles. We can logically infer then that the sphere we can't see is Love; which is Consciousness or the Masculine. Symbolism is a powerful thing; that which we can't see within the 2D Egg of Life is Love (or formless Consciousness). But there are other ways we might be able to deepen our confidence and see something very poetic reveal itself in the process.

You see, the Egg of Life is symbolic of the initiation of life forms as it represents the binary system of origin cell formation in biology. The binary sequence, if you recall, is 1, 2, 4, 8, 16, 32, and so forth. It doubles each time, and this is how all multi-cell life forms start. There's more though, because we humans start out this way but eventually mature to have roughly 80–100 trillion cells and none of this is static as the average cell has a lifespan of five to seven years.

So, each second your body regenerates about 2.5 million new cells to replace the ones that die off. This is a continuous process until you die; it never stops and so every second you're literally and figuratively not the same person you were a second ago. Each five to seven years, you don't have one single cell that's the same.

Except for eight cells. You guessed it: the original eight cells of the Egg of Life never change as they're immortal and they are held about two inches above your perineum, which they call in yoga your Mula Bandha or "root lock." This location is the geometric center of your body: again, sacred geometry extends to everything. In Yogic and Tantra traditions mastery of the Mula Bandha is considered a sacred practice as it's considered the seat of your Pranic or Life Force energy and the master key to awakening your Kundalini, which is considered a powerful gateway for reaching an expanded state of Consciousness.

As above, so below. As within, so without. As Rumi poetically stated: "You're not a drop in the ocean, you are the entire ocean in a drop." I can list one hundred other quotes by all sorts of gurus, sages, mystics, and teachers, and they all point at the exact same thing in the words of their time. And here we see it reflected back within the Egg of Life, the only eight immortal cells within us. Love and Truth, Masculine and Feminine, Consciousness and

Existence; however you wish to see or label it and the six universal Principles of Oneness, Compassion, Growth, Health, Abundance, and Harmony. And, of course, the Masculine contains within it its three constituent attributes and the same goes for the Feminine and her three constituent attributes. It's immortally encoded within these eight immortal cells within each of us; it's literally the original cellular blueprint we carry within us for our lifetime here in Earth school.

We have one more piece of the Flower of Life puzzle to solve—the outer circumference—and we'll get there also via a small but important detour. I promised to revert back to the *Zona Pellucida*, which in biological terms is the double-walled lining of the egg of a woman. Here's an image of what I am referring to.

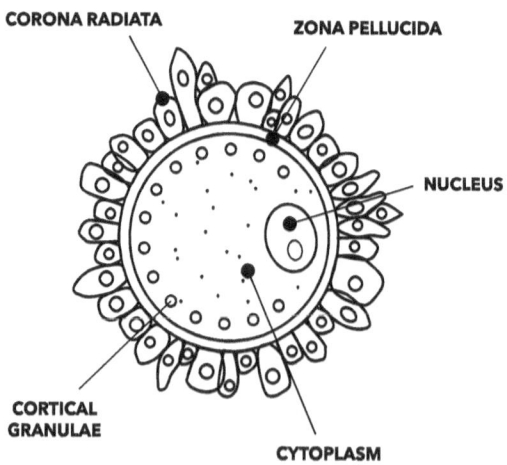

In sacred geometry everything holds a meaning; there's literally nothing superfluous no matter how poetic and aesthetically beautiful the final form might be. It's pure art, on all levels including mathematically, yet every line, shape, or dot of ink serves a purpose and has a deeper meaning. It's well-known by scholars that the double-lined circumference of the Flower of Life is not ornamental; this wasn't an artist that got a little carried away and figured he or she would add one more circumference circle. It holds mathematical significance and math is what ultimately proves out all sacred geometry forms.

The Flower of Life represents all of Creation itself and what is more symbolic and representative of Creation than the egg of a woman? The egg of a woman symbolizes—epitomizes even—fertility. And what is fertility but the potentiality of creation? Now, if we extrapolate what we already discovered about the inner circle of the Flower of Life—Love—we can now start to wonder what that outer lining of the *Zona Pellucida* might represent.

We discovered earlier that Love is the hidden fundamental power that animates all of Creation, so what could Love possibly be held within if it's the fundamental power already?

Source.

It cannot be any other way or any other thing. Once again, whether you call this God, Creator, Spirit, Monad, Yahweh, Great Spirit, Infinite Intelligence or The All makes absolutely no difference whatsoever. Whatever floats your boat, these are just labels.

It's Source, though, I promise you.

So, here we are: we solved for the final puzzle piece and we can now complete the Flower of Life within the Love+Truth Framework.

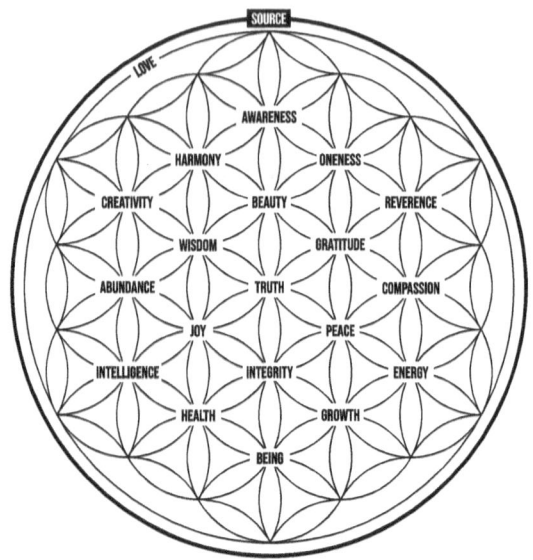

> "The pure impulse of dynamic Creation is formless; and being formless, the Creation it gives rise to can assume any and every form."
>
> —KABBALAH

Kabbalah is a branch of Jewish mysticism within Judaism; it recognizes the Torah but is grounded in the esoteric teachings contained in the Zohar, which is a commentary on the Torah accredited to the second-century sage Shimon bar Yohai. For all intents and purposes, Kabbalah centers around the esoteric or spiritual teachings within Judaism and therefore in many respects fits closer to other ancient wisdom teachings and mystery schools like those of Egypt than the Jewish religion as we know it today.

At the core of Kabbalah is the Kabbalah Tree of Life. And guess what, we can retrace the Kabbalah Tree of Life in the Flower of Life. Now, I am not a Kabbalah scholar, so I am going to abstain from making any comparison or analysis of what the Kabbalah Tree of Life represents within Kabbalah. There are also two versions and I don't know which one is considered more pure, so to speak—since Kabbalah is ultimately a form of religion, my guess is this is just another example of how religions tend to "bastardize" over the course of history through human interpretations.

For instance, at this time, there are 900+ versions of the Bible and all sorts of branches of Christianity ranging from the Catholic Church to the Mormons and everything in between. All of these proclaim to hold the true word of God yet differ wildly in their interpretation of the Bible and Christianity.

In my personal journey, I have come to discover that all major religions hold profound truths within them and can offer rich teachings, so I draw wisdom from all of them. I just don't believe in middlemen, which is the institution of religion. We each have a direct connection with Divinity, so I prefer not to have the static on the line of human middlemen in the form of clergy. This is a strictly personal choice and I fully respect and honor everyone else's freedom of religion within the confines of the Golden Rule. Freedom of religion—any freedom, really—can truly only exist when it's fully reciprocated.

But, after that sidebar, let's get back to the Kabbalah Tree of Life. The below graphic shows how the Kabbalah Tree of Life can be retraced within the Flower of Life. As you'll notice, Beauty is shown within parentheses as in some versions of the Kabbalah Tree of Life this node—called "Sefirot" in Kabbalah—is not present and in others it is. Again, I don't know the history or significance of that particular node within Kabbalah; but, for the point I am demonstrating, this detail is irrelevant so we can leave this detail for the scholars to debate.

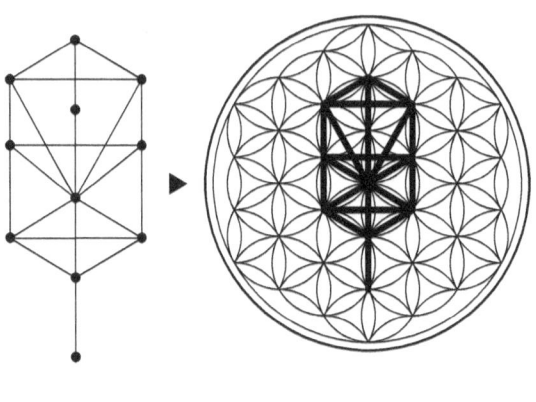

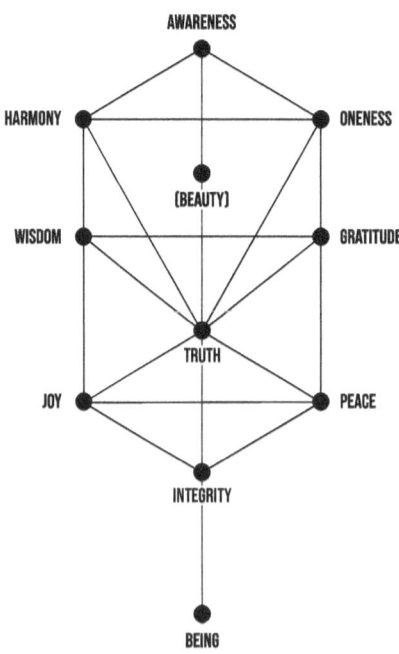

You see, I have a confession to make. None of this is truly mine. It's all coming through me from a higher source; I am just the communication vessel that was selected and although I could share more it's irrelevant. What's most important to know is that I am not special, I am just the typist, to put it crudely. The whole Love+Truth Framework is just that, a teaching framework of Higher Knowing. It's not the absolute Truth and should never be confused with that; it just points at something that is universal Truth and that's all we can ever do with words. Please always remember where we started: "The Tao that may be spoken is not the enduring Tao."

The primary reason I am including this slight digression into the Kabbalah Tree of Life is to show you two things and these are master keys to the beauty, depth, and magic contained within the Love+Truth Framework. First, this whole teaching framework is dynamic, alive, and multilayered. It's not a termination point but a starting point. As I was writing this book and channeling what I received into words, layer upon layer of higher wisdom was revealed to me step by step. So much so that I had to start making judgments about what exactly to include in this book because if I just kept writing I might fill 2,000 pages. What it showed me is that the depth of this teaching framework is endless. I just covered the basic relationships, but much like Metatron's Cube, there are an infinite amount of other geometric connections you can create between the Architecture, Gifts, and Principles coupled with Love, Truth, and Source.

Each time you do this—play with it if you will—something else will be revealed to you. I've been doing this for two months now as I am writing this book and I am just blown away by the layers and layers of direct knowing that reveal themselves if you interact with this teaching framework like this. And it seems inexhaustible; the more I interact with it the more I see.

Again, I didn't design this and clearly the Flower of Life has been around since antiquity, so I have no claims on that whatsoever. This whole teaching framework and the entire outline of this book came to me in a single download while I was driving to the beach on May 1, 2022, and then it took me 1.5 hours while I was on the beach to write out the entire outline. The next day I started writing. So, that's the first master key: this teaching framework is not a fixed religious or spiritual doctrine. It's a living and breathing framework for you to now bring alive. Run with it, play with it, interpret it whichever way serves you best as long as you use it with the embedded sacred intention: make your life the richest and most authentic expression of your spiritual art—let it serve you in becoming a true Poet.

> "Your heart knows the way, run in that direction."
> —RUMI

Which brings me to the second master key. This book and the entire Love+Truth teaching framework is unequivocally intended to fully empower you. You are your own guru, mystic, and sage. We are each our own healer. Nobody can heal you, only you can. And you have all the answers within; sometimes they just need to be peeled loose where guides and books like this one might serve as a peeling tool.

But don't ever confuse the tool for the one doing the true peeling. Please don't ever outsource your Power to a middleman; all the Power contained in this universe is within you already. You are both the sculptor and the sculpture, always have been and always will be. You also know how to do this, and through remembrance we each restore what we might have temporarily forgotten as we came here to this Earthly plane. All you have to do is follow your Heart. Your Heart knows the way; she will masterfully guide you through the labyrinth of Maya and help you walk through the fire. You are already a true Poet within, and your Heart knows what the Mind can never grasp. Follow the whispers of your Heart, that's the only way to traverse the pathless land to where you deep down wish to go.

With these two master keys in mind, let's revert to the Kabbalah Tree of Life, and this time I am going to refer to the far-right version which has the Love+Truth Framework superimposed on the Kabbalah Tree of Life within the Flower of Life. What I am going to show you next is me interacting with the teaching framework.

So, I literally just look at this sacred form and allowed it to inform me what it wants to reveal to me. I realize the naysayers of esoteric teachings will laugh at this and see it as some form of intellectual folly. I don't see it that way; in fact, I know differently. You see, the moment you realize, accept, and fully embrace that absolutely nothing in this universe is coincidental, something shifts inside you, a portal of sorts opens. It's always been there; it just opens up. Everything in this universe is infinitely intelligent in its design and operates by perfect law and order. There simply are no flukes, accidents, coincidences, or random events. No such things exist, it's all by perfect and absolutely flawless design, every last-minute detail. There's also information in everything. Literally, you can focus on a single strand of grass, and it will inform you something.

So, the first thing I noticed is the center line with Truth in the middle node. What this tells me is that Awareness realizes Truth through Beauty, and Being realizes Truth through Integrity. Beauty is Feminine as it's the coalescence of Creativity and Reverence; Integrity is Masculine as it's the coalescence of Intelligence and Energy; hence, Awareness (which is Masculine) realizes Truth through the Feminine and Being (which is Feminine) through the Masculine.

Just on this center line I can go several layers deeper; for instance, Truth is the center point between Awareness on one pole and Being on the other. Awareness is in the heavens, Being is on the Earth, and Truth, which is Existence of Life itself, is where they meet. I can keep going, but I won't because my main aim is here to show you how you could choose to interact with the framework and not pre-chew all the answers as what wants and needs to be revealed to you might be different than it is for me.

I will explore some other ones just to demonstrate the interacting with this teaching framework. On the left and right axis I can see a progression. Joy and Peace can be seen as most closely related to Life on the Earthly plane. Wisdom and Gratitude can be seen as most closely related to the Mental plane, and Harmony and Oneness to the Spiritual plane. That's a progression that holds information and that's just one way to interpret this; there are countless others.

Sacred geometry forms can also be used. For instance, there's a triangle that forms between Joy, Peace, and Integrity or a diamond shape if you connect Truth as well. These geometric relationships hold information. There's a direct vertical line from Joy, through Wisdom, to Harmony—I can probably write three pages on all that informs me. Similarly, there's a vertical line that runs from Peace, through Gratitude, to Oneness.

As you can tell, it's inexhaustible and this is just the Kabbalah Tree of Life, which is only a fraction of all the possible relationships contained within the whole Flower of Life since there are twenty-one "nodes" to interact with within the Love+Truth Framework if you include Love and Source.

I will share one final one because I want to address this discrepancy within the two versions of the Kabbalah Tree of Life. Let's assume Beauty is not a node. What does that possibly inform us? One way to interpret this is that Awareness (the Masculine) can realize Truth without Beauty. Let's think about that for a moment. So, this informs us Beauty is possibly a "tool" or stepping stone, if you will, for Awareness to realize Truth, but it's not essential in that it can also be realized without this stepping stone.

If we view this in the context of higher levels of Consciousness where we attain a significantly heightened level of Awareness this makes total sense. We grow beyond needing Beauty, which is the Feminine, which is Polarity, to realize Truth. Going beyond Polarity (and Duality) is what we call enlightenment. All of this just by interacting—playing—with this teaching framework in the context of the discrepancy of the two versions of the Kabbalah

Tree of Life. Perhaps you're starting to see what I mean there are no coincidences, everything is flawless, and everything holds information that can reveal something to us.

> "I created a vision of David in my mind and simply carved away everything that was not David."
> —MICHELANGELO

Of course, the statue of "David" symbolizes the perfect Divinely created "man" or better yet, true Poet. And we are each a true Poet with unimaginably beautiful poetry within us. Just like David, all we need to do is carve away everything that's not the true Poet within us. You are both the sculptor and the sculpture and everything you see laid out in this book within the Flower of Life is already within you—no exception. It's that simple and has always been hiding in plain sight. There's nothing on this Flower of Life that you don't already know, not a single word you're not familiar with already, even if you have forgotten to express some or all of it into Life itself as we all do when we enter life here in Earth school.

It's that simple, yet admittedly not so easy.

The Truth is, it's not so easy because the world informs you to look for the answers in the Outer World and that search will always prove to be in vain. All of this, the entire universe, is already contained within you. All the answers, all that spiritual poetry, it's all there waiting for you to be rediscovered.

All change starts within.

None of us can single-handedly change the world; we're not asked to do so as that's not our responsibility. But we are 100 percent responsible for our little sliver of it. We're an invaluable piece of the mosaic of humanity, indispensable in and to all of Creation or you simply wouldn't be here. You are truthfully that important. The only real question is, will you make your little sliver of our shared physical reality as important as it is to all of Creation? Will you muster the courage and spiritual fortitude to go deep within and rediscover all your greatest spiritual art and then express this into all of Creation like a true Poet?

> "Nothing happens to any man that he is not formed by nature to bear."
> —MARCUS AURELIUS

I cannot promise it won't be without challenges or some pitfalls; facing yourself and slaying all your inner dragons isn't always pretty. Healing old wounds and trauma invariably has its dark moments. Overcoming deep pain and inner suffering is not a well-marked or paved road. I am just telling you the Truth; this isn't always going to be a merry pony ride.

What I will promise you is that you are infinitely capable of doing this. In fact, you came here to do this; you chose to be here during these chaotic times of upheaval and change in the world and walk through the fire. Deep down you know this, or you would not be reading this right now or have gotten this far into this book. You are the Phoenix Rising and deep down you know it's time to walk through the fire.

I can promise you all of this because I am you, except I already walked through my fire. Not because I wanted to, not because I am some sort of preordained spiritual prodigy, and definitely not because I am part of some elite cosmic star seed lineage. The humble reality is, the universe left me no choice. I went kicking and screaming, holding on for dear life to everything I had ever known only to have the universe strip me so naked there was seemingly no other choice left. I did it the hard way; I needed an epic fall from grace to realize the only way out was through.

There's a far more graceful way than the way I did it; just live this book and that path will unfold for you. Whatever else you need will appear as you venture onto the pathless land. Teachers will show up, books will present themselves, workshops, retreats, and all sorts of helpers and fellow travelers will join you along the way. How exactly I can't tell you; that's safely guarded within the Unknowable of the universe. I have just seen enough to know I can trust it.

But you must go within as that's where all the gold is. It's all already within you, hiding in plain sight. When we go within, we change ourselves and when we change ourselves, we in turn change the world.

If you wish to see a more beautiful world, express more beautiful spiritual art into all of Creation. The ripple effects are enormous; you will never know the full extent and all the ways in which you're affecting this world in profound ways.

If you ever get momentarily lost or disoriented, if there's ever a stubborn fear or doubt that simply won't let itself be released, just remind yourself of this just to get your bearings back.

> "Love is the secret sauce,
> Truth is the only way."

From one Poet to another, I see you, and the view is magnificent.

CONCLUSION

"Love that shines from within cannot be darkened by obstacles of the world of consequences."
—PYTHAGORAS

THANK YOU. Thank you for getting this far into this book but moreover thank you for Being you. I hope this book was valuable to you, that there were some or perhaps many nuggets of wisdom that will help you on your journey. Frankly, I secretly hope it stirred your Soul.

Writing this book certainly stirred mine. It's been a deeply humbling experience as I've never experienced anything quite like this before. I've been writing almost daily for about ten weeks, roughly producing a chapter each day, and never in my life have I gone on a journey of discovery within like this. Not in my wildest dreams could I have imagined a mere two months ago I had this book in me, let alone that I was about to write it.

CONCLUSION

Sometimes the Divine touches us as if to confirm our deepest held wish. Throughout my spiritual journey into the pathless land, my deepest wish has always been to know so I can trust. But how can you trust what you cannot see, cannot touch, and cannot prove? This book showed me the answer to that question.

What we cannot see sees us. What we cannot touch touches us. What we cannot prove proves itself all the time in everything. That was my gift wrapped within this book; I truly hope you find your own gift within it.

> "Worship the Teachings, never the Teacher.
> The true Teacher knows he's still a Student,
> the true Student knows she's already the Teacher."

Upon receiving this book, there was also a message given to me. It's the statement written above, and it echoed in my Inner World every day while I was writing this book. By now, it's been imprinted on my conscience and memory as if written in stone.

We're living in very special times, a time of chaos and upheaval as humanity and Mother Earth are transitioning to a new timeline. Many changes are upon us, and these all must occur as the natural evolution of mankind. There will be growing pains, confusion, and what appears like Chaos, but all of this is just the natural progression as we move through the release phase of the adaptive cycle of change of humanity and our planet. Phase transitions work like that, the collapsing of the old while the new starts to arise but hasn't fully taken form yet. What appears like total Chaos at the surface is truthfully governed by infinite Order obscured from sight.

What all of this calls for more than anything is coming home within yourself to your source of Power deep within. No more outsourcing to middlemen. You are your own Sovereign Being, Divinity expressed into form. Your magnificence is indescribable; words could never capture your true potential for greatness.

So, I want you to know I am nothing special, nor is anyone else. Worship the Teachings, never the Teacher. You are your own Teacher. Don't look up or down on anyone; we're all just walking each other home, as Ram Dass used to say. If you toss away everything contained in this book and take just that one point away, this book has served its purpose already, and anything else is a bonus.

Your ability to see all of this for yourself hinges but on one thing: self-love. Love yourself like the universe loves you, and all else will flow from that.

This whole book drips with references to art and poetry, and all of that is not just my wooly way of writing cute prose; it's fully intentional. Spirituality is art; you are spiritual art. All of Creation is art; even science is art. There's as much poetry in mathematics and quantum physics as there is in music or painting. Your role as a true Poet—if you choose to be one—is to be an alchemist that transmutes everyday Life on this Earthly plane into spiritual art.

It makes no difference what you do, pick whatever makes your Heart purr and stirs your Soul—follow your bliss, as Joseph Campbell would say—but do it as a true Poet. Make it an expression of your most beautiful spiritual art. Play, dance, laugh, and sing with Life itself; become fluent in the language of the Heart to tune into the intelligence of Life itself and allow it to guide you.

Within the Outer World, we each take ourselves way too seriously but pay little to no attention to ourselves in our Inner World. The object of *the* one Infinite Game is reversed: we don't take ourselves so seriously within the Outer World, but we pay all sorts of attention to ourselves within our Inner World.

That Inner World is the eternal wellspring of all your knowing and all the spiritual art within you that wants to be expressed into the Outer World. That's where all the gold is and all the great alchemists before you knew this. They didn't transmute lead into gold; they left the lead of the Outer World and turned to the gold within. There is but one destination, one singular purpose, in all of this, and that's for each of us to discover the fundamental Power that animates each one of us as well as this entire universe and whatever might lie beyond.

Love.

It's that simple, I promise you.

LOVE + TRUTH

> "As you start to walk on the way,
> the way appears."
> —RUMI

We've covered a lot of ground in this book so far, and yet we have barely scratched the surface. There are layers of depth in all I touched on that I cannot possibly capture in a single book, and I know without a shadow of a doubt there's even vastly more depth that's as of yet invisible to me. This is exactly the way it's supposed to be; Earth school and the many dimensions beyond are spiritual scavenger hunts. We go through a succession of mastery classes and progress as we go all the way back home to Source.

As fascinating as all these possible dimensions beyond are, here on Earth school, each of us is asked to master but one singular aspect or level of Consciousness, and that is Christ Consciousness. Whether you're a devout Christian, a traumatized former Christian, or none of the aforementioned, please don't get hung up on the word Christ here as the "man" named Jesus Christ was merely symbolic for this level of Consciousness, so there's no religious connotation in this whatsoever. Christ Consciousness points at an enlightened state of self-realization, the highest octave of Consciousness accessible to us on the dense Earthly plane.

Whereas learning about dimensions like 3D, 4D, 5D, and beyond has some utility and definitely makes for great dinner table conversations, we shouldn't lose sight of the fact that the true work here on Earth is ascending into Christ Consciousness. That's our day job; the rest is for fun conversation during off-hours. I say this tongue in cheek but this is serious business. Many on the spiritual path are getting lost in the esoteric doldrums of New Age spiritual fluffiness. Wizardry in memorizing and being able to regurgitate all sorts of arcane spiritual information is just another form of getting lost in the cobwebs of your mind. This path tends to lead seekers to prophesize about their Pleiadean royal star seed lineage, live their lives by their astrology charts and tarot cards, and talk all sorts of spiritual jargon but all of it remains entirely ungrounded. I am not picking on astrology or tarot cards—they're tools I reference also at times—but the pathless land can be a challenging land to navigate and an easy place to get a little lost as spirituality is not about what you know, it's all about Being, or in other words, how you live Life itself.

If your spiritual path doesn't change the way you do the dishes, you're not on the path you think you are. Spiritual art has no dress code, no specific language, and doesn't hinge on how well you can do the acrobatics in yoga or knowing what house your Moon was in yesterday. It makes no difference if you can sit in an ice bath for thirty minutes or never dipped a toe in one. And it certainly makes no difference if you talk about the Buddha like he's been your neighbor for ten years, yet you're still triggered daily and spew out all sorts of ugliness toward people you think are still asleep. For all its mysticism, where the rubber meets the road in true spirituality is how you live your life. Who you are and how you show up for Life itself, all the rest are inconsequential details.

> "The experience of life in a finite, limited body is specifically for the purpose of discovering and manifesting supernatural existence."
> —PYTHAGORAS

The world is not in good shape. It's not all "love and light" out there; there's deep Darkness which is all rooted in low levels of Consciousness. I'll say it again; we're in a race to raise human Consciousness. Hence, none of our worldly problems are our real or actual problems; they're all infinitely solvable—practically overnight in evolutionary terms—except not at this collective level of Consciousness. So, this Christ Consciousness is not trivial business. Mankind's future depends on it, and the good news is we don't need everyone to level up; we just need a critical mass to reach the tipping point, which, due to the logarithmic scale of Consciousness, is infinitely doable. But to reach this critical mass, we do need more true Poets expressing true spiritual art into all of Creation. Not just some casual spiritual noodling with all sorts of look-good fluffiness that simply doesn't move the spiritual needle enough to tip the scales.

So, you can see this book as an operating manual on how to live your life as an expression of spiritual art; it's by no means the only way, as the pathless land has no defined paths and never will. It's not perfect and by no means complete, but it makes ascending, growing, and evolving toward Christ Consciousness something that's actionable. Live this book, and you will inevitably become a true Poet. I truly wish you'll go on this inner journey so you can experience all the miracles contained in the truest expression of your spiritual art. I cannot promise you attainment of Christ Consciousness in this lifetime, but I can promise you it's within you. I can also promise you the only way there is through remembrance and going within.

You must go within; that's where you'll find all the answers.

CONCLUSION

The higher octaves of consciousness I am inviting you to reach for and rise up to are not trivial, easy, or even convenient at first. But I don't just see the potential in you; I know it to be there. I know who you are in Truth; you don't need me to sugarcoat things, cuddle you, or serve you spiritual baby formula. You're magnificent, so much more than you could ever imagine, and your potential is limitless. You are Divinity itself, and it's my mission to remind you because this world needs you. This world needs your spiritual art.

Heck, I need your spiritual art; I want to see it shine bright and touch me at my deepest core. I want you to penetrate me with all your Divine brilliance. I crave it. And who am I but this whole universe. I am, but the whole ocean in one drop, and so are you.

So, my dear true Poet, show me your mastery, bedazzle me with your artistry, hit me with your most exquisite spiritual poetry. I invite you.

Actually, that's too soft and sugary. I dare you.

Love & Truth,
Robert

ACKNOWLEDGMENT

The King of Righteousness waved his scepter of wisdom

and the grace of knowing came my way.

The Sacred Ibis flapped his wings thrice, and the peace

of understanding took flight.

Then Hathor revealed to me her true nature and effervescent

beauty and all doubts burnt in the fire.

There I am, lead in the ashes.

Alchemized through Resurrection.

Here I am, reborn, gold anew.

In Deepest Gratitude to the Most High,

RA

ABOUT THE AUTHOR

ROBERT ALTHUIS is a certified Medium, sought-after spiritual mentor, and author of the Amazon bestseller *Never Enoughitis*, his first book published in 2021. He was an Ivy League-educated Fortune 100 corporate executive and later a highly successful entrepreneur when he experienced a spiritual awakening in 2015. In the ensuing years, as he deepened his pursuit of spiritual wisdom teachings, including becoming a certified Yoga instructor (RYT-200), his intuitive capacities of claircognizance and clairsentience blossomed and fully opened up.

In recent years, as Robert started to divest his business portfolio, he founded the Sacred Wealth Collective, a mindfulness organization dedicated to inculcating Love+Truth as the philosophical foundation for leaders and organizations as well as those seeking a deeper purpose and fulfillment of Life itself.

These days, most of his time is dedicated to serving as a spiritual mentor, keynote speaker, business advisor, or board member and instructing at various workshops and retreats year-round.

For more information or free resources, please visit www.robertalthuis.com.

ADDENDUM
SACRED GEOMETRY & MATHEMATICAL POETRY

SACRED GEOMETRY IS A VAST SUBJECT, and there are volumes of books written on the subject, and still, not everything has been said or explored. So, this Addendum is just to highlight a few aspects of sacred geometry, numbers, and mathematics referenced in this book at greater depth. However, if this overall subject interests you, I highly encourage you to study and explore it further as there's a fascinating universe of forms, shapes, numbers, and mathematics to discover, which overwhelmingly reveal a mesmerizing architecture and design to what we call reality.

> "Mathematics is the alphabet with which
> God has written the universe."
> —GALILEO

At its very core, Sacred Geometry can be seen as the mathematical bridge that helps us explain how an infinite force field of energy (i.e., consciousness) is able to express itself into form.

Form, we know, is made up of geometric patterns, and we can see this very clearly in nature, where we can easily retrace the Golden Ratio, the Fibonacci Sequence, and all sorts of geometric forms, shapes, and patterns. All geometric forms, shapes, patterns, and numerical sequences have a mathematical foundation or underpinning, and this extends to the fractal patterns we see throughout the universe. So, it can be said the entire universe is mathematical in nature. Nassim Haramein, a renowned physicist, even states, "anything considered spiritual or metaphysical is just physics we do not yet understand."

Now, all of this makes sense logically because our scientific understanding has reached far enough that we know without a shadow of a doubt that the entire universe known to us doesn't evolve completely randomly or haphazardly. Scientifically, we don't necessarily understand all of it or how it evolves and does what it does, but we do know the entire universe evolves intelligently and in accordance with certain laws and principles, many of which we've started to decipher and be able to translate into mathematical equations.

Sacred Geometry extends far beyond mere mathematics, though, as these geometric forms, shapes, and patterns hold information within their structures, and this information is recognized by our mind on both conscious and deeper subconscious levels. This is why Sacred Geometry can be retraced in everything from ancient religious symbols to coats-of-arms and even modern-day corporate logos.

Most of all, what Sacred Geometry points us at is the harmonic dance between art and science in all of Creation in the same way that, at our personal level, there's a harmonic dance between art and science in the Creation of our spiritual art. And ultimately, the only reason to read on in this Addendum or study this subject in greater depth is if you feel it will help you refine your spiritual art.

> "There is geometry in the humming of the string, there is geometry in the spacing of spheres."
> —PYTHAGORAS

Let's start with the very basics, which is numbers. Even this is a science in and by itself, as you can't even start with this subject until you define the number system. I will keep it to the ubiquitous base-10 system that's prevalent in our world, although the base-12 system is still widely used in certain applications and the Babylonians famously used the base-60 system, which has been argued by many to be superior. Then again, the ancient Mayans used a base-20 system, so if you would ask them this question, that would be their preference.

It's important to note that even though we call it a base-10 system, from a Sacred Geometry and mathematical perspective, the number "zero" is not actually a real number even though the base-10 system starts with 0. In the same way, "10" (or 20, 30, 40, etc.) is considered a transitional number or placeholder like "zero," so we're really only concerned with the numbers one through nine, and this holds especially true for all instances where we reduce any number to its digital root (i.e., adding the integers of any number until you arrive at a single-digit number between one and nine).

NUMBER 1—ORIGIN OR SINGULARITY

The 1 is the circle, unbroken and unending, as well as the point at its center. It is the oneness, origin, singularity, or Source that all Creation comes from, the realm of infinite possibilities not yet distinguished into separate entities of form. In sacred geometry, the circle is the foundation from which all the other forms are built. As we've seen previously as well, the circle also represents Consciousness (or Heavens in Taoism).

NUMBER 2—DUALITY

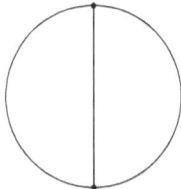

The 2 is the line created by the first movement of Consciousness away from the single point of source. The line divides the circle, which creates a new dimension, and—just as a cell splits in reproduction—Creation begins. The 2 then represents duality, the perception of otherness through which the One can experience and understand itself. Anything and everything of form in our physical reality is rooted in duality, which is ultimately Maya or illusion.

NUMBER 3—TRIAD OR TRINITY

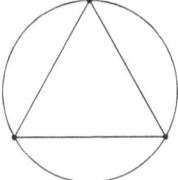

The 3 is the triangle or tetrahedron, the first shape to contain space and create a plane or surface. The duality becomes multiplicity, and Consciousness expands. There are many examples of the Triad in various aspects of Life: mind-body-spirit, past-present-future, mother-father-child, sun-moon-earth, length-breadth-depth (three-dimensional reality). Of course, then there's the Holy Trinity of the Father-Son-Holy Spirit.

NUMBER 4—SQUARE

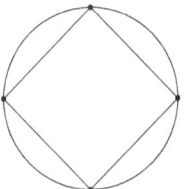

The 4 is the square or hexahedron, which offers support and stability through its even, balanced, and symmetrical shape. In Taoism and many other ancient wisdom traditions, the square symbolizes and is associated with the Earth, the solid world of form we live in. There are many 4s in the manifest world: 4 seasons, 4 directions, 4 phases of the Moon, 4 Earthly elements (Earth, Air, Fire, Water).

NUMBER 5—PENTAGRAM

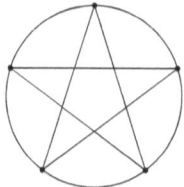

The 5 is the pentagram, an ancient symbol of regeneration and transformation. It is also a symbol of the human form, with head, arms, and legs outstretched, welcoming experience. It is through our 5 senses that we navigate the material world. Often mischaracterized as a Pagan or Wiccan symbol, its use actually predates these schools of religion as the pentagram has represented the four earthly elements and ether (also often referred to as spirit) since antiquity.

NUMBER 6—HEXAGRAM

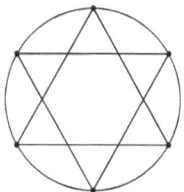

The 6 is the Star of David or star-tetrahedron, two perfectly balanced, interlocking equilateral triangles representing the Masculine and the Feminine. It symbolizes the Hermetic principle of "As Above–So Below" or, in other words, the meeting of spiritual realm with the material world. The star-tetrahedron is also symbolic for the Merkaba, the torus field around the human body. The 6 brings harmony, cooperation, and growth through balance.

NUMBER 7—SEPTAGRAM

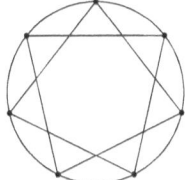

The 7 creates the septagram (also called heptagram or septogram), a seven-pointed star drawn with seven straight strokes. The 7 symbolizes the mystic and the philosopher, the number of creative, mental activity, and spiritual evolution. The 7 relates to cycles of time and the movement of the sun and the planets as seen from Earth. Many vibrational things, such as chakras, colors of the rainbow, and musical notes (A through G), come in 7s. There are also seven wonders of the world, and in many cultures, 7 is considered a lucky number.

NUMBER 8—OCTAGON

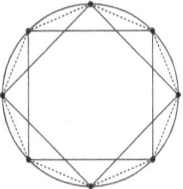

The 8 is the octagon, the intermediate form between the circle (Heaven) and the square (Earth). As the 4 doubled, it is the number of ascension through transcending the material world via spiritual realization. The 8th step on the musical scale is the octave, which brings harmonic resonance and a sense of fulfillment. The 8 is also symbolic for success, health, realization, and abundance in many cultures. Finally, the octagram or 8-pointed star, which forms two squares angled at 45 degrees, is a revered symbol across many religions, including Hinduism, Buddhism, and in Christianity represents the Order of Melchizedek of which the Bible states Christ was a Priest forever (Hebrews 5:6).

NUMBER 9—COMPLETION

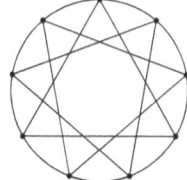

The 9 is the completion of the creative cycle. It brings attainment, compassion, and vision for the future through the wisdom gleaned from the journey through the other numbers. As the 9 symbolizes the terminus point of the cycle, it's also associated with releasing, letting go, and making room for the new. However, the 9 is not an endpoint, but merely the closing of the circle, carrying us back to the 1 to begin the next evolution, the next cycle, the next stage or phase of Life itself. The 9 has very unique mathematical properties and is universally considered to be the most sacred number; Tesla even held the belief that the number 9 represented a mystical key to our universe.

NUMBER 9—MATHEMATICAL POETRY

To demonstrate why the 9 is so revered in sacred geometry and numerology, we're going to have to delve into some of its unique mathematical properties just to reveal a small glimpse of its mathematical poetry.

There are 360 degrees in a circle—which we stated earlier symbolizes the "Heavens" or Consciousness—and the digital root of 360 = 9 (3 + 6 + 0 = 9). If we now cut the circle in half, we have 180 degrees, which again has a digital root of 9. Cut 180 in half, and you have 90 degrees, and we once again see a digital root of 9. This continues with 45 degrees, 22.5 degrees, 11.25 degrees, and so on and so forth.

Next, not only does every multiple of 9 itself (e.g., 18, 27, 36, etc.) have a digital root of 9, but every integer, no matter how large, multiplied by 9, reduces to a digital root of 9. The 9 is the only number that has this mathematical property.

No less distinctive is the fact that when you add 9 to any number between 1 and 8, the digital root will reduce to the original number as if the 9 was never added. For instance, 5 + 9 = 14 = 5 or 7 + 9 = 16 = 7.

These examples are just illustrative as there are too many of these remarkable mathematical "coincidences" (hint: that's an oxymoron) of the powerful 9 to list them all, and they're not just purely mathematical. We can find them in countless measurements of area (e.g., 1 square foot = 144 inches = 9) as well as time (e.g., 3,600 seconds per hour = 9), and we encounter this phenomenon in something as geographically and culturally diverse as the 4 Hindu Yugas (Ages) and the Mayan calendar and precession cycle. Heck, even Plato's "perfect number" of 5040 has a digital root of 9. I think you get the point; the list is literally endless—the number 9 is truly magical.

Please don't memorize any of this unless you really want to; it's not important to accumulate trivia data in your mind, as all I am trying to point to is the magic and mathematical poetry that's interwoven into the fabric of Creation. If you can just see the magic, you "know" all you truly need to retain.

> "A stone is frozen music."
> —PYTHAGORAS

As you might recall, all of Creation or the Finite World of Form has its underpinning in the harmonics of vibration and frequency. In that way, everything we see and can touch in physical reality is frozen music. There's a harmonics of vibration and frequency that's native to our universe; it's the tune of all of Creation, if you will, which includes us, humans, as well. Whatever is in harmony with this tune will be coherent, and whatever is not will be dissonant to the fundamental energy that permeates the entire force field of Consciousness.

In terms of our physical body, coherence is what creates homeostasis and regeneration, whereas dissonance is what causes illness and degradation. All of this is well-known and documented, so it would be illusionary to think vibration and frequency has no effect on our mental health. In fact, we know it does, as we can measure brainwaves and coherence or dissonance within the various brainwave states. Moreover, abrasive sound—so-called "music torture"—has even been used as a form of torturous coercion by militaries the world over, and we don't even have to go to this extreme. We have each put on a radio channel or walked into a place where the music was abrasive to us. The music genre might be different to each person, but the triggering is real and overwhelming when it happens. So, clearly, the significance of the harmonics of vibration and frequency is real and undeniable, no matter how much many like to play it down or dismiss it entirely.

Now, there are a total of twelve notes in our Western musical scale, with the thirteenth being equivalent to the first, only one octave higher. There's a very precise mathematical relationship between the same notes at various octaves in that the frequency of the next note higher is exactly twice the Hz, and each lower note is half the Hz. So, the A note in the native tuning pitch of A4 = 432 Hz would have A3 = 216 Hz and A5 = 864 Hz, and so on and so forth. This is all exact and mathematical in nature; all of music, in fact, is.

Below is a table showing the comparison of digital roots between the conventional "concert pitch" A4 = 440 Hz tuning standard as conventionalized by ISO and A4 = 432 Hz tuning standard, which has its origins in the Pythagorean tuning standard.

Note	A4 = 440 Hz Tuning		A4 = 432 Hz Tuning	
A / Octave	Frequency	Digital Root	Frequency	Digital Root
A_0	27.5 Hz	5	27 Hz	9
A_1	55 Hz	1	54 Hz	9
A_2	110 Hz	2	108 Hz	9
A_3	220 Hz	4	216 Hz	9
A_4	440 Hz	8	432 Hz	9
A_5	880 Hz	7	864 Hz	9
A_6	1760 Hz	5	1728 Hz	9
A_7	3520 Hz	1	3456 Hz	9
A_8	7040 Hz	2	6912 Hz	9

There's a plethora of books, articles, and research on this subject as well as a library of videos you can find on YouTube, and you will find the opinions differ greatly. All of this is a fascinating area to study, but there's also an intuitive way of coming to "know" all you really need to understand. Cymatics is the study of sound and vibration made visible, typically on the surface of a plate, diaphragm, or membrane. When the output of frequency is made visible, as it is in cymatics, the patterns that emerge from frequency are visibly coherent (i.e., orderly and beautiful) or dissonant (i.e., chaotic and ugly). In essence, cymatics makes visible to us what is "life" and what is "anti-life" in terms of frequency and vibration. So, a shortcut would be to just look up some cymatics videos; there are literally thousands of them.

Finally, I am not here to convince you of anything, just to open doors to show you this entire universe has a mesmerizing mathematical poetry that's interwoven into every fiber and aspect of what we experience as physical reality. Once you see, you cannot unsee.

> "The seen is the changing,
> the unseen is the unchanging."
> —PLATO

We'll complete this Addendum with a quick analysis of the Platonic Solids, the five fundamental building blocks of reality named after Plato. What I am specifically attempting is to show you—once again—the indisputable connection with the number 9.

Before we do so, let's do a quick review of the language of geometry, so we establish a baseline of the definitions. See also the graphic below; faces and edges are relatively straightforward to understand. Each "vertex" is a corner and what's important to note is that each vertex has an interior angle and an exterior angle. There's a mathematical relationship between the interior angle and the exterior angle of a vertex, but I am going to skip over that as it's not relevant for what we're after as we're principally concerned with the interior angles of the five Platonic Solids.

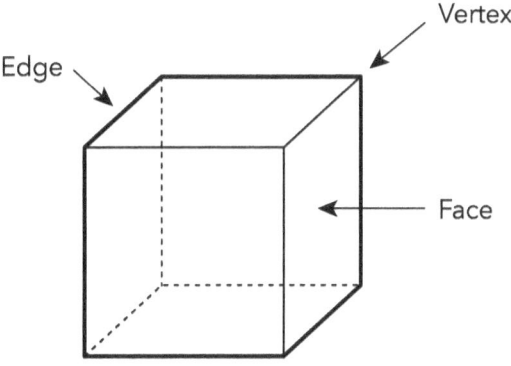

With these definitions in place, let's now look at how we would go about calculating the interior angles for each of the five Platonic Solids. We'll use the below graphic to guide us along.

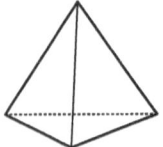 ### Tetrahedron

4 faces
4 vertices
6 edges

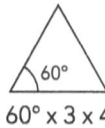
60° x 3 x 4
720°

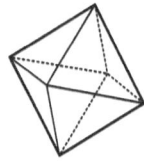 ### Octahedron

8 faces
6 vertices
12 edges

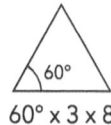
60° x 3 x 8
1440°

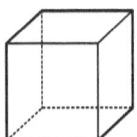 ### Hexahedron (Cube)

6 faces
8 vertices
12 edges

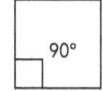
90° x 4 x 6
2160°

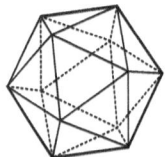 ### Icosahedron

20 faces
12 vertices
30 edges

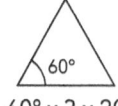
60° x 3 x 20
3600°

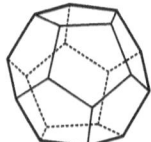 ### Dodecahedron

12 faces
20 vertices
30 edges

108° x 5 x 12
6480°

Just for illustration purposes, let's take a closer look at the Hexahedron or cube, as it's perhaps the most familiar form to us of all the Platonic Solids. As you can tell, the interior angle of any face of this shape is 90 degrees. Since each Hexahedron face has four vertices or corners, the total degrees of each face is 360 degrees. The cube or Hexahedron has a total of six faces, and therefore, the sum total of the interior angles is 2160 degrees. And guess what the digital root of 2160 degrees is? That would be 9 as 2 + 1 + 6 + 0 = 9.

The math works the same for each of the Platonic Solids, and the corresponding sum total of degrees for each of them has a digital root of 9.

I trust by now it's become evident that there's something very special about the number 9 and its relationship with all of Creation. And truthfully, this is just skimming the surface, as there are entire books devoted to anything from the mathematics hidden within the Platonic Solids to how these primordial shapes relate to the harmonics of vibration and frequency, which leads you to the term "frozen music."

If this topic has your interest, by all means, delve as deep into it to satisfy your curiosity as it's a fascinating field of study. However, all of that is well beyond the scope of this book, nor is it essential to become a math whiz to create your most beautiful spiritual art. The only thing that's important is to become open to the magical and, at times, mystical intelligence that underpins all of Creation, which we experience as our physical reality.

Because if you can just see that, you can see the Divine's fingerprints in everything, in all of Creation, and most importantly, maybe yourself.

Once you see, you cannot unsee.

www.ingramcontent.com/pod-product-compliance
Lightning Source LLC
Chambersburg PA
CBHW030507080526
44586CB00011B/95